More Praise for *The World Is Open*

"If you wonder how schools will evolve in the information-rich Internet Age—if you'd like to 'see' what that looks like—this book will show you. Dr. Bonk provides compelling examples of twenty-first century education, and his stories will leave you wondering why we aren't doing more to ensure that online and blended learning opportunities are available to every student. Picking up on Friedman's theory regarding the democratization of the workforce, Dr. Bonk explains the ramifications for learning in a globally connected world. This book paints almost endless possibilities in a world where we can now connect young and old across time, culture, language, and geography. It will leave you wanting to open doors for students everywhere."

—Julie Young, president and CEO,
Florida Virtual School

"Taking his inspiration from Thomas Friedman's *The World is Flat*, Professor Bonk's book *The World is Open: How Web Technology is Revolutionizing Education*, is a personal account, written in an unabashedly post-modern stream-of-consciousness style, of how the Web of Learning has changed him and is transforming the world. Like Friedman he writes from the American experience but draws global implications. This is a book that all involved in eLearning should dip into for inspiration."

—Sir John Daniel, president and CEO,
Commonwealth of Learning

"It has become a truism to say that the world in which we live is changing rapidly. The task now at hand is to understand the trends and harness their power. In no area is this more important than in education, where we must meet the challenge of a high-quality education for all the citizens of the world. And in Professor Bonk's new book, *The World Is Open*, he provides a powerful tool to help us meet that challenge. He argues that because of the Web 'anyone can learn anything from anyone at anytime.' But his work extends beyond this basic premise. He defines and documents the specific trends that are influencing how and where learning takes place so that they can be put to use by a wide range of audiences. This important book helps us deliver the education revolution."

—Gaston Caperton, president, The College Board

"Curt Bonk has captured the essence of the wondrous digital empowerment practices and philosophies in today's highly networked world. From his book, you will learn that educational technology entrepreneurship is a splendid kind of virus to be infected with."

—Paul Kim, chief technology officer,
Stanford University School of Education

"We have an educational economy of information abundance confronting an educational delivery system that was built for a time of information scarcity. Bonk outlines a practical and comprehensive road map for navigating the explosion of open educational resources and how they can be used to prepare ourselves and our students for a lifetime of learning and discovery."

—Lev Gonick, vice president, Information Technology Services;
chief information officer, Case Western Reserve University

"In the age of 'fingertip knowledge,' curiosity is the key to learning. Curtis Bonk's *The World is Open* book provides a powerful perspective of how we organizations and individuals can harness the power of global knowledge and content to drive performance and learning."

—Elliott Masie, chair, The Learning Consortium at The Masie Center

"Curtis Bonk opens our eyes to the world of open education, where learning can take place anytime, anywhere we have access. This book is filled with powerful stories that paint a new picture of what learning can become if we understand the potentials of this new Web. It's a must read for educators, and, more importantly, for learners."

—**Will Richardson**, co-founder, Powerful Learning Practice, and author, *Blogs, Wikis, Podcasts, and other Powerful Web Tools for Classrooms* as well as the highly popular edublog, *Weblogged*

"*The World Is Open* is such an inspiring story for the twenty-first century. The subject matter is especially important to me because I use online learning technology to learn and to teach. I love how the stories of people using technology to learn make the book so relevant. Not only is each story inspiring and motivational, but they are also practical, providing many ways for readers to open their own world of learning."

—Adora Svitak, 11-year-old teacher, author, speaker

"Technology has historically been an appendage to education because it has not been integral to the mission of dispensing information. Dr. Bonk provides a glimpse into the future of learning, in which technology plays a central role by fostering an egalitarian knowledge frenzy where learning is open and unconstrained by classes and schedules. Bonk exploits Web 2.0 technology to make a quite compelling case."

—David Jonassen, distinguished professor, Educational Psychology and Learning Technologies, University of Missouri

"Professor Bonk's insightful book provides a panoptic and inspiring rendering of our new era of pervasive access to learning resources and social networks for open education. What a fun read!"

—Roy Pea, professor of Learning Sciences and Education, Stanford University and director, Stanford Center for Innovations in Learning

"Online learning is an important innovation that expands opportunities for students through improving access to new pathways. *The World is Open* brings new ideas, provides deep insight, and encourages a new way of thinking about education. The book also provides key strategies, resources, and tools for e-learning that will help administrators, teachers, parents, and students globally."

—Susan Patrick, president and CEO, International Association for K-12 Online Learning (iNACOL)

"A very interesting read, that is equally applicable to educators, trainers, learners, managers, strategists as well as technology specialists. We are at the brink of educational evolution and the ten trends of WE-ALL-LEARN provide a framework of how we can embrace this evolution. Education is no longer a luxury but a human right—we are all learners and WE-ALL-LEARN. The world is open and it is now time to embrace that openness for the benefit of society. This book is a must have for all, that has real life examples with technologies that are available now."

—Stefano Ghazzali, CMALT, FHEA, FRSA, program development manager, Manchester Business School, University of Manchester

"*The World is Open* gets to the heart of the way ten key technologies are changing the way the world learns and making a flatter world possible. Dr. Bonk offers a new and exciting way to look at the transformation of education from the classroom to an open world of learning technology. Because it is accessible and readable, *The World is Open* will appeal to a wide range of audiences from educators to business leaders. I'm glad to see that the power of social networking in education is recognized for the transformative power that it will bring."

—Shirish Nadkarni, CEO and co-founder, Livemocha

"Curt offers an insightful and perceptive view of the technological trends that are converging to transform learning to become more global, collaborative, personalized, empowering, ubiquitous, and open. Filled with enlightening and inspiring real-life stories from those successfully using these emerging technologies, this book on open learning trends will be an eye opener and useful guide for many!"

—Gary H. Marks, executive director and founder, Association for the Advancement of Computing in Education (AACE)

"Openness may be the previously missing ingredient that finally enables meaningful educational reform by increasing transparency, affordability, local control, and accountability. In this timely volume, Bonk provides a wonderfully readable look at where openness is taking education, what it means for learning, and what should excite or concern us about the future."

—David Wiley, associate professor, Brigham Young University; chief openness officer, Flat World Knowledge; and founder and board chair, Open High School of Utah

"A riveting guide to the future of learning and education. This book should be compulsory reading for all who seek to understand the driving forces of this century."

—Joon Mo Kwon, CEO, Nexon Corp

"Those who know Curt are used to insightful advice and predictions delivered in an innovative style. *The World is Open: How Web Technology Is Revolutionizing Education* does not disappoint! It is a chance to relive much of recent history of technology-enhanced learning but then discover innovative ideas to take forward within a practical framework. All this is enhanced with stories and examples presented in a way that cannot fail to enthuse all those who read them to find their place in the new world of open learning."

—Nigel Banister, chief global officer and CEO, MBS Worldwide, Manchester Business School

"Virtual worlds, mobile learning, social networking . . . these are just three of the ten key trends that Curtis Bonk has identified in his informative book on the future of learning. Drawing on examples from around the world and through the use of illustrative stories, he brings to life how changing technologies and social trends are impacting learners of all ages."

—Heidi Fisk, executive director and co-founder,
The eLearning Guild

"The current economic crisis is punctuating the shift from an industrial to a global knowledge economy and society. Profound changes in learning are at the heart of this transformation as people and organizations can be plugged into a global, open platform of networked knowledge and intelligence. Read this extraordinary book to understand how."

—**Don Tapscott,** chairman, nGenera Insight; adjunct professor,
Rotman School of Management, University of Toronto;
and author of thirteen books about the new technologies in business and society,
most recently *Wikinomics* and *Grown Up Digital*

"In this thoughtful new book, Curt Bonk's research and observations mirror what we in iEARN have seen since 1988. Teaching and learning are being impacted by connective technologies in ways that creative education practitioners discover daily. No longer is information, wisdom, and critical analysis the sole domain of libraries, 'experts,' or even teachers in the front of passive students who absorb what they are told. The Internet and other technologies reveal that students, with invaluable teacher facilitation, can learn through interaction with people anywhere in the world, coming to their own critical conclusions, posing new inquiries, and generating amazing intellectual and creative work.

Just as importantly, students are comfortable with change, easily adapting to new technology tools and taking for granted that learning is not just something done during school days, but is a life-long endeavor. An early iEARN pioneer from Argentina noted that 'No one knows so little that s/he cannot teach another and no one knows so much that s/he cannot learn from the other.' Professor Bonk's illustrative stories of how technology can enhance learning confirm that through technology students can go beyond learning *about* the world to learning *with* the world."

—Ed Gragert, executive director, iEARN-USA

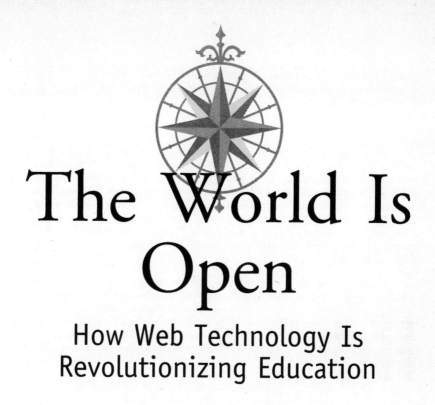

The World Is
Open

How Web Technology Is
Revolutionizing Education

Curtis J. Bonk

JOSSEY-BASS
A Wiley Imprint
www.josseybass.com

Published by Jossey-Bass
A Wiley Imprint
989 Market Street, San Francisco, CA 94103-1741—www.josseybass.com

Library of Congress Cataloging-in-Publication Data

Bonk, Curtis Jay.
  The world is open: how Web technology is revolutionizing education / Curtis J. Bonk.
    p. cm.
  Includes bibliographical references and index.
  ISBN 978-0-470-46130-3 (cloth), ISBN 978-1-118-01381-6 (paper)
  ISBN 978-0-470-52671-2 (ebk); ISBN 978-0-470-52672-9 (ebk); ISBN 978-0-470-52673-6 (ebk)
  1. Internet in education. I. Title.
  LB1044.87.B66 2009
  371.33'44678—dc22

                                                                          2009013925

Printed in the United States of America
FIRST EDITION
PB Printing 10 9 8 7 6 5 4 3 2 1

This book is dedicated to the memory of Chris Essex (February 19, 1965–April 17, 2007), student, teacher, instructional designer, writer, rocket builder, music lover, podcast partner, colleague, technology guru, and friend to all, who helped show me and countless others the open learning world.

Contents

Prequel: Sharing . . . the Journey

GIVING AND SHARING

Former U.S. president Bill Clinton's 2007 book, *Giving: How Each of Us Can Change the World,* provides a simple yet powerful message of hope, optimism, and change. Throughout the book, Clinton effectively captures a giving spirit through dozens of fascinating vignettes. One example is John Wood, who quit his job at Microsoft in order to build thousands of libraries as well as computer and language labs, while making educational scholarships available to children in such places as Nepal, Laos, India, Cambodia, and Vietnam through a program called Room to Read. To make this program work, there are thousands of givers who donate books, software, money, and other resources for Room to Read libraries and educational programming.

In addition to Wood, there is Woods, or, I should say, legendary golfer Tiger Woods, who founded the Woods Center, where volunteers offer mentoring in math, science, and technology to youth of Southern California. Of course, Clinton also highlights AmeriCorps, an organization he was instrumental in creating back in 1993 during his presidency. AmeriCorps teachers travel to places such as South Africa, inner-city Los Angeles, and hurricane-ravaged New Orleans to give their time, talents, and educational services.

Reading Clinton's book is certain to turn any reader into a giver. Clinton's wide-ranging compilation of riveting stories draws the reader to visions of how giving something, however seemingly small or inconsequential at the time, can make a huge difference. People around the world are contributing to efforts to diminish world pollution, discover cures for prostate cancer and AIDS, bring attention to the need for global peace, and provide support to victims of natural disasters and emergencies, such as those devastated by the major tsunami that hit South and Southeast Asia on December 26, 2004, as well as those caught in Hurricane Katrina just eight months later.

Each of us has something to give—time before or after work, physical labor and sweat, innovative ideas and other types of mental effort, money and tangible materials, and unique talents and skills—that can make a positive impact on the inhabitants of this planet. In parallel to acts of giving there typically is some sense of sharing—the sharing of stories, visions, kindness, wealth, sense of duty, resources, and so on. Indeed, sharing is as much a part of giving as giving is a part of sharing. Sharing is actually defined as an act of contributing or giving something. And sharing is what this prequel—and perhaps life—is all about.

If giving creates hope for someone, then "sharing" potentially multiplies this process to include everyone. In effect, giving, though vital to sustain and enrich human life on this planet, is often unidirectional (that is, going from a giver to a receiver), whereas the fruits of sharing more often spread in myriad directions. Sharing may, in fact, represent a synergistic expression or culmination of giving in which what is provided or shared is duplicated, reused, and further dispersed to people that you did not initially intend or imagine benefiting from the act. What is evident is that acts of sharing take place in a highly interactive dynamic; such complexities aside, there is significant overlap between acts of giving and sharing.

Instead of trying to bring to life all acts of sharing here, I focus primarily on sharing in educational settings via learning technologies, while briefly recounting aspects of my own personal journey related to such sharing during the past couple of decades. In the twentieth century, educators were often referred to as givers—those who give back to society without asking for much in return. Such individuals give their time to educating learners at all hours and on any day of the week. They offer their talents in particular subject matter areas, and they invent imaginative ideas and activities so that others can be motivated to achieve at a high level. Of course, such giving is a model for each succeeding generation of educators.

In the twenty-first century, however, opportunities for educators to share may actually eclipse opportunities to give. In contrast to giving to a particular student, classroom, or school, sharing denotes an impact that is much more far-reaching, or at least potentially so. Now, with the emergence of the Internet and, concurrently, online sharing, you can have an impact on anyone anywhere on this planet at any time of the day. In particular, sharing has increased in salience within teaching and learning environments due to unique possibilities afforded by online collaborative technologies.

FIRST WAVE OF TECHNOLOGY: DRILLING LEARNING

Until recently, technology has been a key reason for the lack of sharing in education. What was on one person's computer was solely for his or her use and not to be transmitted to others, because that would only encourage cheating or lazy thinking. Key examples of this perspective included programmed instruction and computer-assisted instruction (CAI) in the 1960s and 1970s, which were by-products of the behaviorist movement made popular by the famous Harvard psychologist B. F. Skinner and his followers. At the time, technology was primarily used to reinforce learning. With such perspectives came the shaping of people in small steps toward a skill using what many opponents labeled "drill and kill instruction." Shaping trumped sharing. Individualism overrode collaboration. *Result: sharing was virtually nonexistent in that first wave of educational computing technology.*

SECOND WAVE OF TECHNOLOGY: ENHANCING LEARNING

As programmed instruction and its reinforcement style of learning "finally" faded away, many educators in the 1980s and early 1990s began to use technology to expand or broaden what learners could accomplish in basic skill areas such as math, science, reading, and writing as well as other subjects and in even less clearly defined learning pursuits. No longer were they limited to using technology to narrowly focus on discrete facts and dates and pounding them one nail at a time into the brains of awaiting learners. There was a huge and highly welcome funeral procession for programmed instruction and CAI.

I witnessed part of this mass burial firsthand when conducting my master's degree research in a number of schools in Wisconsin during the summer of 1987. I had students using dozens of convergent thinking software packages intended to enhance logical thinking, problem solving, hypothesis testing, classification skills, deductive reasoning, and making inferences. At the same time, I tested a similar set of divergent software packages for fostering originality, brainstorming, spatial reasoning, recognizing patterns and relationships, and designing original works in poetry, art, drawing, animation, and music. This was a far cry from the canned drills of most technology deployed in schools at the time.

Instead of limiting students' educational opportunities to a set of predefined standards or objectives, this wave of software elevated or extended learning beyond what anyone could do alone. Such technology tools worked with and expanded upon human cognitive capabilities to enable highly valuable and novel learning outcomes. Although the second wave of educational computing technology was not especially designed for sharing and collaboration, it was a means to enhance human mental functioning. *Result: technology was a cognitive tool to enhance human thinking and reasoning.*

THIRD WAVE OF TECHNOLOGY: EXTENDING LEARNING

By using the second generation of educational technology to "enhance" learning, rather than hammering it in, educators started focusing on computers as cognitive tools that would augment mental functioning, thereby enabling learners to accomplish tasks that were not previously possible. My dissertation project on critical and creative thinking computer prompts embedded in WordPerfect in 1988 and 1989 was a prime example of augmenting learning with technology tools. Such learning enhancements were also found in supplemental resources such as practice exams, current topic readings, outlining and concept mapping tools for writing papers, rudimentary simulations, and other course study aids packaged on floppy disks and later on CDs, which were often glued or taped to the inside cover of the mighty textbook.

This approach was quite common from the late 1980s to the mid-1990s. Unfortunately, sharing was not typically embedded in such efforts, though one could share the disk. In addition, most often the technology provided by the textbook publishers was something that the teacher used to demonstrate, teach, show, and explain key concepts, and was not for students to try out or use to test hypotheses, brainstorm ideas, or collaborate with others. A focus on manipulating and measuring individual learning remained entrenched across all phases of technology design, implementation, and evaluation.

When the Web emerged as a viable educational tool in the 1990s, educators began to experiment creatively with it. At that time, the focus changed from using technology to enhance learning to using technology to extend what educators do. This was a third generation of educational computer technology.

For example, at Indiana University from 1996 to 2000, we used third-generation tools such as Web conferencing to organize interinstitutional collaborations between pre-service teachers in Indiana and Finland. This project soon expanded to include classes in the United Kingdom, Peru, Korea, South Carolina, and Texas. Students discussed case problems seen in schools and suggested solutions to each other based on their course readings. With such projects, class discussions could take place on the Web late at night, long after the course lecture was delivered and even after the instructors and their assistants had gone to bed. Ideas were not only shared internationally, but they were also saved online for the next class of students to read, reflect upon, and use.

Activities that extended learning environments also took place in K–12 and corporate education. In K–12 classrooms, for instance, projects and initiatives such as Keypals, the GLOBE (Global Learning and Observations to Benefit the Environment) Program, the Journey North, and Kids as Global Scientists pushed learning well beyond traditional walled classrooms so that children could share their papers or scientific findings with peers in other schools, geographic regions, or countries. They might even have a live videoconference between two or more schools to share their curriculum projects and ideas. Such outreach programming and culturally beneficial activities were intended to foster global awareness and appreciation of cultural differences and similarities by youth around the world.

In corporate training, this third generation of tools enabled learners to work in teams with others in their organization located in different parts of the world using asynchronous discussion forums, Web conferencing, and online chats. Such global worker-training activities built corporate efficiencies and expanded productivity in ways never previously imagined.

As these examples illustrate, it was during the 1990s that online educational activities were taking off in seismic proportions beyond the four walls of the classroom. *Result: ideas related to using technology to share began to crystallize. However, sharing was primarily limited to sharing papers across locations, sharing opinions in discussion forums, and sharing ideas via e-mail.*

FOURTH WAVE OF TECHNOLOGY: TRANSFORMING AND SHARING LEARNING

Though perhaps impressive, all of these activities in the third wave of technology amounted to nothing more than light-touch sharing by today's Web 2.0 standards, where user sharing, contributions, and participation are the norm. Just where such efforts will lead remains something of a mystery, as most educators today have simply walked through an initial passageway leading to a rich labyrinth of sharing opportunities. Many—afraid to upset any colleagues, students, administrators, supervisors, or other stakeholders—remain hesitant to wander further inside the possibilities of the Web 2.0. Some lack adequate support and training. Others lack time or interest. There are many reasons to stand for months or even years at the doorway to transformative technology change in education and simply peer in.

As a result of these barriers, sharing, for the most part, continues to be incidental to the course or learning experience goals and objectives, and not the prime motivator for teaching or training with technology. Many educators operating from this perspective fully admit that sharing educational resources, materials, and ideas has wonderful side effects (for example, gaining new colleagues, increased global awareness, automatic course updates, and so on). Their main focus, however, is on enhancing or extending the learning of those enrolled in their classes. Unfortunately, their direct concerns and ultimate reach typically do not include students in other classes or institutions or students who are unable to enroll in their classes for whatever reason. This perspective may change in the coming decades as online and nontraditional learning and learners become the norm.

What should be clear by now is that using technology to enhance and extend teaching and training environments was relatively painless. The next phase of educational technology, which sprouted wings in the late 1990s and is still evolving, relates to using technology to transform the curriculum. Transforming education with technology has not been as widely adopted as some perceive, but an avalanche of change is under way.

Now with fourth-generation educational computing technology, such as the Web 2.0, educational courses are being entirely rethought and revamped to take advantage of authentic learning and real-world audiences for collaboration and interaction. For example, there are online corporate reports for business classes to analyze and discuss, Web-based surveys and polls for research courses to access and perhaps verify, digital movies produced by students and shared via YouTube for cultural anthropology courses, Google maps embedded in architecture or urban studies courses, freely available podcasts of Spanish radio for language courses, and live language lessons via Skype. Students can record, communicate, and debate real problems or cases that one or more of them have encountered, instead of debating canned ones from textbook publishers. And, equally remarkable, the answers to those problems might come from someone that they will never physically meet. *Result: sharing in this fourth phase of technology integration is much more flavorful and multimedia rich; undoubtedly, it will soon be widely accepted as standard educational practice.*

SHARING TAKES ROOT

Despite hundreds, if not thousands, of such transformational teaching examples, there are endless bumps in this road. For instance, during the late 1990s, Murray Goldberg, former computer science professor from the University of British Columbia, built a high-profile user community around his extremely popular course management system, WebCT. Though he did not anticipate it, this community sprang up from a fast-growing user base for his product, thanks to his broad and insightful grassroots efforts. Allowing instructors to initially use his product for free did not hurt either.

During this growth phase, Goldberg started dreaming of what it would be like if instructors using WebCT shared content, course resources, ideas, and even teaching styles or approaches. As president and founder of WebCT, he hoped that instructors using WebCT (and similar course management systems) could browse through the shared online content and write to each other for permission to use the resources that they had found. And even though there were 150,000 courses in WebCT format at the time and 50 e-mails a day from an active and thoughtful user group, only two people were willing to put their courses up on display for others to view; a mere two courses out of some 150,000. This certainly was not the exciting sharing culture that he and other online learning pioneers had envisioned. What went wrong?

Well, there were two gigantic barriers to sharing online content: *ownership* and *copyright*. Some worried about who actually owned the materials and whether they would benefit if they shared such content. Others were nervous that corporate lawyers at publishing houses would see the course resources that they were using without proper copyright clearance and engage in some type of legal action. Still others noted concerns about the piracy of their materials.

As the red flags of copyright and knowledge ownership were raised, Goldberg and many others hit a wall on sharing. They grasped the new possibilities for online communities of instructors but lacked the process for this to actually happen. Instructors wanted to share, but they simply could not, due to many internal policies, rules, regulations, and administrative mandates as well as external fears, barriers, and concerns on the part of the publishing industry—not to mention fast-changing legal requirements from state and federal governments.

Part of the problem was the newness of online learning. Today, educators and the institutions and organizations they work for have a better, though still imperfect, understanding of what the prevailing laws allow in terms of copyright. These same institutions and organizations also have established more effective internal copyright policies and procedures. Another part of the problem was the fact that the primary reward system for most instructors in higher education was research based; it rarely, if ever, revolved around pedagogical inventions or the sharing of such inventions. And still another issue was the emphasis on individualism in most educational settings (such as individual teaching, individual learning, individual assessment, and so on), rather than on collaboration. Overcoming such fears would take more than a few years of familiarity with online learning environments and sharing content within them.

As these barriers began to crumble, numerous signposts of the coming tidal wave of change appeared. One key historical marker occurred late in late 2006 when *Time* magazine named "You" as the person of the year in recognition of the growing use of online technologies that empower people. As made evident in that issue, people can contribute to learning and comment on the learning of others, instead of passively receiving it. At the same time, the copyrighting of scarce knowledge in the centuries prior to the Web 2.0 gave way to the sharing of vast stores of human creativity and innovation after the Web 2.0.

Centuries from now, historians will note that in the early 2000s we entered an age of knowledge and information abundance. For every fully copyrighted document or e-book, there were now several others to pick from that were free to use and share with others. As an added sweetener to the free and open access movement, often these materials could be expanded, remixed, and reused in totally novel ways. A nonprofit organization called Creative Commons rose up to help individuals share and build upon the works of others while abiding by the assigned copyright designation and rules. With Creative Commons, the tools were now available for the person creating an educational resource to provide freedoms to others who might want to share, remix, or commercially use it. As this happened, the term "ShareAlike" became increasingly used in place of "copyright."

Contributing or giving to others is what both the Web 2.0 and Bill Clinton's *Giving* book are all about. The Web 2.0 is about sharing. We share podcasts of what we have found online as well as podcasts we have produced. We share ideas in our own wiki or contribute to existing wiki pages found in Wikipedia or WikiQuotes. We share our courses and educational resources with others.

We also subscribe to what others want to share with us. We subscribe to particular online news shows, postings from insightful bloggers, channels from YouTube video creators, and a plethora of other online content. What all these events mean is that you, the people, control your educational experience, instead of someone else controlling it for you.

Thanks to visionary people like Murray Goldberg and the emergence of Web 2.0 technologies, there is now a resounding buzz in education about sharing. During my travels the past few years to places like China, Spain, Taiwan, Thailand, Korea, Ireland, the United Kingdom, Iceland, and Saudi Arabia, people have been talking about sharing and the possibilities that it holds for education. It is starting to make sense, especially when experiencing a budgetary shortfall or economic crisis.

This was not the case just five or ten years ago. For instance, when I gave more than a dozen talks on e-learning in four different cities in Australia in August, 2000, and mentioned sharing, a common refrain I heard was that "sharing may work over there in the United States, but it will not work here." This mantra was repeated when venturing over to Finland nearly a year later, and the year after that to New Zealand, Korea, and, yet again, Australia. Ironically, in the United States, I heard the same comments, only in reverse—it may be viable in those other countries you have been visiting, but not here, not now, not anytime.

Like Murray Goldberg, my optimism on how online sharing and collaboration could change education around the globe had taken a serious blow in the early part of this decade. It really did not matter where I was; each place I stopped provided the same gloomy news, the same questions, and, generally, the same resistance and reluctance to share. I could have been standing in the middle of an international airport filled with educational professionals from hundreds of countries all headed in different directions and each of them would have stopped and stated the exact same thing: "We do not share in my country, period."

Not only did most educators work alone and apart from others, but they also did not want their educational materials to be exposed to or exploited by a world community that might critique or mismanage them. These trepidations were not minute or restrained, but enormous, pervasive, and intense.

THE GLOBAL EXPANSION OF SHARING

Fortunately, the sharing pioneers kept chipping away at such fears. With each passing year, education and training professionals in K–12 schools, colleges and universities, and corporate, nonprofit, military, and government training settings have all become more comfortable with sharing educational ideas, content, and best practices. Time, experience in teaching with online resources, modeling and examples of others, and general Web familiarity have broadened the views of those once hesitant or reluctant. Sharing has become a prominent part of the educational lexicon. It is part of what you do when you teach, design instructional materials, or evaluate instructional innovations. You share resources and materials in online portals and content repositories, you place your best practices up on display in the Web for others to learn from, and you share your results. Learners and potential learners from every corner of this planet benefit from the sharing.

Sharing now permeates society. Our casual sharing can have an impact on a child or an adult in rural parts of Cambodia, Chile, Chad, or Canada. Let's briefly look at Canada, as an example.

In northern portions of the Canadian provinces there typically are no roads, except during cold winter seasons when ice bridges can be formed. Given these physical constraints, education is often shared electronically. In parts of Northern Ontario, thousands of First Nation individuals lack paved roads, plumbing, and other amenities that many of us take for granted. Amazingly, however, many have broadband access to educational opportunities through programs such as Contact North and the Good Learning Anywhere Project. And, as noted below, with this access at their fingertips, these learners in Northern Ontario, as well as learners in any other corner of the globe, can engage with and share course materials from MIT and numerous other universities for free. Why? Because these resources have been shared!

Although examples of educational sharing might not be in the news as frequently as the examples of giving that Clinton documents, they are no less common. Many universities and educational organizations are sharing online course materials and information resources, including MIT's OpenCourseWare (OCW) initiative—a plan to place every single MIT course on the Internet for free.

When Charles Vest, then president of MIT, announced this bold OCW initiative on April 4, 2001, many wondered about MIT's actual intentions as well as the ramifications for institutions of higher learning and beyond. Just a couple years after Vest's announcement, there already were hundreds of courses online and thousands of hours of free content. Given its more than one million visitors each month, the MIT OCW project is certainly making a monumental impact. Testimonials found on the OCW homepage come from individuals in dozens of countries including Croatia, Argentina, Nigeria, Morocco, Indonesia, the United States, and China.

So momentous is this initiative that OCW courses from MIT have been translated into Spanish, Portuguese, Thai, French, German, Vietnamese, and Ukrainian. Thanks to such efforts, a large percentage of the world population can now learn from one person's initial idea to share. Other esteemed universities such as Johns Hopkins, Tufts, Notre Dame, Utah State, Carnegie Mellon, Korea University, the Open University in the United Kingdom, and a consortium of universities in Japan, including the University of Tokyo, have followed the lead of MIT in placing some of their course content online for free.

As such courses are shared, the world naturally nudges forward as a better and more enlightened place to put up your tent, open up your laptop, and live and learn. Though some are quick to note that typically there is no instructor grading student work within OCW courses, extensive learning is possible without instructors. Self-paced, exploratory, and personally directed learning is certainly a legitimate and vital educational activity, and often much more exciting, pleasurable, and beneficial than teacher-directed learning. Keep in mind, however, that at this time exploring such resources does not lead to any course credit or a degree. The recent emergence of online entities such as Peer 2 Peer University and the University of the People, which exclusively use such open education content, may change that.

Not only are course materials being shared, but so are podcasts or online audio files of lectures, conference keynotes, student presentations, and other valuable educational resources. People are sharing ideas in their online blog posts. In effect, anyone living in the twenty-first century with Internet access can be a journalist. Furthermore, current discoveries and new theories no longer have to wait years in the professional publishing pipelines to be read, discussed, commented on, and revised. Life at Internet speed is highly accelerated, personal, engrossing, and exhilarating!

MY SHARING JOURNEY

The sharing of thoughts, initial research, collaborative ideas, and announcements within a blog or personal homepage helps both the sharer and the receiver. For instance, the results from the simple sharing of a blog post may evolve into a magazine or journal article, or even a book. And with free and open access journals, open source books, and even wikibooks, sharing is amplified from a simple blog post or a rough idea scribbled on a napkin in a restaurant to a series of ideas with collaborative partners around the world. Many scholars today are putting up full books on the Web for anyone to download the entire text or pieces of it as needed.

Not only have I seen such sharing in action, I have personally attempted to develop a series of sharing tools and resources. During late 1998 and into 1999, about a dozen doctoral students and I developed many sharing tools and associated resources for an undergraduate textbook in educational psychology published by Houghton Mifflin. The goal was for students and instructors who used the book to share instructional activities, events, and ideas online. They could also find advice, examples, and templates for their teaching. We called the resulting textbook sharing site and portal INSITE.

When done with INSITE, we expanded on these ideas with a free global resource for college instructors and corporate trainers called InstructorShare that was developed through CourseShare, a company we formed to help share educational resources with the world for free. The goal of InstructorShare was to facilitate the sharing of learning resources and materials with the global education community. With Instructor-Share, instructors in higher education and trainers in corporate settings could share media elements, book reviews, pedagogical innovations, and conference information within more than two hundred communities in distinct fields or disciplines. An important feature was that instructors also could asynchronously or synchronously discuss their use.

Although InstructorShare was quickly used by thousands of people, copyright issues and concerns made us take it offline after a few years. Nevertheless, it remains a model for online sharing. Now more than a decade later, dozens of other online repositories (databases of content or learning objects) and referatories (databases of links) exist, including popular sites such as MERLOT (USA), Connexions (USA), CAREO (Canada), and Jorum (UK).

And though we decided to terminate the InstructorShare project, we did not give up on sharing. In fact, during the greater part of the next five years, my team also built a series of sharing portals including Book-storeShare, UniversityShare, LibraryShare, TrainingShare, and Publi-cationShare; only the latter two remain operational. LibraryShare, for instance, indexed digital libraries and online library resources as well as hundreds of public and university libraries in North America. Similarly, BookstoreShare was designed to lead users to the increasingly vital world of free or open access digital books. UniversityShare, in contrast, offered a virtual map to the homepages of colleges and universities around the planet. The only commercial product we developed, SurveyShare, became the most widely used result of our efforts, with tens of thousands of people each year developing online surveys with it and hundreds of thousands taking them for free. Users of SurveyShare could collabora-tively build and share their surveys and survey results with their colleagues and friends.

Human sharing epitomizes this fourth wave of technology. Each tool, system, resource, or course built online must have sharing opportunities or consequences for it to be highly valued and used. Fortunately, the world is becoming filled with such virtual sharing devices and options.

OTHER SHARING QUESTS AND QUESTORS

As pioneers in this online sharing journey, we were intent on finding ways to share the knowledge of the world by assembling a compendium of links to all the online libraries, bookstores, and universities we could locate. These were lofty goals, but many organizations and institutions are now building online libraries and content aggregation sites that do just that and much more. For example, personnel from Google, in collaboration with some of the foremost public libraries, colleges, and universities, are digitizing scores of books with the goal of being the primary source on the planet for the world's knowledge. Millions of accessible e-books from Google, or at least pieces of them, are now shared with a fast-growing online world community. And this has been expanded by the launching of Google e-bookstore near the end of 2010 with over 3 million books to choose from.

Not satisfied with these choices? Well, a coalition led by the Internet Archive is building a free digital library of Internet content. With its own ambitious book-scanning project, the Internet Archive is in head-to-head competition with Google. Incentive comes from the fact that officials at the Internet Archive do not want Google to be the only knowledge-providing game in town. And they are faring quite well in this contest. By early 2011, there were 2.6 million open access text documents at the Internet Archive (including more than one million digital books that can be freely printed). These high-profile races to store the world's knowledge notwithstanding, just think of the innovative ways in which educators in developing countries could use the millions of free and open access books now available online.

The global pursuit toward digitization of knowledge objects is not just about books. The Internet Archive is attempting to index the entire Web. In the "Wayback Machine," for example, one can look up Web pages by year, month, and date. The Internet Archive not only looks backward but also to present and future states of the Web. By September 2009, the Internet Archive had indexed some 150 billion Web pages. And as of early January 2011, it had indexed 420,000 movies, films, and videos; about 760,000 audio files (including more than 86,000 live music concerts); around 60,000 maps from the United States Geological Survey; 34,000 free software tools; and a vast array of open educational resources. This is one ambitious project!

Reread those numbers and then pause for a moment and think about how much learning can now take place not just at this moment in time or particular year, but for decades or even centuries to come. Think of all the human lives that such educational resources might touch and change for the better.

As these colossal scanning and indexing projects unfold, sharing is no longer debated or resisted; instead it is a key part of what it means to be in education, no matter what setting you are in. These numbers tell us that we are a sharing species. I believe that such acts of giving and sharing may ultimately define who we really are as human beings.

With such momentum, the conversations surrounding sharing have vastly changed. When I travel to different countries and cities today, the reactions are much different from what they were in 1999 or 2000, or even just one or two years ago. I witness new possibilities for sharing with each journey I make. When in Taipei in July 2005, I met with Lucifer Chu, who has donated hundreds of thousands of dollars of his own money to translate MIT courses to traditional and simplified Chinese in a project called the Opensource Opencourseware Prototype System (OOPS). Lucifer is a highly energetic, funny, and charismatic leader who is changing the world through translation efforts and the ensuing sharing.

Fortunately, Lucifer's OOPS project is hardly a one-act play. Sharing is about connections and one phenomenal resource for making them is, in fact, called Connexions. A November 2006 visit to Rice University in Houston, Texas, where the Connexions project is headquartered, confirmed that they had developed one of the fastest-growing and most widely used collections of online scholarly material in the world. As of January 2011, Connexions contained over seventeen thousand course modules available for download in such areas as physics, history, music, computer science, nanotechnology, and biodiversity, resulting in over one hundred million page hits each month. With the innovative ideas of Professor Richard Baraniuk, the founder and one of the chief architects of Connexions, the Connexions people were not merely housing an extremely large repository of educational materials—they were building a powerful set of free software tools and resources to expand these sharing and collaboration efforts.

A similar and somewhat more established site, MERLOT, evolved out of the California State University Center for Distributed Learning in the late 1990s. By January 2011, it contained more than twenty-six thousand content resources and could boast ninety thousand members around the world using shared online resources as well as evaluating them in a peer-review rating system. Each time I explore MERLOT, I find the resources it contains stunningly impressive. And, as later explained in this book, if I am a teacher, I can just as quickly connect to Curriki for free K–12 contents or to the Global Text Project for free and open access digital textbooks intended to help educate disadvantaged populations in Africa and developing countries around the globe.

But the journey continues. Just four months after my November trip to Rice University, I was back on that campus in late March 2007 to attend a Hewlett Foundation grantees meeting. This gathering in Houston brought together those with funding from the foundation to share experiences about the open educational resources (OER) that they were developing, promoting, and evaluating—this was a meeting of sharers about sharing. Without a doubt, the OER movement is the single most fascinating and globally life-changing educational event to occur in the past few decades. It may be the pinnacle outcome of the Internet. Indeed, OER has far-reaching consequences. Simply stated, as education is shared and consequently transforms the lives of millions of youth, so too are economies and international relations transformed, leading to further transformations in personal self-esteem and the potential for minor as well as major educational achievements and untold new competencies.

JOINING THE SHARING REVOLUTION

It does not matter where I travel or with whom I communicate now, the stories I hear are much different and, at times, exceedingly optimistic. The seeds of sharing have successfully grown and ripened into assorted educational fruits. No longer are there mass protest rallies against online learning or the sharing of such resources and learning. Visits to various cities in Mexico, Australia, Singapore, Malaysia, Saudi Arabia, the UAE, Korea, and Canada in 2009 and 2010 confirmed this for me. At each stop, people asked me if it was acceptable to videostream my talks. In response, I quickly told them to podcast, videostream, Webcast, pubcast, or do whatever they wanted with it. And feel free to post my slides, my talk abstract, picture, or bio as well. All education should be shared. The more we share educational resources, the more the knowledge of this planet is opened to its learners.

So what can you share to help education around the world?

1. **Mentoring:** You can sign up to be an online mentor, coach, or tutor in your area of expertise. Many professional organizations today, such as those in engineering, business, and nursing, include some type of mentoring services.

2. **Course Content:** If in postsecondary education, you can share instructional content you have created in places such as MERLOT or Connexions. If in K–12 education, perhaps contribute to or use Curriki or one of many online lesson plan sharing sites. Those in corporate, nonprofit, or government positions should talk to your training directors or chief learning officers about what sharing is possible within your organization. And informal

learners and citizens of the world can create a course homepage or shell, podcast, or online instructional videos wherein they share educational ideas and experiences.

3. **Join the OCW Movement:** At an organizational or institutional level, you can share entire courses or programs in the OCW movement. Administrators need to consider putting forth proposals and strategic plans for such.

4. **Guest Expert:** You can be a guest expert in an online chat or Webinar. You might also podcast a lecture on a topic and place it on the Web for others to access for free, such as in iTunes. Along these same lines, you could videostream a lecture you give in a class, at a conference, or in a workshop for free distribution to the world community.

5. **Collaboration:** You can sign up at ePals or Keypals to engage in online collaboration with another school. You could also share cultural artifacts or lessons for such collaborative activities and events. At the corporate level, you can share software problems and solutions, new product training, and additional intellectual capital in wikis, blogs, podcasts, or other appropriate technological outlets.

6. **Translator:** You could volunteer to translate open educational resources or OpenCourseWare in your native tongue.

7. **Portals:** You can create, index, or aggregate educational portals of online content. You can also market or showcase any new or consistently useful portals that you find.

8. **Evaluator:** You can help in the evaluation or rating of online content. You could also develop the methods and forms of evaluation to be employed.

9. **Software Developer:** Software developers can offer open source or introductory free versions of their software or special discounts for education.

10. **Blogger:** You can blog on current events in education to share what is happening. At the same time, you can add hyperlinks within your blog, thereby stretching your post to other valuable educational resources, documents, trends, and events.

This list offers only a fraction of what is now possible. Clearly, opportunities for sharing our educational lives are exploding. This is a key part of the giving that Clinton was talking about. Sharing education is among the most powerful acts of giving that human beings can engage in. And such educational sharing can take place in a wide variety of formats.

Sharing can be casual among friends who teach the same course and want to benefit from what each other has developed or accomplished. Such collegial sharing might involve a new instructional activity to test out, or a video you've just found in YouTube, CNN Video, or the BBC News and Videos. Each instance of sharing among these friends and colleagues, casual as it might be, allows for innovations, changes, and new ideas to be piloted and perhaps someday flourish in other disciplines not originally intended. Online educational sharing is often creative, spontaneous, and somewhat haphazard. As a result, it is virtually untrackable. But as evidenced by the millions of visits to these sites each day, it is happening!

The scope of online sharing certainly varies. It can occur among just a few individuals or perhaps benefit only a single person for it to have value. At the same time, it can be used by teams, schools, local communities, countries, regions, or the world community. Sharing can be sensed in a fleeting moment in time and then dissipate. It can also be much more lasting and even viral, thereby spreading to people far beyond the originally intended audience and recurring a million times over.

The fourth generation of educational technologies has not only made sharing possible, but also highly encouraged. For millions of people spread far and wide across this lovely planet, these technologies are indispensable; this is how countless individuals today spend the learning-related aspects of their lives. Consequently, stories of sharing in education will be part of teaching and learning lore for decades to come. Teachers will continue to be givers, but everyone involved in education or training, no matter their role or capacity, will be sharers as well as sharing receivers.

There are no shortages of sharing opportunities today, nor will there be in ten, twenty, or a hundred years from now. With each passing generation, sharing will become increasingly synonymous with education, because sharing, like giving, is at the forefront of what it means to be human. Each person walking this planet will be expected to share his or her ideas, talents, expertise, wisdom, products, computing power, bandwidth, scientific discoveries, and educational materials with others using various forms of online technologies. Such is life in the twenty-first century and beyond.

As in Bill Clinton's documentation of how giving can change the world, through sharing, anyone can make a small dent in solving educational problems and implementing progressive educational reforms. What will you share and where might your journeys in this exciting arena lead? I hope you find time to share your results.

Please let me know what transpires. I look forward to hearing about your innovative sharing pursuits.

Curtis J. Bonk
Indiana University
April 2011

Introduction to the Open Learning World

COOL SUMMER DIGS

Our first week in Hope, British Columbia—a small town on the banks of the Fraser River—has been exciting. This area of B.C. is extremely lush and vibrant, covered in vegetation and full of waterways. We have begun work at Welqámex—a once large settlement on a now uninhabited island—where we are currently hacking through dense forest under-growth to re-establish paths across the site.

I now consider myself proficient with a machete and a hatchet (skills that I didn't expect to acquire), and I am surprised at how much work precedes an archaeological excavation. We are building trails, clearing deadwood from archaeological features, setting up sieving stations, and even digging and building an outhouse. It's tiring, but at the end of the day when we turn around and look upon all that has been accomplished, the hard work is immensely gratifying.

Despite being overgrown, the forest is beautiful, and I have observed many wild plants, some of which were used regularly for clothes and food by the Stó:lō people. On a daily basis, the thirteen of us are the only people on the island. The island is secluded and mostly cut off from the modern day hustle and bustle. With the sun shining through the canopy of the tall cottonwood and maple trees and the birds calling, I can sense an energy in the forest, perhaps from those who once lived there, and it is very spiritual. We work closely with members of the Stó:lō community, and their stories and guidance help to bring our work alive. In so many words, it is beautiful work in a beautiful place.[1]

You might be wondering just who this hatchet- and machete-wielding person is. You might also be scratching your head as to why I start this book about a technologically sophisticated and open learning world with a story about outhouses and clearing walking paths from dead and rotting trees. Perhaps this makes you equally curious as to when it was written. Well, the writer's name is Lily Henry Roberts, and she authored that short reflection on Wednesday, July 2, 2008.[2] As Lily indicated in her story, that July she was located on an island near Hope, British Columbia, a city of some six thousand people less than a hundred miles east of Vancouver. During the academic year, Lily is an undergraduate history major at UCLA and a member of the women's rugby team. As such, she is perhaps just the sort of hardy person who is meant for a machete-wielding adventure in the thick forests of Canada. But UCLA remains in her hip pocket when she's up in Canada. You see, Lily is part of the Archaeology Field Program sponsored by UCLA's Cotsen Institute of Archaeology and run through its International Education Office.

These archaeological dig projects are open to anyone over the age of eighteen, not only UCLA students and alumni. You do not even have to be a college student to participate. While the vast majority of those who enroll are traditional college students, many are not. Even more intriguing, given sufficient time, interest, and money, you or I could sign up for this program. During the summer of 2008, some 138 people were enrolled in it. In recognition of their learning during the program, they each received twelve credits at the end of their digging efforts. These students were engaged in archaeological projects not only in western Canada, but also in Ecuador, Chile, Peru, Panama, Albania, Italy, England, and Catalina Island in the United States.

Lily and many other students and instructors at seven of the UCLA dig locations blogged about their summer adventures. These online diaries help connect them to anyone with Internet access. And through their blogs, those of us who cannot physically be there with them can be armchair Indiana Joneses![3] Here in Indiana, that sounds mighty appealing.

The Internet is an amazing learning resource. Through one simple online tool—blogging—we are quickly immersed in information related to what archaeologists around the world do for a living. With blogs and other Internet tools and resources, field school experiences can now be shared and discussed with thousands of people on a daily basis.

The site instructor from UCLA, Dr. Anthony P. Graesch, also posted to the Canadian group's blog site.[4] He explains that the way in which archaeological research is typically portrayed in television and the movies is often well beyond the actual, more mundane activities of archaeologists. At the same time, he notes that the rich and complex history of the Stó:lō people cannot be found in textbooks.[5] History is embedded in the landscape itself. You must be there and experience it! Blog posts like his spread hope that all of us can learn from shared online experiences. Perhaps it is fitting that he is blogging from Hope!

For those who cannot commit six to ten weeks of their time, student and instructor blogs, program press releases, and embedded pictures serve as brief forays into the history of these First Nation people. Those who have the time and interest, but who wish to travel beyond North American settings, have plenty of options. While Lily and Colleen are in British Columbia, UCLA archaeology graduate student Jamie Aprile is in Albania. Her July 14, 2008 blog post is rich with detail about the excavation and recording activities her team is conducting.[6]

As in the blog about the Canadian summer dig project, the postings from Albania share firsthand experiences of students and instructors as they work the site. In addition to blogging and e-mailing coordinators back at UCLA about their progress, these young archaeologists use technologies such as global positioning systems (GPS) to help them find and record information. Just like Lily, Jamie is quite pleased to be out of the classroom and in the real world. However, that real world is no longer just hers. In the twenty-first century, Web technology has arisen to help learners like Jamie freely share their experiences with people they do not know and will likely never meet. As Jamie's post divulges, archaeological work is not a holiday for those enrolled but requires much sweat and dedication.

Much of these efforts are the brainchild of UCLA archaeology professor Ran Boytner, codirector of the Chile dig in the Tarapaca Valley where pilot versions of the Archaeology Field Program have been evolving over the past several years. He is accompanied by seventeen students, making Chile the most popular of the summer dig destinations. When he first dreamed up the idea, Boytner expected

UCLA students to be the primary beneficiaries. He was soon in for quite a surprise. Students have been pouring in from all over the world. And why not? They are digging in some of the driest, oldest, and most interesting sites in the history of human civilization. Such projects offer adventure, work, learning, personal reflection, collaboration, and greater cultural awareness.

Boytner stated that in a good number of field schools, students fail to learn proper techniques and are treated as "inexpensive labor."[7] Many are turned off by that educational approach. He argued, "We are sending students into these immersion programs where we put students front and center. It is our job to prepare the next generation of scholars, and more importantly, philo-archaeologists—people who like archaeology."[8]

What is unique is that the UCLA project transports students from the classroom and into genuine research environments. As such, it apprentices them for possible professional lives as archaeologists and other occupations where categorization, analysis, attention to detail, and teamwork skills are critical. In effect, these intensive weeks in the field prepare them for life. With the blog-posting activity, however, this is more than an apprenticeship of 138 people. The Summer Digs project is also a virtual apprenticeship for thousands or perhaps even millions of online Web surfers. With these online posts and summaries, Boytner and his colleagues are helping to train the next generation of archaeologists, anthropologists, and historians. It is quite plausible that many people stumbling on their blog posts from Chile or Peru a few years, decades, or even centuries from now might become quite energized by them and decide to take a class in archaeology or even enter the field.

What do those enrolled find in these adventures? Discoveries range from ancient pots to pieces of gold to Chilean mummies to llama feces.[9] Throw in a few skulls and bones, a bit of ancient petroglyphs or collections of rock art, and intriguing native rituals, stories, and customs, and there is much to write home about in one's blog postings. Students can also update their friends and family in e-mail reports as well as text messages from their mobile phones. Admittedly, however, with limited Internet access in such locations, at least at this time, these students must often travel quite a distance to find a way to submit their posts. Given connection speeds, their blog updates are often done through e-mail back to UCLA main offices.

What is interesting today is that with the emergence of the Web, we can go from a live experience during the day, and a few hours later record it for near-eternity in a blog posting or Web site entry. Real-world archaeology becomes recorded and amplified through the Web. Our life experiences are immediately shared and, at the same time, permanently stored. As this happens, our identity in this world is altered and our status is temporarily elevated, if only for a few weeks. The Web becomes a way to communicate findings and build social networks for one's research as well as notable personal pursuits. The use of blogs and other Web-based recordings of our daily events extends our existence and identities into cyberworlds.

Of course, the Archaeology Field Program is just one example of a host of real-world projects that anyone can sign up for. Nonprofit organizations such as Earthwatch and Greenpeace have been operating for decades with volunteers. What is unique is that the Web offers such organizations the opportunities to spread their messages with a variety of online resources, including pictures, fact sheets, videos, news, events, and blog postings. Earthwatch even boasts a YouTube channel and a Facebook group. Not to be outdone, Greenpeace has an online discussion forum anyone can join as well as blogs from activists with embedded videos and pictures that are quite captivating. They also have Greenpeace TV, which offers online documentaries, Greenpeace podcasts, and many interesting environment-related games you can play for free online.

These types of organizations can now more directly promote science, global citizenship, and opportunities for human learning through online means. The Web has become prime real estate for educational programming about the environment, climate change, history, politics, and nearly any topic you can think of. What few people realize is that as the Web becomes our preferred learning platform, nontraditional learning is suddenly the norm. Lifelong learning dreams discussed decade after decade in the twentieth century are quickly being realized in the twenty-first.

Just as these various UCLA summer digs were going on, Discovery News featured the remarkable findings of David Thomas, a doctoral student in the archaeological program at La Trobe University in Melbourne, Australia. Unlike the UCLA students, Mr. Thomas could not make personal appearances at the dig sites he had in mind. The reason was simple—they were located in far-too-dangerous regions of war-torn southern Afghanistan. Because he could not travel there, the options he had to conduct his research were rather thin. Fortunately, Google Earth came to Thomas's rescue. Using this Web resource, high-resolution images enabled him to find and chart up to 450 sites that appear to be significant from an archaeological standpoint.[10]

With one online resource to support his research, Thomas does not have to raise funds for his airfare, food, and lodging. He does not have to leave his family and friends and travel thousands of miles to conduct his research. And he does not have to worry about being shot or decapitated once there. All he needs now is a computer, a reliable Internet connection, and the patience to make careful observations. With those things in place, Thomas has located numerous camps, mosques, reservoirs, dams, and military installations that the archaeological world did not know existed. When I spoke with him in August 2008, David told me he preferred actual "digging" and "doing" to remote forms of archaeology. As he put it: "Although my family is probably glad that I sat in front of the computer screen, Google Earth isn't and shouldn't become a substitute for getting down and dirty. . . . [B]y actually visiting the area, we would find many more sites which don't show up on Google Earth." Nevertheless, with such tools, David has become a discoverer of culture without leaving a physical trace of his being there. His footprints are electronic ones. And although he told me he never feels in danger even when he is in quite "dodgy destinations," such as Libya, Sudan, Syria, and Afghanistan, I reminded him that perhaps thanks to Web technology his head is still attached. In contrast to the UCLA Archaeology Field Program, this is an example of how learning can begin with the virtual in the hopes that one day it will move to back to the physical. How many other exciting discoveries are simply awaiting such innovative Googling efforts?

Thanks to the Web, we can all be adventurers, explorers, writers, dreamers, and learners. At times we move from physical to virtual and other times in the reverse. And, as Thomas has shown us, sometimes virtual journeys are much more preferred and viable than physical experiences. As these stories reveal, the learning world is now open.

It is open in the forests of Canada. It is also open in the deserts of Chile and Egypt. It is open in Albania as much as it is open in Afghanistan. You can now explore it too. Physically, virtually, or both.

THE PREMISE

If this book could be shortened to its narrowest point, it would exist as a one-line proclamation that states, "Anyone can now learn anything from anyone at anytime." As the stories in this book reveal, it does not matter if you are a scientist on a ship in Antarctic waters or a young girl in a Philippine village—you can learn when and where you want and from whomever you are interested in learning. What's more, these two individuals—the scientist at sea and the girl at home—can now communicate and learn from each other in a matter of seconds, or, alternatively, when the other is sleeping, or even weeks, months, or years after the initial contact. Granted, such learning usually requires access to the Internet, or at least to a computing center.

But therein lies the premise of this book—as a member of this species known as human, you learn. You learn every day. In fact, *we all learn*—all 6.7 billion of us. And, as the stories above reveal, multiple technologies have arisen almost in unison to open up such learning to each of us at every waking moment. To simplify a highly complex situation and set of events, ten key technology trends that directly and indirectly impact our learning in the twenty-first century are incrementally revealed in this book using a model called "WE-ALL-LEARN."

A few years back, Thomas Friedman argued that our world had been flattened by many technologies, most significant of which is the Internet, with its ability to find nearly any piece of information we might seek in the exact moment of need.[11] As he showed, the commerce-related implications of this premise are enormous. However, Friedman was focused on social and economic flatteners brought about by technology and the associated changes in organizational structures and business practices. In contrast, this book explores territory that Friedman only touched upon briefly in his excursions, while also forging ahead into some lands he left uncharted.

At its hub, this book and its corresponding framework address how Web technology offers new hope for educating the citizens of this planet.

It is the opening up of education that ultimately makes a flatter or more robust economic world possible. In the twenty-first century, education trumps economy as the key card to participation in the world. It is education, after all, from which robust economies are built. So when there are momentous shifts or megatrends occurring in education, they must be explored, documented, grasped, and exploited ethically as well as thoughtfully. Instead of Friedman's "flatteners" or the highly touted "megatrends" of John Naisbitt, however, I shall call the ten learning technology trends that are transforming education and life in the twenty-first century "openers," as in the door opening to untold learning opportunities for billions of people.[12]

TEN OPENERS: (WE-ALL-LEARN)

1. **W**eb Searching in the World of E-Books
2. **E**-Learning and Blended Learning
3. **A**vailability of Open Source and Free Software
4. **L**everaged Resources and OpenCourseWare
5. **L**earning Object Repositories and Portals
6. **L**earner Participation in Open Information Communities
7. **E**lectronic Collaboration
8. **A**lternate Reality Learning
9. **R**eal-Time Mobility and Portability
10. **N**etworks of Personalized Learning

As will become evident, while Friedman was documenting his three "p" words—new economic *players* from China, India, and Eastern Bloc countries, a flattened *playing field* resulting from collaborative technologies, and more horizontal and less hierarchical management *processes*—three different ones were simultaneously emerging in education. In education, the "p" words relate to *pages* of content, *piping* for that content to run through (that is, a technological infrastructure), and a *participatory* learning culture. Instead of economic might fostered through online technology, the converging learning trends offer untold intellectual might. The triple convergence in education, then, underpins and hastens the vast economic opportunities that Friedman and others have discussed during the past few years. And that is the premise of this book.

WHERE IS PLATO WHEN YOU NEED HIM?

We are living in a time period of the most monumental changes and challenges to arise in education since Plato held his first classes at his famed academy, Hekademeia, later known as Akademeia. Even in those days, learning in different locations and times was facilitated by technology as teachers and learners were shifting from exclusive reliance on oral traditions to instruction that included the written word. This, of course, was a historic transformation for the people of this planet because learning could now take place beyond a singular geographic location and moment in time. Learners could read Plato's thoughts and ideas, instead of having to be there for the live event. Plato, in effect, was the first known distance educator.[13] Still, the prime delivery of education in the fourth century BC was via speech from the expert instructor or mentor to awaiting learners.

Fast-forward a couple of millennia and those same oral traditions—as well as the associated teacher- or text-centeredness that they promote—still pervade all levels and forms of education. What a time traveler would quickly discover is that in most cases teaching has not really changed much since the days of Plato, even though the technologies for learning have progressed dramatically, especially during the past century. This book is an opportunity to take these time travelers to different rooms and learning situations, including boats, trains, subway stations, and even alternative worlds and dimensions, where the status quo for teaching and learning is definitely not the one you and I experienced growing up.

Most people remain unaware of the enormous number of these nontraditional learning venues and opportunities or are hesitant to use them when they are. Not surprisingly, the field of education is replete with highly thoughtful yet cynical articles about how little technology has improved the state of education. Some of these articles ask how comfortable Plato and his student, Aristotle, might be in visiting a typical school or teacher education classroom today compared to, say, Hippocrates making a similar visit to a medical school building.[14] Such articles will invariably note that while the medical field has decided to make use of advances in technology to train its students and thereby benefit society, the techniques that surround the field of education have not really changed much. For instance, large-screen televisions, projection units, marker boards, prerecorded videostreamed or podcasted lectures, and PowerPoint slides are simply more of the same teacher-centered past. Since the 1960s, the "distance" in distance education has too often meant how large could the lecture halls and classrooms be and still allow learners to view the screen.[15] It remains eyeball-to-eyeball learning. Today's teachers, much like those in preceding generations or even millennia ago, remain the masters of some content area that must somehow be imparted to students and then rigorously assessed.

What is perhaps different today is that technologies are actually leading to major changes in teaching and learning, especially in the opportunities to learn. As this occurs, students are taking on the roles of teachers, and those formerly known as teachers are better positioned as guides, tutors, and mentors. Millennia of highly intractable instructional approaches and limited educational opportunities have begun to give way to something different. In the span of just a decade or two, with the escalating use of the Web and its associated technologies for learning, educational practices have greatly expanded beyond the time-and-place rigidity of fourth-century BC teaching and learning environments. Today, as we are seated in just the first few years of a new millennium, educational institutions and training organizations are being forced to modify or significantly change the instructional practices that they have used and often found highly effective (at least from internal and external accreditation criteria) since they were established. Of course, changes of any type rarely come easily or without much heated questioning, controversy, and debate.

It is only now that far-reaching changes in the education of young and old are possible with learning technology. Decades ago, Charles Wedemeyer from the University of Wisconsin pointed out that over the centuries, technologies—including books, the telegraph, the postal service, the telephone, the radio, the television, and computer-assisted learning—have extended the time-space dimensions of learning.[16] With each of these inventions, learners could learn when and where it was feasible for them. The reliance on eyeball-to-eyeball learning, which had been pervasive since Plato's Academy two dozen centuries ago, is no longer as prevalent in schools, universities, and corporate training institutes, and may not even be preferred by the learners or their instructors. But the technologies of the twenty-first century are more numerous and qualitatively much different from those of preceding centuries. Online bulletin boards, e-mail, chat rooms, iPods, mobile phones, wikis, blogs, and interactive headgear all provide for enhancements of the traditional teacher-centered past, as well as providing opportunities in which learners have a voice and can engage in more personally meaningful projects. Such technologies provide ways for all of us to learn.

What was accomplished previously with textbooks and classroom lectures has shifted to other resources and learning technologies. This shift effectively frees up face-to-face classroom time for addressing personal needs. With such personalization, it is truly the age of learner-centered and empowered learning. It is time to push forward new learning proposals and goals, not just for a particular classroom, program, or institution—as important as it is to do so—but to reflect on this impact on a more global scale. Today, we should be striving to take advantage of unique and low-cost learning opportunities and formats available for students of any educational need, monetary status, background, or age level.

Of course, for the learning faucet to be truly opened, the learner needs access to the Internet, or, at least, access to the resources available from it in print or a digital format. For most members of this planet, such access will begin with their mobile phones. As those with Internet access realize, we have all just lived through a decade of rapidly expanding and extremely intoxicating use of the Internet for instruction. In less than ten years, we have shifted from e-mail and relatively simple online services and activities to opportunities for downloading massive amounts of high- and low-quality videos, producing and sharing music online, connecting multiple sites in full-motion videoconferencing, and engaging in online chats with dozens of friends or experts simultaneously. However, the coming ten or twenty years will assuredly be even more fascinating and tumultuous. Each decade, distance-learning historians seem to document the extensive lineage of distance-learning technologies and resources that have helped shift when, where, and how learning occurs. However, it was not until recently that enough factors converged to offer the possibility of learning about nearly any topic in any discipline to any connected learner or classroom. It can happen today. And it is now often there for free!

Imagine for a moment that you are that time traveler mentioned earlier. If you walked out of ancient Greece or Egypt into a modernized classroom today or into an online course that did not require a physical space, it might cause your heart to pause—not due to the physical journey, but due to the intellectual ones that are now possible. You might interact with Plato not simply by reading his famed *Republic* under the shade of an oak tree, but within a virtual world or simulation. Or perhaps you might meet him in an online role-playing exercise with another student who has taken on his persona. And Plato's various dialogues or Aristotle's works on rhetoric, physics, or politics might be entered into a wiki that you might index, cross-reference, and perhaps even enhance or meaningfully alter through audio recordings or hyper-links to still other Web resources. In effect, the learning technologies of today not only extend the places and times in which learning can occur, but they also offer changes in the types of learning that are now possible, as well as the range and location of learners who can take advantage of them.

THIS IS NOT YOUR PARENT'S EDUCATION

The world is very different today. Anyone reading this book has witnessed and likely participated in at least some of the educational transformations mentioned above. And these were not incremental changes that could be gradually sipped over the past two-and-a-half millennia. Instead, for the most part, they have been available in a one-gulp-only variety. Add to this challenge the fact that there are massive technological innovations and shifts to suddenly chug down, and you have serious problems. Such changes are on the scale of a child's Happy Meal soda that has been supersized by a McDonald's in Texas. Suffice it to say, the educational drinks now available in the early stages of the twenty-first century are definitely not the same ones that our parents or grandparents consumed. We have a vastly different educational world in which to quench our thirsts for knowledge. Therefore, it makes sense to step back for a moment and reflect on the key changes in education that have opened the education world since your parents and grandparents entered their first school buildings and classrooms.

I began this writing quest in June 2007 exactly one hundred years and two months after my grandfather, George Goronja, second generation from Yugoslavia, was born in Milwaukee, Wisconsin. My Grandpa George entered his first primary classroom around the fall of 1912. Contrary to what the many educational critics contend, this classroom was much different from those he would have entered today had he lived to see his hundredth birthday like his older brother Steve. Grandpa George would often tell me that when he got to West Allis Central High School, he walked in the front door and walked out the back door. He did not go home; instead, he kept walking to the Allis Chalmers plant near his parent's house to help in the manufacturing of farm tractors where, despite being laid off during the Depression, he spent more than forty years working, mostly as an inspector or foreman. He was, at times, joined at Allis Chalmers by my grandmother, mother, father, and uncle, all of whom, in contrast, managed to complete their high school educations.

If we could travel back in time with him, we would see that the educational opportunities of a century ago were phenomenally different from what we have today. To begin with, Grandpa George did not have podcasts made of his school lessons in case he missed class. He did not have instructors who waxed eloquently in their blogs about how a particular class or module was going or who inserted supplemental course links in that blog. He never received an e-mail message that linked him to wondrous electronic course resources made available through the Web. There were no virtual worlds to explore for hours on end where new forms of communication and interaction could transpire. Grandpa George and his classmates could not move about to computer labs and media rooms in accordance with their interests and learning pursuits or think about entering and exiting a course at any time of the day. Instead, their learning was pinned down to a particular time, teacher, and place.

I am also certain that my grandfather could not create his own learning materials with some of his classmates that could be edited by still other peers, experts, instructors, or complete strangers in a wiki. Of course, my grandpa never Googled anything, or sent messages with his phones to classmates with reminders of an assignment that was due, or accomplished important course-related activities with his mobile phone or handheld computing device. Nor did George and his class-mates ever engage in virtual discussions and interactions with team members from within their own classes. Equally impossible was the ability to send a question to or seek advice from an ever-present tutor or mentor at any moment and conceivably receive an immediate response. Yes, someone from a local community might enter a class for thirty minutes or an hour, but after that, such an individual was typically long gone. Not today! Online tutoring and mentoring is not just possible, it is a key aspect of education among all age groups from primary schools to corporate training environments to those in senior-citizen activity centers.

The educational world in which our parents and grandparents grew up has significantly and permanently been altered; and so has the learning world experienced by most people reading this book. Books, crayons, pencils, overhead projectors, tape recorders, and blackboards have not disappeared entirely, but learners are increasingly relying on online resources, electronic ink, virtual presence, and digital displays. Some may participate in this educational world using what might now be deemed more traditional technologies for educational delivery, such as laptop and desktop computers. For others, it will occur with MP3 players and iPods strapped around their arms or waist when jogging or connected to a car radio system when driving. For still others, especially those in Asia, this learning transformation will take place with their mobile phones and other handheld technology—at first in small bits or minilearning programs, but soon, with advances in content engagement and screen display units, in larger doses and longer formats.

Education in the coming decade will be as pervasive as the watch or the mobile phone was in the last. What happens when watch knock-offs you see in Malaysia, Thailand, or Singapore are no longer fake Rolexes, but instead devices equipped with hundreds, if not thousands, of free course-related programming hours from MIT, Stanford, Cambridge, or Harvard, as well as with options for more informal learning pursuits? How might such products be promoted and exchanged? Just how cool will it be to have a phone or watch loaded with educational content to view on the train, plane, or bus? Will such items be disposable or resalable? Will fake or real MIT instructors be delivering such content? And will content need to be delivered at all or just be there when needed? In a couple of decades, we may have every single lecture ever recorded in any language as well as all encyclopedia and fact-book content embedded in our watches or mobile phones and be able to subscribe for free to have them continually updated. Do you now see that this is a learning revolution? If so, are you ready to enlist your services?

ENHANCE, EXTEND, TRANSFORM, AND SHARE LEARNING

We humans keep adding to the mix of technologies and resources for enhancing, extending, and transforming learning. A course or learning experience might be enhanced with test questions, simulations, online cases, or other resources available in some type of digital format. It might be extended through collaborative technologies, social networking software, and virtual worlds wherein learners meet and interact with experts, peers, and other instructors they might never have encountered otherwise. And this course might be transformed through participatory learning avenues, such as when learners add to a wiki, participate in an online discussion, or produce problems or cases for each other to solve online and later evaluate or modify the solutions.

But today our metaphors reach beyond enhancing, extending, or transforming learning with technology to notions of sharing that learning. Unlike the use of technology that might only touch the learners in one's class, training program, or organization, today a thought or idea can truly make an impact on anyone anywhere on the planet. It might not be today or tomorrow when that thought or idea is needed. However, once posted to the Web, it will likely be reflected upon or employed by someone sometime in the future. It is that sudden trend toward sharing educational resources, beyond any other development outlined in this book, that is fueling change in education and opening new doors to optimism and human potential. And perhaps it is human nature—we humans love to connect, exchange, share, remix, and reinvent. We also like to share our expertise and see that the areas in which we are expert are placed in good light. So it is with that mind-set that many of us give our time for free to resources like Wikipedia. Perhaps this sharing culture has not suddenly emerged, but was in hibernation, waiting for the right moment to appear. With the wealth of learning technologies today, the time has certainly come.

A few decades ago, software designers and engineers were not likely to share code and build free tools for the world community (though many definitely wanted to). Likewise, educational institutions were not expected to share their courses and course materials with competing institutions or with learners not enrolled in their programs. In those dark ages of just a decade or two ago, instructors locked down their content. As a result, few humans would ever see or hear them in action. Even their colleagues in adjacent rooms or in the same department would rarely if ever venture inside to view their daily performances. And students caught sharing content or ideas were treated as irresponsible citizens if not criminals. But such acts are common and increasingly encouraged here in the twenty-first century. Today, sharing learning is a mantra heard around the world. Do you believe in the power of sharing?

WE ALL NEED TO PARTICIPATE IN THE OPEN EDUCATIONAL WORLD

Given that these technology trends apply to all learners, each of us has a stake in them. No one who wants to participate successfully in this world can put further learning on hold. We, the learners of this new world, need to rally around the learning tools, materials, and resources that we have in order to improve the educational backgrounds of everyone on this planet, and, in doing so, their social, cultural, and economic status and future life possibilities. That is a human and moral imperative.

New and exciting educational technologies appear each day. Anyone attempting to track and test most of them has likely gone at least a tad loopy in the process. The framework provided here—WE-ALL-LEARN— is an opportunity to pause and make sense of the wealth of technologies appearing each day, and hopefully give a few people back some sense of sanity as well as shared optimism about our collective future.

Corporate executives who are interested in making sense of technology trends today and planning for new forms of training and education in the coming decades will benefit from learning more about the WE-ALL-LEARN framework. IT managers can use it in long-range planning for employee training and forecasting meetings and reports. Training managers in corporations or government agencies can also take advantage of the stories, ideas, and examples given here to help justify e-learning initiatives and strategic plans. All of these individuals will want to take advantage of these trends in a financially attractive, efficient, and strategically beneficial way.

In schools and higher education institutions, administrators might use the ideas in this book in making decisions about where to place valued resources. Those in teaching and learning centers might employ the WE-ALL-LEARN framework, or some spin-off of it, to train instructors and staff on the multiple overlapping education and technology trends and the parallel wealth of online teaching possibilities. University deans, for instance, might use it for faculty retreats. In addition, the framework might be particularly valuable to higher education administrators wrestling with key technology or enrollment decisions.

Instructors, housed in different educational sectors or working within various educational levels, might use this book to discover educational resources, tools, and activities that they might embed in their instruction. Even the more hesitant or resistant instructors, trainers, and staff in schools as well as corporate training organizations today might also find the resources in each chapter and underlying framework valuable. Of course, some of the content might provide a wake-up call that says, in effect, that educational options are not declining anytime soon. It might also provide instructors with ideas to discuss and debate with others.

Parents, too, will find many things to consider in raising and helping to educate their children. Their perspectives might help school boards, technology leaders, librarians, and teachers to thoughtfully plan for new technologies. And their children will be a great sounding board for the ideas expressed in this book and any learning technology purchases or strategic plans for their schools.

Finally, and perhaps most important, government officials and politicians reading or accessing this book will discover that there are many exciting new possibilities for enhancing the learning of people in their respective communities and regions of the world. Although concerns about health care, global warming, and security are pervasive, education is the $64 billion question. Politicians running for office can no longer ignore it. Witness Barack Obama's successful presidential campaign, which relied on a rich array of Web-based social networking and communication technologies. Of course, YouTube videos, blogs, podcasts, virtual worlds, and social networking sites increasingly include information about particular political candidates. Those in office, as well as those seeking it, are beginning to realize the educational possibilities of such technologies. In the midst of lawsuits, bans, and hearings related to many emerging Web technologies, it is time for all government officials to grasp the educational potential of Web technologies and provide additional funding and research support as part of twenty-first-century policies and solutions. They should recognize and appreciate the use of blogs, podcasts, online videos, and social networking tools in recent election campaigns and understand that many free Web technologies and open-access learning resources are widely available to educate their citizens. Now is the time to take advantage of these tools in schools, colleges and universities, workplaces, and beyond.

Despite a daily barrage of technology-related announcements and news stories, many people still fail to see the obvious direction in which education is headed. Much of the reason is that education is a highly reactive and slow-moving industry. Unfortunately, it is only when a calamity strikes that some of the openers discussed in this book have become more accepted and taken advantage of. As an example, learning on the Web became highly desired during the SARS crisis in China as well as in the aftermath of Hurricane Katrina in New Orleans. There really was no other way to learn. No doubt deadly flu viruses, earthquakes, tidal waves, floods, and severe winter storms have had the same effect in many villages, cities, and regions of the world. Online learning, in some format, often became the only option.

It is also certain that the global economic crisis we currently find ourselves in, as well as crises to follow, will bring citizens across the planet to appreciate the range and depth of learning now possible online. To upgrade their skills, countless people will be downloading free podcasts, reading and commenting on e-books, watching online videos from the BBC and CNN, and exploring various learning portals. They might also look up an event or topic in Wikipedia or find needed medical information from an expert Web site. Those concerned about quality should be aware that anyone connected to the Web can now find learning resources from every single course that MIT offers and explore them for free. More impressive, for those in China who lack sufficient English language skills, much of the free online course content from MIT as well as that of other universities has been translated to traditional and simplified Chinese and made available to them on the Web without cost. You will read about the people behind such efforts in this book.

As critics point out, not everyone has benefited from Friedman's flatter world. The current economic predicament adds an exclamation point to such arguments. Tens of millions of people might find themselves unemployed after many years of service while millions more fear a similar fate. In the twenty-first century, it is the Web that offers them hope for a better future. Parents, educators, politicians, corporate executives, and those in government training agencies need to be more informed of the learning potential of the Web and find innovative ways to harness it. If you want a decent job in the coming decades, you'd better start looking online for ways to continually expand and fine-tune your skill set. There are many openers and much for you to learn online. It is time you became aware of your expanding options for an education and joined this revolution in learning.

EMBEDDED STORIES

As I considered interviews and key contacts for this book, it was clear to me that I needed to hear from the creator community as well as the user community. In each chapter, therefore, I attempt to capture some of the diverse and global nature of open education from those bringing exciting learning technologies to us as well as from those who are learning with them. Many of the people spotlighted in this book are leaders of a particular project, educational resource, learning tool, or technology trend in education. A few have their feet firmly planted in two or more innovations or trends and were difficult to place in a particular chapter. You will read anecdotes involving corporate training innovators and leaders, creative K–12 teachers and administrators, renowned scholars or researchers in higher education, community leaders, scientists, entrepreneurs with creative technology talents, and students of all stripes.

The UCLA Summer Digs and Afghanistan stories offered at the start of this book are meant to place the open learning world on full display by showing a couple of nontraditional learning possibilities that are now available to learners of all ages and backgrounds.

- These stories detail how learning has shifted from the classroom to real-world settings. In the twenty-first century, more opportunities exist for learners to take charge and engage in personally empowering learning pursuits.
- Both anecdotes illustrate how anyone can participate as a student or casual observer. You do not have to be a designated full-time student to benefit from the countless learning opportunities that the Web now offers. And learning need not only be formal. Informal learning is a large chunk of what happens today.
- Summer Digs reveals how a simple technology like a blog can impact anyone learning anywhere.
- At the same time, with Web technology we do not even have to travel to better understand human culture or engage in most any learning pursuit of interest. The tale from Afghanistan demonstrates that even physically inaccessible regions of the world may be reachable via different types of technology.
- As with social networking tools such as Facebook and MySpace, friends sent to dig locations on different continents can stay in touch and learn from each other through their blog postings and other online communications.
- There are millions of armchair archaeologists who now rely on the Web for their knowledge explorations and associated exchanges.
- Personal learning quests and associated information can be posted today and replayed years later for anyone to benefit.

- Summer Digs is a story from many corners of the world of those involved in a giant quest to understand human civilization. It is not just a story of learning in North America or one dominant perspective or paradigm, but a global story that expands each day.

Keep in mind that these are just a few examples of the learning potential of the Web.

In fact, each person highlighted in this book has an interesting story to tell. For many, it is a story of how they developed a technology tool or resource that epitomizes a particular trend. For others, it is a glimpse of how they used a tool or resource to change the world, or at least a small portion of it. Still others with whom I corresponded have played key roles in pushing along a particular trend or opener and promoting it to the masses.

Their stories will, at times, highlight what they originally intended or expected. At other times, the story will focus on the specific results and current state of their learning journey. In still others, the future directions and implications will be more salient. Hopefully, these stories will inspire others to extend and advance one or more of the ten trends outlined here or to initiate a wholly new trend or educational opening. In addition to the Summer Digs and Afghanistan stories, this book contains dozens more such anecdotes from quite diverse locations around the planet. And the Web is filled with millions more. I encourage you to explore them!

WE-ALL-LEARN

Face it, we all learn. We all learn in many different learning styles and forums not only in order to survive and eke out a living, but to be productive and successful in whatever human pursuits we want to go after. Professional golfers, pharmacists, lobbyists, marriage counselors, truck drivers, and stock market traders all learn. Kindergarten children, second-grade teachers, first-year college students, medical interns, and university administrators all learn. Sheepherders, miners, fishermen, outdoor adventure guides, pole vaulters, and online instructors all learn. We are fortunate to be living during the sudden emergence of an energizing mix of learning-related trends that can enhance the learning of any one of these types of individuals. When these trends are combined, learning is more global, collaborative, rapid, mobile, ubiquitous, participatory, authentic, and free and open. The open world offers us daily doses of electrifying learning possibilities.

I do not argue with those who allude to the pervasive digital divide. Nor will I claim that these ten trends are equally distributed, apparent, or even possible across cultures today or in the near future. What I can say is that they will make learning more a part of any culture, though to different degrees.

Web technologies have blown the doors to educational opportunity wide open. Schools, colleges, universities, government agencies, and corporate training organizations not only need to take notice, they need to take action. This book provides a framework for doing just that.

The ten converging educational openers detailed in this book confront both established as well as newly formed institutions and organizations. Of course, many corporate and higher education administrators continue to act like the captain of the Titanic facing the tip of the iceberg. What is simultaneously remarkable and yet troubling, perhaps, is that these trends may only be the tip of the proverbial iceberg. They will not disappear anytime soon and there is much more than meets the eye that can impact human learning. What will more likely happen is that they will lead to still further educational technology discoveries and inventions that will even more radically shift the balance of power from institutions and organizations as well as from instructors and tutors toward individuals, young and old, rich and poor, seeking to learn. As the WE-ALL-LEARN model will make apparent, we are in the midst of a grand shift toward personalized learning environments and more complete and open learner participation.

Don't look back. The educational world of your parents and grandparents no longer exists. And it is a far cry from Hekademeia. Sure, some of the goals might be similar, but most of the listening and recitation techniques that had seemingly worked for millennia no longer hold up as the primary drivers of education.

It is my hope that this book will start a dialogue about how the various educational technology trends and openers relate to one another and might, in the near term, coalesce. Discussion also needs to unfold on how these openers might accelerate access to education by those living in poverty or without adequate access to learning technologies. The open educational resources (OER) movement described in this book will grow with each passing year. As this happens, it will shift all-too-common fixations with technology and information access issues toward those related to education and learning.

My own travels across many parts of this planet have forced me to rely on most of the learning technologies outlined in this book. I have taught classes while in Iceland, the United Arab Emirates, the United Kingdom, China, Chicago, and Washington, D.C., back to my students at Indiana University (IU), where I am housed. Some of these events were synchronous or real-time, whereas others were asynchronous. In addition, I have designed and tested a series of tools and learning portals for sharing and collaboration online. And my own research has explored emerging technologies such as podcasts, wikis, blogs, online and blended learning, and shared online video such as YouTube.

Though I am no Indiana Jones, in my travels I have witnessed hundreds of incredible educational events and activities firsthand. After these events, I have often sat down with those involved and have heard wondrous stories related to how human learning has changed through the use of emerging technologies. And, as the tales of this book and those in the companion Web site (see WorldIsOpen.com) reveal, such stories are now often expected to be captured, archived, and shared so that many others can learn from them. You too can now share your own stories of learning and teaching success with technology in the World-IsOpen learning community.

You can also find a free companion e-book at WorldIsOpen.com and at Scribd.com, a document-sharing site, which is discussed in Chapter Seven of this book. Though the chapter titles in the companion e-book are exactly the same as what you will find here, it contains entirely different material from this book. In addition to a free companion e-book, you will find all the references and Web resources mentioned in both books at the WorldIsOpen site for you to browse, read, and explore. You might share the Web site and associated e-book with those in Third World countries and with others who lack sufficient resources to buy this book. I hope that it can contribute, in some small way, to the open learning world. Given that they each contain different stories and ideas, reading both books should give you an enhanced sense of the unlimited and quite exciting possibilities for learning today. At the same time, there are untold millions of ideas and resources that are not mentioned in either book.

What *The World Is Open* book and associated Web resources make clear is that what we now have is a seismic wave of educational possibilities. This wave makes possible the notion that we all can learn what we need to learn when it is required or thought valuable. Of course, that is what we are ultimately on this planet for—to learn and to grow. WE-ALL-LEARN, so let's make it so.

We All Learn

I USTREAMED YOUR USTREAM: NOW THAT'S A TWITTER OF AN IDEA!

As someone who is used to giving over a hundred talks each year and whose blog is titled TravelinEdMan, my schedule in early November 2007 was part of a routine I had come to expect. First, there was a trip to Washington, D.C., to present some of the ideas for this book at the University of Maryland, followed by a presentation at a public health conference in the Walter E. Washington Convention Center a couple of hours later. I flew home the next morning only to return a few days later for a similar sequence of events; this time to keynote a disabilities-related conference, followed by a talk at Northern Virginia Community College, which my friend Nantana Wongtanasirikul had arranged.

As that session ended, a couple of monitors two feet behind me switched from my presentation slides to my Monday night Web 2.0 graduate class back at Indiana University (IU). Within seconds I could view my students back in their Indiana classroom from this classroom in northern Virginia via free Internet-based videoconferencing. They presented to me and I to them. It was the Internet2 at its finest. I could attend a conference in D.C. all day and not miss my class back at IU. In a couple of hours, I thought to myself, I would get a break.

This time I would get a day at home before traveling to the Atlanta Convention Center for a set of four talks at the Georgia Educational

Technology Conference (GAETC). Flying back from D.C. the second time, however, I realized two things: first, my personal gas tank was close to "E" for "essentially out of energy," and second, I was not yet ready for any of the talks in Atlanta. Fortunately, I had an entire day to prepare. Atlanta was a one-day affair—soar in on a nonstop flight from Indianapolis in the early morning, deliver my four talks in succession, and then fly back that night. I hoped to sleep on the plane each way.

Needless to say, GAETC was a grueling experience. By the time I got to my fourth and final talk that afternoon in Atlanta, I was pretty well spent. Worse, the conference organizers had asked me to synthesize the key points of my three earlier talks that afternoon in this final "best of" talk that would likely be my most dreadful talk of the year. I had fifteen minutes to catch my breath and refocus. When I returned, I made a mental list of the challenges I faced—a relatively small crowd, my body was dragging, I had extremely sore feet from making the mistake of wearing brand-new shoes, my vocal cords were about used up, and I was just about out of the free prizes that I could toss to the crowd to distract them.

Could it be worse? Yes. I quickly found out how bad things could get. Just as I was pondering what to do, Vicki Davis, a teacher from Westwood Schools in Camilla, Georgia, decided to plop herself down in the second row. Her selected location was right in front of where I would be presenting and just behind my suite of remaining props and prizes. I had heard about her popular blog, "The Cool Cat Teacher," but we had never met before. I thought to myself, "Oh man, now I am going to be blogged to the world by the Cool Cat Teacher. I am toast, I am really toast! I am not ready for this." Then Vicki decided to go for the jugular and said, "Do you mind if I Ustream your talk?" "Ustream?" I asked "What is that?" Vicki politely smiled and replied, "It is a way to broadcast your talk on the Internet. And it is a free service. People who cannot attend your 'best of' talk will be able to see it." I soon found out that anyone with a Webcam and an Internet connection could create a Ustream account and broadcast his or her captured events to an unlimited audience. Music, talk shows, sports, politics, meetings, speeches, and special gatherings—it is all there in Ustream.

When she finished describing it, Vicki added, "Oh, and I will Twitter it as well." Now Twitter I had heard of but had yet to see anyone actually use it. With Twitter, friends can sign up to receive updates on activities automatically through e-mail, instant messaging, and the Twitter Web site. Social networking tools and resources like Twitter enable people to quickly connect and share information—the maximum length of posts is 140 characters—with those who have similar ideas, backgrounds, and interests. I realized that people used Twitter to let others know what they are doing or thinking at any given moment during a day. People might note that they are "off to the library," "cleaning the fish tank . . . let me know if you want to help!" or "drowning in a grant proposal." Often such short posts are made through a mobile phone. Vicki was about to let her entire Twitter subscriber network know that she would be Ustreaming my talk. When done, she was going to write a blog-post reflection about my performance that would likely be read by thousands of her blog subscribers and casual browsers. Now, here was one connected teacher!

Given all that, it took just a few seconds to say, "Sure, go for it." I now realized that having my talk on Ustream would make my audience unknowable and perhaps much larger than any audience I had had all year. Things were looking up or at least becoming much more interesting. My body quickly went from butt-dragging tired to highly inspired. I decided to muster all the remaining energy I had for this final talk and leave no regrets. Why not, I was being Ustreamed to a live audience—potentially to the entire connected world, which is over one billion humans! To up the ante even more, those who later read her Blogger post might watch the saved file in Ustream. Within mere minutes, people around the world who received Vicki's announcement on Twitter were logging in to see the show. To my amazement, my colleague, Dr. Bernie Dodge at San Diego State University, was saying hello to me and relaying questions through Vicki. Dodge, the inventor of the now famous WebQuest activity, is someone you want to have answers for. When Vicki casually let me know that Bernie was watching my talk via the Web, it was yet another layer of pressure and a simultaneous shot of adrenaline.

I soon found out that one of my IU students, Jennifer Maddrell, was also tuning in. At the time, Jennifer was working on a master's degree in our distance program in Instructional Systems Technology. She was also a cohost of the weekly Webcast show Edtechtalk, which features the latest news from the world of educational technology to improve teaching and learning around the globe. She got wind of the Ustream event while attending a conference in New York City and sent a warm message to Vicki for me as well. After the event, Jennifer sent me an e-mail titled, "You Ustreamer!" Then she said, "I was Ustreaming from a conference in New York, when I saw a Tweet [a post to a Twitter account] from Vicki Davis in Twitter that she was Ustreaming YOU! So, at my conference we Ustreamed us watching your Ustream. Cool . . ." Yes, how cool was that? One of my students was watching me present on a topic she was interested in, but it was not during a class at IU. She was not even in the audience for my conference talk. Instead, at the exact same moment my talk was given, she was in a session at an entirely different conference in a city 850 miles away; yet she still could benefit from my presentation as it was happening.

"Ustream a Ustream," I think to myself. Wow. There must be thousands of educational uses for just this one tool. The world of education is opening up before our eyes. And it is truly open and much of it is now free! With Ustream, or some other system, we could bring education and technology leaders from around the globe together for a live event addressing serious issues such as Internet access, the digital divide, and the cost of textbooks. As Live Aid and Farm Aid concerts did in the 1980s and 1990s to help farmers keep their farms, with such resources we could gain global attention and support for education resource and technology needs in different Third World countries or regions of the world. We might name it "Live Ed" and include the best education thinkers and activists from around the planet. It is worth a thought. Okay, who will start Live Ed?

There are so many Web technologies today that, if we combined them, they could extend and amplify the learning possibilities for anyone with an Internet connection. According to Vicki Davis, "We live in a place where we may be streamed, captured, photographed, filmed, and 'snagged' at any time and at any place. It is the publication of our lives like we've never seen before and it opens up opportunities for many of us!" She goes on to tell me that many of the things I crave already exist. There is a wiki page of all educator Ustreams called EdTV. There are online conferences for those who cannot attend live ones such as the K–12 Online Conference. And, if I am still not convinced, she says there is a space on the Web for discussions of issues on K–12 education called Classroom 2.0 Live Conversations that has some eight thousand members. For those wanting to know where technology in education makes a difference, these sites are surely inspirational. For the time being, however, the notion of someone "Ustreaming my Ustream" will remain novel enough to motivate me when speaking on an empty tank!

THE WEB OF LEARNING

Do you have a favorite place to visit for a vacation? I know of a place more than a billion earthlings have already visited and vow to come back to. Given that you selected this book, I am wagering that you already have been there and quickly became engrossed in the stunning landscapes that surrounded you. A casual tourist, perhaps? Or maybe you are an expedition leader or field guide on a return visit. No matter what your role or purpose, it is a place you want to come back to again and again for nostalgic reasons as well as for the exciting and timely new explorations that are possible.

Most readers will already recognize that what I am talking about is the "Web of Learning." It is a somewhat magical or mystical place where teaching and learning never end. Unlike traditional stand-and-deliver classes, the sun never truly sets in the world of online learning. Fortunately, the hearty explorer will find that the lights rarely flicker or fade in the Web of Learning.

Sure, you can assume the role of teacher or learner when in the Web of Learning. But you can also be a learning escort, concierge, coach, media designer, planner, or anything you really want to be to facilitate your own learning or that of others.[1] And if such responsibilities do not fit your style, there are hundreds of additional roles or avatars to select from or personally create. So why not partake in it? It is a gigantic learning party that is happening each and every day. And this is one party you do not want to miss! Most of the time, you do not even need an invitation; instead, the invitation to learn exists at a mouse click.

Once you arrive, you will discover that you are not simply using the Web of Learning; instead, like the Borg in the television show *Star Trek: The Next Generation*, you are now a part of it. Your actions—contributions, reactions, comments, and designs—have been assimilated into the corpus or being of the Web of Learning. What you do there has a chance to influence any learner or education professional anywhere on this planet, and someday in this century, with the arrival of interplanetary coaching and mentoring, your contributions will be felt far beyond planet earth. If you post your learning activities or practice tests to the Web of Learning, learners in other geographic regions of the world can use them in preparing for their examinations or in checking their understanding on a topic.

Language and culture are, of course, valid concerns. As machine translation devices increase in accuracy and usability, though, your resources can be quickly converted for those not familiar with your particular language. In addition, they can be modified and adapted by a savvy instructor teaching learners who are younger, older, or less or more experienced than your own. Equally important, opportunities to bridge cultural differences arise when instructors share their ideas with other instructors. But is this Web of Learning spinning out of control? Some would say definitely yes. Others might further contend that Internet technologies need extensive revamping and upgrading to be ready for the proliferating uses in education that now appear on the horizon.

When I ask audiences where online learning is beneficial, a common response is "everywhere." Although one would not exactly call this an intellectually deep answer, there is some merit to it. The branches of the "Web of Learning" extend into all types of learning settings, both formal and informal. My friend Jay Cross, who coined the term e-learning, has written in depth on the informal learning avenues that are not only more available via this Web of Learning but are now required to survive.[2] Learning can be a spontaneous, on-demand decision in a community of learners who are making daily pilgrimages to the Web of Learning for casual insights. It can also be more thoughtfully and purposefully designed.

The Web of Learning impacts younger and older learners. Sometimes this happens simultaneously, as when retired workers and nursing home residents mentor primary school children, or vice versa, when well-wishing youngsters send hellos and encouragement to those in fairly lonely nursing home care. Though still controversial, there are applications of online learning that illustrate its relevance with extremely young children in preschool and primary school settings involving reading, writing, speaking, and listening skills. And in college and university settings, there are millions of freshmen in biology and chemistry courses conducting online experiments, senior students in accounting preparing for chartered examinations with online resources, graduate students in law school debating court cases, and music majors across a range of course levels practicing their music, hearing how instruments sound as they age, and listening to historical recordings of experts. At the same time, professionals in the workplace, such as engineers, human resource personnel, accountants, and customer service representatives, are continually upgrading their skills when needs arise and when time permits. And they are choosing to do so online.

The Web of Learning is part of a personal as well as professional lifestyle. Brothers can share the results of their online learning with brothers, sisters with aunties, and moms with dads. Sure, some of it may be strange and curious facts or funny stories, but there are learning lessons in there nonetheless. Personal and professional friend networks pop up in Facebook, Bebo, MySpace, and LinkedIn, to share one's ideas, connections, and current events. What is clear is that this Web of Learning extends to all age groups, all walks of life, and learners in all corners of the world and beyond.

If the Web of Learning had existed in 1950 to enhance the learning possibilities and ultimately the competencies of just one learner on the planet, we would have still considered it transformative, albeit in an extremely small way. This one learner would likely have been paraded around as some type of learning prodigy or spectacle. He or she would have been *Time* magazine's Person of the Year.

But the Web of Learning has done much more than that. The cat is truly out of the bag. During the past decade, millions of people have taken and completed at least one online course. Millions more are enrolled and participating in an online course at this very moment. The Web of Learning has changed the learning potential of those in every country of the planet from Antarctica to Zambia. There is no denying that your own learning potential has dramatically changed with access to it. And with this sudden opening of potential come new learning accomplishments, jobs, success stories, and goals. We are witnessing a massive uncovering of human potential.

What will someone find in this Web of Learning? At first glance, there are tools for learning at deeper levels as well as skimming or browsing possibilities. With some resource guidance and support, you will quickly come upon a sea of educational tools, resources, and objects, each vying for your attention and later use. Some pop up to smack you squarely in the face, whereas others take more subtle routes to getting your attention, but may do so repeatedly until it happens. Notices of podcasted events on nearly any topic imaginable, online conferences and virtual meetings, lifelike simulations, intriguing virtual worlds, and online games are soon found. But there is more. There is always more! There are cultural and historical databases and timelines of information related to long since departed civilizations. There are links to digital resources from online museums and libraries documenting the birth and death of such cultures. And there are portals of learning resources and centers devoted to these particular cultures and people. Further, community-developed resources—such as wikis, which any person on this planet could design or contribute to—can further support, extend, and even transform what is known about that culture. What a diverse array of resources—and each of them can be thoughtfully integrated into a particular course or across a series of them.

Given these possibilities, what is simultaneously mind-boggling and yet understandable is that many education and training professionals are stymied when entering this Web of Learning. Why the trepidation and hesitation? Well, in comparison to academic courses and other learning experiences of just a decade or two ago, when one good textbook and a supplemental reader or study guide may have sufficed, today there is an endless stream of announcements related to educational resources for one's courses and programs. These announcements typically add to the dozens of learning portals and resources already found and utilized in a course. There are a fast-growing number of discussions, collaborations, explorations, and assessment tools, as well as thousands of resources that might find their way into online course activities. Given this array of instructional possibilities, it is not surprising that many simply choose to ignore the Web of Learning altogether or incorporate it in the most minimalist fashion. This book can help the hesitant or resistant by offering a model or framework for reflecting on what is possible and organizing or compartmentalizing such activities.

Gone are the days when the lecture was the dominant mode of course delivery and deemed the essence of a successful course experience. My own research during the past decade in postsecondary education as well as corporate training shows that online lecturing is a minor component of a total online course experience. It is true that although online formats allow and, at times, even encourage lecturing, it is just one of many instructional choices at one's fingertips, and a minor one at that. In contrast to its dominance in face-to-face settings, of which those reading this book are all too aware, lectures and direct forms of instruction might account for less than 10 or 20 percent of an online class.

The instructional approaches of choice in online environments are more collaborative, problem based, generative, exploratory, and interactive.[3] There is more emphasis on mentoring, coaching, and guiding learning than in the past. My memories from secondary or even college training would be vastly different if my learning had been one of discovery, coaching, collaborating, and being personally guided. There was, of course, some of that, but it was too intermittent to radically alter the authoritative lecturing approaches that were dominant at the time.

Clearly, there is a need for instructional approaches that are more active and engaging and in which learners have greater control over their own learning. Words such as "ownership," "control," "engagement," "relevancy," and "collaboration" are among those shaping the learning-related dialogue of the twenty-first century. And these are also the key principles or components underlying effective online instructional activities and events. Those involved in professional development or the training of adults in the workplace will readily recognize the above list of words because they are embedded in the adult learning lexicon. They almost beg the question of why anyone would want solely to rely on face-to-face instruction when working with adults.

Understanding the ramifications of the Web of Learning is still very much a work in progress. Not all technologies foster engaging and cognitively rich information processing and networking. Technology by itself will not empower learners. Innovative pedagogy is required. And the approaches will vary with the type and age of students. In postsecondary spaces, online communications and interactive tasks and events between and among students and instructors, trainers, or tutors are often referred to as the heart and soul of online learning, especially in higher education. In contrast, corporate training, until recently, has tended to rely more heavily on self-paced and preselected materials.

Primary and secondary learning often utilizes a combination of approaches, such as relying on self-paced materials and practice examinations when students are home and interactive online experiences when at school. And military training might place an emphasis on real-world embedded training, games, and simulations—the focus being on carrying out some action followed by bouts of reflections on such actions.

Because the Web of Learning contains opportunities for all such approaches, emphatic statements about which ones it is best suited to support are naive and, at times, quite silly. It is a space that is evolving. It is such a new and interesting place for learning delivery that the experience base of any one person is not enough. No one knows the entire space and all the educational possibilities and resources that reside within the Web of Learning; this would be impossible. But one can test out and gradually master strategies for harnessing its energies and resources.

In some respects, the Web of Learning is effectively a monster with thousands of heads and tentacles, each possessing its own knowledge nuggets and with a great appetite for consuming, as well as making available, more information. And though some of those tentacles might be severed, or perhaps even a few heads might be chopped off entirely, new ones sprout up in a few days or perhaps just a few seconds. This is one monster worth looking at and exploring! Certainly some of the information found inside is incorrect (witness Wikipedia vandalism and trolling) or exists only at the surface level of learning. But much of it is educationally relevant and continually evolving. There are games, 3-D worlds, online conferences and professional meetings, podcasts on nearly every education topic imaginable, world and city maps, virtual museum tours of famous exhibits, and countless visual records of human history. So many resources can be embedded in online courses and programs. Granted, such resources are not the same as physically touching or directly viewing the real object or event, but they can be useful approximations of it, functioning in the same way as a picture in a book or a drawing on a marker board.

The Web of Learning, therefore, becomes a place where learners are empowered; they are entrusted with choice in their learning paths or journeys. Perhaps above all other aspects of Web utilization, the power of choice is what sets the Web of Learning apart from other forms of learning. With opportunities to make personal decisions related to their explorations and potential online discoveries, learners develop a sense of ownership and self-directedness or self-determination. They are finally free to learn, seek knowledge when needed, and are able to express in creative ways what they have learned, as Carl Rogers repeatedly advocated in his *Freedom to Learn* books way back in the twentieth century.[4] Of course, there are constraints related to the relevancy and accuracy of the information found online, but for a change, learners are taking control of their own learning paths.

As you explore this book, regard it as part of a personal pilgrimage into what you can do online. It is purposefully not laced with prescriptions or specific activities, though there are dozens of stories and projects outlined from which to draw your own conclusions and design your own learning ventures.[5] It is not only meant for education professionals, but also for anyone with an interest in learning, and in the learning-related technology transformations facing each of us each day. This journey into the Web of Learning should be exciting for everyone, because we are all learners. Enjoy your learning travels!

FLAT, SPIKY, AND OPEN

Thomas Friedman's *The World Is Flat: A Brief History of the Twenty-First Century* provided a very broad view of the massive social changes occurring in every sector of society since the dawn of the new millennium as a result of a variety of technological innovations.[6] Friedman insightfully noted how economic, political, and social worlds have been flattened by ten key trends or events. Leading up to a discussion of these so-called flatteners, Friedman delineates three distinct eras of globalization.

The first era of globalization began with Columbus's journeys that opened up trade between the Old and New Worlds. This era was more about the power of brawn the and muscle than brain power. Globalization 1.0 was rooted in the global expansion of countries as seen in the accords and treaties between them. Going global, therefore, was a question asked at the country or regional level, not at the organizational level. And it was unfathomable at the individual level.

The next era of globalization, Globalization 2.0, which lasted from about 1800 to 2000, entailed multinational companies finding new markets and labor in other countries and regions of the world. As

Friedman notes, at first falling transportation costs underpinned such actions, and later the falling costs of telecommunications was a key contributor. Toward the end of this era, advances in telecommunications and computing power were used to form unique collaborations between and within companies. Still, there remained barriers to seamless and ubiquitous global collaboration at the corporate level.

In the third era of globalization, however, it was not countries or corporations competing and collaborating. Instead, it was the dawn of a new age; it became possible for globalization to include the direct involvement and participation of any person on this planet. In Globalization 3.0, singular individuals from all corners of the planet were empowered to participate in the world economy in ways previously unimagined. They could now pool their knowledge, skills, and ideas to create new products, organizations, and documents that in turn could be employed by still others located anywhere in the world.

What this all meant was that by using Web tools and resources, more people could connect with other people than at any moment in history. And each day such collaborations are growing. It is in this age that millions, if not billions, of people can read, refine, and share a new idea or opinion. Such collaborations will undoubtedly result in a wave of innovations and inventions not before possible. Creativity by the masses, for the masses.

As Friedman documented, individuals in this millennium have acquired new powers and freedoms to participate socially, politically, and educationally with others around the world. Clearly, the emphasis in his book was on economic powers and the new workforce available from India, China, and former Eastern Bloc countries. Numerous stories in *The World Is Flat* describe how collaborative technologies expand the possibilities for forming new businesses and distributing valued goods and services by anyone for anyone. Friedman heralded the fact that employees and work teams can spring up from nearly anywhere on the planet and at any time they are needed. He appropriately pointed out that new management processes combined with online technologies encouraged unique forms of team collaboration and associated product development. Such coinciding events have opened up a more level economic playing field for billions of people. Friedman referred to these three parallel trends—a flattened playing field brought about by collaborative technologies, new economic players within that playing field, and changes from vertical and hierarchical management structures to horizontal ones—as a triple convergence that was "turbo-charging" the flattening process.

Using a series of personal anecdotes, Friedman insightfully describes the convergence of various technologies—be they mobile, wireless, personal, or virtual—that buttress and nurture new forms of collaboration, globalization, and personal expression. Such technologies are central to the social and economic developments that, in his words, flatten the world. Such flattening enables companies around the globe to compete with those in more developed countries. As evident in the ten flatteners listed below, many of the societal changes Friedman outlined are more economic in nature, rather than the education- or learning-related changes discussed in this book. At the same time, there is much overlap.

1. 11/9/89: The Berlin Wall came down
2. 8/9/95: The company Netscape went public
3. Workflow software (for example, PayPal and eBay)
4. Open sourcing (self-organizing collaborative communities, such as Mosaic, Apache, Wikipedia, Linux, Mozilla-Firefox)
5. Outsourcing (such as the Y2K problem)
6. Offshoring (for example, to China, Mexico, Thailand)
7. Supply chaining (such as Wal-Mart)
8. Insourcing (UPS fixing Toshiba laptops)
9. Informing (for example, Google, Yahoo!, MSN Web Search)
10. The steroids: digital, mobile, personal, and virtual (for example, wireless, file sharing, VoIP, video camera in phone)

Friedman pointed out that the technologies of the twenty-first century allow for collaborative forms of economic growth that were not possible before. The convergence of these ten events, according to Friedman, resulted in economic flatness.

Others, such as Richard Florida, contend that the world is not flat, but instead, is rather spiky.[7] From this perspective, innovation, and thus economic development, rests in certain cities, countries, and regions of the world more than others. Such places amass greater creative and intellectual capital as well as financial resources to support innovation centers and research parks. These creativity-rich centers and cities (such as Bangalore, Chicago, Singapore, Beijing, Dublin, Seoul, Tokyo, Taipei, London, Vancouver, San Francisco, Boston, Helsinki, Berlin, and Sydney) can attract, harness, and develop talent more effectively than others. A creative class of people moves freely among such cities. They are attracted to the opportunities found there. From Florida's viewpoint, although shifts in these economic development powerhouses can and do occur, technology has yet to equalize this development and perhaps never will.[8] Rather than equalize the peaks, hills, and valleys, he suggests that the top political challenge of the early part of this century is to lift up those in the economic valleys without "shearing off the peaks."[9]

Perhaps there is a way to understand and plan for Friedman's notion of flatness and Florida's spikiness. Education, when open to the masses, is a tool for economic flattening that, when effectively used, can greatly assist those in the valleys while still enabling those at or near economic summits to find ways to keep climbing. Today, education is opening for us in ways we've never seen before. As Richard Straub points out, we have open societies, open source systems, open standards, and open educational content.[10] As the director of development at the European Foundation for Management Development (EFMD), which links twelve thousand management professionals in over seventy countries, and the former director of Learning Solutions at IBM, Straub, if anyone, should have his finger on the pulse of this openness. As he accurately points out, management structures are opening up with values such as empowerment, tolerance, lifelong learning, participation, cooperation, and individual freedom. This is a significant departure from the traditional top-down command-and-control hierarchies that often fueled the exploitation and general distrust of the workers, bureaucratic governance, and overregulation.

Straub argues that open environments for work and learning foster the freedom, participation, creativity, and innovation that both Friedman and Florida seem to be seeking. He is not the first nor will he be the last to suggest that. Nearly two decades ago, Alvin Toffler forecasted a dramatic and democratic shift in power in business and industry, and the world in general, in which relationships between people, organizations, and even nations would be transformed.[11] As always, Toffler was spot on. Here in the twenty-first century, managerial decision making is giving way to work teams just as swiftly as teacher lecturing in schools and universities is giving way to self-determined learning, mobile learning, and problem-based curricula. It seems everyone in business is employee-centered while everyone in schools is now learner-centered. The reins of power have indeed shifted as Toffler anticipated.

According to Toffler, during this "powershift," the focus must be on knowledge. As he contends, "[D]espite exceptions and unevenness, contradictions and confusions, we are witnessing one of the most important changes in the history of power." He further argues, "For it is now that knowledge, the source of the highest-quality power of all, is gaining importance with every fleeting nanosecond."[12] The most momentous of these powershifts, however, is not from particular people, political parties, organizations, or nations, but from shifts in relationships to the access and control of knowledge as this global society finds its way in the twenty-first century. With the creation of the Web just as Toffler's *Powershift* book was being published and the more recent emergence of what some call the Web 2.0, it seems we are now living in Toffler's future.

In the midst of this flatter yet spikier world with massive shifts in power and control, we need to reflect on the training and education of the creative class of people assuming this power. Education in the twenty-first century is mightily different from how it was in the previous one. Jay Cross argues that we live in times wherein informal learning outstrips the more formal variety.[13] In his seminal book on the topic, *Informal Learning,* Cross provides a wealth of evidence that both schools and businesses are increasingly reliant on informal learning for daily survival, especially in work-related settings. Such observations reinforce the views of Friedman, Florida, and Toffler in critical ways because they highlight the link between informal learning and innovations in business management and overall productivity. Organizational support for informal learning can result in more motivated employees who work in engaging communities of practice in this more flattened work world.

But informal learning does not just start when one enters the workplace; it is part of the experience of each person on the planet, young or old, rich or poor, male or female. A young worker spends most of her learning hours in what would be deemed more informal situations. There are no credentials that this worker receives from going to the Web to learn what a wiki is, or to view a map of a country she intends to visit, or perhaps to buy Cross's book—yet each of these information searches entails learning. The new technologies of the Internet have propelled us into the actualization of informal learning pursuits. These same technologies have transformed learners and learning and provided more flat *and* more open management structures.

The macro-level perspectives contributed by Friedman, Florida, Straub, Toffler, and Cross give us clues that help us make sense of this ever-changing world. Technology and location both matter in this open world; location is all too often the determinant of accessibility to Web technology. Successive waves of learning tools appear every few years, if not every few months or weeks, within a highly global work-and-learn society where free and open content proliferates and access perpetually expands. Technologies such as wikis, blogs, virtual worlds, mobile devices, and electronic books make the learning revolution unmistakable and exhilarating. Such tools bring us to an age of educational and economic participation and personalization unlike no other. Education and economy go hand in hand and are equally affected. Certainly, to some degree, the barriers have come down to make it a flatter economic and social world. At the same time, it remains rather spiky. But for education, a colossal shift has commenced toward informal and nontraditional learning pursuits chosen by the learner where much of the content is free and open. There can be no doubt that the watchword of this century is openness.

Open education can help liberate people who were previously exploited by economic gamesmanship and command-and-control hierarchies. Freedom to learn will foster attitudes of freedom to work for oneself. As this happens, it will place such individuals in positions that provide a sense of personal dignity and self-worth. A proliferation of creative expression, as well as a sense of global connectedness or shared humanity, will crystallize within the valleys and peaks, enabling every new learning participant who is connected to the Internet, and thus to free and open educational resources, to experience high levels of success. This book introduces you to dozens of the revolutionary leaders creating this openness for you, as well as many of those who have already reaped enormous benefits from open learning. It is likely that most of the people discussed in this book do not realize that they are so central to the magic that we are witnessing in learning and education today. But clearly they are. They *all* are!

THE WEB 2.0

The evolution we have all experienced during the past decade from the Web 1.0 to the Web 2.0 has made each citizen of this planet aware of the vast educational possibilities now available for all ages of learners. We see it daily in the news we encounter or the communications in which we engage. First intended as an interconnected web of knowledge and artifacts, the Web is not unlike the content storage and retrieval business plan of the ancient library at Alexandria. Today, however, the goals of the Web extend far beyond the mere digital existence and interconnection of knowledge. Donald Tapscott and Anthony Williams argue that "[t]he Internet is becoming a giant computer that everyone can program, providing a global infrastructure for creativity, participation, sharing, and self-organization."[14] As they accurately point out, we have moved from the initial stages of the Internet as a gigantic newspaper to a place where you can easily connect with the authors, editors, or readers of such articles, and contribute your perspective or resources. We have shifted from a culture that passively received content from the Web to one that actively participates in it by adding content.

Like Tapscott and Williams, Friedman alluded to an assortment of technologies—including Skype (a tool for to talking over the Internet for free using "Voice over Internet Protocol" or VoIP), Wikipedia, blogs, Web searching tools, and collaborative software—that are making an impact in educational arenas from highly developed to Third World countries. With such technologies, the world has definitely become more free, open, deep, rich, and personally empowering for those attempting to learn or relearn something. And there are countless reports of additional technologies specific to the education world.

Those in Generation X and Y who are entering colleges and universities as well as the workplace are known for being savvy about such technologies. Without a doubt, they are pushing corporations and institutions of higher learning to raise the bar of the possible to allow employees to have a greater voice in strategic planning and students to have greater control over their own learning. Certainly, most educators and trainers today have witnessed such individuals boldly carrying their MP3 players and mobile phones, while satisfying addictions to e-mail, Web browsing, and instant messaging. We have also seen the growth of for-profit colleges and universities offering degrees and special services online. What's more, places such as Stanford University are furnishing students with their own wiki about campus life and activities as well as posting popular lectures to Apple iTunes.[15] A few miles down the road, San Jose State University has designed a virtual glimpse of campus life for potential students using Second Life. To the north, the University of California at Berkeley has decided to make its course lectures available for free in both iTunes and YouTube. And this is clearly just the start of what is to come.

Emerging educational technologies and resources are allowing for a more learner-centric focus in education where the learners are active instead of the more passive mode of instruction that has existed for centuries. During an invited presentation at MIT on December 1, 2006, John Seely Brown argued that in this new participatory educational climate, learners become engaged in a culture of building, tinkering, learning, and sharing.[16] When I talked to him during a conference at Rice University in Houston a few months later, Brown reiterated these points. The combination of free and widely distributed educational resources with tools that enable learners to add to or comment on such resources or build entirely new ones begins to redefine what learning is—it becomes production or participation, not consumption and absorption.

A week after Dr. Brown's talk at MIT, *Time* magazine published an article by Claudia Wallis and Sonja Steptoe related to bringing schools out of the twentieth century.[17] These authors argued that innovation and creativity, communication, interpretation, synthesis, collaboration, problem solving, and interdisciplinary insights are the types of skills that need to be emphasized. The ability to creatively combine, weave, and interlink knowledge is more vital than restating sets of facts, names, and dates. Among the key required skills of our time include the ability to work collaboratively with people from different countries or geographic regions. Students need greater sensitivity to different cultures and languages, including more exposure to such languages as Mandarin Chinese, Spanish, and Korean. They need to build such skills through real-world experiences and projects. And thoughtful use of new and emerging technologies is one way for this to happen.

In their article, Wallis and Steptoe remind us of a wry joke, akin to the Plato and Aristotle scenario I detailed in the Introduction, that often circulates among educators. They note that Rip Van Winkle could suddenly find himself in the twenty-first century after sleeping for a hundred years and would be taken aback by massive changes found everywhere in society except in schools. Schools, he would quickly recognize. As Wallis and Steptoe point out: "American schools aren't exactly frozen in time, but considering the pace of change in other areas of life, our public schools tend to feel like throwbacks. Kids spend much of the day as their great-grandparents once did: sitting in rows, listening to teachers lecture, scribbling notes by hand, reading from textbooks that are out of date by the time they are printed. A yawning chasm (with an emphasis on yawning) separates the world inside the schoolhouse from the world outside."[18]

However, schools do not have uniform curricula or philosophies, and many are in the midst of transformative change, with Web 2.0 technologies being part of the reason for such changes.

Two weeks after the article by Wallis and Steptoe, *Time* magazine brilliantly followed up that article by naming "You" as the "Person of the Year."[19] It recognized the shift to an age where users generate and contribute ideas to the Web instead of simply paging through content submitted by others. The realization that users or learners were important was no longer lingo to be reiterated by the education community but was being widely accepted by society as a whole. Everyone participating in society as a digital citizen in any meaningful degree had come into contact with emerging Web 2.0 technologies that granted them a voice and a vote, and turned up the volume on their contributions.

In effect, the year 2006 signified the trend toward empowering technology users with Web 2.0 technologies that allow them to generate ideas online instead of simply reading and browsing through someone else's.[20] We now use the "read-write" Web, not just a Web from which one passively consumes or reads information. Included in the new Web were wikis, podcasts, blogs, online photo albums, and virtual worlds such as Second Life. Web 2.0 tools and resources bring people together to share, collaborate, and interact. Web technologies can now network individuals to accomplish more than any one person could alone. With a new blog appearing every second and a world that is seemingly filled with wikis and subscription podcast shows, "we" are now the Web; each of us is the Person of the Year.

With enhanced bandwidth, reduced storage costs, increased process-ing speed, and the growing acceptance and expectations of rich multi-media, emerging Web 2.0 tools and resources such as YouTube, Second Life, Flickr, MySpace, Facebook, and Blogger are increasingly popular and integrated into the culture. And as such participatory technology becomes easier to use and thus more widespread, more people have found a venue in which to contribute their unique talents, with the possibility of their ideas and insights being recognized and utilized not only locally, but also publicly and internationally.

Clearly, many of the same technology trends that Friedman docu-mented are having a significant impact on the world of learning today. Without a doubt, the increases in bandwidth, reductions in storage costs, continued enhancements in processing speed, and ubiquitous access to multimedia and hypermedia learning formats have radically transformed education and training during the past decade, and especially during the past few years. As the technologically advanced Japanese and Korean cultures demonstrate, there is now ubiquitous access to learning with personal multimedia players, mobile phones, and other such devices. Of course, as such participatory technology becomes even easier to use and increasingly accessible around the globe, education environments across sectors will continue to shift and transform. Ideas of one learner or instructor may be shared with anyone anywhere on this planet and at any time. As this occurs, educational information and resources will no longer be local but global.

In an *Educause Review* article, Bryan Alexander notes that many resist the shift to the Web 2.0 due to the lack of clear definitions, differences in determining exactly what qualifies a tool to be labeled as Web 2.0, and the seemingly temporary or fleeting nature of the field.[21] However, he further argues that we need to look beyond questions and concerns related to such labeling, especially given the many powerful implications already appearing in different educational sectors that are directly linked to Web 2.0 technologies. Actual projects, practices, and conceptual implications trump problems in labeling.

For Alexander, initial educational uses of the Web, or the Web 1.0, were for making available pages of content for learners to browse or read. The Web 2.0 relates to microcontent or streams of revisions to a Wikipedia document or daily blog postings and hyperlinking that can be saved, shared, copied, and quoted. In our time-crunched society, it is much easier to start a wiki entry or compose a blog summary of an event, than it is to write an article or a book. And when posted, there is some immediate sense of personal empowerment or identity. Whether we will become a society of writing dabblers as a result is difficult to predict. At the same time, simple writing attempts in one's blog could expand into magazine articles, speeches, and books.

Learning technologies will continue to appear to stimulate our thinking not only about what is possible in Thomas Friedman's flatter economic world but in Richard Florida's more spiky one as well. The Web 2.0 is also in the land of open education where human beings participate in their own learning quests. These interactive technologies have brought hundreds of millions of us to the realization that we will always be learning. Soon the entire planet will recognize this need. When it does, there will be declarations that the world is now open for the education of all the citizens of this planet.

DECLARING THE WORLD OPEN FOR EDUCATION

In June 1776, Thomas Jefferson, with the help of John Adams, Benjamin Franklin, and several others, toiled on a draft of the Declaration of Independence. The writing that took place during the ensuing weeks would effectively serve as a foundation of a country for centuries to come.

Jefferson and Adams would each live five more decades and witness the results of the ideas expressed in the Declaration of Independence as a new nation and a new way of governing rose up and rapidly expanded. Both of these remarkable figures played a key role in testing out the document when serving as the second and third presidents of the United States.[22] When they both passed away a few short hours apart on July 4, 1836, some fifty years to the day since the Declaration, their ideas for a democratic government in which people actively participated in the processes, activities, and management of it were in full view. Suffice it to say, their dreams have had a massive impact in many corners of the world.

Fast forward to September 14–15, 2007. On those two days, a meeting convened by the Open Society Institute (OSI) and the Shuttleworth Foundation in Cape Town, South Africa, resulted in a different but equally revolutionary declaration. It was an effort to help people become aware of the growing movement toward free and open educational resources, technology, and teaching practices as well as to promote their distribution and use. Like Jefferson, Adams, Franklin, and others centuries prior, the goal of this movement's leaders was to provide access to ideas and opportunities. In this case, however, the intent was for people to pursue their educational dreams and aspirations.

At the Cape Town meeting, thirty people were brought together from quite diverse perspectives, occupations, and parts of the world. Their ultimate declaration begins with this statement: "We are on the cusp of a global revolution in teaching and learning. Educators worldwide are developing a vast pool of educational resources on the Internet, open and free for all to use. These educators are creating a world where each and every person on earth can access and contribute to the sum of all human knowledge."[23] The document goes on to discuss a new age of teaching and learning, as well as advancing the culture of sharing. This culture, like that of Jefferson's political scene of the late 1700s, is a much more participatory one than what had been experienced in the past.

Numerous barriers to these dreams and visions exist, of course, including insufficient Internet access, as well as incompatibility between technologies, lack of awareness, lack of interest, and frustration.[24] Still, Internet access is not required to participate in this revolution because many open educational resources can be transferred to CD or computer hard drives. At the same time, groups such as the Internet for Everyone campaign, announced in the summer of 2008, are working to make Internet access available in every home and business in the United States. A broad coalition of companies and organizations such as eBay, Google, the Free Press, and Educause promptly signed on as well as many Internet luminaries including Larry Lessig, Yochai Benkler, and Jonathan Zittrain, all of whom are highlighted later in this book.[25]

The signers of this twenty-first-century education declaration outline three strategies to realize their vision. First, they call for educators and learners to actively participate in this movement by creating, promoting, and using open educational resources. Second, they ask for authors and publishers to release their resources openly. Third, they encourage governments, boards, and higher education administrators to make OER resource initiatives, collections, and ideas a priority. This declaration was not meant as a final document but as an evolving one. Different organizations around the world are welcome to use it as a base for their own open education declarations, contextualizing and modifying the original document for their own particular needs. Those at the Cape Town meeting focused on open educational resources (OER), such as free and open course materials, games, books, lesson plans, software, and other materials. At the same time, they realized that there are many open education initiatives that will spring up in other areas that may not be possible today or cannot be labeled at this time.

Among the American representatives at this signing event were Jimmy Wales from the Wikimedia Foundation, known for the development of Wikipedia among many other free and online wiki-related resources. Alongside Jimmy was Richard Baraniuk, professor at Rice University and founder of Connexions, a fast-growing online resource of educational content, such as courses and textbooks. Like Jefferson and prominent figures from the era of the American Revolution, both Wales and Baraniuk have been accused by many as being nothing more than idealistic dreamers. Educators, parents, scholars, and politicians have raised red flags about quality, use, assessment, and access of such OER. The irony is that these concerns are raised while their Web platforms are used by millions of learners around the world. The development, promotion, and use of their tools and this coinciding declaration are just a start to something much grander.

In an open forum article in the *San Francisco Chronicle* on January 22, 2008, Wales and Baraniuk argue that this movement can radically change the world of education.[26] They ask us to imagine worlds where the cost of textbooks and supplemental learning materials would no longer keep students out of community colleges and other institutions of higher learning but are free. They push further in suggesting that such resources might automatically adapt to different learning styles or situations. Equally important in their push to widen access to open education, such resources could be quickly translated into the language of the user. As they note, the OER movement itself was but a dream a decade prior to this declaration. Now it is possible for anyone with access to the Internet to "author, assemble, customize and publish their own open course or textbook."[27] And emerging ways to license that content make it legal for others to use and remix it.

Wales and Baraniuk both realize that we are just at the threshold of the exciting new world of open education. For them, "Open Education promises to turn the textbook production pipeline into a vast dynamic knowledge ecosystem that is in a constant state of creation, use, reuse and improvement."[28] As this happens, learning will be more customizable and specific to the learner's true needs, not prescribed by someone foreign to that student, classroom, school system, university, or culture. They hope that with increasing access to OER, people will work together to "transform the way the world develops, disseminates and uses knowledge."[29] This is not just their hope. This is their declaration!

On January 24, 2008, just two short days after the open education declaration was made public, some 695 people had signed it. I was number 695. By July 4, 2008, another 900 names had been added. I received an e-mail that day from Elliott Masie, head of the Masie Center and an internationally recognized futurist, reminding me that "learning" is at the root of the freedoms and sense of independence that we enjoy. He goes on to say: "The ability of a society and an economy to make learning a prime and core value—from elementary school, through high school, on to college and into our work and vocational lives is essential."[30]

Masie's sentiment would likely resonate with those signing the Cape Town Open Education Declaration. Unlike the earlier American Declaration of Independence, the document they have designed is an open digital one for anyone to sign, including you; visit www .capetowndeclaration.org/. As additional people and organizations become aware of OER, unique collaborations and conversations in this area will undoubtedly ensue. Akin to the release of the Declaration of Independence, making public this open education declaration is critical in realizing those dreams. The coming decade will likely include many battles and skirmishes over this one document and the philosophy behind it. We need the foresight and intellectual might not only to prevail in some of these clashes, but to make the world a better place for learning. Fifty years from now, this declaration could lead to a radically new world of education, where learning is freely available for every citizen on the planet.

NOW WE-ALL-LEARN

We are experiencing ten key learning technology trends across the planet that are opening access to both formal and informal education. As these trends proliferate, they nudge us into a culture where knowledge sharing is the norm. Open source software is, naturally, one of these key trends. But this is no longer exclusively a discussion about how Apache or Linux can help corporate servers run more cost effectively. Instead, the conversation has shifted toward access to free and open educational resources that can have a direct impact on learners and teachers. For instance, when colleges and universities, such as Berkeley, MIT, the Indian Institutes of Technology, and the Open University in the United Kingdom are sharing their course materials with the world, it is time to stand up and take notice.

Fortunately, such events are not limited to English-speaking countries; ambitious people in other places are simultaneously translating such knowledge and making it available for millions, if not billions, of potential learners in their own cultures. Learners are now collaborating with peers from around the planet, as well as being mentored by experts and practitioners from other countries or regions of the world. It is a time when learners can catch up on their studies or personal interests while sitting at a bus station, commuting in the subway, or resting outside a lecture hall on a warm, sunny day. In effect, educational resources are available faster than ever before and in larger doses. And such resources are often free to access, build upon, and share with others.

While learning is being opened up to masses of people that previously did not have access, it is also opening up in new forms to those who already did. Learners of all ages are increasingly engaged in formal as well as informal learning, which is highly mobile and often ubiquitous. In such a world, each of "you" will need to continue learning in order to stay employed. Given that every education professional today can swiftly access these amazing learning resources and events, there are thousands, if not millions, of examples that could be provided and stories that could be told of how the world of learning has become opened up in revolutionary ways. I have selected just a few resources and people to highlight here that were involved in the creation, marketing, implementation, and evaluation of such educational technologies and resources.

The ten educational openers addressed in this book, as well as the three converging macro trends underlying them, are detailed briefly below. The first-letter acrostic or handy mnemonic for the ten openers is WE-ALL-LEARN. This memory aid can help us better understand the possibilities of the Web of Learning.

Some of the openers relate to creating or finding information and resources and making them available on the Web. Other openers concern the infrastructure for locating, selecting, and using such resources and generating ways to access them. And still other openers involve participating in and personalizing these resources. Of course, there is overlap across these openers. The framework provided here is just one attempt to categorize or make sense of the seemingly infinite resources, tools, people, and activities found online. The acronym WE-ALL-LEARN was purposefully chosen to denote my rising optimism for learning and education. During the coming decade, other more innovative frameworks and schemes will be designed and hopefully extensively used by learners, instructors, trainers, and anyone entering the Web.

I do not mean to imply that all the world's learning problems have been solved or that they are even close to some type of resolution. My primary goal in designing the WE-ALL-LEARN framework was to divide up online resources in such a way that educators, trainers, teachers, freelance lecturers, instructional designers, and others would be able to more easily and more actively employ them in their own instruction, rather than avoiding the Web at all costs.

A second and no less important goal, naturally, is to use WE-ALL-LEARN to champion a reduction of the digital divide. Many of the stories embedded in the chapters of this book provide markers that this is indeed already beginning to happen. Granted, there are billions of individuals on this planet who as yet do not have access to the Web. I do not mean to discount prevailing digital divide concerns. This is a serious global issue, which perhaps a book such as this can help make more salient. Still, although the majority of the global population has yet to own a computer or participate in Web-based learning activities, it is likely that thousands more people obtain access each day and can, therefore, participate in the new forms of learning outlined here. Now, with WE-ALL-LEARN, we have a framework for reflecting on the learning opportunities that can be provided across educational sectors and geographic regions.

The emergence of the Web and enhancements in bandwidth offered by Internet2 capabilities is a given. In fact, all ten openers utilize Internet technologies and the associated bandwidth. The first opener, however, is perhaps the most directly linked to Web capabilities and technologies. It is, in fact, two openers—the proliferation of Web access and the availability of digital books and online documents. Even without lightning-fast access to the Web, there are enormous learning opportunities that were not possible a decade or so ago.

TEN OPENERS: (WE-ALL-LEARN)

1. Web Searching in the World of e-Books
2. E-Learning and Blended Learning
3. Availability of Open Source and Free Software
4. Leveraged Resources and OpenCourseWare
5. Learning Object Repositories and Portals
6. Learner Participation in Open Information Communities
7. Electronic Collaboration and Interaction
8. Alternative Reality Learning
9. Real-Time Mobility and Portability
10. Networks of Personalized Learning

As the WE-ALL-LEARN framework indicates, we are no longer participants in Aristotle's world where one could conceivably read from every book or document written. In the twenty-first century, no one can know all. However, we all can learn. And the vital signs of intelligence in this century are related to access and use of knowledge when needed. Knowing where to look, how to access, and what to focus on are the powerful strategies of today.

The "WE-ALL-LEARN" metaphor is purposefully intended as a bold goal for society. It offers a temporary road map for how to enhance the educational possibilities of all learning participants on this planet. Still, there is no assumption that this is happening for most people today. Dire digital divide problems pervade every society, culture, region, and city. Still the world of education is opening. The remaining chapters of this book show how, why, where, and when this opening process is happening. They also offer clues on how this opening process can flourish in communities where it has yet to appear.

As with Friedman's flattened economic world, there are three larger trends that provide a superstructure for discussing the ten educational openers. These converging macro trends are:

I. The availability of tools and infrastructure for learning (the pipes)

II. The availability of free and open educational content and resources (the pages)

III. A movement toward a culture of open access to information, international collaboration, and global sharing (a participatory learning culture)

As indicated earlier, this triple convergence is different from the one Friedman elaborated in his book. This convergence does not focus on global economics and the new players, playing field, and processes that have emerged to flatten the world. In education around the globe, there is a different convergence related to the "pipes," or online infrastructure, the pages of online content, and a participatory learning culture brought about, at least in part, by the Web 2.0. In this convergence of education openers, many of the tools for Web-based collaboration, searching, and participation are the same as what Friedman outlines. The technologies and processes that have flattened the world economically have simultaneously opened it up educationally. The ultimate goal, of course, is expanded opportunity for learning in this more open educational world.

Competing and collaborating economically can follow or occur during such learning.

The convergence of these three macro trends has put in motion opportunities for human learning and potential never before approached in recorded history. Of course, all three components are needed. First, the pipes must be in place. These pipes—Internet access and bandwidth, preferably free and ubiquitously available for the highly mobile— provide the infrastructure for the management, supply, and distribution of free and open educational content. The first, third, seventh, and ninth openers most directly relate to such infrastructure issues.

All ten openers are clearly indicative of the second macro trend related to the proliferation of online content. For instance, much of what is later discussed in this book regarding the first opener also concerns the second converging trend related to the availability of online content such as digital books. In effect, although piping is important, online educational resources must be available, useful, and needed. Still, the second macro trend is most symbolized by the fourth and fifth openers with freely available online course contents and gigantic portals of rich educational content. With these two openers in place, each of us now has access to an endless sea of online portals that contain links to billions of pages of educational content.

The laying of the vast technological pipes with an overflowing store of educational content is only part of the story. In effect, though people can perpetually explore online content and materials to learn, a final ingredient is needed to truly open education for more democratic participation and personalization. That component has to do with culture and psychology as much as technology. Thus, the third macro trend electrifying all of humankind today is the creation of a culture that collaboratively builds, negotiates, and shares such knowledge and information: a participatory learning culture. If the resources and infrastructure are in place but the education community, as well as society as a whole, fails to maximize their power, then millions of unique learning possibilities will be lost. As we shall see, the sixth, eighth, and tenth openers highlight this trend more than the others.

Although the economic world may not be flat or level enough for everyone, the stories in this book will demonstrate that it is open for everyone, including those who do not have access to the Internet. That news, more than anything, may shock the critics who spell out perpetual doom for those on the other side of the digital divide. I for one am not willing to accept such gloomy views. Everyone who uses Web-based collaborative tools or portals to donate or volunteer time, talent, money, or other educational resources is potentially opening up education and affecting those without Internet access. Read about the Room to Read, 1kg, and TwinBooks programs in Asia. Web-based technology is making a huge difference in the lives of those lacking Internet access and computing technology of any kind.

In the end, the people, ideas, and technologies opening up the world of education have something to say to each of us. We all learn in this wonderful Web of Learning. The following ten chapters will not only detail each of the educational openers related to the Web of Learning, but the combined stories, examples, and tools discussed within them will also show that we are entering an age where the use of WE-ALL-LEARN will help us all learn. With that in place, the closing chapter will recount the journey and offer glimpses of a few interesting trends that may still lie ahead.

To Search and to Scan

OPENER #1: WEB SEARCHING IN THE WORLD OF E-BOOKS

FROM TERAFLOPS TO PETAFLOPS TO FINGERTIP KNOWLEDGE

Costs have plummeted for bandwidth, storage, and processing. Those wanting to connect to the Web can now find broadband access as they walk the streets of a town or into a café or bookstore. No worries if they want to download what they find online. They can download the world's knowledge if they so choose. As anyone who has visited a computer store can tell you, the cost of storing two hundred gigabytes of information is what it used to cost for a mere gig a few years ago. And computer clock speeds, once impressively measured in megahertz statistics are now available in multiple gigahertz rates.

Remember those predictions in the 1980s and 1990s that we will soon have a supercomputer on our desks or in our laps? Well those days are here now.[1] At the present time, however, supercomputers are measured in teraflops (that is, a trillion floating-point operations per second) and soon petaflops (that is, a quadrillion floating-point operations per second), thus pushing back dreams of desktop supercomputing to that land far off in the distance once again.[2] Of course, anyone who owns a computer today can claim ownership over the supercomputer model of yesterday.[3]

Oops, did I say that soon we'd have petaflop speed? On Monday, June 9, 2008 a machine appropriately named Roadrunner was the first to reach it. Built and tested by IBM in Poughkeepsie, New York, and soon to be housed at the Los Alamos National Laboratory in New

Mexico, Roadrunner was able to perform a thousand trillion calculations per second or petaflop speed.[4] To put this in perspective, Roadrunner is twice as fast as IBM's Blue Genie, which was the prevailing fastest supercomputer ever built. At the time, Blue Genie was three times faster than any previously built machine. Roadrunner has the computing power equivalent of 100,000 laptops. From a human perspective, if all 6.7 billion people of planet Earth had a calculator and performed one calculation per second, it would take forty-six years to accomplish what Roadrunner can now do in a single day.[5] Although the $100 million price tag was earmarked for technology to ensure nuclear weapon safety, it will undoubtedly also benefit those in engineering, medicine, and science. This race for machine speed and storage capacity will hopefully lead to the design of new biofuels, drugs, and computer simulations.

The impact of a new race of supercomputers will be felt in education as well. Already the convergence of these three factors—bandwidth, storage, and processing speed—has made resistance to online teaching and learning much more futile than back in the 1990s. This trio of trends has fueled the uploading and indexing of books, articles, videos, audio recordings, and other content online. The Web is now filled with a plethora of educational content, including online modules, courses, and programs that can be used to address diverse learner needs.

Chris Anderson, editor-in-chief of *Wired*, notes that when placed online, content no longer has to serve a mainstream audience.[6] Instead, it can address a few select people who might purposefully access it or simply stumble upon it. In his widely acclaimed book, *The Long Tail: Why the Future of Business Is Selling Less of More*, Anderson showed that e-commerce companies can stock more goods, and hence sell more products than conventional companies that had to focus on the hits in their limited shelf space.[7]

A similar trend is occurring in online education where instructors, schools, universities, and corporate training units can make more resources available for students to browse at their fingertips. Rural schools, for instance, can contract with outside services or organizations to provide courses or experiences that are beyond the capabilities of their own staff. John Seely Brown refers to this phenomenon as "niche learning opportunities."[8] No longer are schools limited to offering a finite number of courses with a predetermined list of resources. Students can pursue their passions. And they can do so with a like-minded community of practice.

Passion-based learning fosters deeper knowledge about a subject area. And the mentors and other experts found in associated learning communities that a student might join can help apprentice such learning. As Brown notes, such participatory learning combines the acquisition of skills and competencies related to a field or topic with gradually becoming an active member in that world; these are the initial stages in the development of what Brown calls "learning 2.0"— a life filled with options, choice, flexibility, and openness. Because storage costs are low and often free, learning is more individualized and available on demand. Never before in the history of humankind has so much choice been offered.

As the Web swells with content and resources, there is more choice in where and how to learn. An answer to nearly any question can now be found online at Internet speed and readily printed out. Corporate training guru Elliott Masie refers to this as the age of "fingertip knowledge" where memorizing lists is much less important than being savvy at accessing such lists. As Masie puts it:

> Have you noticed how we are memorizing less? It is due to a combination of Fingertip Knowledge and an increased confidence that information can be easily accessed from our devices and networks. . . .
>
> There are serious implications for the lowered expectation of memorization in our instructional designs. How do we recognize that our learners may not, and perhaps should not, memorize key information? Rather, we may want them to be able to navigate to the information, which, in some instances, is safer since things may change. In other instances, the information may not be useful until situations arise.
>
> The lowered levels of memorization and the increased use of Fingertip Knowledge have huge implications for how we design and deliver learning activities.[9]

We are just at the initial stages of Web use in education and training. Masie's notion of fingertip knowledge skills is among the strategies that have arisen to help learners cope with increasing information demands and opportunities. Questions abound. Is Masie a learning prophet or will the wetware we carry inside our skulls combine with the software we carry around on our belts or in our handbags? And when it comes to memory and knowledge, is less more, or is more really more? Perhaps we need our internal memory stores for split decisions that come up, and our technology-driven memories for other activities. In the midst of these questions, one must keep in mind what Albert Einstein and many since have long noted: "Information is not knowledge."

BOB AND TOM FINGERTIPPING PRESIDENTS

As apparent in many of the interviews presented in this book, fingertip knowledge and a functional Internet connection can get you information on just about anything you need. This next story illustrates the point. I was having lunch in College Station, Texas, on Friday, March 30, 2007 with my long-time colleagues Bob Slater and Tom Reynolds. Bob and Tom had recently eased out of the charter school business and were doing a bit of reminiscing. They were reflecting back on all the time and effort they put into it, and I was enjoying listening to them as I could see Masie's ideas of fingertip knowledge explicitly as well as implicitly in many parts of their stories.

Back in August 1999, Bob and Tom decided to take up George W. Bush, then governor of Texas, on his offer to create innovative charter schools that would empower student learning. Creating a charter school is not easy. Bob and Tom had to go through an arduous process requiring many meetings in Austin, hunting for a place to put the school, and on-site visits. Still they were committed to it. As professors at Texas A&M University at the time, it was not a typical job expectation. However, they had a novel idea that swiftly came to fruition: a high-tech campus focused on "inquiry-creativity" in Bryan, Texas—the Brazos School for Inquiry and Creativity. The Brazos School served at-risk high school students who had dropped out or been literally kicked out of the local public high school.

Bob and Tom had teamed up to do something about the serious student motivation and retention problems we hear about each day. As discussed in a special report by *Time* magazine and the *Oprah Winfrey Show* on the high school dropout crisis in America a year earlier, nearly one in three students in America was dropping out of school.[10] Worse still, almost one-half of African American, Native American, and Hispanic youth failed to graduate.[11]

A couple of years later, a report from America's Promise Alliance on fifty of the largest cities in the United States provided even more depressing news.[12] In those fifty urban areas, the average graduation rate was just slightly above 50 percent, with Detroit and Indianapolis taking up the rear at 24.9 and 30.5 percent, respectively. How can high-ranking education officials in either of those cities be hired back with such numbers? With more than one million high school students in the United States dropping out each year, Colin Powell, the former U.S. Secretary of State and founding chair of the Alliance, claimed that "it's more than a problem, it's a catastrophe."[13]

As our lunch progressed, it became clear to me how the charter school designed by Bob and Tom directly addressed this huge motivational dilemma. First of all, they planned for a school rich in meaningful, student-centered learning. Students would be empowered to learn. To accomplish this goal, the school environment had to be an invitation to learning instead of the same old boring routines these kids had seen year after year. The layout for the Brazos campus was quite simple: one large, well-lit, clean room with an assemblage of hanging plants and about twenty Internet-ready computers that could be wheeled to whenever the learning was to take place. With forty high school students in the school, two students were paired to work together at each computer station.

Tom explained to me that the curriculum consisted of assignments addressing a couple of state standards handed out each Monday morning. Five days later, the entire Brazos school would meet and students would share their findings in compact yet interactive PowerPoint presentations. The beauty of this approach, according to Tom, was that the students knew ahead of time that their work would have an immediate audience. With weekly goals connected to state standards, freedom to explore personal interests, and large audiences for their products, the same students who were indifferent or had been dropping out of school, were now succeeding and dropping in. The problem was no longer getting students to stay; more often, it was getting them to go home.

Keen use of fingertip knowledge was continuously evident. If they were assigned inquiry tasks to research the lives of former U.S. presidents such as John Adams, William Henry Harrison, Abraham Lincoln, or George H. W. Bush, such information would be at their fingertips when they looked it up online or found it on a CD. Week after week, these kids displayed their fingertip knowledge skills by accessing information at just the right moments in their presentations or when questions arose: skills that would carry increasing value when they went to college or landed a job in the real world. Not surprisingly, much learning success was happening in Bryan and their other charter school locations in Texas. These were the same children that many schools and teachers had basically given up on and did not want to see again.

What soon became more interesting is what happened when the landlord of the building in Bryan, originally from Hyderabad, India, showed up one afternoon and observed the students working. He was so impressed that he invited business acquaintances from Houston to see this innovative school. They too became thoroughly charged up by all the passionate and interactive learning they saw taking place. In the midst of this excitement, they hired Bob as a consultant to fly to Hyderabad in the summer of 2003 to help them start an inquiry-creativity school there.

While sitting at dinner on the night he arrived, Bob leafed through a copy of the local newspaper. In it was a story summarizing a speech made the day before by India's President A.P.J. Abdul Kalam, in which he described a pressing need for the exact type of school that Bob had been sent there to develop. Bob nearly fell off his chair, not from lack of sleep, but due to the rush of adrenaline pumping through his veins.

With such serendipity hanging in the air, Bob wanted to connect with the president to tell him his ideas and perhaps arrange a meeting. This was his moment. The stars certainly had been lining up. But just how does a professor from the United States who is in India for the first time in his life do that? Of course, his answer was the Internet and locating the right fingertip knowledge. And once his fingers started typing a few search terms, it was relatively easy to find. Sure enough, the e-mail address of the president of India was listed on the Web. Chuckling to himself about his ten-digit prize, Bob sat down that evening and e-mailed President Kalam, describing the "inquiry-creativity" model of schooling he had been developing and the theory behind it. Then it was time for some serious sleep.

The following morning when Bob awoke and checked his e-mail in-box, he could not believe his eyes: there was a reply from President Kalam himself.

In the e-mail, Bob discovered an invitation to meet with the president, provided that he could come up to New Delhi to Rashtrapati Bhavan, the Presidential Palace. Though he had heard that President Kalam was known as the "People's President," Bob could not help but be flabbergasted. After checking his pulse a few times, Bob replied that he would be happy to meet with him. Next, he had to rearrange his schedule so he could fly up to Delhi sometime during his one-month stay in India. Ten days later, Bob flew from Hyderabad to New Delhi where he met with the President of India for about an hour and a half. During their conversation, they discussed many issues related to education and the knowledge society, two of Bob's favorite topics.

Such is life on the Web. Fingertip knowledge has the potential to get you anywhere and help you meet anyone. Interestingly, for several years after that fateful meeting, President Kalam, who continued in office until July 2007, incorporated some of Bob's ideas into his speeches. How did Bob know that? He found President Kalam's speeches on the Internet, where they can still be found today.

Now imagine, if you can, the millions of people connected each day online who have an interest in improving education, learner creativity, and student retention in schools. There are endless opportunities for using the knowledge and information at your fingertips to connect with school principals and headmasters, heads of government agencies, and educational researchers like Bob and Tom. Your fingertip actions can make it happen. You might be shocked at the responses or assistance you get. The world is definitely open!

What is clear is that technology access is a key part of learning in this century. A project started in India in 1999 called "Hole-in-the-Wall" provides access to computer kiosks in the slums of New Delhi and other parts of India. The Hole-in-the-Wall project was started by Sugata Mitra, a physicist and chief scientist with NIIT, a well-known technology training and software leader based in New Delhi.[14] His vision was to provide educational access to children in the poorest slums of India. This project gives poor children a chance to learn and increase their digital learning skills. Among the skills they are learning is the value of fingertip knowledge—how to acquire the right information when you need it.

A WASTE OF BANDWIDTH?

In my many travels, I have had to rely on Internet access from hotel rooms, business offices, pubs, airport terminals, Internet cafes, university computer labs, and wherever else I could acquire it. One such situation occurred on Friday, December 8, 2006 in Taipei, Taiwan. Taipei is known for being a city with more Wi-Fi hot spots than any other place on the planet; there are thousands of access points.[15] I woke up one morning in Taipei to find an e-mail from my former student, Bude Su, now a professor at California State University Monterey Bay. She told me that Seymour Papert, an MIT professor and one of the foremost authorities in the field of educational computing, had been in a life-threatening accident in Hanoi the day before. She had read about it in a very brief online article from Boston.com.[16] It turns out that Papert had been speaking at a conference and was walking back to his hotel when he was hit by a motorist.

Seymour Papert was the designer of the programming language Logo. Logo enables young children to program computers and, in turn, robots—while learning concepts of geometry years before they might be more formally taught it in school. Papert also had been the brains behind a hugely popular laptop program in Maine. He was a key advisor of the One Laptop per Child project, which came out of the MIT Media Lab where he had worked for decades prior to retirement. He wrote popular books and papers on students constructing knowledge when using personal computers long before PCs were widely adopted in schools. Papert was a leading figure in artificial intelligence, learning theory, computer science, children's thinking, and constructionism. He had worked with the famous Swiss psychologist Jean Piaget during the 1960s. And he was perhaps dying in a foreign land.

I had read Bude Su's e-mail, but I was yearning to know more. Papert, whom I knew and had seen speak on several occasions, was one of my idols and perhaps the most prominent figure ever in the field of learning technology. What could I do? First, I sent a quick thank-you to my former student and asked her to keep me posted with updates.

Then I searched the Web for more information. I came upon a few newspaper articles, which provided the same sketchy information but not much more. At last, I found a familiar Web site that provided more news coverage and was written from a more personal perspective than what one might find in an online news report. It was Andy Carvin's Weblog, Waste of Bandwidth, which had what I needed.[17] Here, I found pictures of Papert, personal stories that Andy was able to relate from meeting him, a summary of what he meant to the field, and links to Papert's Wikipedia page that had still more news.[18] A colleague sent him the following e-mail that he included in his blog post:

> i am in still in vietnam at the ICMI conference. i have to just tell people the news, at least those i think will be interested. On tuesday afternoon, Seymour Papert got run over. He hit his head, and has had to undergo emergency neurosurgery. We are deluged here with well-wishers, and people flying in, so forgive me if this is very terse. His chances of a full recovery are not good but they are not zero. Everyone here is doing what they can—the local people here are just marvelous. Everything that can be done is being done.

Andy then elaborated on his personal interactions with Papert and reminded readers of the professor's long list of accomplishments. I was deeply thankful for Andy's touching post. So was the entire world of learning technology. His story contained content that traditional media would never have included and may not have been aware of, such as the following:

> I remember when my friend Patsy helped organize an education technology conference about 10 years ago, and Seymour was invited to be the keynote speaker. When the session was done, he had the opportunity to wander the conference and see other presenters. Instead, he wanted to go to the playroom where a group of kids were playing with toys, both high-tech and low-tech. In a matter of moments, Seymour dropped to the floor and got on his hands and knees. He then passed his time by playing with the toys while masterfully getting the kids to talk about what play means to them. I sat down against the wall, legs crossed, and watched him work his magic. I learned more about education from

observing him construct Lego buildings with these kids than any book I've ever read on epistemology.

Perhaps the irony was that Papert was apparently talking to his colleague about how they could improve the traffic flow in Hanoi with mathematical models just as he turned and was hit by the motorist. The following day, he was still in a coma after undergoing emergency neurosurgery.

As time passed, the Web began to satisfy my need for additional information on Papert. It came via e-mail, online news sources, blogs, and Wikipedia, which I could quickly access from my various hotel rooms as I traveled in Taiwan. He was made the news story of the day in Wikipedia alongside the death of former Chilean dictator, General Augusto Pinochet. Despite the myriad sources, the story remained incomplete. To my dismay, the only updates I found more than a year and a half later were from his personal homepage, as well as Wikipedia updates. The last news from Wikipedia sources indicates that he is doing well at his home in Maine, thanks in large degree to his rehabilitation team, which is employing the same experiential, hands-on techniques to aid in his recovery that he championed during the past few decades.

Thanks to my online learning network, I had the news that I needed even though I lacked daily access to more traditional U.S. news media. I was able to access many photos of Papert and pictures of his books to use in talks in Taiwan as well as Thailand a week later. In Hsinchu, Taiwan, about one to two hours south of Taipei, I had the opportunity to visit an elementary school known for its exceptional staff and their way of fostering student creativity. The students' creative products were on display throughout the building.

I took the opportunity to act as Papert himself might act. As described in Andy Carvin's blog post, Papert has always been interested in children's play. What do they learn from building, creating, designing, interacting, and tinkering? In the 1980s, he endorsed students taking apart computers and putting them back together. Unlike many personal computers today, they were anything but cheap in those days. Papert would interview children about their strategic moves and what made using computers so enjoyable.

With Seymour Papert in mind, I entered the computer lab of this school and asked a sixth-grade student what he was doing during his computer time and what interested him the most when using computers. He replied that he enjoyed playing games, sending messages to his friends, and exploring. For this young person, the power of the Web was in opportunities for play as well as exploration and collaboration. Papert was right again. But it was information I found online at my fingertips during that trip that reminded me of Papert's views. And from Internet hot spots in Taiwan, such online resources on this learning pioneer were amazingly easy to access.

FASTER THAN A FORD?

Throughout history, human learning has always had one foot firmly planted in the production of knowledge and the other in disseminating and enabling access to such knowledge. Today, the Web provides the foundation for both. In terms of knowledge access and dissemination, tools for searching and finding information such as Yahoo!, Google, and MSN Search expand and organize one's educational quests. Some people get it; others simply do not.

My friend and mentor, Dr. Brian J. Ford in Cambridge, England, has wrapped his brain around this issue of access for several decades, and his views are more optimistic and historical than most. Brian was working with computers in the 1970s and first wrote articles on computers thirty years ago. He has been on the Internet since 1993 and his personal Web site, first launched in 1996, records forty thousand hits a day. Run a search on Google for "e-learning professor scientist" and a link to information about Brian is at or near the top of the list each time, out of 1.5 million search hits from sites around the world.

Before detailing a few of his ideas, it is important to note that Brian is a leading scholar in the field of biology. In addition, he is an independent scientist, prolific author, internationally known re-searcher and scholar, popular interpreter of scientific issues for the general public, lecturer in many countries, current and former fellow with many universities, former director of British Mensa, and BBC television and radio personality. He hosted a TV game show, *Computer Challenge*, which is likely on TV somewhere in America as I write this.

But the list goes on. Brian is also a pilot, piano and keyboard player (who began by jamming with rock guitarist Dave Edmunds), popular cruise ship speaker, award-winning photographer, scuba diver, and trained marksman. What caught my attention is that he is author of a satire on science and education that claims to be a book with the world's longest title of over forty syllables.[19] It's too long to include here. Where would someone with such a background and interests file his publications and reference information? Why, on the Internet, of course.

In trips to London and to the University of Leicester in the United Kingdom during the past few years, as well as in our hundreds of e-mail conversations, I have had many chances to discuss emerging technology trends with Brian; in particular, e-learning and access to such learning. I could see that this extraordinary man was enamored with the Web of Learning. Perhaps, this biologist viewed it as a Web of Life.

Despite all his accomplishments, when I first met Brian in March 2005, he had taken up residence at the University of Leicester with the express purpose of conducting e-learning research under the tutelage of Dr. Gilly Salmon, the United Kingdom's e-learning guru. Why? Well, he realized that every college and university around the planet now had a Web presence, but this presence needed to extend beyond online books, presentations, and lectures. Brian knew that much of the content found online was backward looking, or even deficient. He pointed out that little research was being done on the quality and interactivity of such content. And he set off to do some new research, as well as take account of the work others had done.

I could sense from our many discussions that there was a revolution brewing, and he wanted to be a researcher, teacher, and advocate within it. Brian had taken up similar duties during preceding generations of educational delivery technologies—correspondence, radio, television, and computer-assisted instruction. He told me that as had happened throughout human history, new educational doors were opening. But the pace of such change today was much more rapid, and as a result, the opportunities were more diverse and extensive. With time and distance no longer barriers to learning and access to scientific discoveries, Brian sees a new era opening up in front of our eyes. He tells me it is truly a revolution in learning.

Brian had done a previous fellowship at the famed Open University in Milton Keynes and had witnessed firsthand the power of correspondence courses, including television lectures at "ungodly hours" that could be recorded and watched at a later time—as many times as one wanted. That too was a revolution, because learning no longer had to take place at the school, college, or corporate training setting. Instead learning happened at one's home while wearing slippers and quietly sipping one's favorite brew.

Brian told me, "The Web simply offers access at speed. But just because something is good, doesn't make it a good read." As such, resources and materials that might be posted online are not automatically an improvement over other choices or more palatable. Nevertheless, the human race has entered a period that has immense and unparalleled implications for teaching and learning. Links to new ideas and resources are available in the blink of an eye. You might be amazed with the resources that you can mold, shape, and reuse for educational gains.

Brian wanted me to think about just how much the speed of access had changed since Newton's times at Cambridge where he, too, is based. He asked me to think still harder and consider life hundreds of years earlier. I tried this thought experiment, but my years of searching in Google and Yahoo! had clouded my judgment. When I returned home from a trip to the United Kingdom in January 2007, Brian sent me an article he had just penned for *Laboratory News*. In it, he openly wondered how productive he would have been if he had been required to ride on horseback to get to the university library, as had been the case five hundred or six hundred years prior. In addition to the arduous journey to the library, he would still have to find information once inside. Worse still, the scholar would need to wait for days, weeks, or months for a scribe to produce a copy of any document that corresponded to his interests.

The printing press reduced time scales for the producers as well as consumers of knowledge. Now time might be measured in minutes, hours, or days, instead of weeks or months. And multiple copies of learning materials could swiftly be made available for learners, not just at one location, but anywhere with a postal code and enough money to purchase them. Brian reminds us that recordings of lectures on cassette have been used for decades, and photocopiers have saved incalculable amounts of time. He sees the single idea of digitization as having reduced the time lapse from months or hours to mere milliseconds. And with it, educational opportunities open up and multiply! As Brian describes it, "The Internet, however, is the ultimate miracle. A mouse click takes you to the library; you can search not only for titles, but for content. Google, Yahoo, and the rest are digitizing books everywhere. Now, if you need to access comments inside a book from the other side of the world, we are down to milliseconds. The fact that you can search instantly for any term—in any book—is something that you could not do with the printed word. Digitization alone has made that possible."[20]

In May 2008, I caught up with Brian on a beautiful day in Atlanta. Even though he was about to speak to a group of microbiologists about his new theory related to the intelligence of cells, our discussion quickly turned to the evolution of educational technology over the past few decades and the features of e-learning that were dramatically expanding educational possibilities. I asked Brian about his involvement with the evolution of learning technologies since his initial work with the BBC and even before that. He told me:

> When I was a kid, I can remember seeing the occasional bit of film or a tape locked away in a drawer; or a rare book. And if I happened to bump into a friend who might ask me, I could show him that very page on which the section of text that interested him was situated. Now that book, if I wish to, that tape, that film, that photograph, can go straight on the Internet. The Internet conveys immortality. It confers permanent immortality on fleeting realities. And, as a result, things you have forgotten in the bottom of a dusty drawer, are out there forever, digitized for everyone to access, anytime they like, and wherever they are in the world.

Yes. Digitization could conceivably make every idea in every existing book available for educational as well as noneducational uses. For Brian, such possibilities represent the most gigantic advancement in history for teaching and learning. And we are swiftly moving from possibilities to actualities. As proof, many such digitization efforts—especially those related to e-books—are noted in this chapter.

Though there are innumerable controversies made salient in the media related to book-scanning projects, such issues are actually relatively minor episodes in the larger human evolutionary script—one that opens up education to the masses. In part, the digitization projects outlined here are meant to indicate just how early we are in this movement. However, one should not get too sidetracked or lost in all the discussions of tools and projects for creating electronic content such as e-books. It is vastly more important to realize that the ultimate goal is the availability of learning tools and the elevation of teaching and learning on this little planet. It is also crucial to remember that this is just the first opener of the WE-ALL-LEARN model. There are nine more to come, each with its own exciting educational possibilities as well as surrounding controversies.

ABOUT TO BE GOOGLE-IZED

As we all know, learning from most classroom training is too quickly forgotten, especially when not used. We also know that many of us spend extensive time each day searching for information, and most of our findings are not relevant to our needs and interests. A better approach to learning is to provide knowledge when it is needed. Given that more than 70 percent of corporate learning is informal, providing information on demand is often the only viable option.[21] Knowing that the requisite information is highly accessible avoids us spending our days in endless searching and cataloging. It can help us find what we need in small, yet understandable chunks that are ranked by relevancy and called up when needed. Learning is no longer imparted from a teacher or trainer. In this new world, learning quests are purposefully chosen, self-directed, and immediate.

As learning shifts from acquiring and assessing knowledge to searching and finding knowledge, companies like Google accompany most learning journeys. In making this point, John Ambrose, senior vice president of strategy, corporate development, and emerging business for SkillSoft, argued in his article, "On Demand: The Googlization of Learning," that the most effective employee training programs blend an assortment of online information resources and tools as needed.[22] Many of these come courtesy of Google. He is right. We now have Google Scholar to acquire articles written by a well-known academic. We also have Google Maps to find the location of a reception for that person. And there is Google Video to watch this scholar deliver a lecture or conference keynote as many times as one wishes. There is also Google Blog, Gmail, Google Groups, Google Earth, Google Book Search, Google Images, and so on. The world has been Google-ized.[23] Google, Google, Google, Google, Google, and for good measure, still more Google.

For many people, Google is their favorite company and they relish spending time on its sites. Many Google resources are for educational purposes. For instance, Google Earth alone has more information than anyone can possibly learn in a lifespan. As with the David Thomas story in the introduction to this book, learners can explore buildings, waterways, country boundaries, and road systems in Google Earth. Such a tool is a godsend for many geography teachers. In one demo, the user is taken to Ayers Rock, Mount Everest, the Grand Canyon, and Diamond Head. In another, key buildings in cities such as Rome, London, New York, and Calgary dance in front of one's eyes. Those tired of exploring landmarks in Google Earth can look in the other direction and explore stars, planets, and constellations using the special "Sky" button. There are millions of stars and galaxies to explore in "Sky" mode.[24] Adding layers of information such as constellations can help one navigate these heavenly bodies. One can also explore high-resolution images from the Hubble Space Telescope, which is overlaid on top of Sky images with additional information on different objects available with a simple mouse click. Back in our own solar system, the learner can see animations of the orbits of different planets.

The brightly colored images are amazing and inspiring. The world is truly open with Google Earth and Sky. If this represents the Googleization of learning, I am all for it. I did not have such tools available to me when growing up. Two hundred million galaxies to explore whenever you feel the need? This is a monumental historical event!

Marissa Mayer, vice president for search products at Google, noted that "Google's mission is to organize *all* the world's information and make it universally accessible and useful."[25] Think about how foolish such goals would have seemed a decade or two back. Imagine what goals companies like Google might have a decade or two from now. Organizing *all* the world's information. For whom is this being organized? By when? Who will decide what qualifies as information? How will it be made accessible? How will it be put to use? And with the explosion of information in most any discipline today, can such goals ever be reached?

If Google succeeds in indexing all of the world's information, then the online searchers of the world will have no choice but to enter Google. And this is no small number of people. A report by comScore of Reston, Virginia, revealed that there were 750 million people searching online in the month of August 2007.[26] Those individuals generated over 61 billion searches. Of those, 37 billion, or 60 percent, were with Google. The largest percentage of searching did not emanate from North America or Europe but from the Asia-Pacific region. If Google meets its stated goals, in perhaps a decade or two, these same individuals will be successfully searching online for everything humankind ever thought of and recorded.

There is talk that Google founder Sergey Brin is interested in creating artificially intelligent agents or technologies to help with our information search needs.[27] A few years back there were even rumors that he wanted to implant a chip in your brain that could help access answers to questions as needed. Just think of something and your mobile phone or some type of audio device could whisper or text you the answer.[28] Imagine how such a device might impact standardized tests, certifications, and quiz shows. More important, contemplating the potential of any artificial agent support might allow some to see that having the equivalent of the *Encyclopedia Britannica* in one's head is no longer a defining feature of an intelligent person. Instead, people need skills in problem finding and problem solving, information synthesis, knowledge collaboration, originality, and critical analysis.

With all the resources available through Google and other online portals, significant learning is no longer discrete knowledge or facts learned at a specific event. The sheer volume of information is too enormous to expect anyone to know it all. To deal with the overwhelming amount of new knowledge generated in any field, learning is increasingly equated with access. Our learning access might come from online or face-to-face meetings with mentors. It might also be a derivative of work with virtual teams. It can come from online instructors, online repositories, and electronic portfolios of life experiences. Google and other search tools are simply fueling a trend toward making learning available on demand for learners. It is our intellectual café for learner-centered learning.

Oddly enough, some educators are heard chatting during lunch about their "Google jockeys." No, this is not horse racing or a specially designed line of men's underwear. A Google jockey is a participant in a class presentation who finds the terms, ideas, and Web sites mentioned by a presenter and displays them for the class as they are mentioned or needed.[29] Apparently, a professor at the Annenberg School for Communication at the University of Southern California (USC) coined this term. He found that having a designated Google jockey could help students keep track of the wide range of ideas he discussed in his classes. Such practices utilize a tool—Google—which students commonly rely on anyway and may seek out after class. They might also learn some new search techniques during the Google jockeying process. There is an air of spontaneity and empowerment when a class has a Google jockey. The concept is simultaneously humorous and refreshing.

When it comes to Web access and associated tools, Google seems to have it all. And much more is in the works in its experimental labs. Soon your browser will be able to display your search results in different ways, such as in a time line or map view by using Google's technology to extract key dates and locations from the search results. These more visual types of views might be helpful when locating information related to key events, people, organizations, and places. More is more, and that is exactly what Google offers.

THE GREAT GOOGLE SCANNING PROJECT

Where can you get your fill of this "more is more" world? Google Book Search is one such place. Formerly dubbed the "Google Print Library Project" or simply "Google Print," Google Book Search is a monumental effort to bring the world of books to everyone's fingertips. Its partners include the University of Michigan, Harvard, Stanford, Oxford, and the New York Public Library, just to name a few.

Google Book Search is being developed for the betterment of mankind. There are four possible book views: (1) *Full views* for those where Google has permission to publish the entire book as well as for books that are out of copyright; often the latter types of books are in the "public domain," which currently means any book published prior to 1923; (2) *Limited view*, which includes a few preview pages from the book that can be browsed and where one can conduct multiple searches; (3) *Snippet view*, where one can search a book and find up to three snippets of information for each search; and (4) *No preview* option, which simply has information about the book and links to find or buy it.[30] The hope is that exposure to a book, in any of the four formats, will increase the chance that it will be purchased.

With such options and undoubtedly more on the way, we are in the midst of a digital book revolution. Do you want the works of Charles Darwin, John Dewey, or William Shakespeare? Do you want to read *The Iliad* or *The Odyssey* by Homer? Various complete editions now exist. Anyone can just pop into Google Book Search and read them online, save them in PDF format, or print them out for later reading. Imagine the possibilities for instructors and self-directed learners around the globe as books are increasingly found online and not just in the library. Think of the creative works that an instructor or her students might make with pieces of either of these epics.

Despite the huge potential, there are many problems facing Google and its book search project team. As with most new technologies that make previously sold content free, the publishing industry threatened lawsuits against Google, although some have been recently settled. But by scanning only a page or two of a book that is for sale into Google Books and providing links to Amazon, BookSense, Abebooks, Barnes and Noble, and a Google Product Search comparison, the publishers actually can benefit from having such content online.

Google has contracts with dozens of respected institutions to provide books for Google to scan.[31] The University of California (UC) system alone has agreed to supply 2.5 million books over a six-year period.[32] That translates to more than 400,000 books per year. Currently, the UC system is being asked to deliver 3,000 books per day. Now that is a lot of books!

The UC system is not alone in these efforts. Librarians at the University of Michigan threw a party on February 1, 2008 when they successfully scanned their millionth book. Perhaps shortly after that party, many of them came to the sobering realization that they still have 6.5 million more to go, not counting the thousands of books that are likely added to their holdings each year.[33] It is difficult to fathom what a million books looks like. According to their "million books" Web site, this amounted to 361,441,145 pages of text containing 70,000,000,000 words in 428 languages on 135,432 subjects by 351,028 authors.[34] If weighed, the site noted, such books would amount to 750 tons. The storage of this amounted to 43,008 gigabytes of information. In length, this would have been 146 miles of books laid end to end, which would roughly equate to a trail of books from Washington, D.C., to Philadelphia. This was no small feat. In fact, it took 436 University of Michigan library staff members to complete it. Certainly, it was worthy of at least one huge bash to celebrate, and it must have been one fine party.

Paul Courant, university librarian and dean of libraries, told me that they expect to complete the balance of the scanning by 2010. My rough mathematical calculations tell me that is nearly 9,000 books per day counting weekends and holidays. Whew! They must have a lot of scanners. According to Dr. Courant, his staff is moving "thousands of books at a time to the scanning facility, and reshelving them as quickly as they come back." Score a touchdown for the maize and blue!

Despite such celebrations and meeting these goals, there are huge quality-control concerns related to the Google Book Search project. In January 2008 I spotted a feature article on the Google book scanning project in *Campus Technology* by Dian Schaffhauser, which said that many bloggers are poking fun at the apparent lack of quality control at Google.[35] It seems that there are many books with hands, arms, and fingers of the person scanning prominently displayed with important text pages. This is a valid criticism. I know when I pulled up Darwin's *Origin of the Species*, which had come from the Stanford University Library, the scanner's fingertips were at the bottom of various introductory pages. Could it have been that person's crude attempt at fame? "Look here, Mom and Dad, I am famous! Anyone reading *The Origin of the Species* for the next few hundred years will first be seeing my fingers." So much for the evolution of this species!

Different companies are competing to be the first one up the summit. Everyone wants to get to the top first—to have the world's knowledge. But what happens when such knowledge is murky? I decided to browse Darwin's masterpiece in Microsoft's Live Search Books tool. Though still in beta version at the time, I saw crisper text and no embedded body parts of the person doing the scanning, but each page took slightly longer to load than the same pages from Google. Of course, the quality of the original from the Cornell Library that Microsoft used might have been better.

They are each racing. As they do so, company officials, experts on retainer, and board members are making decisions about the learning needs, expectations, and capabilities of the citizens of this planet. Each company, Microsoft and Google, among others, is vying for supremacy in our digital age. Not just words, but also cartoons, photographs, diagrams, and other cultural artifacts will be available to anyone on the Web.

Quality concerns will undoubtedly continue to mount, but these projects offer learning opportunities to each connected citizen of this planet from Nairobi to Katmandu to Busan, and from Mexico City to Minsk. Such individuals will want to be connected. They will seek educational opportunities that their parents and grandparents may not have had. For both personal as well as economic reasons, the books scanned into these sites will raise the value of one's planet earth membership card. Among the more popular scanned textbooks will undoubtedly be those addressing language learning, as well as books on entrepreneurship and starting a business. And when features such as expert videos, animations, or audio are added or embedded within such books, there will be an even greater learning explosion.

Before such projects as Google Book Search and Live Book Search, Amazon.com established a program in November 2003 called "Search Inside This Book" that allows one to explore a book prior to buying it. A customer can search for words or content that she needs before selecting the book for purchase. After just a week, Amazon reported that full-text searchable books had 9 percent higher sales than those without it.[36] In late 2005, Amazon was back at it with a couple of other programs in the works with giant book publisher Random House as a partner. One of their inventions would allow someone to purchase just the chapters needed from a book. So a teacher wanting to upgrade her technology skills during the summer could just purchase the portions that are relevant to her from a voluminous book like this one. A second program will allow Amazon customers to upgrade their purchases by adding an electronic version of the book. In effect, they will not need to physically access the book to use its contents.[37]

When writing this section, I received an e-mail from Books24x7, a subsidiary of e-learning courseware company SkillSoft, announcing that it will offer a new service called "Chapters to Go." Now corporate customers can download chapters on hot topics from leading authors as PDF documents for offline reading and printing. Included in such downloads are their notes and bookmarks. They have made available full-text searching of thousands of digitized professional and reference books. With that, busy executives might have less downtime when commuting, traveling, or on a "vacation."[38]

Other e-book companies, such as ebrary, are based on a business model with subscription fees that allow for multiple people to access, search, and view the contents. According to Donald Hawkins, ebrary acts as a photocopier on the Web and charges fifteen to twenty-five cents per page.[39] Given that model, the company wants the user to find content so she can pay for it. In June 2008, ebrary announced a partnership with Ambassador Books and Media to offer nearly seventy thousand e-books and other electronic content for purchase to single users or institutions in a multi-user access model.[40] It now seems, after years of ups and downs, that there are finally some success stories for those in the e-book business to share.

As with any contest, there ultimately comes a time to announce the winners and losers. The news I received May 27, 2008 declared Microsoft the loser in the controversial book-scanning battle. The company had not just lost; it had done so to its top competitor. Microsoft started ten months later than Google and apparently spent much less on the project, and could not catch up without a significant monetary influx.[41] So after scanning some 750,000 books and indexing eighty million journal articles, it was shutting down the Live Search book and search programs.[42]

The apparent excuse? According to a post to the Live Search blog by Satya Nadella, senior vice president of Search, Portal and Advertising at Microsoft, they felt a need "to focus on verticals with high commercial intent, such as travel."[43] He recommends that instead of continuing to scan books, companies with search engines might be better off "crawling content repositories created by book publishers and libraries." So rather than create one hell of an online library by scanning every book in sight, Microsoft would rather crawl to content placed on the Web by others. Fortunately, the books and articles that they have already digitized will remain available online; however, no additional scanning will occur. Microsoft had galloped hard to get to this point. Exhausted, they were done. Race over? Not quite yet.

ALIGNING AGAINST GOOGLE

A few months before Microsoft surrendered to Google, an announcement sat in my e-mail in-box about a new online library that apparently had beaten Google, at least according to several academics.[44] What is it now, I wondered? Beaten Google? Microsoft could not beat them, so who did? And beaten them at what? I knew that Google would prefer not to take a seat in the second row to anyone, especially not when it comes to digitizing books. Well, it seems I was sleeping again. I found yet another stunning development within the Web that could ensure that WE-ALL-LEARN. At the time, I did not realize that another organization, the Open Content Alliance (OCA), had made available more than 100,000 books in little more than one year. According to their Web site, the OCA was conceived in 2005 by Brewster Kahle of the Internet Archive, in partnership with Yahoo!, not only to provide access to scanned books, but also to multimedia content—in effect, "public access to a rich panorama of world culture." The goal is to have a representative collection of "the creative output of humankind."

Perhaps instead of rushing to judgment that it has beaten Google at its own game, the existence of the OCA grants us an option to having Google control the electronic storage and distribution of so much of human history and knowledge. As Kahle noted in an October 2007 interview in the *New York Times*, "Scanning the great libraries is a wonderful idea, but if only one corporation controls access to this digital collection, we'll have handed too much control to a private entity."[45] In contrast, the OCA is a large community of interested participants who help build collections of materials that everyone can use. Nonprofit organizations like the Sloan Foundation have helped fund many of the scanning costs.

OCA members are well on their way to meeting their goals. By February 2008, there were eighty major institutions and research libraries in the OCA.[46] Participants include Harvard, Indiana University, York University, Rice University, Xerox, Adobe, Yahoo!, MSN Search, O'Reilly Media, and dozens of other organizations and institutions. Additional members included the Getty Research Institute, the British Library, the Smithsonian Institution, the Boston Library Consortium, the University of Toronto, and Microsoft. Yes, Microsoft was on this team now. Apparently, though Microsoft lost in the great scanning race, it is encouraging libraries to work with folks like the Internet Archive.[47] Hewlett-Packard Labs has also thrown their hat in by providing the scanning equipment, and Adobe is providing software licenses for its Acrobat and Photoshop software.[48] For those worried about too much corporate sponsorship, much of the funding for the OCA is coming from the Sloan Foundation, which has been quite active in the online learning world for the past decade.

OCA members are digitizing more than 12,000 books a month and had completed over 230,000 books by July 2007. In about an hour, they can scan two three-hundred-page books with estimated costs of ten cents per page.[49]

This is simply amazing! How large might this online collection of books become in five, ten, or twenty years? And they are not talking about trivial books, but comprehensive, seminal works such as the John Adams collection from the Boston Public Library and the James Birney Collection of antislavery materials from Johns Hopkins University Libraries. Other examples include texts on the Gold Rush and Western expansion from the Bancroft Library of the University of California at Berkeley, art and architecture books from the Getty Research Institute, and publications from the Metropolitan Museum of Art. History, art, architecture, and much more, are being preserved.

While all this was shaking out, Kahle and the Internet Archive found time to spearhead another project in San Francisco, namely the Open Library project. The Open Library, in effect, is the gigantic, digital card catalog for the OCA and beyond. Unlike Big Brother Google, the Open Library embraces Web 2.0 technology such as the use of commenting on or reviewing the online books. It will be a free, fully open, and comprehensive archive that records the discussions and reviews of its users. Basically, it is attempting to become a richer and more personally directed reading experience than the present options at Google and other online book sites. More important for academic partners in the OCA and likely others, there are no links to book publishers or enticements to buy the books; either the entire book is there or nothing at all. As with Wikipedia, unpaid volunteers will generate many of the contributions to the Open Library.

One of the Open Library project leaders is twenty-one-year-old Aaron Swartz, who is building a free online book catalogue for the Open Library that anyone can edit using specialized wiki-like tools. Though only twenty-one, Swartz comes with nearly a decade of relevant experience. At age fourteen, he helped author RSS, a Web tool for alerting people of new blog posts, news headlines, and podcasts. RSS came from a fourteen-year-old! Four years later, he did what most eighteen-year-olds with technological savvy and sufficient gumption do—he started a new a company. Swartz cofounded Reddit.com, a social news ranking Web site whose traffic grew so fast it was bought out a year later by Condé Nast in October 2006.[50]

Swartz' posted biography reads like those of most highly productive creative geniuses. A self-proclaimed writer, activist, and hacker, Aaron was homeschooled after an "intolerable" year of high school at North Shore Country Day School, where he had a scholarship, in Winnetka, Illinois, a suburb of Chicago. Soon, he was building award-winning database-backed Web sites and he coauthored RSS.[51] Then in 2002, after reading an article about Creative Commons, a nonprofit organization devoted to helping copyright holders make their works available according to different restrictions, including unrestricted access, Swartz was inspired to offer his services. He quickly wrote to Stanford Professor Larry Lessig, the founder of Creative Commons, who invited him in to take a lead role in a key technology used at Creative Commons called RDF. Through Lessig's support, he was even accepted into Stanford, where he spent a year before other projects grabbed his attention.

Currently, Brewster Kahle has convinced Swartz that his talents are needed in the Open Library project. In this project, one of his key goals will be to create "a comprehensive Web page about any book ever published."[52] Swartz hopes to build a site where one can find interesting books on what some might deem obscure topics. He will help determine how millions of dynamic book records will be stored and used. Like those at Alexandria before him, Swartz is attempting to catalog and provide access to the great works of the preceding centuries all in one place.[53] Just suppose by age twenty-one you had accomplished so much that could benefit humankind with such a project. As the doors to learning open wider, there will be thousands of young people like Aaron Swartz who change the world using technology, creativity, and high energy.

The Open Library was not set to start business until March 2008, but a demo site was created in mid July 2007. It did not take me long to browse this great wonder of the modern world. When I ventured there, the first book I came across was Henry James's *An International Episode* from 1892, contributed by the University of California at Berkeley. It was three decades prior that I wrote a critique of one of James's short stories in my freshman English class at the University of Wisconsin at Whitewater. But I only had a book, a black-ink pen, and a pad of paper. Today, I can download the book, search its contents online, and soon magnify pages of it. Yes, I can do that at the Google site as well. But in the Open Library there are sticky tabs indicating the pages where the keywords I searched for appear. Adding to my sense of excitement, I click on such tabs and go right to that material.

Books at the Open Library have additional features and advantages. For instance, *An International Episode* comes in a number of file formats. Those who use the embedded "flip book" tool get the sense of a physical book. And if people want to purchase bound copies, Lulu.com, a company that offers print-on-demand and self-publishing services, allows anyone to create their own book covers and associated artwork and then print the book for a minimal charge (the sample online ones are just $8). In the works are a series of collaborative tools for sharing book annotations, bookmarking, creating user-defined collections, and a tool for embedding passages from other texts that automatically trace back to the source document if one cares to read more.

I can also read reviews of the book. I find one with a full five stars. I too can write a review of *An International Episode*, which anyone else coming to retrieve this book can then read. Soon I spot a link to audio files of the book made by LibriVox. These files are in the public domain.

Upon clicking, I find that I can listen to the complete audiostream of the book using my computer, or I can download the six individual episodes, each read by a different reader, in three different formats, including one for my iPod. More interesting, I can listen to a male or female read the book. I can also listen to someone from the United States or the United Kingdom read it depending on the accent that I prefer. So many choices for just one book! It dawns on me that someday this same book will be available in dozens or even hundreds of languages. I can write a review here as well, but first I must sign up for my virtual library card. Of the nearly four thousand people who have downloaded this audio file, I am the first to write a review.

Heading back into the Open Library, there are thousands more books to download. How about *Tom Sawyer*? In just a few minutes the entire thirty-six-megabyte file is copied onto my machine. The considerable number of online book resources and tools now available assures me that Jay David Bolter was right; we are living in "the late age of print."[54] Today, hypermedia capabilities, along with participatory learning opportunities of the Web 2.0, extend electronic print into the domains of sound, images, videos, and animations. It is a much more flexible and interactive learning environment. And any marking, comments, or links placed within that electronic document are a form of collaboration and sharing that heretofore could only exist in the minds of those who could perceive such connections or interrelations between media elements and information.[55] Today those links are in full view for anyone to see. The entire world can now share and elaborate on passages or ideas within such works as *Tom Sawyer* or any other online book in the Open Library. I can write a review and cross-reference other online resources, which others reading my review can browse and reflect upon. *Tom Sawyer* is no longer a static document, but one that begins to come to life. Additional Web 2.0 tools will certainly amplify such capabilities.

ALL THE WORLD IS A STAGE—WRITING BOOKS FOR THE WORLD

Google, Microsoft, and the OCA are hardly the lone providers of free book access. For example, the Global Text Project intends to develop more than one thousand free open-source digital textbooks. The goal is to help educate disadvantaged populations and people in Third World countries who simply cannot afford to buy paper-based books or to access the ones they need.

College students are helping in the process. Remember final assignments in school that you put a lot of work into? Now think about the final course projects and other scholarly works produced by graduate students in their various classes around the world that are often discarded when the class ends. Instead of another semester of seemingly wasted effort, in the Global Text Project, their examples, glossaries, exercises, and sample tests might serve as supplemental materials for a free book that a professor is writing. Or perhaps these same students might write the chapters. It is important to note that the students would gain from such a real-world experience. At the same time, their creative energies and talents would be set free rather than contained or confined to a single course or program.

The Global Text project was spearheaded in January 2004 by Professor Richard Watson at the University of Georgia. Watson's graduate students wrote the first version of the book, *XML: Managing Data Exchange*. Students at Georgia and at other places around the world have continued to enhance and extend that book. According to Watson, with $200,000 of funding from the Jacobs Foundation in Switzerland, some initial pilot testing of the ideas is about to take place in Ethiopia, Uganda, and Indonesia. Textbooks already have been developed in business, agriculture, education, and science.[56] You can find titles such as *Classical Mechanics*, *Introduction to Physical Oceanography*, *Principles of Toxicology*, *Introduction to Economic Analysis,* and *Social and Cultural Foundations of American Education*. Two new books on business fundamentals and introductory information systems will soon be available in English, Chinese, Arabic, and Spanish. An April 2008 blog post from Watson indicates that the project is being warmly received in Africa and the Middle East.[57] A network of contributors, funders, users, and other participants is being formed. Momentum is building!

All of their work is kept in an open document format (ODF) using OpenOffice; they also publish these documents as PDF files. More important, because ODF is XML-based, they can publish to any media format. Though funding for proof of concept remains an issue, they are finding success in updating books that are out of print (after getting the original author's permission, of course). The primary focus of the Global Text Project is business, science, and technology books. As Watson told me: "We have done a pilot in Ethiopia of the IS book and successfully engaged students in providing feedback, via what we call Student Quality Circles, to authors to improve chapters. We want to create more active and reflective learning as part of the project so that the books are under continuous improvement."

Imagine that you contributed to such a book as a graduate student in 2009. Years later you travel to a more modernized and literate Kenya, Pakistan, or Vietnam, either professionally to deliver a speech or more personally while on vacation, and someone recognizes your name and thanks you for the free online book. Or imagine that someone simply sends a thank-you card to your professor who forwards it on to you. The latter is already happening! And it is connecting the people of this planet to help them learn in ways not previously possible. As this occurs, WE-ALL-LEARN!

Although the Global Text Project is still in the initial stages and may fail, there will undoubtedly be other noble projects like this which spring forth to help fill in the huge chasm in the digital divide that seems to widen each day. There is little doubt that free textbooks, how-to manuals, reading packets, novels, encyclopedias, and other reference-ware will be available at no charge, in multiple languages, and for numerous technology devices. There will be no reverse pivot here. The march toward free and open source books is coming at a brisk pace. Those who benefit from an education where none occurred previously will be most thankful.

This is not the only initiative attempting to bridge the digital divide. Yale, Cornell, Microsoft, and three United Nations programs for health care research and global online research in agriculture and the environment have banded together with two key publishers—Springer and Elsevier, as well as a hundred other publishers—to provide free journal access to health care workers, such as doctors and nurses, researchers, and others, in developing countries.[58] Imagine the lives this unique partnership will affect.

This U.N. effort is not simply for one or two journals but thousands of them. And it is not just a few countries or people benefiting from this grand scheme, but more than a hundred countries and untold millions of people who will ultimately benefit from enhancements in health care, farming, and environmental information. Access to environmental journals alone comes from more than three hundred publishing houses, scholarly societies, and scientific associations and includes more than 1,200 scientific journals and titles, such as *Botany and Plant Biodiversity, Energy Conservation and Renewable Energy, Climatology, Population Studies and Migration, Oceanography and Marine Biology, Ecology and Wildlife Conservation,* and *Social Sciences and Desertification.* Add to that list those in health care (over 3,750 journal titles) and agriculture (958 additional journals), and you begin to get a sense of the true scale of this effort. There is grand knowledge sharing happening in the Web.

And this is not simply about research; a great many of these journals relate to practice. In health care, for instance, there are publications such as the *Journal of Dental Education, Journal of Second Language Writing, Medical Education,* and *Journal of Continuing Education in Nursing.* There is access to journals in psychology, psychiatry, law, anthropology, toxicology, engineering, genetics, and a host of other disciplines. Of course, these journals are not all in English; some are in Portuguese, Spanish, Russian, Chinese, Italian, German, French, Japanese, and even one in Ukrainian. And many are available in multiple languages.

With one project, a world of current scholarship and practice is at one's fingertips. Momentum is building. In battling the escalating cost of college, many professors are purposively deciding to donate their textbooks and writings to the world.[59] Someone can find the latest research on a topic, as well as how to implement it or put it into practice.

And that's just some of what is happening today. What announcements will come tomorrow or overnight while I sleep? Perhaps I should discuss the California Open Source Textbook Project that seeks to significantly reduce the $400 million that the state of California spends on textbooks each year. Or perhaps I should include information on the One Million Book Project being led by Carnegie Mellon University. The One Million Book Project is an attempt to design a universal library that will foster creativity by offering free access to all human knowledge. It already has 1.5 million books scanned and available for browsing. The enormous volume of announcements in new learning technologies and education is beginning to make my head spin.

How can we keep up with new developments? And where is the leadership in education to make sense of these fabulous initiatives?

BLOWING DANDELIONS

While organizations are busy creating free books or scanning thousands of them, many people are taking matters into their own hands. Numerous well-known authors have taken a stand to write or edit books and allow free downloads of them to anyone with Web access. For example, back in October 2005, my good friend Terry Anderson, professor and Canada Research Chair in distance education at Athabasca University in Canada, decided to do this with an edited book, *Theory and Practice of Online Learning*.[60] A year later, he was delighted to tell me that it quickly had fifty-five thousand downloads.

Some might argue that interest in free online books is short-lived. When I inquired about the book a couple of years afterwards, I discovered that Anderson's book remained a hot commodity, and this was four years after the original publication date. In January 2008 alone, more than six thousand full HTML downloads and another thousand PDF downloads were made. Chapter Three on strategic approaches to online learning received an additional twenty-three hundred downloads. On top of the book and chapter downloads, Anderson's e-book had over seven thousand hits. That may not sound impressive to professional writers, but for academics, that is a huge audience. It was so successful that he came out with a second edition that is also free online.

Most academic books do not sell many copies. Normally, Terry might have sold five thousand, or if lucky, ten thousand copies of such a book, and would have had much more modest exposure. But with free Internet downloads, any world citizen online can access his work. According to the Creative Commons copyright notice he selected, anyone can read, print, and freely share the content in whole or in part with proper attribution and for noncommercial use. At the same time, he restricted copyright so that no one could create derivative works, such as by altering or building upon his work and selling it personally. Such copyright is less stringent than the typical book publisher's exclusive rights licenses, which often force authors to go through unwieldy permissions policies and, worse still, result in more limited readership and use.

Terry has taken a stance. If online learning is to be successful, then the resources to support it should be easily accessible and free. When I spoke with him in Edinburgh, Scotland, in September 2006, he noted that the royalties he gave up were quite minimal. What he maximized was his reputation. Though he never mentioned or took credit for it, he had also taken an ethical and moral stance to educate the people of this planet. He had maximized their learning possibilities. Such returns are not easily equated with dollar signs and cost savings as with most corporate return on investment (ROI) calculations. Still, there are likely hundreds of thousands of readers of his book. That is quite an impressive ROI! With one decision—to make his book free to the world—his influence quickly extended far beyond the audience that most academics total in their entire careers. As Don Tapscott and Anthony Williams note in their book *Wikinomics*, "In today's information-soaked environment, writers and content creators need to find ways to permeate people's consciousness. Giving away content and building loyal relationships are increasingly part of the arsenal creators use in the battle for people's attention."[61]

I believe Terry has done more than that. He has contributed to the free and open learning culture that is growing in our midst. People like Terry, and there are now thousands of people just like him, are becoming ardent members of and contributors to the WE-ALL-LEARN movement. Can there be a more obvious book that should be freely available over the Web than one related to helping teach and learn online?

What if a cadre of scholars became unhappy with the normal book review process and their lack of control over it and took a similar approach? It is not unusual for book publishers to dictate everything to the author—the title, table of contents, figures and tables used, model names, resources cited, order of chapters, length of chapters, types of examples provided, and so on. On top of that, in the next stages, they predetermine the cover design, marketing strategies, and cost with minimal, if any, input from the authors. In such a model, author creativity is virtually nonexistent. But what if the middleman is cut off from the deal? Or what if both worlds—the traditional publishing world and the free e-book world—could coexist?

Cory Doctorow has proven that such a scenario is now possible. In fact, he epitomizes this movement. Doctorow is coeditor of Boing

Boing, a highly popular blog related to technology, culture, and politics, with a daily readership of 1.7 million people. Doctorow, a thirty-eight-year-old native of Toronto now living in London, is also author of several award-winning science fiction novels that are available for fans to download and read for free.

His first published novel, *Down and Out in the Magic Kingdom*, was simultaneously published by Tor Books in physical format and placed online in a free electronic format under a Creative Commons license that encouraged his loyal readers and those who stumbled upon it to copy and share it as many times as they wanted. Within a day, there were thirty thousand downloads of the novel and unknown additional copies made.[62] Three years later, the book had been downloaded more than 700,000 times from Doctorow's Web site alone; it is impossible to track other downloads of his book. The novel also has been reprinted a half dozen times during that period and translated into more languages than Doctorow can keep track of. This development is not entirely new, by the way. The same approach was chosen nearly a quarter century ago with *Ender's Game*, the very first novel to be made available for free online, way back in 1984 on the DELPHI online network. Like Doctorow's work, it also appeared in physical form thanks to Tor Books.[63] With this free access, Doctorow's work has received extensive exposure and recognition, including winning the Locus Award from the popular science fiction and fantasy magazine by the same name.

Through electronic publishing, Doctorow's career took off. He has worked for the Electronic Frontier Foundation in London, and served on the boards of many organizations, including the Participatory Culture Foundation, the Open Rights Group, and Technorati. Invites, speeches, meetings, and so forth, are all common experiences. Though he dropped out of four different universities without completing a college degree, his reputation as a first-class blogger, writer, and thinker earned him a one-year stint as a visiting professor at the University of Southern California (USC) during the 2006–07 academic year. At USC, he was the first Canadian Fulbright Visiting Research Chair in public diplomacy.

Simply put, e-books opened many doors to Doctorow that otherwise would have been nailed shut. Though he was perhaps once thought to be on the fringe, the mainstream is now frantically trying to keep up with his insights and movements. At the same time, those alongside him on the e-book fringe have bonded with him and helped promote the digital publication movement. As Tapscott and Williams point out, greater opportunities for emotional bonding between authors and their reader community are possible when timely and free information is conveyed online.[64]

When I e-mailed Doctorow in April 2008 about my interests in open access content such as e-books, he replied with a draft of an article, "Think Like a Dandelion," that was about to appear in *Locus Magazine*, in which he noted the following:

> If you blow your works into the net like a dandelion clock on the breeze, the net itself will take care of the copying costs. Your fans will paste-bomb your works into their mailing list, making 60,000 copies so fast and so cheaply that figuring out how much it cost in aggregate to make all those copies would be orders of magnitude more expensive than the copies themselves.
>
> What's more, the winds of the Internet will toss your works to every corner of the globe, seeking out every fertile home that they may have— given enough time and the right work, your stuff could someday find its way over the transom of every reader who would find it good and pleasing.[65]

As this quote brings into full view, Doctorow firmly believes that bits are meant to be copied and distributed, not copyrighted and protected. He finds that copying or sharing work actually helps him make more money. He argues on his homepage, Craphound, that enlisting "my readers as evangelists for my work and giving them free e-books to distribute sells more books. As Tim O'Reilly says, my problem isn't piracy, it's obscurity." He adds that by giving away books, he gains a wide range of ideas about how to make money from them. Such a philosophy garners him exposure and insights into the worlds of publishing, education, and emerging technologies that no one else on this planet has. Small wonder he is a popular speaker, writer, consultant, and activist.

Terry Anderson and Cory Doctorow have opened the world by boldly placing their thoughts and ideas on the Web for anyone to read, download, or critique. They are definitely not alone in their online experimentations and visions. Anyone can now post online books and other documents and offer them free to the world. As with Doctorow's dandelion metaphor, those taking such a stance will have readers in every corner of the globe. At the same time, those seeking royalties for their creative work but lacking a publisher can self-publish their books using services such as Lulu, AuthorHouse, and BookSurge; the latter of which is owned by Amazon and offers print-on-demand services. Book publishing options abound. There are many dandelion seeds yet to be blown.

THE END OF THIS SEARCH

Web searching, digitization, and the creation of content to search for is the first opener. There are overlaps with some of the other openers, but this is where WE-ALL-LEARN begins—one must search and find content. And powerful content is certainly now available to each of us. We can thank the Googles, Microsofts, and Yahoo!s of the world who made their search technologies and resources available. We should also thank those at nonprofit organizations such as the OCA, the Internet Archive, and the Global Text Project, which have given vast book-related contents to search, including free books, open-access journals, and downloadable research articles. And we should send notes of appreciation to Terry Anderson, Cory Doctorow, and anyone else who intentionally provides free online access to books and other documents they have written or edited.

Each of these individuals and organizations is pushing ahead new frontiers of Web content accessibility, portability, and learnability. As such, they have an impact on the potential for individual learning pursuits as well as collaborative knowledge quests.

A Web filled with digital book content is just the first step in the WE-ALL-LEARN perspective. We have to provide access to such books and documents to people with minimal technology infrastructure. What happens, though, when these books are placed in the hands of those who never had such access? Will there be a sudden rise in literacy tutors, trainers, and specialists to help them take advantage of such opportunities? Will unique collaborations spring up among these early pioneers in the digital textbook revolution? There is no doubt that the increased access to electronic books and other Web documents and objects has an opportunity to transform education.

In a world where WE-ALL-LEARN, it is educational professionals who must design creative and educationally beneficial uses of these technologies. Without their creativity, ingenuity, and persistence, much of what Google or the Internet Archive is doing today would be pointless and ultimately worthless. Though many are self-learners in casual explorations, many more learn from using this content in accredited online learning classes and programs. The following chapter pushes into this second opener—the world of fully online and blended learning.

E-Demand Around the Globe

OPENER #2: E-LEARNING AND BLENDED LEARNING

A COURSE FUNERAL?

Why write a chapter on the demand for e-learning when my friend Jay Cross points out that formal courses are dead?[1] Instead, one should look at informal courses, which comprise 70 to 80 percent of our learning. And there is no busywork with informal learning—it is all directed toward accomplishing a personal goal or task, not something artificial or imposed by an instructor. The notion of a standard course with all its prepackaged curricula is dead. Instead, workers of today need just-in-time and on-demand learning. Workflow learning where one might download some needed materials when a problem or situation arises is the mode of information delivery in the twenty-first century. And with the education technologies available today, work-flow learning is a reality.

Even if formal courses are dying, there is still a need for ideas on how to facilitate learning at the dawn of the death of such courses. Clearly, Cross and others leading this death march realize that e-learning is one of the key instigators for a mass burial.

THE GROWTH OF E-LEARNING AND BLENDED LEARNING

Since at least Plato's era, technology has allowed time and distance to exist between learners and instructors. For Plato's students, it was the invention of writing. Move the clocks forward more than a millennium, and we would find Norwegian instructors taking advantage of the geographic distance that writing permitted by shipping assignments to students in distant villages.[2] For others since then, the education diversifiers have included the printing press, telegraph, phonograph, radio, television, satellite, computers, and now the Internet.

With each wave of technology, educators make renewed promises regarding the impact of such technology on education. Correspondence and other forms of education delivery have a rich history in the United States and around the world. John Heyl Vincent, a pastor and later American Methodist bishop from the Chicago area, even noted that "the day is coming when the work done by correspondence will be greater in amount than that done in the classrooms of our academics and colleges."[3] And he said that in 1885. Today courses are not just available in correspondence mode but also via real-time Web conferencing tools, radio, CDs and DVDs, television, online chat, mobile phones, and many forms of technology-enabled learning environments. Distance educators continue to experiment with each newfangled technology as it appears.

Along these same lines, there has been a christening of innumerable centers and institutes for e-learning or blended learning during the past few years. These centers have a mission to find, document, and showcase the best online learning practices and provide labels for some of the activities that they employ. It seems that at every stop I make, there is a new building or institute that has just been opened. It does not matter if I am visiting the University of Tampere in Finland, York University in Toronto, the Open University of Malaysia in Kuala Lumpur, or the University of Glamorgan in Wales—there is increasing funding devoted to distance learning and emerging educational technologies. In many places, governments are pouring in money. They are making long-term investments in their people.

These resources are appearing in response to the constantly changing student populations found in schools, colleges, and training organizations. The learning clientele is becoming more and more diverse each day, and the addition of technologies, as well as centers that monitor and evaluate their use, allows these learning organizations to diversify even more. This diversification stems from many factors, including increased access to learning, lifelong learning pursuits, recertification needs, immigration, longer life spans, better course marketing, and so on. And a growing number of technologies and delivery mechanisms connect this diverse array of students together. One course might rely on asynchronous technologies, such as online discussion forums and practice tests. Such approaches allow for flexible work schedules since learners can participate at any time and from any region. Another course might incorporate real-time chats with guest experts, online Webinars, and videoconferencing. These technologies provide a sense of caring from the instructor or expert as well as immediate feedback to participants' questions and concerns. Many courses today combine such approaches.

Suffice to say, you can feel the shift toward the engagement and empowerment of learners in multiple delivery formats and activities. There is choice. So much choice! And I have yet to mention the possible inclusion of animations, games, and simulations as learning tools or online cases, scenarios, and problems. Despite debates still raging today about best approaches, there is no one best technology and no one best instructional approach. There are so many options.

E-LEARNING IN SCHOOLS

Send Me to NotSchool

I have been tracking online learning for nearly two decades now. June 24, 2004, sticks out in my mind as a day filled with radically new ideas for online learning. It was a lovely Wednesday morning in Lugano, Switzerland. My colleagues and I jogged up and down city streets talking about the upcoming keynote speaker for the Ed Media Conference. His name was Professor Stephen Heppell from the Ultralab at Anglia Polytechnic University (now Anglia Ruskin University) in the United Kingdom. We had read about some of the innovative learning technology ideas coming from the Ultralab, and this was our chance to hear from the person who had founded it some fifteen years prior in 1989.

After our run, my five colleagues and I found an open row near the back of a very crowded auditorium. Heppell did not disappoint. He is someone who looks to the future but has many creative ideas in the present as well as the past. As an example, he talked about how modern Web-based "pirate" radio projects were similar in spirit to programs broadcast from ships off the coast of Britain that circumvented the BBC's restricted playlists during the 1960s. He then showed virtual curators displaying items from a national museum on the Web, which invited people to share stories that they might have about the objects. After that, he played kids' multimedia works wherein they strung together pictures of people as they age from one to ninety-five. During his riveting talk, Heppell demonstrated that young students can create multimedia work at the level of university students if they are allowed to follow their passions.[4] In his view, the better models of learning included choice, empowerment, creative expression, meaningfulness, and individuality.

Exciting ideas to be sure! However, there was one concept that had me inching up on my seat for a better view—NotSchool.net. "Did he say NotSchool," I whispered to my U.K. colleague Jim Hensman sitting to my right. "Yes," Jim answered, "NotSchool, have you not heard of it?" It was then that Heppell had me hooked.

As he spoke, I was reminded of Ivan Illich's somewhat radical assertions about the ineffectiveness of schools as institutions of society.[5] In the introduction to *Deschooling Society*, published in 1970, he wrote that "we have come to realize that for most men the right to learn is curtailed by the obligation to attend school. . . . Universal education through schooling is not feasible."[6] Illich advocated a self-directed learning mode in which "educational *webs*" would "heighten the opportunity for each one to transform each moment of his living into one of learning, sharing, and caring."[7] Such sentiments sound highly similar to the social networking and other participatory learning opportunities of the Web today.

Illich did, in fact, advocate for new types of networks and "opportunity webs," which would be readily available and would expand access to learning and teaching for everyone. He also discussed how new kinds of media, radically different from television, could empower the learner and encourage free expression just as seen today with YouTube and other shared online video formats. Illich also wrote about skill exchanges and opportunities of peer-matching networks offered through technology. Although he was amazed that simple technology-assisted exchange programs had not been established in the early 1970s, the emergence of the Web a few decades later gave us many such resources and programs. Illich also thought that an assortment of reference materials, learning objects, freelance educators at large, and peers with similar interests could help a student define her learning goals and offer her an apprenticeship that was better than that found in traditional schools. If such resources were freely available, even better! Such things now exist. It is clear that he was decades ahead of his time.

For Illich, there were three purposes of a good education system. First, it should offer unlimited resources for any learner at any point they are requested. Second, it should allow individuals who want to share knowledge or expertise to find those who would like to learn from them. Third, the system should allow all who want to present an idea, issue, or resource to the public to be able to do so. Learning should be open regardless of prior degrees or certifications. And such learning need not subject learners to obligatory or lockstep types of programs; nor is there a need for a designated teacher who is the custodian or the master of ceremonies within such prescribed and typically boring curricula. Illich assumed this alternative access to education would come in the form of explorations in one's physical community. However, as Heppell was now showing us at the Ed Media conference, these explorations were quite possible in virtual spaces, which were much more scalable and replicable than physical ones.

Perhaps Heppell had read or met Illich. In 2001, some three decades after *Deschooling Society* and a year before Illich's death, Professor Heppell and his friends at the Ultralab helped start NotSchool. NotSchool helps the kids who normally slip between the cracks of traditional schooling. In a nutshell, NotSchool is a national, Internet-based project in the United Kingdom that helps some five hundred to seven hundred young people each year who have not done well in the regular classroom due to problems like bullying, phobias, travel schedules, reluctance to learn, pregnancy, and assorted other reasons. It is aimed at students aged fourteen to sixteen who have been out of school for an extended period and have failed to learn from traditional education channels including home tutoring. In effect, it is an alternative school of last resort.

As the name implies, NotSchool provides a new model for education. Learners are called "researchers" and teachers are termed "mentors." In line with Illich's ideas about good schooling, other human support is provided from subject-matter experts, buddies (undergraduate and graduate students), and "governors," who are often prominent people who did not do well in school themselves. Internet connections and various technologies are provided for NotSchool children. Online technologies are used for student creative expression, not simply to force them to turn pages of content.[8] With its willingness to move to more flexible student-driven learning schedules, NotSchool has given many students renewed confidence while engaging them in content that really matters and that is important to employers of the twenty-first century. More than half of those who entered the initial phase of the NotSchool program received some sort of formal accreditation and nearly one-third wished to stay involved after that point.

Given the motivational problems in schools today, perhaps we need to start building thousands of NotSchools in cyberspace rather than more of the brick-and-mortar variety. If more kids learn, the experiment will have been worthwhile. Perhaps other forms of alternative schools will arise like NotSchool—schools that take advantage of traditional and online forms of instruction for truly powerful blended NotSchool learning. Interestingly, when I visited Anglia Ruskin University two years later, I found out that Heppell had left the Ultralab for a post in Dublin. Not too surprisingly, the Ultralab eventually closed down, but NotSchool lives on!

NotSchool is just one example in a sea of online programs and initiatives. Given the mind-boggling numbers of people currently enrolled in online courses, this chapter can only scratch the surface of what is currently happening in the online learning world. Daily news reports, white papers, and conference announcements indicate that emerging technologies—such as podcasting, coursecasting, wikibooks, video blogs, and mobile learning—create instructional opportunities that previously were unimaginable.[9] As these reports reveal, there are countless informal and nontraditional learning events and situations where online courses and resources are making an impact.

Consider the video-based blogs, or vlogs, that detail happenings at the Monterey Bay Aquarium, a space shuttle liftoff, a peace rally, or an immigration rights meeting. Or think of the local as well as worldwide educational ramifications of a nightly educational podcast featuring current topics and controversial issues in the field of education. And when a community-built wikibook is freely available to explain a new and confusing topic to any of the people on this planet with online access, it is difficult to ignore. In all three of these examples, we have communities of educators and concerned citizens sharing their knowledge and expertise for the benefit of others. And all three already exist.

Along with such opportunities come new perspectives. My own research indicates many instructors around the world are building and sharing knowledge because they want to help the world, as well as personally grow from such sharing. Although there are mounting concerns about the expertise, authority, and accuracy of those doing the sharing, such acts can perhaps bring everyone on this planet to a baseline of knowledge from freely shared content that is learned without instructor support—"Level One Knowledge," if you will—from which to expand to other levels with additional formal and informal training from instructors, tutors, and mentors. Learning at Level One does not create immediate expertise, but oftentimes, learning online in a self-paced fashion can enhance one's skills if the content is properly designed and the study is seriously undertaken.

The continued emergence of innovative educational technologies and associated instructional applications is a given. What is in question is whether they will be utilized in online teaching and learning to a significant degree. There will always be first adopters and pioneers who swiftly grasp and affirm the applicability of such innovations in nearly every educational example or situation they come across. They are the learning optimists and visionaries who push learning just beyond the reach of the latest attacks from the critics. For them, potential online learners are everywhere. There is the salesperson learning the features of a new product while she is traveling to see a distant client. In the same household is her son, Stan, who is a high school student retaking geometry during some free moments in the summer. Stan's older brother happens to be a soldier learning Arabic online before heading on a mission to the Middle East. And his sister is a pre-service teacher taking a few online courses at her university while on an internship at a Native American reservation. A few miles away lives Stan's grandfather, who is now retired and is learning—through special education portals and tip sheets found on the Web—how to work at his local library with individuals who have visual and hearing impairments. The scenario is fictional, but e-learning optimists and pioneers will swiftly point out that these are just a few of the educational possibilities available within the Web.

Although there are scores of online learning optimists and pioneers, as well as myriad examples of innovative uses to justify such optimism, there are also many who admittedly are more hesitant, reluctant, or resistant about technology's role in education. Like medieval European sailors who hugged the shoreline and relied on familiar landmarks, many teachers will not give up the lecture, the canned drills, rote instructions, and twenty years of dog-eared lecture notes. In education, our safekeeping selves too often suppress our risk-taking selves. But with such safekeeping comes an earth with a different sort of flatness—a dreary sameness that greets traveling learners with scenes of familiarity, accompanied by redundancy, complacency, and dryness. In a word, boring!

But the Web offers something beyond such dull and flat learning. It is an openness that is pushing ahead toward the untried and untested, not clinging to the past or perpetually gripping the shores of the known world. New mind-sets can help break down barriers to educational access and open new doors to learning. Of course, some will cite legal or ethical concerns, whereas others will see plagiarism around every corner. Still others will suggest administrative nightmares. And there will be those who simply do not see how online learning can benefit their area or discipline. For such folks, the Web may be everywhere, but it serves no legitimate purpose in teaching and learning environments. They have yet to see the new oceans of learning that are now possible.

The Indiana Ocean

Perhaps the most rapidly growing area of online learning is at the primary and secondary levels. In fact, the stage is now set for explosive growth in primary and secondary school settings. A major study was conducted in 2007 by Project Tomorrow and e-learning leader, Blackboard, of over 230,000 students, 21,000 teachers, and 15,000 parents from 3,000 schools across the United States.[10] Among the findings, it showed that nearly half of high school students and one-third of middle school students are interested in taking courses online that are not presently offered at their schools. Besides gaining access to certain courses, other reasons they were interested in online courses included working at their own pace, the possibilities of extra help, personal interest in the area, and the ability to take more advanced courses. One in five, in fact, had already completed an online or distance course at their school or on their own.

Students were certainly willing and interested in online learning. What about other key school stakeholders, such as teachers and parents? Just 3 percent had taught an online class, but nearly half of the teachers surveyed had taken one. More telling, perhaps, was that over three-fourths of teachers felt that technology made a difference in student learning. Unfortunately, these positive feelings about technology failed to translate into online learning support among these same teachers. A mere 18 percent indicated that online classes would be a good investment for increasing student achievement levels, as compared to 42 percent of parents. Perhaps these teachers were simply concerned about losing their jobs. Perhaps they should be!

As surveys like this reveal, online learning is gaining attention in K–12 settings. At about the same time, a report from the North American Council for Online Learning revealed that forty-two states had significant supplemental or fully online programs or some combination of both.[11] The authors noted that these reports are increasing in complexity because the categories used to describe the delivery of instruction—fully online, supplemental, and face-to-face—are becoming extremely blurred. As this happens, for-profit companies are stepping in to provide online services. In fact, one such company, K^{12} Inc., grew so fast from 2005–07, that it filed for an initial public offering of stock. In its prospectus, it reported an annual growth rate of 35 percent and was serving twenty-seven thousand online students in 2007. Half of the online learning programs surveyed in this report experienced 50 percent growth from the year before, and another 40 percent grew by 25 percent or more.[12] Growth seems to be the key word in K–12 online education. Already, there are well-known virtual school initiatives and significant enrollments in states such as Utah, Missouri, Florida, Idaho, Mississippi, Virginia, Illinois, Ohio, and Michigan.

I can almost trip over the offices of the largest online learning high school in my state on my way to work. The Indiana University High School (IUHS) began in the late 1990s as an experimental project. Today it enrolls nearly four thousand students taking classes and another fourteen hundred in diploma-granting programs. When I met with Bruce Colston, director of the IUHS in June 2008, he informed me that many of their courses offer students a choice between correspondence or online versions. Courses with such options include advanced composition, art history and appreciation, and introductory-level courses in German, as well as advanced-placement courses in calculus, English, chemistry, and American history. Again, as the world opens up, new educational options are provided. Those worried about quality need only see that graduates of IUHS have been accepted to prestigious universities, such as Duke, Northwestern, Emory, and Parsons School of Design, as well as many regional colleges and universities.

Students come to IUHS from varied backgrounds and needs. Some are behind in their studies. Some are hoping to graduate from high school early. Some are in the military. Some are incarcerated. Some are homeschooled. And at least one is a ballerina. In her quest to become a professional ballerina, Kathryn Morgan enrolled in the IUHS to focus on dance full time and pursue an apprenticeship with the New York City Ballet. Kathryn loves the flexibility. As she explained, "I need something that lets me work on my time. The online courses have been really great. I love getting the feedback so quickly." Contrast that with Zachery Meunier who at age seventeen is quite the political activist. While interning for Indiana Congressman Baron Hill, Zachery has learned a massive amount of information that he would not have learned in a traditional high school. This young Democrat and hopeful political campaign specialist has also helped with events for Hillary Clinton in her bid for the U.S. presidency. Like Kathryn, Zachery loves the flexible schedule and notes that "If I had been in a traditional school, it would have been impossible."

Study at the IUHS is not constrained to U.S. borders. When Karen Fennell and her husband decided on a five-month sailing adventure in South America and the Caribbean that would take place from January to June 2006, they had three daughters who quickly asked to come along. Caitlin was a semester ahead in college, Lydia had graduated from high school a year early, and their third daughter, Bridey, was a sophomore in high school at Lake Forest Senior High School in Illinois.

The older two could easily convince their parents that they had the time available for this journey, but Karen did not want Bridey to fall behind her classmates. In the coming weeks, she extensively searched for nontraditional learning alternatives that would enable Bridey to keep up with her coursework while accompanying them on this sailing adventure of a lifetime. After many dead ends, she contacted Bruce Colsten at the IUHS. "Of all the schools I contacted," Karen told me, "Indiana was the most willing to be creative and think outside the box. Bruce simply said to me 'let me see what we can do.'"

Bridey was soon enrolled in IUHS courses in French III, English, precalculus, and history. So off they went. Well, not so fast! First, they had to travel to Arcaju, Brazil, to pick up the new forty-six-foot catamaran that they had custom built. Inspired by a popular B-52s song to "roam around the world," they named their sailing vessel the "S/V Roam."

Once at sea, they realized that finding libraries on the different islands they planned to visit would be difficult. Because all her courses were essentially self-taught, Bridey would have to prioritize the time available at each stop. She downloaded homework when in port so she could complete it during the passages between stops. Though some might not call it work, she spent about four hours a day looking out at enchanting bay views or sitting among coves of lovely palm trees while doing her homework. When at sea, she really had no choice but to work within view of the seemingly endless Atlantic Ocean, as studying below deck was sure to cause a headache from the rocking of the boat.

Another challenge confronting this family of sailors was figuring out how Bridey could turn in her assignments and take her tests. Each IUHS midterm and final exam had to be proctored. However, parents or relatives could not take on such a role. The Fennells, however, found options that met their needs as well as the requirements of IUHS. As learning pioneers, the family had to think creatively. With IUHS approval, they often got dock masters to be exam proctors. One time, they even got a captain from a Portuguese boat to monitor and sign; fortunately, he understood English. And later on, when in the Grenadines, they found a retired teacher to help. When complete, all exams had to be signed by the proctor, placed in a sealed envelope, and then delivered via the postal service. Bridey's assignments, however, could often be uploaded to a designated course drop box on the Web or e-mailed directly to the instructor.

Learning her lessons was also accomplished in unconventional ways. Although her parents were not able to help with most of her homework, Bridey could practice her French lessons when asking for directions or ordering groceries on many of the islands where they docked. After days of learning alone at sea, Bridey came to enjoy these authentic learning opportunities. And she did learn these lessons well; in fact, she got straight A's in her four courses. Bridey was not the only one who was productive on the ship. Karen, a psychiatric social worker, started working on a book of her own. Her husband, Steve, ran his home-building business from the helm of the boat by communicating each day with one of their sons back in Chicago.

In addition to Bridey's self-study learning from a distance, the S/V Roam housed a family who had, in effect, become online teachers. Eldest daughter Caitlin found a way to be a teacher and mentor to children thousands of miles away. She embraced this more open learning world by creating a program with the Lake Bluff Elementary School back home, which would monitor the family's journey and use Caitlin's accounts for activities and discussions in a geography class. The kids logged in every few days and read and discussed her journey updates. These activities gave Caitlin a sense of meaning and focus during the trip. She was not the only one who found solace in Web writing; most of the family, in fact, blogged and posted updates about their journey while traveling. As they traveled from coastal cities such as Salvador and Recife in Brazil to Tobago and Trinidad and on to the Grenadines, St. Lucia, Martinique, the Dominican Republic, and the rest of the Caribbean, Bridey experienced increasingly faster connection speeds.

The longest stretch at sea was a ten-day journey from Brazil to Tobago. It was here that Bridey really had to plan her study time wisely. Keep in mind that she remained a full-time high school student while walking through villages and meeting people she would never have met otherwise. Though not a specific class assignment, she gained an immense amount of cultural knowledge, as well as insights into the educational technology available in that part of the world.

The last stop of the journey was Charleston, South Carolina, where much of the family has now relocated. In all, they traveled five thousand miles. Each day, and perhaps each mile, was part of a unique learning adventure for Bridey as well as a teaching opportunity for Caitlin.

Karen and I chatted on June 6, 2008, two full years after their voyage at sea ended. Bridey was graduating that evening with high honors from Wando High School in Mt. Pleasant, near Charleston. The high school was three times bigger than the one she left in the suburbs of Chicago. When times were tough, Bridey relied on the organizational and self-directed learning skills that she gained while with the IUHS. Karen confided that too often these critical life skills are not taught in schools. Essentially, taking online classes has prepared Bridey for entering the real world.

In Karen's words:

> The confidence she gained in being self taught, locating the post office and Internet connections in each port, and finding the time to download enough materials since there are target dates to get everything accomplished was enormous. There was a 4–5 month timeline for completing all her courses. There were specific assignment deadlines. She would know that we would be leaving an island tomorrow and have to think about how much stuff she needed to download for her next assignments. She also realized that her parents did not know the materials so she needed to learn it all by herself. Bridey had to create a plan of study and then do it on her own. She has shown she could teach herself when needed. If she now has a bad teacher, she simply goes back to IU mode and thinks about how to teach herself the content.

Bridey then explained:

> Studying while sailing gave me the chance to explore the world outside my comfort zone, while I remained a student. I am proud that I learned how to organize my time and be in charge of my education. My teachers at IU encouraged me to contact them when needed and they bent a lot of their rules to talk to me outside their office hours to fit better with when I was in port.

She added:

> I am also proud that I did something most of my friends thought was outrageous. My friends said that they would never want to be stuck on a boat with their parents, without their friends and social life. My social life

changed drastically. My sisters and I became closer and a really great evening was sitting on the tramp on the front of the boat watching the sun going down over the ocean, hoping to see the elusive "green flash" as the sun dips down below the horizon.

Pushing the borders out still further, the IUHS is currently creating programs for adults in Indiana who never finished high school. In addition, it has recently formed a partnership with Paxen Group of Melbourne, Florida, to help with an accelerated online high school completion program geared for the military. Word is getting out. Interest in IUHS online courses and programs is coming all the way from Nigeria, India, and China. For example, the IUHS is negotiating with Chinese officials to offer a Western-style high school experience in China. If successful, it will use expatriates living in Beijing as teachers. The expectation is that the correspondence option would be preferred over the online experience. Whatever the format selected, such a school would prepare Chinese teenagers for university study abroad. It will undoubtedly be highly popular.

Mandarin in Michigan

Due north of my home state of Indiana is Michigan. This is a part of the country in deep economic crisis as it responds to the collapse of the automobile industry in the Midwest. In response, Michiganders have turned to education as part of a strategy to become more technologically and globally minded and connected. As a sign of things to come, in 2006, Michigan state lawmakers passed a bill requiring all high school youth to complete at least twenty hours of meaningful online learning experiences as part of their high school degree. For most this means enrolling in at least one online course.[13]

Michigan high school students are thus entering the more open learning world, where they will engage in online field trips, blog about such experiences, communicate with other students in threaded discussions, and track their progress in electronic portfolios of their work. Perhaps just one chance Web site visit or exploration will expose some of these students to career options and possibilities of which they had not been aware previously.

When exploring the online guidelines for this program, choice and options are highly apparent. In fact, Michigan lawmakers and educators are willing to accept a wide continuum of online learning experiences in these twenty hours ranging from teacher-led to blended to teacher-facilitated and finally to self-paced formats. As you move down this continuum, the teacher fades into the background. Those wanting to know the advantages and disadvantages of each option need only see the online learning guidelines in the Michigan Merit Curriculum.[14] Given these options and guidance, this program certainly seems like a winner!

Unlike other states, students and parents in Michigan likely yawned when this bill was passed. At the time, Michigan already had nearly 7,000 students enrolled in online courses through the Michigan Virtual School (MVS).[15] Started in 1999, by 2008 the MVS had over 100 part-time instructional positions along with a couple of full-time teachers serving 11,000 students from 1,100 Michigan schools. The average class size was roughly 20 students per section. Dan Schultz, senior development and policy adviser of the Michigan Virtual University, told me that enrollments were expected to top 15,000 in 2009.

More than two hundred different courses are currently offered by the MVS. Skills learned in these courses include gathering and analyzing data, evaluating the accuracy and appropriateness of information, communicating ideas to others, and conducting online research. Naturally, through these online experiences, Michigan students will also become adept at creating and sharing electronic documents and navigating through hundreds of Web sites and other online resources. These courses are equipping Michigan teenagers with lifelong learning skills.

Another impressive development in Michigan is a project that began in the Confucius Institute at Michigan State University (MSU) that supports the teaching of Mandarin to K–12 students.[16] As a backdrop to this program, one should realize that more than two hundred Confucius Institutes have been developed in some sixty countries throughout the world as a means to promote Chinese culture and language as well as enhance global relationships.[17] Through agreements with the Confucius Institute, a university in China typically sends the Chinese teachers to the partnering university, which must provide the housing, staff, and matching monies.

In partnership with the Michigan Virtual University, the Confucius Institute at MSU offers every high school in Michigan one free seat in the program. In the fall of 2006, MSU started offering online Chinese language classes to more than 240 high school students.[18] According to Dr. Yong Zhao, the executive director of the MSU Confucius Institute, about 1,000 students from eight states have taken the online course. And there will be about 300 in the fall of 2008 as well as another 300 in the spring of 2009. The Mandarin course requires four days per week of self-study. A fifth day each week is spent in live audio conferencing originating from the MSU campus with native Mandarin speakers. The instructor meets with groups of three to five students using a tool called TeamSpeak while communicating with headsets.

High school students are not the only ones benefiting from these institutes. Anyone can learn some new Chinese words each day with a service offered by the Confucius Institute called "phonecasting."[19] Just dial in and receive your free three-to-five-minute Chinese lesson for the day. In this age of mobile learning, even Chinese fortune cookies can be replaced with similar online learning quickies.

Yong Zhao is also excited by the opportunities for teaching Mandarin through interactive online games. When I contacted him in July 2008, he excitedly told me that one massive multiplayer online game called Zon already had six thousand registered users from some forty countries. And it is still in beta! He quickly added, "We have also been teaching Chinese to community college students in Second Life." Phonecasting, massive gaming, Second Life, audio discussions with real Chinese professors—their innovative technology experimentations are helping the world learn Chinese. Stay tuned to Mandarin in Michigan. More is in the works.

When I pressed Yong a bit about why all this is happening now and how it reflects our more open learning world, he said:

> Online seems to be the only viable way to meet the rising demand for Chinese language instruction worldwide. With good design and expertise, we can deliver high-quality instruction worldwide and reach our audience in an unprecedented way. If technology is truly addressing a problem perceived by educators and political leaders, the uptake is fast. So one insight about online/technology uses is to find the niche. When we start

something new, we should try innovation instead of fixing the old. I can see the online Chinese instruction activities here at MSU-CI (Confucius Institute) will be captured as a major case for understanding and pushing open the world for learning and education.

And what of the high school students back in Michigan? One fifteen-year-old student, Michael Martin from Fennville High School near Holland, said that "Chinese seemed like a language that no matter what career I want to go into [it] could help me out."[20] A decade or two from now, Michael and some of his classmates in this program will likely be Michigan entrepreneurs and government officials. This will put Michigan at a distinct advantage over other states because many of the companies we all will deal with in the future will be Chinese.

So, what happens to teachers in this brave new world that Michigan is helping lead? They are learning online, of course. In 2003, the Michigan Virtual University launched LearnPort for Michigan teachers to receive free online professional development. To date, LearnPort has built more than a hundred courses.[21] There are also more than 135 online community rooms where teachers can discuss course ideas and change. And these rooms are busy! In five years, this professional development portal has already served over thirty thousand users.

Now those teaching in the Upper Peninsula find immediate connections to those in Lansing, Kalamazoo, Flint, and Grand Rapids. Teachers in farming communities can find out what works in inner-city Detroit schools. Each teacher is on equal footing whether he is from award-winning Norman A. Miller Elementary School in rural Cement City or a more upscale suburban Detroit school such as Bloomfield Hills Middle School or a private one in Auburn Hills.[22] Given that Detroit is the headquarters for the charity Urban Farming, which has helped bring to life five hundred family-sized gardens across the city, rural school teachers in Cement City might find they have a lot in common with their more urban colleagues.[23]

I have seen these types of learning programs work all over the world. In fact, Professor Emeritus Lee Ehman and I created a similar type of professional development program for rural teachers in southern Indiana, though it was more blended and smaller in scope.[24] It was exciting! Online, a teacher is a teacher is a teacher. It is ideas that matter and the ability to share them and the willingness to accept them from others—not the car in which a teacher drives to work or the schools from which he got his degrees.

Virtually Young in Florida

Before Michigan made these impressive announcements, all media attention related to K–12 online education seemed focused on Florida. Back in 1997, the Florida Virtual School (FLVS), known then as the Florida Virtual High School, was one of the first online K–12 schools in the country.[25] As someone who was perpetually bored in high school, working on schoolwork from home or wherever one happened to be sounded intriguing to me and seemed like it would help to address the serious student motivation dilemma in the United States and many other countries today. I remember meeting FLVS officials a couple of years later at the Florida Educational Technology Conference (FETC) in the Orlando Convention Center and being impressed by their information and instructional design ideas.

In April 2001, I finally had a chance to sit down and talk with Julie Young, FLVS president and CEO. Julie was seated across the aisle from me on a bus ride to dinner during a symposium organized by Jones Knowledge called "Go the Distance." She quickly informed me that the FLVS started with just a few dozen students in 1997, but since then it had grown to nearly six thousand students taking one or more online classes. Her insights into the world of K–12 online education made a lasting impression on me. Not surprisingly, with such leadership, the FLVS has received many recognitions and awards.

When I asked Julie for updates in July 2006 and then again in April 2008, she noted that the growth had continued. With state appropriations of over $50 million, during the 2006–07 fiscal year, the FLVS had over 52,000 students from grades 6 to 12 enrolled in more than 87,000 half-credit courses.[26] These half-credit course enrollments were expected to exceed 100,000 during the 2007–08 school year. By 2007, FLVS was offering ninety different courses including ten advanced placement courses taught by more than 400 full-time and 176 part-time teachers. Like Michigan, she added, it also offers online courses in Mandarin Chinese.

Such impressive numbers did not happen overnight; instead, they came from rigor, depth, innovation, and quality in all aspects of the FLVS. According to Julie, the technology tools of choice for FLVS instructors and students include e-mail, chat, discussion boards, Web conferencing, and telephone. When I asked her about any learning results that she did not anticipate, the first thing that came to her mind was the enhanced student ability to speak clearly with an adult. When in online programs like FLVS, students can no longer hide behind their more vocal peers. Regular one-on-one interactions and discussions with an adult strengthen FLVS students' communication abilities. Other improved student competencies include organizational skills and self-initiative as students take responsibility for their own learning.

At the same time, online environments require extensive reading and writing. This translates into a significant development of skills in these areas as well. Such gains in literacy skills are a huge win in a state such as Florida that has a large immigrant population and is perpetually focused on the literacy deficiencies of its residents. Finally, despite students' mistaken beliefs that they know all that there is to know about technology, Julie mentioned that many admit to learning new technology skills, such those involved in Web conferencing, VoIP, and even simple PowerPoint presentations.

Let's recap what she said for a moment—presentation, communication, organization, reading, writing, and technology skills. Not bad. Now throw in increased motivation and ownership for learning and you really have something to write home about. Small wonder that people are looking at FLVS as a learning model for the twenty-first century.

Julie noted another amazing benefit of online courses in K–12 schools:

> We've had students from the life management courses write that they've improved their ability to communicate with their families as a result of the course. One student who had been running with a rough crowd wrote that he realized he had made poor choices that had adversely affected him and his family, and the course taught him how to turn things around for himself. He actually said that he believed the course and the teacher saved his life. It doesn't get much better than that.

No, it certainly doesn't.

Julie and her colleagues have witnessed firsthand the educational transformation of the past decade brought on, at least in part, by online and blended learning. When I asked her about the new open world of education, she said that she basically agreed with Thomas Friedman that increased information access combined with new forms of information exchange, collaboration, and teamwork have huge ramifications for our personal, educational, and work-related lives, and that not all of these developments are positive. As Julie put it, "I think this new world of open access provides for students some exciting and unprecedented opportunities for learning. It also presents new dangers."

Then she added:

> Part of my passion as an educator is to help other educators understand how vital it is that we be willing to pioneer within this new "open" world on behalf of our children. If you think of pioneering days of old in this country, no one would have dreamed of sending children out to forge a trail to the West ahead of their parents. Yet, so many parents and educators today are willing to throw up their hands and say that they just aren't good at technology or they are just too old to change their way of teaching. That's the equivalent of sending our kids into a wilderness with no map or compass. We have to be willing to provide the maps and the compass so that when they get out into this new open world of instant access, they will have guideposts, warning signs, and even a moral compass to keep them on a productive path.

With Julie Young at the helm, thousands of students are on productive paths, making FLVS a clear online learning leader. As a sign of this leadership, FLVS not only services the state of Florida, but since 2002 it also teaches students from other states; today the FLVS extends to thirty-five states. (Unlike in-state students, those outside Florida pay a tuition fee.) Could foreign countries be next?

Julie informed me that excellent support provided by the State of Florida enabled the FLVS to develop high-quality courses quickly. Many other states delayed their online learning initiatives but soon wanted to ramp up fast. To do so, they turned to FLVS for their courseware, training, consultative services, and even to enroll their students in FLVS classes. For example, when Appleton, Wisconsin, school officials were exploring online learning, they turned to FLVS for a model as well as for associated support. The FLVS has effectively taken its years of hard work and specialized knowledge about online learning and turned it into a national clearinghouse for quality online courseware and instructional design. When it comes to online K–12 education, they are a known brand. For many, they are *the* brand.

In a recent interview, Julie Young indicated that she would like Florida and other states to adopt the Michigan policy to complete some type of online experience before obtaining a high school degree.[27] Once again, Julie's vision of how the benefits of online learning could help all students took a step forward. In the summer of 2008, the State of Florida passed a new law that significantly expands online learning opportunities starting in the fall of 2009. This law requires all public school districts in Florida to create fully online options for their students from kindergarten through high school.[28] If they cannot, they must either partner with other districts to accomplish such goals or contract for such courses and programs with online learning service providers. The FLVS is once again working in partnership with school districts to help them meet the new online learning requirements. Unlike other states that have delayed online learning programs and initiatives, Florida has a resident expert with a huge track record who knows what quality online learning looks like: the FLVS. And the FLVS can help with virtual learning from soup to nuts—technology, training, and courseware; you name it, FLVS has it. To top it off, the FLVS has more than a decade of experience partnering with local districts to work from. In a few years, enrollments of 100,000 student may look quite small.

With this bold move, Florida is perhaps the first state to pass a law that encourages its youth to obtain their high school degrees without ever setting foot in a physical classroom space. Now this is a revolution in learning.

Such novel state laws and policies open up the world of learning for millions of young people in Michigan, Florida, and soon other states and regions of the world. The hope is that students who enroll in online programs will learn the organizational, leadership, self-confidence, and self-directed learning skills that Bridey Fennell learned. I would love to see my own state of Indiana create such mandates, policies, and opportunities, but it continually flirts with online learning initiatives—one day announcing them, and the next day pulling back on their funding.[29] It is a yearly battle here that is undoubtedly occurring in many other cities, states, provinces, and countries.

E-LEARNING IN FOR-PROFIT UNIVERSITIES

A Phoenix Has Risen in the Distance

As online learning has moved from its infancy to its adolescence, the number of instructors and students affected by online course practices and activities has grown tremendously. Since the turn of the century, a tidal wave of online learning courses, programs, and ideas has continued unremittingly. The ride has undoubtedly been bumpy and unforgiving for some, but an accelerating trajectory for others.[30] During the past few years, reports from the Sloan Foundation as well as some reports of my own have documented online course and program enrollment data in the United States and around the world, both in fully online and blended learning environments.[31]

Blended learning has been receiving the bulk of the attention during the past years. A blended environment, taking advantage of both face-to-face (FTF) and online methods, has advantages that other delivery systems do not. Blended learning has been a key aspect of training in corporations such as IBM, Microsoft, and Oracle as well as in higher education institutions such as the University of Pretoria in South Africa and Beijing Normal University in China.[32] It is conceivable that blended learning will soon have an impact on nearly every college, university, corporation, institution, or organization involved in training or education on this planet.

Given these developments, more educators and trainers need to understand what they can accomplish in these environments. They are seeking guidance, stories, and examples of what works or might work. As more people graduate from fully online and blended programs, such degrees are earning increasing respect and acceptance in the workplace, as well as in higher education.[33] And when basketball superstar Shaquille O'Neal of the Phoenix Suns earns his MBA from the University of Phoenix in a blended program, there is intense media attention and increased awareness from the general public.[34]

Adult education and training is experiencing explosive growth around the globe. Fully online universities such as Capella University, U21 Global, Western Governors University, and Jones International University, as well as those with significant online programs, including the University of Phoenix and Walden University, have emerged to fill this gap. Each of these institutions has a unique story to tell.

Let's start with a well-known and somewhat controversial story. The University of Phoenix, part of the Apollo Group and listed on the NASDAQ, now has more than 100 campuses and 160 learning centers.[35] Of its 330,000 students, approximately 200,000 attend online.[36] That there is a university in the United States with one-third of a million students is mind-boggling! That the majority of them are earning degrees offered through online instruction by a company that is on the stock exchange leaves no room for debate as to whether we are in the midst of a revolution in learning. Small wonder that the University of Phoenix is creating a research center that seeks to understand best practices for teaching nontraditional adult learners.[37] University of Phoenix officials have also reacted to self-service student needs by offering specially designed "drop-in" centers.[38] Unlike the problems of face-to-face instruction with students dropping out, with online education, they are now dropping in! How cool is that?

That does not mean there are no problems at the University of Phoenix. The university has gone through two presidents in recent years—Todd S. Nelson in early 2006 and Brian Mueller in late June 2008. There are some rumors that at least one of their departures was due to differences with hard-charging, visionary Apollo Group owner and billionaire, John Glen Sperling.[39] The University of Phoenix also has had to respond to its share of lawsuits and allegations, student complaints, and scholarly debates.[40] It has been consistently attacked by traditional institutions and scholars for low standards and highly aggressive marketing tactics. In the midst of this sea of controversy, it continues to grow and grow, and grow some more. It is now the largest private institution in the United States. It serves a population that averages thirty-five years old and is about two-thirds female.[41] Centuries from now, historians may write a more complete story of how this phoenix off in the distance rose up among the ashes of traditional education to change the life stories of millions of adults. Time will tell.

Not every online course or idea tested in higher education finds success. Courses and programs ideal for online environments are those in which the content constantly changes, such as in medicine, management, and engineering. Another area often targeted is supplemental materials for professional degree and certificate programs in fields such as accounting, nursing, and dentistry. Carefully crafted online materials can often be made available to learners long before revised textbooks or lecture materials. Courses with heavy doses of writing, such as English, journalism, and many others in the social sciences, are also ideal for online learning with all the tools for writing and collaboration found there. Along these same lines, any course that relies on supplemental aids and resources can now use the Web. Despite arguments to the contrary, online learning can also offer individualized feedback to students in high-enrollment face-to-face classes where there is a lack of a personal connection with other students or the instructor.

These are just a few brief examples of where online learning makes a difference. As stories later in this book will reveal, online learning can also help in situations where the students are spread out over a vast geographic region (for example, in the provinces of Alberta or British Columbia in Canada) as well as where individuals need to work full-time due to family commitments. Online learning allows working adults to continue their education and training when time permits.

One example is Christopher Brownell, professor at Fresno Pacific University. It is 6:31 PM on June 28, 2008. Professor Brownell reminds me that he had attended a few talks of mine the previous month when I was on his campus. He would love to acquire a doctorate in math education, but cannot leave his current post to do so. He is searching for something "delivered in a blended format, with minimal physical relocation requirements." Brownell adds, "I am in my late forties with a family, mortgage, etc." He finds that math education programs in the more prestigious, traditional universities, which he prefers, are not flexible enough for his needs. As he puts it, "What never ceases to amaze me these days are schools that hold to very strict residency requirements for their programs. These work for the twenty-somethings with very young or no children, but once your life begins to be entangled in others' lives the uprooting becomes much more messy."

Brownell is exactly the type of nontraditional learner that the University of Phoenix and other online institutions target. A few years ago, I talked with Brian Lindquist, vice president of academic affairs at the University of Phoenix, about their blended and online programs. Brian informed me that although blended learning enrollments pale in comparison to their face-to-face and fully online programs, this was the fastest growing of their three delivery systems.[42] As he describes in my *Handbook of Blended Learning,* they even offer two flavors of blended—one for more geographically dispersed learners that requires fewer face-to-face sessions and one where students are more local and can physically meet more often.[43] Perhaps one of these solutions will appeal to Brownell.

Though not everyone who takes advantage of blended learning at the University of Phoenix is a basketball star like Shaquille O'Neal, there are millions like Christopher Brownell. They are settled physically but not mentally. There is so much more that they want to learn. Opportunities found via the Web are now their primary solution.

People like Brownell should not only look to a particular institution for a solution. Sometimes online and blended learning opportunities stretch across institutions or organizations in consortia. In fact, online learning is often the linchpin in the formation of unique education and training partnerships among businesses, government agencies, and higher education institutions. Over the past decade, online learning has been readily adopted by adult learners. This is due in part to the variety of educational options presented by institutions such as the University of Phoenix and others.

The E-Learning Skyline of Minneapolis

Let's look at Capella University, headquartered in Minneapolis, Minnesota. It was founded in 1991 by Stephen Shank, former CEO of Tonka Corporation and assumed the name "The Graduate School of America" (TGSA) in 1993. Four years later, it received regional accreditation, and in 1999, it changed its name to Capella University. In 2006, Capella became a publicly traded company. Dr. Mike Offerman, the vice chairman and former president of Capella, informed me that as of September 2008, it had twenty-four thousand students enrolled from all fifty of the United States as well as from forty-five other countries. Of those, more than four in five were pursuing master's or doctoral degrees. According to the Capella Web site, the regionally accredited university offers more than a thousand online courses for twenty-two different degree programs in over a hundred areas of specialization. Popular programs include such areas as health care, public safety, information technology, psychology, education, and business.

By being fully online, Capella can focus entirely on the needs of working adults. This focus has resulted in rapid growth. Enrollments hit ten thousand students in 2004, fifteen thousand in 2006, and then nudged over twenty thousand in 2007. As skills needed to succeed in the workplace continue to change and people live and work longer, Offerman believes that there will be an ever-increasing need for institutions like his to serve those currently in the workforce. He is impressed by the diverse backgrounds of adult learners and what they bring to the learning equation. He told me that his passion stems from seeing adults get a second chance at realizing their educational dreams and career aspirations through online universities and programs such as his. Offerman said, "What really surprises me and keeps me engaged in adult higher education are the wonderful stories of personal achievement and overcoming of considerable obstacles by adult learners who are able to finally achieve their dreams." One student in Capella's social and community services doctoral program describes his experience as follows: "Getting a degree online, I feel like I am on the cutting edge. I like being a pioneer. I find myself writing so much more than you do at traditional universities, and I feel like I am really becoming a true scholar. I find myself learning about my colleagues so much more, and I end up really learning about new concepts and widening my horizons. That is the beauty of online education."

Capella, and thus adult online learning, is on the move. In 2007, Capella's revenues increased more than 25 percent to $226 million. The bottom line was $22.8 million in income for Capella, which was 70 percent higher than the year before.[44] Such growth has resulted in hundreds of new hires. And though many of these people teach from home, most of its Minneapolis employees are consolidating into one primary location at 225 South Sixth Street. This skyscraper, affectionately known as the "Halo" for its distinctive roof, will soon to be renamed the "Capella Tower."

Capella Tower is not the typical headquarters for an online learning company. With fifty-six stories, it is the second-largest building in the State of Minnesota.[45] Given its commanding presence in the Minneapolis skyline, people will no longer be thinking banks, plazas, and financial centers when they cross the Mississippi River from Wisconsin to work or to shop at the Mall of America. Instead, they will see and think about online learning. The sky is the limit! And innovative online universities like Capella will be radiating the light that encourages thousands of members of the human species to become a bit more enlightened each day. Capella executives certainly chose their building wisely.

From Flour Power to E-Power

Capella is not the lone online learning success story in Minneapolis. Walden University, another institution known for distance and nontraditional forms of learning, is less than a mile away. Walden is situated in what is called the Mills District of Minneapolis, the name being a reminder of the days when Minneapolis was the flour milling capital of the world. With four key degree-granting schools—School of Management, School of Health and Human Services, School of Psychology, and School of Education—it is somewhat reminiscent of the offerings of Capella. This seems odd—two institutions of higher learning just one mile apart and offering similar courses and programs. I have to remind myself that they do not compete for students in the Minneapolis area but for students in the world.

Degrees at Walden include those in psychology, public health, nursing, management, child development, software engineering, public policy, and mental health counseling, among many others. I am familiar with Walden because their students are housed on my campus in Bloomington for a couple of weeks each summer as part of their residency requirements. In addition, they have full access to our research libraries throughout the year from wherever they are located. During the past decade, I have given talks to Walden instructors and administrators on a couple of occasions and have met with several of their students. I always walk away impressed. Like Capella, Walden has provided thousands of working adults with learning options that can lead to enhanced self-esteem, more money, and job advancement.

"Walden U.: A Working Paper," written in 1969 by Harold "Bud" Hodgkinson, a faculty member at the University of California at Berkeley, got a few people thinking, talking, and eventually creating Walden. The following year, Walden emerged from Hodgkinson's concept of a more student-centered university.

Success did not happen immediately. For the better part of the following three decades, Walden was a smallish university of under a thousand students. But enrollment has most definitely exploded in its fourth decade. The reason appears to be a combination of new management and gargantuan appetites for higher education and the online learning tools that make it possible to meet those desires. In 2001, private tutoring giant Sylvan Learning Systems (now owned by Laureate Education, Inc.) acquired a 41 percent interest in Walden and took a controlling interest the following year. Since then, the number of students enrolled in Walden University has skyrocketed. Enrollments of two thousand in 2001 snowballed to eight thousand in 2003, thirteen thousand in 2004, and twenty-eight thousand in 2007. Alumni figures stood at six thousand in 2004, but quickly mushroomed to twenty-five thousand in 2007. Imagine working for an institution in the midst of such growth! The opportunities must be incredible.

Out of curiosity, I contacted my good friend Peter Young, who was working on a doctorate in Applied Management and Decision Science in the College of Management and Technology at Walden. At fifty-two, Peter did not want to go back to school full-time because he would lose his position as senior instructor of Marketing and Strategic Operations at Notre Dame de Namur University (NDNU) in California. As a recent Fulbright Scholar in the Republic of Belarus and former director of Undergraduate Business Programs at NDNU, Peter is not the typical student seen on college campuses. Instead, he brings his rich experiences with him to his online classes at Walden.

Peter told me that the program has unfolded just as the Walden counselors indicated it would. According to Peter, the instructors take their jobs extremely seriously and deliver what he feels is a quality education. He found that the program incorporated a skillful mixture of traditional academic engagement between students and instructors by using technology in every aspect of the coursework. Still, he was surprised that the attrition rate in his particular program was running close to 90 percent—by the time of his dissertation, only three of the original thirty-five students were left.

Why the drops? It is likely that some of this stemmed from family and work commitments, program length, program costs, and pricey textbooks. At the same time, relatively easy admission policies may have granted access to students who were not prepared for the engagement and interactivity required. For still others, it was probably the multiple residency requirements that drove them out. As Peter discovered, much of this "residency" time was geared to first-time students rather than to those with extensive higher education backgrounds like him. Most likely, it was a combination of these and other factors, including familiarity with online learning, time, and personal motivation that caused the retention problem. Time, of course, is the centerpiece of any online learning retention explanation.

Based on his experiences, I asked Peter where he thought online learning was headed for the adult education market. He responded that because of the drastic population growth projected for the United States and other parts of the world, combined with increased access to education, he believes that "the sky is the limit." He also suggested that these increased educational opportunities will result in heightened competition for middle and higher-end employment. As this occurs, people will be searching for more relevant education that is applicable to current work topics and needs. In addition, as technology use increases in the workplace as well as in learning places, individuals who adapt to it better are the ones who will be successful. Finally, as energy, transportation, and physical engagement costs mount, online education will be the vehicle for greater numbers of people to enhance their well-being. With escalating oil prices, the costs of a laptop computer and high-speed Internet connection might now be lower than paying for the requisite gas to attend face-to-face class sessions.

As this happens, issues related to online learning quality will need to be addressed, however. According to Peter, rigor, quality, and depth of programs will be watchwords for online education. As he puts it, "[T]he stigma is all but erased now for online education—though programmatic and academic standards must be maintained and honed for it NOT to become simply an *ordinary commodity in the future*."

With the explosive growth of Walden and Capella, thousands of Peter Youngs are gaining rich and personally relevant educational experiences and needed credentials. Something is clearly happening in the State of Minnesota, and in Minneapolis in particular. Already known for its creative spirit and high literacy rates, Minneapolis has become a major hub for online learning. Flour mills of the 1800s and 1900s have been replaced not by "mind refineries," but by mind and learning opportunity openers. The history page from the Walden University Web site states that it moved its academic offices from Naples, Florida, to Minneapolis because it sought accreditation in a region that was open to nontraditional post-baccalaureate education.

Perhaps other states and countries will view online learning as a major industry to take advantage of and begin to fill its old warehouse districts and half-full skyscrapers with thousands of employees from other e-learning companies and organizations. Education no longer takes place solely in squared-off rooms and small corner offices, but in as many formats as one can imagine. With both positive and negative ramifications, education has evolved into big business for bigger people; it is no longer the province of little tots in one-room classrooms. Politicians, educators, and business executives need to devise ways to encourage Web-based experimentation and innovation in education so that more Capellas and Waldens materialize to educate the citizens of this planet, while keeping goals for high-quality learning experiences front and center.

Extending Our Minds over to Denver

A little over seven hundred miles to the southwest of Minneapolis-St. Paul is another hub of e-learning—the Denver metropolitan area. In 1993, Denver-based Jones International, Ltd., set about creating a totally online university, now known as Jones International University (JIU). At that time, there was no existing viable course management system that could support the complexity and scale of what Jones had in mind, nor was there any appropriate electronic library. So Jones created both and started aggressively evangelizing the concept of online education.

Subsequently, in 1996, Real Education, Inc.—the predecessor to eCollege—also designed a course management system. At the start, it had a single client, the University of Colorado. It now services some 650 distance learning programs. eCollege is popular in both K–12 and higher education settings.

Accordingly, two of the earliest course management systems and the first online electronic library totally supporting a university were created in the Denver metro area. This is not happenstance. The Denver-Boulder area is loaded with high-growth technology companies and technologically talented individuals. With this technologically rich culture, it is not surprising that many of these firms and individuals are interested in ways to help people learn with emerging technology.

Stop by the Jones offices today and you find out that Jones International, Ltd., has consolidated all of its educational activities into its Jones Knowledge Group, Inc., subsidiary. This education and media giant had very humble beginnings. Jones International is wholly owned by Glenn R. Jones, who started a cable television business with a $400 loan against his Volkswagen. Jones Intercable, Inc., later became one of the top ten cable operators in the United States. Success was not immediate but had to be earned, and earned it was. In fact, Mr. Jones, trained as an attorney, had to personally string cable in small Colorado cities—Georgetown, Evergreen, and Idaho Springs—for his original company, the Cowpoke Cable Company.[46] His first piece of office equipment is said to have been a sleeping bag to bed down in his prized Volkswagen Bug. Both he and his car surely were driven.

Such determination and ensuing growth helped springboard Jones into many phases of technology-enhanced learning, as well as radio, telephony, software, and entertainment markets. Among his educational inventions was Mind Extension University (ME/U) in 1987. ME/U used cable television networks to serve thirty thousand students who were completing courses remotely from more than thirty different colleges and universities. With ME/U, Mr. Jones was the first to deliver college courses directly into homes using a special cable TV channel.

Many new populations of learners were served from this one innovative idea. Education was finally reaching people in rural and remote settings who lacked easy access to higher education or who simply wanted to learn more. At the same time, education was now available within the hotel rooms of travelers who previously were stuck watching local sports or news. Of course, such educational programming also enabled those in urban settings to seek degrees while they worked full-time.[47] As a member of the latter camp in the mid 1980s, I know full well about this as I relied on TV-based courses to qualify for graduate school while simultaneously working full-time. After changing the name from the Mind Extension University to Knowledge TV, the popular channel had close to fifty million subscribers in the United States, Mexico, China, Thailand, Poland, Romania, Holland, and the Scandinavian countries.

Mr. Jones continued testing new technologies for delivering education to those in need. For instance, he experimented with the digital American Memory Project at the Library of Congress, a free and open-access Internet portal rich in American history and creativity. He saw the power of sharing sounds, images, maps, and moving images that was now possible online. He also started using the Internet as the return communications loop for Knowledge TV from Thailand back to Denver. As these pilot tests succeeded, Mr. Jones decided that an Internet Protocol infrastructure for education would be even more efficient than a cable channel. Soon after, Knowledge TV was sold to Discovery Communications, which then morphed into Discovery Health Channel.[48]

Even after such deals, Mr. Jones was not content. His vision was to fuse the communications revolution with education. To accomplish this, he set out to bend the direction of the communications revolution toward the service of education while extending the human mind and, in his words, "helping enable the forward progress of civilization." During the dot-com boom, he expanded his ideas for online education into the Jones Empire. One of those ideas was the formation of a global accrediting body that could, among other things, accredit online universities. This entity was the Global Alliance for Transnational Education (GATE).

Mr. Jones was not only concerned with adult education but also the education of young people as well. Beginning with *Make All America a School* in 1989, he had, over time, penned several books on the future of education.[49] In one of these books, *Cyberschools: An Education Renaissance*, Mr. Jones makes the argument that the classroom is often your front room.[50] More than a decade ago, referring to the environment of ancient Athens in Plato's time, he stated: "Let us take notice of *our* environment. It is time now to fuse our knowledge society electronic tools with our great teaching institutions and information repositories. It is time to create a world that is, like Athens was, a great school, a world vibrant with interest and excitement about education, a world where educational opportunity is visible to all and hope is alive, a world that sees the wilderness of information as our new frontier."[51]

Mr. Jones is quite a visionary and an education pioneer with a social conscience.[52] With books like Alvin Toffler's *Future Shock* in his hip pocket, Glenn Jones envisions a world where the barriers to education are lifted and access to knowledge is democratized. It is such a world that I believe we are now entering, and Mr. Jones has been a key individual placing us on this journey. Ellen Waterman, associate dean for Distance Education at Regis University, worked for Mr. Jones in the 1990s. When I met her in Denver in July 2008, she told me, "With initiatives such as Mind-Extension University, Glenn is one of the true visionaries in the whole concept of distance education. He pioneered the use of cable and video in learning on a broad scale."

When I spoke with Mr. Jones the month before, he told me that one of the unique ways in which he hoped to realize such a world was to make certain that the new fusion of education with the tools of the communications revolution did not end up going down the path of mediocrity, as had happened at many pure correspondence schools. It was at that point, he said, that he decided to commit his organization to a level of quality that would enable JIU to become accredited at the highest level. In effect, Mr. Jones wanted to establish a reality where high-quality online learning was possible, and where there was no excuse for not doing it. Accordingly, JIU became the first fully online university to become accredited by a U.S. regional accrediting body, the Higher Learning Commission, a member of the North Central Association. Even JIU's recently accredited doctoral-level programs are fully online.

JIU has degree and certificate programs that are focused primarily on two schools, education and business. Though not as large as Capella or Walden, JIU continues to be an innovative leader in the types and formats of online programs and degrees. At the same time, Glenn Jones finds refreshing ways to push the boundaries of what education actually is and who can participate in it.

I met Glenn Jones a few times at e-learning conferences in 1999 and 2000. Our encounters were smack-dab in the center of the dot-com boom. One of his companies, JonesKnowledge, was actually sponsoring some of my talks at the time. The first time I visited the Jones corporate headquarters at 9697 E. Mineral Avenue, a few miles southeast of Denver in Centennial, I was awestruck. I had heard that Mr. Jones had a fascination with the *Dune* book trilogy, which influenced the creation of his headquarters as well as his management style. Even the parking structure was memorable. There was also his personal "war room" where he could check on his conglomeration of cable TV, media, and e-learning businesses around the country at any time. It was his personal outpost of the Jones Empire. When building it, Mr. Jones even flew to Hollywood to visit with some of the designers of various Star Wars artifacts who influenced the design of his Denver-based war room and associated observation deck.

Mr. Jones described his plans for his corporate headquarters in a 1999 interview: "It was a place where people lived, yet it was a fort. This building was built to replicate some of those concepts. It was built as a very livable building but a place where people could come and strap into the latest technology and fight."[53]

And fight they did! At the same time, much of the building and management structure was set up for sharing and social networking long before social networking became popularized by Web 2.0 technology. Again, a man far ahead of his time!

On July 23, 2008, I had a chance to visit the Jones headquarters in Denver again and present the ideas for this book in his boardroom. When I arrived at the Jones building, all I could say to myself was "What an amazing place!" Mr. Jones and I then had a chance to chat over dinner about the future of this open education world. As always, it was clear to me by the end of dinner that he is always looking to the future and how to makes our lives better in it.

E-LEARNING IN A PUBLIC UNIVERSITY

Online Learning Springs to Life

Though smaller in size than institutions known for having significant online learning programs, such as the University of Central Florida or the University of Maryland, online learning at the University of Illinois at Springfield (UIS) is in many ways equally impressive. I remember my brief visit to the city of Abraham Lincoln in May 2004 to keynote the summer institute of the Illinois Online Network (ION). Showing up in a University of Illinois rain poncho and toting a matching umbrella for my talk on "The Perfect E-Storm" drew a few laughs. Despite the chuckles, online learning was no laughing matter at the time. UIS administrators had recently announced a funded initiative to offer both face-to-face and online options for all their courses and programs by the end of the decade. "Everything?" I asked. "Yes," I was told; all courses taught at the residential campus would also be available online.

While there, I had a chance to glance through the catalog of courses that had already been completed, and snatch a list to share with my colleagues back in Indiana. I checked over this list on more than one occasion just to make sure I was not seeing things. Imagine entering a college or university and being told that you can take any of your courses online or in a physical classroom. Which would you choose? Placing every course online is no longer the stated goal at UIS—due at least in part to administrator turnover—but they continue to nudge closer in that direction.

Nearly four years after hearing the bold pronouncement at UIS, I turned to Burks Oakley for an update. Dr. Oakley is professor emeritus in the Department of Electrical and Computer Engineering at the University of Illinois at Urbana–Champaign. As most people in the higher education world in Illinois and beyond are aware, Oakley has had access to every data point related to online learning in higher education within the state of Illinois ever since Web-based teaching exploded in the mid-1990s.

The first time I met Burks, in November 1998, I had been asked to come to Champaign to present my research on online instruction for a report that had been commissioned as part of new online learning initiatives within the University of Illinois. This initiative was under intense scrutiny and debate at the time. Seated directly behind me at lunch was Burks Oakley with a huge entourage. Whispers from faculty members at my table asking me if I knew that bearded man just five feet behind me indicated that he was a person of great importance and someone I should get to know. Fortunately, a faculty member made a casual introduction as we ended our lunch.

During the decade since our meeting, Burks's name has continued to be synonymous with e-learning in Illinois. From 1997 until 2007, Burks served as an associate vice president for academic affairs at the

University of Illinois. He also was the founding director of the University of Illinois Online initiative. Though currently in semiretirement, he is now a visiting research professor in the Office of Technology-Enhanced Learning at UIS. Given this rich and historically significant background, it is not too surprising that he is known throughout the United States as a promoter as well as practitioner of Web-based instruction. Without much doubt, Burks Oakley, now a tad whiter on top than when I first met him, is the Illinois online learning guru.

Every time I talk to Burks, he supplies me with impressive statistics and pushes my thinking in new directions. He often shares new Web resources related to emerging technologies, along with any of his presentation slides or notes I might want. You see, Burks Oakley is the epitome of the sharing world of education in which we now find ourselves. When speaking with Burks in early February 2008, he informed me that UIS now had 35 percent of its course credits online. According to Burks, students in online degree programs at Springfield pay in-state rates, which makes it extremely cost competitive.

Ray Schroeder, director of Technology-Enhanced Learning at UIS and professor emeritus of communication, informed me that there are sixteen degree programs and four blended programs at UIS, including bachelor completion degrees in history, philosophy, mathematics, computer science, English, and economics, as well as master's programs in legal studies, public health, environmental science, teacher leadership, and human services administration.

Data that Ray forwarded to me months later were quite telling. In the fall of 2008, over half of UIS students took at least one online course, and nearly one-third of students registered solely in online courses. More than 25 percent actually declared majors that were taught online; as a result, many of them never stepped foot in Springfield. In terms of residence of these students, nearly four in ten students had mailing addresses outside of Illinois and 84 percent lived outside of Sangamon, the county in which UIS was located. An analysis of fifty-eight thousand grades for online and on-campus students showed basically no difference between them. With an average age of thirty-five, those enrolling in online master's programs were roughly three to four years older than their face-to-face counterparts. Online undergraduate students were typically nine years older than those on campus.

No one there is surprised by those facts. Teaching and learning online at Springfield is just part of the culture. During the summer of 2008, Ray Schroeder was quoted in the *Chronicle of Higher Education* as saying, "All across the country, community colleges and universities are getting requests for online programs specifically with students mentioning the price of gas."[54] The article goes on to note that summer 2008 course enrollments are not only jumping in Springfield, Illinois, but in Florida, New York, Tennessee, Pennsylvania, and much of the rest of the United States. John Bourne, the director of the famous Sloan Consortium, which is widely known for its research, journals, and conferences on online learning, thinks that we will see more blended types of courses emerge, "half online, half in class."[55] Now that will be a revolution!

Blended and fully online course and program options give students a choice. And choice is especially important for students with full-time jobs or children to raise. As a payoff, those taking both online and campus-based courses took heavier course loads than students just in the online or on-ground courses. Options, blends, alternatives, and any form of nontraditional learning reap huge rewards in the twenty-first century. This is what learning, and, in effect, life now is—full of options.

A recent NPR report indicates that much of the rest of the world is monitoring what is happening at this midsize university.[56] As noted in the report, new students are coming to Springfield. They are coming from Tennessee. They are coming from Ohio. They are coming from Montana. However, they are not forced to drive there like I did in 2004. Instead, they are arriving within seconds via their keyboard entries and mouse clicks. And for instructors, this requires a shift in thinking related to their teaching practices and interactions with students. Fortunately, the e-learning courses and certificates that Oakley and his colleagues spearheaded for college instructors have paid huge dividends.

Although UIS is a campus with an enrollment of fewer than five thousand students, it is having a global impact. That is what the WE-ALL-LEARN model highlights—choice in where to learn, what to learn, how to learn, when to learn, and with whom to learn. At UIS, not only do they understand this, they push this agenda full speed ahead each day. When I chatted again with Ray Schroeder, he indicated that UIS is seeking to establish "a consortium of other mostly regional comprehensive universities to follow the path of the UIS online program." Clearly, the goal is to replicate their successes as well as help others avoid the problems and pitfalls.

UIS is not alone. I have seen this type of institution all over the world, in places as varied as Finland, the United Kingdom, Canada, Iceland, Taiwan, or the United Arab Emirates. The enrollment figures and graphs I receive are nearly identical. In the State of Minnesota, for instance, approximately 9 percent of course credits are received through online education. However, in November 2008, state leaders announced a plan to offer 25 percent of its college credits online by 2015, which is nearly three times the current figure.[57] Online learning is now just an expected component of higher education services. Toss in blended learning to that mix and the mission of institutions of higher learning has been greatly extended during the Internet evolution that created our current learning revolution. It might not be explicitly stated, but it is highly evident nonetheless. Anyone with a position in such a place will tell you—online learning has changed everything.

INTERNATIONAL E-LEARNING

Million-Student Universities

Online education is bustling in nearly every corner of the globe. In Asia, the growth is perhaps even more impressive than in North America. For instance, Ramkhamhaeng University (RU), which is an open university in Bangkok, Thailand, was established in 1971. During a trip there in December 2006, I found out that the university was named after King Ramkhamhaeng the Great, who was the third King of the Sukhothai period in the late thirteenth century. As the inventor of the first Thai alphabet in 1283, he believed in the education of the masses. And the university has educated masses of students in less than four decades. RU now has nearly 600,000 students, many of whom are enrolled in online or blended courses. Let me repeat that—it has 600,000 students! More than likely you have never heard of RU before. Perhaps if it climbs over the million mark, you will.

Imagine running a university of that size! How about one million students? If you live in India, such numbers are already a reality. India's Indira Gandhi National Open University (IGNOU) has 1.8 million students and the numbers are still climbing.[58] Might it soon reach 2 million? What are the class sizes like? When I contacted Dr. Sanjaya Mishra from the IGNOU distance education program in January 2009, he answered these questions as follows:

> I think the University will get to 2 million students by 2010. Normally the addition every year is about 100 thousand. Interestingly, our system does not work in the normal class based way. Mostly the students receive printed learning materials, attend counselling/tutorial sessions (optional, but typically with about 30 students), do assignments, participate in teleconferences and sit in the final examinations. So, in a cohort, the registration of students ranges from 50 to 50,000 depending on programmes. For example, the MA in distance education is below 50, whereas the MBA program is sometimes over 50 thousand. But, as they study mostly asynchronously there is no class size, as such.

Not surprisingly, Sanjaya is helping IGNOU create new programs and certificates in distance education and e-learning. There certainly seems to be high demand for online and blended forms of education in India. This should be an area of high job growth around the world in the coming decade. Parents might want to advise their children who are interested in the field of education or in becoming teachers to explore e-education and e-training job possibilities. Tens of thousands of new e-learning teachers, trainers, instructional designers, media developers, and evaluation experts will be needed.

But what would life be like at a university that adds 100,000 students each year? As a point of comparison, that is more students in a single year than 99.9 percent of colleges and universities in North America have in total. Phenomenal! And just what is it like to be a student in a university that relies on tuition from millions of students to stay afloat? What is it like to be in a cohort of more than fifty thousand MBA students? Is there any personalized attention? Might we soon see such large universities merge across countries or regions to build economies of scale while simultaneously reducing social, cultural, and political divides between peoples of different nations?

As with the growth pattern at IGNOU, the Open University of Malaysia (OUM), which opened its doors with about eight hundred students in 2001, enrolled nearly sixty-five thousand students just six years later. Picture working at an institution in the midst of such growth. There would be a pervasive sense of change. How fresh and alive a place like the OUM is with the feeling that your institution is serving a huge need for your country. Everything there is new—new learners, new tutors, new programs, new procedures, new buildings, and, of course, new ideas. The OUM even designed its own learning management system as well as its own content, model of delivering instruction, and training programs. They have three thousand personal tutors (with thousands more available when and where needed), but there are fewer than a hundred full-time instructors; of those, not even thirty are associate or full professors. No top-heavy tenure-induced systems here! It is a different model for education. Given the novelty and success, it is not surprising that university representatives from the Middle East and other parts of world are constantly visiting the OUM to see how it works.

The OUM offers the gamut including bachelor's, master's, and doctoral courses and degree programs from civil engineering to early childhood education, and from nursing sciences to tourism management. People who want to learn and are eligible can learn. Self-esteem and identity are elevated as e-learning expands their learning possibilities. A visitor to the OUM in Kuala Lumpur as well as RU in Bangkok gets a sense of success and satisfaction. I always find new buildings going up, hear about innovative programs, and meet great people. Still, no one is resting. In January 2009, Drs. Zoraini Wati Abas and Abtar Kaur from the OUM inform me that enrollments had just topped 76,500 and that new programs were being launched that semester for bachelor's degrees in communications, psychology, English studies, manufacturing management, health and environmental management, and multimedia technology. There were also new master's programs in human resource management, project management, instructional design and technology, and software engineering. With all the new programs, thousands more students are likely on the way. The highly creative and ambitious folks at the OUM will likely continue to design dozens of valuable new programs to benefit the people of Malaysia.

E-China

Not too surprisingly, another place of noticeable growth in online learning is China. No one factor can explain it. Many cite continued economic explosion, whereas others say it is due to student demands, geographic needs, government experimentation, and the lack of university facilities. Still others point to SARS as the springboard to its acceptance; the Chinese government, as well as students and educators, could readily see that you could learn online without having to worry about spreading a disease. Clearly an important factor is that millions more people in China are now being connected to the Internet every year. According to a January 2008 report from the China Internet Network Information Center (CINIC), as of December 2007, there were 210 million Chinese with an Internet connection, or just 16 percent of the total population. But these numbers reflected a more than 50 percent increase from the previous year.[59] Imagine the stress such a jump places on the Chinese higher education system. What happens when a country adds 73 million more Internet users in just a year?[60] What happens to entertainment and leisure activities, commerce, government, and community services?

More important, what happens when such numbers enter the realm of education? When Internet access explodes in China so too do the chances that people across the country can learn. More than 93 percent of the CINIC survey respondents thought that the Internet was a useful tool for both their working and learning lives, and about one in six had used the Web for online education. That is twelve million more people using the Web specifically for educational activities than the year before. Then add to that the tens of millions of people indirectly or informally being educated via the Web—through online news (73 percent), online gaming (59 percent), blogging (24 percent), e-mailing (57 percent), searching (72 percent), watching online videos (77 percent), and instant messaging (81 percent)—and you have the potential for a revolution in education.[61] Online music, shopping, banking, and job hunting are important activities, but it is through online education that people grow. And with over fifty million mobile phones in use in China, they are on the brink of a mobile e-learning revolution.

The numbers of people directly or indirectly affected by distance learning in China is difficult to estimate. To clarify this situation, scholars note that China has been marked by three stages of growth in distance education.[62] Correspondence was the primary mode from 1950 to 1978, but was mainly under the arm of special colleges for correspondence education and normal universities. In the second phase, 1978 to 1998, China, as did many countries, developed its radio- and TV-based education by establishing the Center Radio and Television University (CRTVU). CRTVU has grown so large, now at nearly two million students, that one in every ten Chinese students is likely affiliated with CRTVU. The third phase, from 1999 to the present, is primarily one of e-learning. There were about 1.13 million e-learners in China in 2006 and at least 2.7 million in correspondence mode.[63] When university degree students at all levels plus those seeking certificates or specific training are added up, the number of Chinese e-learners could conceivably be over ten million.[64]

One thing is certain—online access to education is gathering momentum in China and will continue to do so for the coming decade as access to the Internet accelerates. What the Internet offers the Chinese people is flexibility in learning, especially for nontraditional and lifelong learners.[65] We can hope that it will soon also be responsive to student learning needs and personalize their learning process. Too often that has not been the case in China.

There can be no doubt that China's higher education system is in heavy expansion mode at the present. And when the country with the largest population in the world pumps up its higher education system and develops online and distance learning to assist in these efforts, the rest of the world should take notice. New forms of online learning delivery, management, and practice will take root in China, and will rapidly add to the knowledge base on e-learning. In the coming decades, the Chinese will not only radically transform the fields of online and blended learning, but they will shake the very foundations of learning.

Need still more numbers as proof? A February 2008 talk on my campus by Professor Lan Xue from Tsinghua University in Beijing indicated that Chinese higher education has burst open from 6.3 million students in 1999 to 17.4 million in 2007.[66] Other data peg the total enrollment at well over 20 million and perhaps at more than 25 million.[67] According to Xue, higher education enrollments increased 40 percent in 1999 and have been growing at a rate of 20 percent annually since then. He noted that China was embarking on a mission to foster a knowledge economy. Such an economy requires the development of a knowledge society to meet the increasing demands for improved social productivity.

Part of this improvement in productivity is expected to be derived from additional monies spent in higher education. In effect, the Chinese government was attempting to cultivate new talent pools from increasing investment in higher education. Smaller universities are being merged or "reengineered" into larger ones to pick up economies of scale. Additional government funding targets university research. The top one hundred universities in China were marked for more monies as a means to improve the quality of teaching and learning. The Chinese want and expect that this will lead to the creation of "world class" universities. However, Professor Xue also noted that the growth of online and blended learning was limited in China's higher education system because only around sixty-seven normal universities are currently authorized to offer online programming.

China will be more than an interesting case to watch; it will provide insights on how other countries should plan for online and blended learning, with or without the same mushrooming enrollments. The growth China is experiencing in higher education at the start of this century is likely unprecedented for any country in the history of humankind. Fortunately, it has occurred in a time of exploding educational options and freely shared content and resources. The e-learning world has found its way to China precisely at a point when China desperately needs such options and opportunities.

I spoke about online learning at Beijing Normal University (BNU) and nearby Tsinghua University in October of 2004. At BNU, I could sense the excitement for virtual learning and technology-based solutions for education. The students were just trickling in from an extended holiday, yet the room was packed with students standing in the back and sitting in the aisles. Still others lined up four to five deep in the hallway peering in. Such enthusiasm is difficult to forget. I walked away with the conclusion that China was poised for the explosion of online and blended learning. Given the numbers above, can there be any other conclusion?

A Free Grain of Rice

When I was growing up, an all-too-common refrain was to eat everything on your plate because there were starving children in Africa, India, and other such overpopulated places. I also remember Grandpa George adding with his deadpan humor to "eat every bean and pea on your plate." It would always get a chuckle from me and make those peas and beans taste slightly better. I am still not exactly sure what this did for starving people in India.

Today Grandpa George might have also asked me, "How can online learning benefit those less fortunate in other countries?" At this point, instead of talking about beans, peas, and carrots, we would have discussed FreeRice.com.[68] FreeRice is a site where you can learn vocabulary words and at the same time feed hungry people with rice. As someone who never did well with vocabulary, I thought I would have a go. As I explored it, I was hooked. As I got answers correct, the points I earned kept me trying for more.

FreeRice is paid through advertisements. As you advance through the game, more advertisements appear below the questions. And as you learn words, you gain points or grains of rice that can be donated to feed hungry people. Answer a question correctly and you have earned twenty grains of rice for donation. The advertisements pay for the rice. Almost immediately, this Web site rapidly received an onslaught of visitors and media coverage. The *Los Angeles Times* said, "FreeRice.com is one of the most ingenious websites of 2007. In the best spirit of the Internet, it offers education, entertainment and a way to change the world—all for free."[69]

Though a mere 830 grains of rice were awarded during the initial day it launched, by February 2, 2008 more than 17 million grains had been donated. By the end of 2007, there was enough activity to feed more than seven thousand people per day.[70] Here is a stunning door-opener for education—a person could learn new words while helping feed people somewhere else on this planet. I am sure my grandfather would have liked this one. I would have preferred it too!

Opening the local paper one day, I discovered that the site was developed in Bloomington, Indiana, by John Breen, who typed in all ten thousand initial definitions after watching his son struggle to find useful resources for the SAT. This is not the first online learning site that began from simple parent monitoring. Tools such as Livemocha and Curriki, discussed later in this book, had similar starts.

Not only does he hope to improve student SAT scores, John Breen is out to end world hunger. This is the e-learning Daily Double—education and nutrition! At his various Web sites, Breen points out that twenty-five thousand hunger-related deaths per day could be avoided with better programs and planning. He knows what he is talking about. Back in 1999, he created a site, Poverty.com, to illustrate the ripple effects of poverty and malnourishment. The UN World Food Program handles the distribution of rice for FreeRice.[71] The initial recipient countries included Bangladesh to help feed 27,000 refugees from Myanmar for two weeks, 66,000 school children from Uganda for a week, 750,000 people for three days who were affected by a cyclone in Myanmar, and thousands of pregnant and nursing women in Cambodia for two months.

Imagine an entire class of elementary or high school students playing this game. How about an entire school or community? How many people might they be feeding while simultaneously increasing their standardized test scores or qualifying for college study? Next, imagine all those who can learn now that they are fed. It is a cycle of positive learning for the people of this planet. Transforming learning into food and back into still more learning! What types of online programs might be next? My imagination runs wild for a moment thinking about all of the free online simulations and games that could incorporate such food donation ideas. Someday such approaches to education and food distribution might be much more common. Let's hope!

RESISTANCE AND RECAP

As shown in this chapter, in the late 1990s, many institutions and organizations began to sanction online courses and programs and track their use. For some, this was like a reenactment of Gold Rush days. Given the intense focus on the technological possibilities of online learning and this rush to be first on the block to offer such courses, most online courseware was substandard. My colleague, Vanessa Dennen, and I labeled it as a time of pedagogical negligence.[72] Unfortunately, this situation remains true today.

E-learning promises gold. What we often are given instead is clunky course management systems that simply show us that a student has completed a course or spent a certain amount of time online. We need better than that. We need innovative, engaging, and personalized learning. Unfortunately, most course management systems fail to provide creative sparks to learning because they only track or map it after it occurs. Providing repositories of information has taken precedence over investing in more intellectually rich and engaging Web-based learning resources. Pragmatic posting of content has taken precedence over the design of deep and engaging learning experiences. Don't give up! Many of the stories in this book, especially those recounted in later chapters, will show you where much successful gold mining is possible. As Chris Dede argues, face-to-face no longer needs to be "the 'gold standard' in education."[73]

As the many journeys in this chapter reveal, the online learning movement has spread across the planet. Still many educators and trainers remain quite reluctant to adopt online learning. Some have too limited budgets for such changes. Some note the lack of time or recognition for use of online technology. Many other resisters note the limited management support they have for such changes. And there is no denying that few were trained for the new job duties of an online instructor. The critics also accurately point out that online courses are often lacking in interactivity and engagement. In a word, much like traditional classroom-based instruction, it is boring. And when learners are handed grades or degrees from little more than electronic page clicking, there are deep concerns, and the pockets of resistance, noted earlier, indeed are warranted.

Such barriers and challenges need to be addressed as online becomes not just an option, but perhaps the major way in which anyone learns. Today online learning may represent a mere 10 percent of the enrollments in higher education and much less than that in K–12 education. But a decade ago the percentages were near zero. A decade from now online learning could conceivably be more than one-third or one-half of all instruction, not only in higher education but in K–12, military, government, and corporate settings as well, because of the convenience, options, and flexibility that it provides. Conditions further spurring this growth include rising unemployment, the need for lifelong learning, an energy crisis, and fluctuating transportation costs. As we rotate classes from face-to-face to online and blended settings, we could become an energized society of Bridey Fennells—confident self-learners who have access to materials and instructors as needed.

Bridey is just one example. There are millions more who benefit from the options that online learning provides each year. It can foster student knowledge sharing and increased awareness of other peoples and cultures. Electronic mentors and coaches can be brought in where needed. Virtual teams can design and share products. When successful in those teams, learners gain new skills needed in this globalized economy as well as a sense of personal control and ownership over their own learning. Ultimately, online learners acquire new skills that help them be more knowledgeable and productive citizens.

We are still in the midst of the first wave of online teaching and learning. Some are in a state of transition to a second wave. As shown in this chapter, much is happening in this first wave in places like Florida, Michigan, Minneapolis, and Denver. Online and blended learning excitement is also alive and well beyond U.S. borders, such as in Malaysia, China, and India. There are also vast challenges faced by each organization, institution, and country that has embraced online learning. In the midst of these challenges, the Web is benefiting millions of learners and teachers around the globe each day. It is here that many teachers find their true calling. It is here that millions now learn. So can you!

It's a Free Software World After All

OPENER #3: AVAILABILITY OF OPEN SOURCE AND FREE SOFTWARE

FREE!

Any Internet user will realize that availability of free and open source software has exploded in recent years. A special report from the March 2006 issue of the *Economist* proclaimed that the open source model for developing software had moved well beyond its origins.[1] Open source is part of a much larger free movement. Chris Anderson, editor-in-chief of *Wired* and author of *The Long Tail,* has an upcoming book called *Free,* which focuses on what happens when digital technologies become increasingly free.

As noted in Chapter Two, storage, processing power, and bandwidth costs are dropping to levels few could have imagined. Anderson calls them essentially free. There is increasing demand and expectations that Web technology will be free. People will not sign up for any new software tool or resource without at least a free trial, or better yet, a free and renewable membership. Emerging businesses in the Web 2.0 economy are more than happy to oblige. Keep in mind that the word *free* has different connotations for different people. For some, the word is related to commerce. For others, it refers to freedom of speech or freedom to change, distribute, and use something.

My colleague Brian J. Ford agrees with Anderson's thesis. He told me that this notion of *free* was something that was important to him because in the United Kingdom, as well as in many other countries, education used to be free but was increasingly being priced beyond the reach of most people. Now the Internet is bringing us back to freer days. As he puts it:

> Education is the most fundamental public resource we've ever had. And, over the last two generations, more and more people on more and more occasions have had to pay more and more money to get it. And suddenly, the glacier is melting. Suddenly, the tide is receding. And education is being offered to larger and larger numbers of people for nothing, for everybody. The whole concept makes me glow with pleasure.

Brian then pointed out:

> The Internet gives us a new form of anti-commerce. What's always mattered in the past has been the mighty dollar, the buck. How you can take your product . . . and make money out of it. Suddenly, the Internet offers people something for nothing. A generation ago, if you wanted a great thing, it would cost you 500 pounds. If you wanted a small watered down version, it might cost you 100. If you wanted the kid's trial version, it might cost you 50 pounds. Now, if you want Photoshop, it will cost you 500 pounds. But if you wanted Photoshop LE, it will cost you zilch. Nothing. That has never happened before and it's turned, it's reversed, the way in which commerce has always progressed for the last two centuries.

As Chris Anderson and Brian Ford remind us, companies like Google and Yahoo! do not sell products and yet make billions in revenues. They each, in fact, give away processing power with free Web searching and storage as well as free e-mail accounts. Yahoo! now has unlimited storage for its e-mail service, Yahoo! Mail. YouTube, recently acquired by Google, was worth billions without ever selling a product. Does "something for nothing" finally exist? Social networking services like MySpace and Facebook do much the same. Anyone who wants to survive must offer free online services today. This makes me wonder how accounting departments attempt to convert reputation, site traffic, and social networks into revenue projections, cash flow analyses, and budgets. Who is training this new breed of accountant who must account for so much free stuff?

Anderson further notes that monies and increased revenues are not the only incentives of this new economy. People are now sharing stuff quite freely. As he puts it, "Altruism has always existed, but the Web gives it a platform where the actions of individuals can have global impact. In a sense, zero-cost distribution has turned sharing into an industry."[2] If sharing is an industry, then that lands us squarely in the world of education where people are known for giving of their time and ideas.

Yes, education can be a land of free sharing. Of course, educators love the word *free* because budgets are rarely flush. So do parents with children and the children themselves. So do seniors who pay school taxes but no longer have kids in school. This word *free*, unlike no other, causes hairs on one's arms to stand up and heart rates to sore. If you are ever asked to speak to a crowd of educators and are not sure what to include, just toss in the word *free* a dozen times, and you will receive rave reviews. In speeches I give, I often chuckle inside as I watch people frantically trying to write down the free resources and tools as I show them at lightning speed. Do they not realize that nearly any technology I can show them today will include a free demo or introductory version? This entire book is filled with the word *free*. Finding free is now as simple as counting one, two, three.

Open Source as Simple as Lotus 1-2-3

Remember Mitch Kapor, former president of the Lotus Development Corporation? If not, perhaps you remember Lotus 1-2-3? It was the "killer application" that spawned much of the age of personal computing (that along with VisiCalc, of course). At least it made many of us accountants and CPAs happy back in the early 1980s.

Well, Kapor is now president of the Open Source Applications Foundation. In a 2005 article in *Educause Review*, Kapor stated that when he searched for the phrase "open source" in mid January of 2005, it returned approximately 28.8 million Web page hits.[3] When I conducted a similar search in late June 2008, it offered me 233 million Web pages. Clearly, that is more than I can browse through in a lifetime. It also informs me that open software development practices have become mainstream. Action in the field of open source software is now prevalent across such domains as gaming, operating systems, security, business management, education, and Web development. The philosophy of open source software is openness of computing code created in distributed or peer-to-peer collaborative development.

As budgets tighten in education and the associated costs of providing education increase, the interest in open source across education sectors mounts. In education and training organizations, some open source tools are available for bureaucratic and administrative software for student enrollments, learning management, and associated financial systems. Other open source tools are more directly related to the teaching and learning process, such as podcasting, wikis, and blogs.

What's the FOSS All About?

Within all this chatter about openness is an emerging gift culture today that is accustomed to sharing knowledge, skills, and ideas. Some talk about the Free and Open Source Software (FOSS) movement as if it were one giant movement. In fact, it is two movements—the free software movement and the open source movement. The free software movement is more concerned with the philosophical freedoms it gives users whereas open source is focused on the economies of peer-to-peer collaboration.[4] Their agendas may be quite different, but as Richard Stallman noted in July 2008, "At a practical level, these two movements' activities do overlap to a large extent. Nearly all software that is open source is free, and vice versa."

I would add that with both of these movements, however, sharing is no longer unusual; it is part of the culture. The seeds for such sharing may have been planted in the hacker culture, which valued sharing craftsmanship in computing. In contrast to the commonly negative hacker connotations related to security breaches, a hacker is more often a term used for computer programming hobbyists and enthusiasts who enjoy designing software and building programs that are clever, aesthetically pleasing, and useful. The free software and open source software fields are filled with such hackers. Prominent names in the FOSS movement include Stallman as well as Eric Raymond, Linus Torvalds, and Martin Dougiamas. The work of these Internet revolutionaries has helped countless individuals complete their technology projects with a new mode of software development and, in effect, become the technology leaders of their own organizations.

Thus, the free software movement and the more recent open source movement, to a large extent, evolved from the hacker culture.[5] Hacker culture is a subculture that in many ways originated from MIT's computer culture of the late-1950s. As craftsmen, computing professionals wanted to be responsible for a project from beginning to end—from identification of the problem, to writing the code, to operating the machine. This hacker culture had a firm belief in knowledge sharing and helping others, including the exploration of computer programming secrets and free access to computers and the availability of information about them.[6]

Among the most fertile soil for hacker culture was higher education, in places such as the Artificial Intelligence Laboratory at MIT as well as computer labs at Carnegie Mellon University, Stanford University, and the University of California at Berkeley. Among these hotbeds, the AI Lab at MIT was probably the best known for its culture of openness, sharing, and collaboration. Many networking, file sharing, and time-sharing systems and tools were pioneered there by hackers.[7]

Today, this sense of sharing has moved beyond the hacker culture. And the fruits of the sharing movement are beginning to be seen in different spheres of education, with innovative and free products available across a range of disciplines. Yet, educational institutions have not really focused on the use of free software for teaching and learning benefits.

Another Boston Tea Party for GNU?

Like the American Revolution, the free software revolution had some of its roots in Boston. Free software arose from the actions of individuals, not government priorities or funding. Although free software had existed for some time, the person responsible for organizing it into a movement with an active nonprofit organization was Richard Stallman.

Stallman is a man with a litany of awards and recognition for his contributions to the field of computer science.[8] Stallman was a hacker at the MIT AI Lab during his days as a Harvard college student in physics in the early 1970s. He continued in the AI Lab for another decade after graduating from Harvard. When at MIT, he designed the EMACS text editor in 1976, which the user manual indicates was an extensible, customizable, and self-documenting real-time display editor.

Stallman, an internationally known computer programmer, quit his full-time job of ten years at the AI Lab in January 1984 to develop GNU, one of the most prominent contributions of the free software movement. GNU is a recursive acronym for "GNU's Not Unix."[9] Imagine quitting your day job to create a product that would be free. This is the spirit of the age where WE-ALL-LEARN. Stallman, as much as anyone, personifies the hope for a brighter and more democratic educational system.

As Levy noted, Stallman was devoted to a vision of sharing.[10] The goal was to work with each other to improve EMACS and other software tools built by the Free Software Foundation (FSF). A portion of an e-mail from Stallman in September 1983 read as follows:

> Free Unix!
> Starting this Thanksgiving I am going to write a complete
> Unix-compatible software system called GNU (for Gnu's Not Unix), and give it away free to everyone who can use it.
> Contributions of time, money, programs and equipment are greatly needed. . . .
> Why I Must Write GNU
> I consider that the golden rule requires that if I like a program I must share it with other people who like it. I cannot in good conscience sign a nondisclosure agreement or a software license agreement.
> So that I can continue to use computers without violating my principles, I have decided to put together a sufficient body of free software so that I will be able to get along without any software that is not free. . . .
> If I get donations of money, I may be able to hire a few people full or part time. The salary won't be high, but I'm looking for people for whom knowing they are helping humanity is as important as money. I view this as a way of enabling dedicated people to devote their full energies to working on GNU by sparing them the need to make a living in another way.[11]

As the e-mail above demonstrates, there was a sharing culture and freedom of inquiry at MIT, and at the AI Lab in particular, which planted the seeds for Stallman's firm belief in free software. Such beliefs fortunately led to his development of GNU, his founding of the FSF with his hacker colleagues in 1985, and his tireless promotion of the cause. When I spoke with him in July 2008, he pointed out that this is a movement that "says it is an ethical imperative for software to be free."

The beliefs of this group are clearly on display in an early report from the FSF:

> The Free Software Foundation is dedicated to eliminating restrictions on copying, redistribution, understanding and modification of software. . . .
>
> The word "free" in our name does not refer to price; it refers to freedom. First, the freedom to copy a program and redistribute it to your neighbors, so that they can use it as well as you. Second, the freedom to change a program, so that you can control it instead of it controlling you; for this, the source code must be made available to you.
>
> The Foundation works to give you these freedoms by developing free compatible replacements for proprietary software. Specifically, we are putting together a complete, integrated software system "GNU" that is upward-compatible with Unix. When it is released, everyone will be permitted to copy it and distribute it to others; in addition, it will be distributed with source code, so you will be able to learn about operating systems by reading it, to port it to your own machine, to improve it, and to exchange the changes with others.[12]

Among the key goals of the FSF was to develop and then distribute software using a "General Public License" (GPL), or what is now commonly referred to as "copyleft" (as opposed to copyright). In stark contrast to typical kinds of copyright that limit the forms and extent of sharing of intellectual property such as computer software, a copyleft type of license protects the right to share such property. Later on, Stallman refined and elaborated on the four essential freedoms of such GNU and GPL software as follows:

Freedom 0. The freedom to run the program as you wish.

Freedom 1. The freedom to study the source code and change it to do what you wish.

Freedom 2. The freedom to make copies and distribute them to others.

Freedom 3. The freedom to publish modified versions.[13]

With these four principles to guide free software efforts, programmers and the users of their programs entered a culture in which the norms and expectations were focused on sharing.[14] Stallman and his colleagues granted users the right to share, copy, and distribute free software at their own volition. At the same time, Stallman keenly viewed users as potential developers who might share their knowledge, skills, and expertise regarding free software with others by asking them to share any modified code back with him and others. This previously insular group of hackers would soon be part of a mass movement. They now had a collective identity and set of norms, principles, and values that constituted the free software culture to guide their day-to-day practices.

A visit to the FSF Web site indicates that the word "free" as they use it is more akin to free speech than to free beer; it is free of any and all restriction. As Larry Lessig noted in *Wired* magazine, the irony here is that you can charge whatever you want for the free software, but you cannot lock up the knowledge related to how it works.[15] By unlocking the source code, others are allowed to learn from it and improve it. One has freedom to "run, copy, distribute, study, change and improve the software."[16]

Stallman's work directly benefits those in education who are often short on funding and infrastructure. When something is free and can be copied onto as many machines as possible, there is a glow in the teacher's eye. Free resources! But the free software movement means much more than saving schools money. In his paper on "Why Schools Should Exclusively Use Free Software," Stallman points out that when you use free software, you have more control over what you can do with it.[17] You can copy and share it. You can let students take it home and put it on any machines there. You can load it on student laptops and they can use it on class work or field trips. You can cooperate with others on projects that use that software and share associated resources, documentation, and other supports without worry of being sued. You can escape any price increases and domination from companies. And the lessons students learn about such free software are lessons for life. Free software is a key part of the more open educational world.

Free software is a crucial development for the field of education. Think about it: copies of free software can be made at no cost, and there are typically no litigation concerns. Because of these freedoms, there are no restrictions stopping people from particular fields, backgrounds, or groups from using or distributing it. In effect, no one can be discriminated against and there is no elitism here. Any user, regardless of social or economic background, gender, race, or educational level, can use that same piece of software, albeit in different ways. As would be expected, however, efficient use of many of these tools often requires a sufficient level of technological knowledge or experience.

In an article highlighting the key differences between free software and open source software, Stallman happily noted that "Tens of millions of people around the world now use free software; the schools of regions of India and Spain now teach all students to use the free GNU/Linux operating system."[18] Now that is some global impact! Stallman has helped open the educational world. However, he laments that the impact is not widely known: "But most of these users have never heard of the ethical reasons for which we developed this system and built the free software community, because today this system and community are more often described as "open source," and attributed to a different philosophy in which these freedoms are hardly mentioned."[19]

The word "free" is a rather difficult concept to pin down; what is free for one person may not be free for the next. For Stallman, it might at times be better to view the philosophy behind this movement as "freedom-respecting" as opposed to giving away free or gratis software. Software could be quite expensive and still respect personal freedoms to study, change, improve, use, copy, and share it.

For those who continue to focus on the economics of free software as opposed to the personal liberties, there will always be constraints to maintaining such resources, as well as to training teachers and students in their use. Adding to this confusion as well as to the hope, some of these "free" items require extensive time, knowledge, and resources to effectively deploy, whereas many other free technology tools are highly intuitive and require minimal support. For learning to be free and open for all citizens, the tools one uses should be easy to deploy and embed thoughtfully in teaching.

Hey Finland Calling

Perhaps more widely known in the free and open source movement is the story of Linus Torvalds. As is commonly known, Torvalds was a twenty-one-year-old computer science student at the University of Helsinki when he released Linux 0.01, the first computer operating system licensed under GNU General Public License. Perhaps more important, on September 17, 1991, it became the first open source software program to be a viable competitor to proprietary software such as the Microsoft Windows system. It took on the behemoth, and that is why it is a giant tale today.

For many in education as well as in business, the immediate response when discussing computer software needs is "anything but Microsoft." The irony is that the first time I gave a talk related to the contents of this book back in late October 2005 at the international E-Learn Conference in Vancouver, a key education official from Microsoft was in the audience. Two weeks later I found myself in Redmond to present my ideas about a more free and open education world to a roomful of Microsoft executives from around the planet. When I was traveling back to the airport with my son, Alex, who joined me on the trip, he told me that their reactions were surprisingly positive. "Perhaps they were just being kind," I replied. Still, if Microsoft officials are studying the open source movement and contemplating how they might react to it, it is worth noting. Imagine if someday all Microsoft software was in fact free, or at least more open.

Back in 1991, neither free nor open source software likely appeared on Microsoft's immediate radar. Both should have been, however. At that time, Torvalds developed the initial Linux kernel—the operating system that is responsible for providing secure access to the machine's hardware and to various computer processes. Soon many in the education and business worlds did take notice, including executives at Microsoft. Though developing Linux was not necessarily part of Torvalds's job, the university knew and supported his work.[20] As with Richard Stallman and GNU, it was a university environment that fostered this sense of innovation and sharing.

In part, such a sharing community could be seen in the now well-known discussions that took place between Torvalds and Dr. Andrew Tanenbaum, a respected computer science professor at Vrije University in the Netherlands and author of MINIX, which was one of the earliest free Unix-like operating systems.[21] A fairly public debate took place between Torvalds and Tanenbaum about MINIX and Linux. These two individuals still maintain their respective viewpoints despite the unquestionable fact that Linux has had a major impact on computing all over the world.[22]

When Torvalds was interviewed by *First Monday* a decade ago about the motivators for open source software developers, he noted that for him it was not fame or reputation, but for a sense of fun in doing what he loved: programming and contributing to the Internet community with usable products others could enjoy.[23] His craft and artwork were now on display. The entire community has different roles to improve a product—some develop code, some test it and report errors or bugs, and still others might create a fix or patch. As he stated in that interview, "Originally Linux was just something I had done, and making it available was mostly a 'look at what I've done—isn't this neat' kind of thing."[24] Torvalds hoped his ideas would be useful to somebody, though he admitted that there was certainly some element of "showing off" in there too.

He noted in a 1998 interview that by making it open source, he ensured that many people could help in the enhancement and refinement of Linux. With so many talented developers working on Linux and testing it for bugs, the product could improve more quickly and broadly than any single programmer could accomplish. As Torvalds points out, no one person could ever think of all the possible uses and potential problems, but a large user community could come close to that goal. I know from experience that you feel an internal high when someone uses your product—especially when it is making an educational impact. As he stated, "A large motivator . . . was just that people started using it and it feels good to have done something that other people enjoy using."[25]

And Torvalds should be quite happy because his little baby is now packaged and used in many creative ways. Some companies, such as Red Hat, make a profit from selling services for the software. And in China, Red Flag Linux is a government initiative aimed at developing China's open source industry. Currently it commands a 30 percent share of the Chinese software market,[26] a market that is pressing on the accelerator. The thirst for open source software products in China will undoubtedly have an influence on the rest of the world. To address this issue, Dr. Guohua Pan from the University of Virginia and I spent much of 2007 writing about the thirst for open source in China as well as in North America.[27]

Like Stallman, Torvalds has contributed to the world of education in ways that he probably never imagined—he has provided a key part of the infrastructure for learning to people of all walks of life and backgrounds.

GIVING BIRTH TO FREE AND OPEN SOFTWARE

For well-known hackers such as Richard Stallman at the AI Lab, software was a "manifestation of human creativity and expression . . . and represented a key artifact of a community . . . to solve problems together for the common good."[28] Stallman and others valued the intimate and interactive way that they could share what they were working on or other activities they cared about, including opportunities to review, comment on, and improve each other's source code.[29] However, during the mid-1960s, corporate management took over many projects that were once the domain of computer hackers. Akin to the factory efficiency of the Ford automobile manufacturing model, this takeover sought to improve computer efficiency through standardizations and specialization of work.

Not too surprisingly, such tactics did not work the same way in computing departments. The craftsmanlike way of working that hackers were known for clashed with the hierarchical way of computing that business brought with it. The latter was stratified based on status and seniority—analysts, programmers, coders, testers, maintainers, computer console operators, computer room technicians, key punch operators, tape jockeys, and stock room attendants.[30] Ironically, the hackers were not simply separated from each other but often from the computers, which were housed in designated computer rooms. The reduced social interaction with their peers diminished the culture of free and open exchange of ideas, and this in turn limited or further curtailed their access to computers and the programs that run them. It was a viciously bad cycle, especially for the self-esteem and dignity of the hacker culture.

Things began to change, however, with the free software movement and then later the open source movement. When Guohua Pan and I spoke with Eric Raymond in January 2006, he told us that the term *open source* first drew media attention in, where else, Palo Alto, California.[31] It was February 3, 1998. This was the day that Netscape announced it would release the source code of its Navigator tool that later emerged as Mozilla 1.0.[32] Instead of the "free" label, often deemed confrontational to the business community, Christine Peterson, an influential figure in nontechnology and intellectual property, suggested the more pragmatic and business-friendly label of "open source." Raymond and many others in the open source movement, including Todd Anderson, Larry Augustin, John Hall, and Sam Ockman, attended the session.

Since that historic event, the term *open source* has been widely adopted to refer to any computer software program whose source code is free to use, modify, and redistribute—typically for its licensed users. An open source software product, in contrast to commercial software, is designed by a community of users or a consortium of organizations and institutions with a joint interest in the resulting product. Such groups also help in the modification of the product and updates. Because the source code is openly available, any individual or organization can download and upgrade it for its own use. Moreover, as Brad Wheeler noted in *Educause Review*, such an organization can usually redistribute copies of either the original or the modified program.[33]

Educational organizations realize many benefits from using free and open source software. For one, there is innovation, creativity, and some sense of voice or control outside of commercial vendors. Now anyone with an idea for educational software can write code or work with others to write code that can benefit people from around the globe. For the first time in the history of this planet, a talented person from any country or province can have a positive impact on any educational idea. Bill Joy, one of the founders of Sun Microsystems, is known to have said that "most of the smart people in the world work somewhere else."[34] Well, with open source, many of these smart people might volunteer their time to work with you. Idea sharing can spark still other ideas and innovations that can have educational benefits well beyond the original goals and intentions of the creators. Communities and interest groups then spring up around such ideas, providing further energy and excitement.

Yochai Benkler refers to such an economy as a "commons-based peer production" model, in which the primary motivator is not money or financial wealth, but an inner passion toward a particular area in which one has interests or skills.[35] And, with the online help of others, you can create something worthwhile or better for some segment of the world. In effect, we all want our areas of expertise to benefit fellow humans. We also want these pursuits to be at their highest possible quality.

We humans give effortlessly to causes we care about. In the past, this often meant money or capital resources. With the emergence of the Web, such giving increasingly is in the form of education and knowledge. And when individuals with similar areas of expertise create online communities with a mission to share their know-how on a large scale, meaningful projects can be undertaken without traditional hierarchical, command-and-control structures, or financial compensation; there is caring and generative human spirit at work. The open source software movement has found a unique way to tap into that spirit.

Such a caring and generative spirit is a beautiful thing to observe or participate in. For example, each day millions of Wikipedian comrades around the world lend their time and skills to the entire Wikipedia corpus. Perhaps it is this beauty that captivates dozens or hundreds of people to refine a page or two in Wikipedia. In the end, we see not only highly useful resources like Wikipedia, but also community-developed how-to manuals, dictionaries, book reviews, summary lists, product recommendations, software code, and countless other products. And such products are free and open for others. Given that mass audience, there are many tinkerers who volunteer their time and efforts to get these products right. The initial invention can even start at the desk of a young college student in Finland and then spread throughout the world in hopes that others will improve it.

The Sakai Is the Limit

My own university has partnered with Stanford, MIT, and the University of Michigan to build Sakai. Sakai is a courseware platform or system that enables individuals or institutions to place their courses on the Web. For instance, one might load papers, reports, PowerPoint slides, and other documents in Sakai. That same person might also put up audio files of lectures, cases and questions for students to discuss online, and course announcements. And systems like Sakai might also have wiki and blogging tools in addition to testing and gradebook systems. They are the shell in which learning later occurs.

I remember sitting in a committee meeting in the fall of 2003 when Sakai was first mentioned. Brad Wheeler, then associate vice president for Research and Academic Computing and dean of IT for IU–Bloomington, announced this possibility. We would be creating code not just for us at Indiana University, but conceivably for anyone in the world community. Millions of dollars of funding for Sakai would come from the respective four partner universities as well as the Mellon and Hewlett Foundations. The open source possibilities did not end there. Work was to be undertaken related to open source assessment tools, e-portfolio systems, and financial management systems. According to Kenneth Green, among the key drivers for this sharing of code was the resulting cash savings by many institutions around the world.[36] In addition, a sense of community emerged among the organizations that later used Sakai or some other open source system. User groups, conferences, and newsletters soon sprang up.

Send in the Moodleman

Open source was not entirely new to me when Brad mentioned it. A few months before the Sakai announcement, I attended the Ed Media Conference in Honolulu in late June 2003. Ron Oliver, associate dean for Teaching and Learning at Edith Cowan University in Australia, recommended that I meet the "Moodle" man. "The Moodleman? Tell me, what is a Moodleman?" I jokingly replied to Ron. Pointing to a group on the other side of the room, he said, "Martin Dougiamas and he is standing over there." Before departing I asked Ron, "What exactly is Moodle?" "Well," he replied, "it is the first open source learning management system."

So my final night on the island I met the Moodleman at the pub in Duke's Waikiki, a seafood restaurant named after the Hawaiian surf legend, Duke Kahanamoku. Martin explained that he started working on Moodle in 1999 because he was frustrated with existing commercial course management systems when he was a WebCT administrator at Curtin University in Western Australia. He had been working on various Internet projects well before the Web became hot—in fact, since 1986. He was particularly disenchanted with the closed systems of most course management systems. He told me the first release of Moodle

1.0 was in August 2002 and, less than a year later, it had more than twenty-seven translations.

Moodle use continues to skyrocket around the world. By late February 2009, Moodle had an installation base of over 620,000 registered users, speaking more than seventy-eight different languages in 204 countries. There are some eighty thousand downloads per month. In addition, there are countless unregistered users and many happy Moodlers!

Like Sakai, Moodle's phenomenal growth is one of those warm and fuzzy stories of everyday people fighting for something better and cheaper than what the vendors are offering, and then succeeding. Martin has an army of code developers who believe in the open source movement. But there are also services sold behind the installation scenes to help those who want to effectively use the tool. It was built to be more in touch with student learning interests and needs. The Moodle philosophy is aligned with what some label as social constructivism. In this philosophy, learners have a voice or say in their own learning, and they benefit from their collaborative experiences with others. Several key social constructivist principles underlie Moodle—helping learners to construct ideas, building products, collaborating, sharing products and ideas, and finally connecting with others who have common interests. Such participatory learning might be seen in the discussion and chat tools, the wiki, and the learner profiles embedded in Moodle. The beauty is that anyone writing code can add additional features or tools based on this underlying philosophy. What has emerged is a community of Moodle programmers building a special environment for social constructivist learning.

As stated on the Moodle philosophy page:

> Once you are thinking about all these issues, it helps you to focus on the experiences that would be best for learning from the learner's point of view, rather than just publishing and assessing the information you think they need to know. It can also help you realize how each participant in a course can be a teacher as well as a learner. Your job as a "teacher" can change from being "the source of knowledge" to being an influencer and role model of class culture, connecting with students in a personal way that addresses their own learning needs, and moderating discussions and activities in a way that collectively leads students towards the learning goals of the class.

Moodle and Sakai are just two of many examples of free online course management systems. There are three benefits that such systems lend to the open learning world. First, they allow organizations and institutions to offer courses and programs that would be too costly otherwise. Second, they make more content available to individuals as well as organizations and entire countries that would not otherwise be able to access them. Third, they create communities of like-minded educators who not only share programming talents and courses, but are interested in improving the human condition as well. Without course management systems and open software to rally around, it is doubtful such individuals would ever meet. With open source tools such as Moodle and Sakai, education takes on a much more global face.

A Few Drupals for a Peace of Ning

But not everyone is interested in courses and delivering prepackaged content anymore. Some might simply want to share personal content and information. Others might want to form groups that share such content. Both are in luck. For instance, free content management systems such as Drupal help anyone to build personal and community homepages. Like Moodle and Sakai, Drupal is open source. There are tens of thousands of Drupal users, many of whom use it for blogging, sharing resources, and social networking. Still other applications are available as add-on modules.

If you are seeking a tool specially designed for social networking communities, Ning, which means "peace" in Chinese, is the place to click on over to. Though not open source like Sakai and Moodle, Ning allows developers to create what are called OpenSocial gadgets and applications using technology developed by Google. And the applications are pouring in—some thirty thousand of them, according to CEO and cofounder Gina Bianchini.[37] Many of these applications, of course, have educational ramifications as they foster social interaction and knowledge sharing.

Along with Bianchini, Ning's other cofounder is none other than Marc Andreessen, the Silicon Valley "whiz kid," who earlier in his career coauthored the first Web browsing tool in Mosaic and then cofounded Netscape.[38] With Ning, founded in October 2004 and launched in early

2006, Andreessen has another hit, and for this one, he migrated from open source to open social.

As of February 2009, there were some 700,000 groups and millions of people using Ning, and it had raised over $100 million of venture capital funding.[39] Once inside Ning, you can join and participate in subgroups of interest, such as groups for artists, meeting planners, digital photographers, high school and university alumni, and corporate social responsibility.

Ning's founders are not totally altruistic. Free version users have embedded ads in their network pages, but there is also an enhanced "Ning for Business" option, which has a monthly fee. This business model has made the company worth half a billion dollars in just a few years. A key reason for this growth is that Ning is a tool that virally expands ideas. With growth projections at over four million such sites within a couple of years, Ning not only energizes viral loops for its members, it is benefited by each network that is formed and then virally expanded. Adam Penenberg describes these "viral expansion loops" as "a type of virtual alchemy that, done right, almost guarantees a self-replicating, borglike growth."[40]

As such, it is an ideal tool for idea sharing and exchange in education. Educators can meet around books, theories, or ideas that promote change in schools, colleges, or other educational settings. Members of an educational network can come from anywhere, not just from a local school, community, or friendship group. When a book on reinventing project-based learning becomes hot, group members can offer perspectives, stories, and experiences from Argentina, Spain, Canada, or the United States. They share photos of their projects as well as powerful videos of others related to their interests.

One popular education-related network called "Ning for Educators" is free of advertisements when used within networks of students in grades 7–12. Created by Steve Hargadon, Ning for Educators has attracted thousands of people from all over the world including Japan, the Philippines, Saudi Arabia, and the Netherlands. This is the ultimate in professional development as well as global exchange for educators. Anyone in the world interested in education can form, join, participate in, or casually browse a group.

Ning for Educators is emblematic of the WE-ALL-LEARN model of this book. These are the educators who are opening the learning world.

Teachers and trainers no longer have to be satisfied with the ideas and advice they obtain from those in their offices, classrooms, or neighborhoods. Now they can post a comment or question to this Ning networld and wait for answers and ideas from newfound colleagues in Asia, Europe, or Latin America. Perhaps, as its name implies, Ning really can lead to peace.

Creating Creative Commons

A creative sharing or participatory learning culture with an extensive and seamless exchange of ideas needs a mechanism for clearing the use of materials that are exchanged. In this culture, there are many tools for being creative as individuals or as collaborative teams, as well as for showcasing the results. Unlike companies, individuals or groups of individuals, especially those in education, might want their work used and modified for still further uses by as many people as possible. Collaboration and sharing are now a common part of the everyday lexicon.

It is difficult for anyone to keep up with the changes that have occurred. Online technologies have exploded at such a brisk pace that the instructional possibilities have advanced far beyond most of the methods and theories in which teachers have been trained. More pragmatically, technologies have increased the educational options for the citizens of this planet well beyond the copyright laws of most governments. At the same time, the procedures one must follow in most organizations and institutions to comply with copyright laws have become chaotic at best. Simply put, the licensing and copyright of the materials has become a huge matter.

Enter Creative Commons. Created in 2001 by Larry Lessig, a high-profile Stanford law professor, Creative Commons is a nonprofit organization devoted not just to expanding access to online materials, but also to the creative use and remixing of them. When exploring the content directory of Creative Commons, you find a rich array of audio, image, video, text, education, and geodata. It is interesting to see the names of organizations and projects with Creative Commons licenses. For example, the Tree of Life (ToL) project, which is hosted at the University of Arizona, has a note on its Web page explaining that it has decided on an "all rights reserved" copyright. However, the materials of this project have different copyright licenses; for example, the ToL glossary allows noncommercial use, whereas its scientific content and learning materials, including text, images, and other media, have more traditional copyright protections built in. WikiEducator, in contrast, has decided on a "Share Alike" copyright allowing anyone to alter, transform, build upon, and even distribute this work. Such a decision is not too surprising given that WikiEducator is a community that passionately believes that learning materials should be free and open. It is a wiki, after all. In contrast, the Freesound Project takes a different approach. As the name implies, this Web site has a collection of free sounds from thunder to drums beating and the crashing of ocean waves. It allows for copying, distribution, and transmission of the sounds and other materials found there but only if proper attributions are made. In addition, derivative works are not allowed from the Freesound Project.

Open courseware initiatives from various universities, which are discussed more fully in the next chapter, each have different copyright designations using Creative Commons. Resources such as Carnegie Mellon University's Open Learning Initiative and the OpenLearn initiative from the Open University in the United Kingdom have thousands of hours of freely available content. Both of these projects have been designated as "Share Alike" but only for noncommercial purposes. In addition, users must give the original author credit while maintaining the same Share Alike copyright for any product derivatives. You can share, copy, transmit, remix, or adapt the work for other purposes. Copyright designations found at Creative Commons help protect public and private universities as well as individuals from for-profit entities that may rip off their intellectual capital.

Creative Commons licenses have been ported to dozens of countries including Finland, Slovenia, Argentina, Japan, and Mexico. Upcoming projects listed at their Web site include Egypt, Guatemala, Vietnam, Turkey, and Bangladesh. With this impact and momentum, there is no denying that Creative Commons is a key part of the movement toward more open educational resources for the world.

The free tools at Creative Commons allow the creator to assign varying rights on use from reserving all rights to some rights to allowing free distribution. At the Creative Commons portal are tools for licensing, mixing, and translating your work as well as various widgets, plug-ins, and add-on tools for your documents, blogs, and Web sites. And resembling a start-up Internet company, Creative Commons Labs, or ccLabs, is developing still other innovative ideas and tools.

An organization like Creative Commons empowers people as well as organizations and institutions. Whereas the GNU Free Documentation License (GFDL) was originally intended as a license for software documentation, Creative Commons pushes well beyond those borders. Creative Commons is the place to go for any author, educator, artist, scientist, and so on who wants to make his or her works available to others in electronic format. Are you an undergraduate student who has created a rock band while attending college and recorded a few songs during jam sessions in your spare time? Might you be a professor who has decided to post your podcasted lectures to the Web? Or are you a teacher in Thailand who has written a manual on the sport of archery? Perhaps you are an agricultural scientist at the University of Calgary in Canada who has preliminary results of a study posted to your blog or homepage. Well, then, Creative Commons might have what you need.

There has been widespread acclaim for Creative Commons. Among the prominent projects or businesses using Creative Commons types of licenses include Wikimedia Commons, Flickr, the Internet Archive, the Public Library of Science, and Citizendium. Various types of documents fall within these projects, including traditional scientific journals, comics, Web portals, movies, and instructional materials. Blogs and podcasts are part of the publication modes that might use Creative Commons. Even bumper stickers fall within its purview.

Larry Lessig has become synonymous with Creative Commons—and with free and open access to information in general. When I asked him if back in 2000 or 2001 he thought that Creative Commons would grow so quickly and have so much influence, he replied, "No. We had no idea. It has been an extraordinary and valuable surprise." His quest is for balance, compromise, and moderation with regard to copyright, instead of a situation in which every scanned handwritten note or podcast posted to the Internet is copyrighted with "all rights reserved." Full copyright might be too restrictive for you when you want others to use your materials or take some aspects of your ideas and repurpose them. The free software and open source materials that Richard Stallman, Eric Raymond, Linus Torvalds, and Martin Dougiamas advocate are possible only if the creator of the code or programming sequence has documented open access to others before someone else attempts to reverse engineer (in other words, steal) the ideas and copyrights them. With Creative Commons licensing, the fruits of individual creativity quickly multiply and reemerge in places not previously considered. And with it, education is opened up to more people.

As digital information dominates our world, politicians must also take notice. In the coming decade, the laws that they pass related to the sharing, use, and recombination of such content will become increasingly crucial and scrutinized. There is little doubt that you will be affected by them. It will be apparent in how, where, and what you learn, as well as how you ultimately affect the learning of others. For everyone on this planet to be able to learn, we need to rethink the monopolies that the recording, publishing, and movie industries have had on the creative inventions for the past century. The creative inventions of this generation and the generations that will follow will be increasingly digital. We, the educators and the learners of this planet, need full and immediate access to this digital content. Who will sign on now to the declaration of open education discussed earlier?

Fortunately, people such as Larry Lessig, who have educational and legal interests and experiences, have emerged to take a pivotal role in this movement toward free and open source content. This is how a trained lawyer such as Lessig has made a difference in educating the people of this planet. Now, how might doctors, biologists, park rangers, or novelists make similar inroads? We all can. We all must. When we all get involved, we all can learn.

OPEN SOURCE AND FREE SOFTWARE FOR ALL

The terms *free* and *open* carry many connotations for different people. Chris Anderson of *Wired,* for example, focuses on the economics of free, whereas Richard Stallman is lead by ethical ideals and the respect for personal liberties and freedoms. What is clear is that the movements for free software as well as open source software are transforming learning opportunities around the planet. Those at the helm of each initiative fully believe that they have designed unique opportunities for promoting education. Whether it is the AI Lab at MIT, the University of Helsinki, or Curtin University in Australia, new free and open learning avenues are possible. People such as Stallman, Torvalds, Dougiamas, and Lessig have shown us the way. Their ideas have emerged from the missions of postsecondary institutions to create, archive, and disseminate knowledge in open sharing communities. With their ideals in place, creativity is nurtured, respected, and disseminated widely.

Free and open source software is a key ingredient in the WE-ALL-LEARN model. With free software tools, especially those that computer programmers and designers around the globe might enhance or augment, there is a growing capital for enhancing education. Of course, there are digital divide concerns. However, once more widespread Web access has been achieved, there are dozens of free tools that may serve as human learning boosters and supporters. Anyone with computer programming or design skills, money, resources, or networks, can now take time to improve the general education level of this planet. They might have an impact on one person. Great! But they might also affect scores of others. To reach toward higher goals, this movement needs you!

MIT in Every Home

OPENER #4: LEVERAGED RESOURCES AND OPENCOURSEWARE

MIT'S IN "VEST" MENT IN OPENCOURSEWARE

Perhaps the most interesting trend in education today is the movement toward open courseware (OCW) initiated by MIT a few years ago. At the most basic level, OCW refers to the placing of free content on the Internet for anyone to use. OCW offers free, searchable, and open access to university resources and course content. For instance, instructors might put up lecture notes, course syllabi, sample tests, media files, course schedules, and other course-related information. However, there typically is no instructor at the site to review or grade students' work.

Ever since Charles Vest made his announcement on April 4, 2001, MIT has received wide-ranging press and praise.[1] Although the goal was to have most of its courses freely available on the Web in ten years, when I spoke with Steve Carson, external relations director, in July 2008, he told me that "we did in fact complete virtually all MIT courses November 28, 2007, [just] six and a half years after the April 2001 announcement." By early 2009, MIT had 1,890 classes online. In effect, its entire curriculum was available for free to the learners of the world.

Adding to such impressive feats, there were at least two hundred mirror sites for the content. Mirror sites provide an exact copy of all the contents at another Internet site, which can speed up downloads, as well as eliminate or reduce costly fees for Internet service provider costs. Of these two hundred mirror sites, some seventy-five or eighty were in the Sahara region of Africa. Local charges are much lower for a hub in

Africa than the tariffs are for accessing materials across international waters.

Since its inception, more than 35 million people around the world have explored MIT's online course content.[2] Carson further informed me that these contents were bringing roughly one million visitors per month and another 750,000 to the translated courses. Keep in mind that although MIT officials expected students and instructors to be the primary users, more than 50 percent of actual users happen to be corporate self-learners who reach out for information when needed or because it's personally meaningful.[3] Educational content from MIT is available to any casual or informal learners looking to update their knowledge on a topic.

All courses at MIT now have a Web presence. Pick a topic, any topic: everything they offer can be yours! Suppose you had an itch to learn about cognitive robotics, rocket propulsion, thermal energy, or air traffic control. You can most assuredly scratch that itch now. Perhaps your partner would prefer to learn about magic, witchcraft, and the spiritual world. Or maybe your teenage son is interested in photography, sculpture, and architecture, whereas his older sister is a premed college student who needs to bone up on biology, chemistry, calculus, or physics. You can all simultaneously explore such course contents, which have been designed by some of the foremost minds on the planet. Even more appealing is that you are not strapped to a particular time and place to do so. Nor must you complete any forms. And there are no checks to write out or campus parking tickets to process. You can explore as much or as little as you want at your own leisure and for free.

The press and acclaim continues to pour in more than seven years later, much of it focused on the humanitarian intentions of this project. This initiative is so popular that *Reader's Digest* even included it in its 2007 list of America's 100 Best Ideas.[4] As Vest stated back in 2001: "This is about something bigger than MIT. I hope other universities will see us as educational leaders in this arena, and we very much hope that OpenCourseWare will draw other universities to do the same. We would be delighted if—over time—we have a world wide web of knowledge that raises the quality of learning—and ultimately, the quality of life— around the globe."[5]

One of the key designers of the MIT OCW project was Professor Dick Yue. When I spoke with him in July 2008, he confirmed rumors that the basic idea for OCW dawned on him when working out on an exercise machine. However, the seeds for this idea may have been placed in his head decades earlier, when, as a child in Hong Kong, he was inspired by an MIT textbook that his father gave him. Now imagine young boys and girls having access to textbook materials, lecture notes, audio and video files, tests, and course agenda for every course at MIT and for thousands of other courses from around the globe. How many youths will be similarly inspired to enter engineering, chemistry, architecture, law, history, or nursing? For Yue, the goal is to reach out to students beyond the physical walls and classrooms of MIT.

As Yue explains it, OCW did not simply spring forth in some sort of eureka moment. Instead, he was chair of a planning committee that was charged with looking into the role MIT could play in the Internet age. Ideas related to their course content were part of that discussion. Yue's committee spent months struggling with what to do. The business plans of other universities attempting to enter the for-profit side of e-learning did not make sense. The economics simply did not add up. And MIT did not care to make an investment in an area where it could not be a leader.

So, with one bold move, MIT would be the first to give away its content, at no charge and with no questions asked. It would lead the rest of the world into an entirely new field called OCW. Yue called this "rational altruism." He said there was a Chinese proverb that effectively says, "Toss out a brick to attract jade." MIT tossed in more than eighteen hundred course bricks and was attracting mountains of jade. In retrospect, it was a fabulous decision. MIT now has many new partners, users, onlookers, and well-wishers. The press has also been quite favorable.

Yue told me that MIT created "a new game altogether." Fortunately, at the time, there was little tension among faculty members. Though some were concerned about whether their creative course designs could be adequately displayed in any type of standard course container, most took pride in exposing their courses to the world. The majority warmly accepted the notion that multiple pairs of eyeballs scanning their content could help improve it. Well beyond minor course edits, many OCW visitors share personal stories and real-world examples that actually end up in later versions of a course. Due to this bold initiative,

MIT faculty members receive practical feedback from all corners of the globe without having to travel. Now these experts can receive a never-ending supply of information to validate their new concepts, formulas, and theories. So much jade!

MIT clearly recognizes the revolution currently taking place in education. Yue stated, "I believe MIT has a responsibility as well as the ability to make a global impact." He added that MIT had flattened the competition by simply offering its content for free. Yue felt that had the competition succeeded in what they were attempting to do by dividing and selling pieces of courses, education would likely not be so open today. From his perspective, those seeking profits from such content were riding the dark horses. Fortunately, Charles Vest and MIT arrived in a series of white chariots and the free and open side of education won out—at least for now.

It is important to realize that MIT has led the way in not only this key opener but in several others as well. It is the open education giant. According to a 2002 report by *BBC News,* the executive director of the OCW, Anne Margulies, stated, "I genuinely think there was an 'a-ha' moment when they said our mission was actually to enhance education." She continued, "Why don't we, instead of trying to sell our knowledge over the Internet, just give it away."[6]

MIT attracted some $30 million from two different foundations to complete the task. There are now thousands of free pages of information and hundreds of hours of video lectures, audio files, and demonstrations from some of the brightest and most decorated professors in the world available to anyone at no cost. As we shall see, this spurred many innovations and spin-off projects.

PAKISTAN'S MIT

I remember sitting in the back of a conference called e-Merging e-Learning in Abu Dhabi on September, 13, 2003. The presenter was Professor Atta-ur-Rahman, the chairman of the Higher Education Commission who also held the position of federal minister and adviser to the prime minister on science and technology and minister-in-charge of the Ministry of Science and Technology. In the midst of his highly impressive talk about expanding Internet networks and bandwidth opportunities in Pakistan, he began discussing the opportunities for Pakistani youth in the courses that MIT was making available. Though there was no instructor grading student work or credit to be earned for such courses, many students in Pakistan were highly motivated to explore the famous courses in computer science, engineering, and physics.

I was stunned. Kids in Pakistan were learning MIT course content from their local schools and homes. Thanks to the creative spark of an idea during a workout by Dick Yue, along with a fair bit of gumption, planning, and commitment by countless people at MIT, those with Web access now had a passport to learn from the best. No longer must they rely on hand-me-down textbooks with outdated formulas and dog-eared equations to solve author-generated problems from years or even decades ago.

An evaluation report from the OCW project at MIT a couple of years later confirmed the utility of these materials for Pakistani youth.[7] For example, in that report, an interview with Saud Khan indicated that he had been using the OCW materials for a few years while enrolled in a master's degree program in telecommunications engineering at Mohammad Ali Jinnah University in Pakistan. One of his professors had been a visiting professor at the University of Massachusetts and recommended that Khan explore the OCW for the digital communications material he desired. Khan pointed out that the OCW gave him materials that would otherwise be too expensive for him to purchase. Moreover, he found the free MIT courses an excellent supplement because they were comprehensive and precise and provided a level of detail missing from some of his courses. He was highly successful in learning on his own with OCW materials.

There is this ingrained notion since the time of Plato and Socrates that a teacher needs to be in the same space as the learner. Not any longer. Students can learn in separate times and locations from the designated teacher or other learners. And they can learn with different types of resources, delivery mechanisms, and assessments. The Pakistani student, therefore, can be intellectually stretched by her access to MIT courses as well as courses from other universities around the globe.

Imagine parents who cannot afford to send their sons and daughters to college but who can still go through an online database of colleges and universities that have placed their course materials online. They might say, "Hey, look at this course at MIT, this new course at Notre Dame, and this program at the Open University in the United Kingdom. If you find something interesting, let me know and I will read it too."

Students and instructors, of course, also benefit. For instance, when Hemalatha Thiagarajan, professor of mathematics and computer science at the National Institute of Technology–Tiruchirappalli, in Tamil Nadu, India, teaches courses on artificial intelligence, she often refers to OCW materials.[8] Given the somewhat prescriptive course syllabi that she must follow, she has little flexibility in her lectures. Fortunately, the OCW materials allow for deeper and fuller coverage of course content. By adding OCW to the mix, her students have greater choice in their learning, and therefore are empowered to explore that supplemental material. The courses also provide valuable learning models and examples for young as well as more established instructors.

Students also benefit from quick access to MIT course content. One student, Kunle Adejumo, extensively used the OCW when in his fourth year of studying engineering at Ahmadu Bello University in Zaria, Nigeria.[9] Though Ahmadu Bello is the largest university in Nigeria, with thirty-five thousand students, it lacked effective Internet access to OCW materials. Even the computer lab did not provide an Internet connection. OCW materials were only available on CD-ROM, which was difficult for him to get his hands on. As a giving person in this open education world, Adejumo accessed the OCW from his home computer and printed out pages from a metallurgical engineering class online. He would then bring these materials to class to help the instructor as well as the other students. Not surprisingly, "they kept asking for more. Finally he downloaded the entire course, printed it and brought it in. The class burst into applause."[10]

Stories like Ahmadu's are not unusual. Rogelio Morales, a metallurgical engineering graduate of the Central University of Venezuela, shared similar stories of how he downloaded different OCW resources and brought them to class where they would be shown, discussed, and shared. Morales noted that many people in Venezuela benefit from the contents. "Not everybody in Venezuela has the opportunity to go to college," he points out. "It's really hard to get into university, so OCW is a great option."[11]

Nader Dehesh, head of design engineering at Saravel Corporation in Iran, is a self-learner. He uses OCW content to explore new courses in the design and manufacturing areas as well as to stay up to date in areas in which he was trained when a student at Allegheny College in Pennsylvania.[12] He is persistent despite the fact that the Internet speeds in Iran are much slower than what he had in the United States

From these few vignettes, it is certain that something interesting is happening here. If there is a definitive symbol for the changing educational times of the twenty-first century, it might be MIT's OCW movement. It is this trend above all others that makes one step back for a moment and take notice. Did anyone in the past century predict that by 2008 people could sit in the comfort of their homes or local libraries and learn from course contents from MIT? If so, did those prognosticators expect that such access would include any course that MIT offered and would be totally free?

The undeniable goal of those involved at MIT is a revolution in education. Perhaps society is finally being deschooled as Ivan Illich wished decades earlier. As Yue stated in the *BBC News* article, "Our hope and aspiration is that by setting an example, other universities will also put their valued materials on the Internet and thereby make a truly profound and fundamental impact on learning and education worldwide."[13]

Though it just began a few years ago, this trend is quickly growing around the planet. Critics might contend that this is English imperialism. In actuality, some ambitious people and projects are now translating MIT courses from English into traditional and simplified Chinese as well as Spanish, Portuguese, Thai, French, German, Vietnamese, and Ukrainian.[14] And the number of organizations involved in OCW is rapidly expanding.[15] Already there are universities in Japan, India, China, Thailand, Vietnam, France, and elsewhere putting their content on the Web for free. With this one innovation called OCW, you can now instantly compare classes and programs offered by institutions in different corners of the world. These comparisons will be more common as additional courses are translated and made accessible. Yes, MIT did indeed start a revolution. It is one that we can join casually from afar and without anyone taking notice, or one in which we can directly take part. Which will you choose?

OOPS, DID I MEAN TO SHARE THAT?

A parallel initiative that had its roots in Taiwan is the Opensource Opencourseware Prototype System (OOPS) project. In OOPS, an army of volunteer translators are converting MIT courses as well as OCW projects from other countries into traditional and simplified Chinese. At the basic level, they translate text from a course. At the next level, they translate audio and video files as well.[16]

In late July 2005, I gave an all-day workshop on online learning in Taipei. My audience was a group of young executives from different companies who had signed up for a leadership academy. With a chance opening early in my schedule, I arranged a breakfast meeting with Lucifer Chu, whom I had been told I needed to meet. My friends informed me that Lucifer had translated the *Lord of the Rings* books into Chinese and made more than $1 million by the age of twenty-six. Appearing within weeks of the December 2001 release of the first part of Peter Jackson's movie adaptation, the timing of Lucifer's translation was perfect. His stroke of good luck resulted in more than 220,000 box sets of Tolkien's translated works being sold within three-and-a-half years.

Lucifer then used roughly half of the first million he made to help translate the MIT courses and other OCW courses into simplified and traditional Chinese. He also used some of the money to found and direct the Foundation of Fantasy Culture and Arts. Though he had amassed impressive wealth from one book translation deal, Lucifer was not a billionaire like Bill Gates or Warren Buffett. By donating such a large percentage of his personal wealth for the good of humankind, Lucifer serves as a potential model for others to follow.

Although I had read articles and stories about Lucifer, I still did not know exactly what to expect. The *Taipei Times* described him in the following manner: "Lucifer Chu is quite possibly one of the nation's oddest millionaires. He lives with his parents, he drives a car that is best described as an 'old banger' and he's addicted to video games and fantasy novels."[17] Apparently, Lucifer woke up one day and asked if he was a better person after accumulating all that wealth and a voice inside him said, "No, you have not changed." So, change his life he did. Now Lucifer's mission is to help as many people as he can to find better lives through online education. With this focus on helping people freely learn through the Web, Lucifer symbolizes the WE-ALL-LEARN motto of this book. Though perhaps preferring to play video games, he is a world changer and educational revolutionary.

Lucifer graduated from college in the late 1990s with a degree in electrical engineering. Only later did he begin work as a professional translator. After becoming famous for translating *Lord of the Rings*, he was host of a ten-minute technology news show in 2003 where he introduced ideas and stories related to technology and Internet resources. During the summer of 2003, the program was experiencing extremely low ratings. The only time there was a spark of interest was when he introduced MIT's OCW program. One mother called in to ask about it, and her questions aroused his interest and changed his life. In February 2004, Lucifer decided he wanted to revolutionize the OCW movement by localizing the MIT OCW Web site for the Chinese people.

Lucifer pointed out to me that the MIT project had cost more than $20 million. His Chinese localization project, in contrast, started with an old computer saved from a junkyard and stored in a university Internet center with official authorization. He was willing to support this project with personal funds because he could relate to it on many levels. For instance, with the translations, Lucifer and others could learn about electromagnetism, a course he did not do well in as a college student. And now he could take and retake it as many times as he wanted from one of the best professors in the world; thanks to OOPS, it was available in his native language.

OOPS was the third organization to sign an official translation affiliate agreement with MIT. In 2005, OOPS had more than 10,000 daily visitors and around 500,000 total visitors. Three years later, in 2008, the total number of OOPS visitors topped 1.9 million with Lucifer expecting this to increase to over 2.2 million in 2009. That is more than 2 million people benefiting from MIT content translated to Chinese— far more than MIT enrollments back in Cambridge, Massachusetts. The brainchild of one person with a funny name has influenced the learning of millions.

Lucifer is now using his influence to sponsor conferences and institutes on OCW and e-learning, as well as to help universities in Taiwan, such as National Central University and National Chiao Tung University, establish their own OCWs. He is also working to translate courses from other universities and countries. In April of 2007, *The New York Times* ran a feature story on him, and a year later he was quoted in the *Wall Street Journal*.[18] With all this attention, the distance between East and West shrinks. The quickening pace of this shrinkage is perhaps the most astonishing aspect of this open world.

Lucifer is striking—relatively tall, bulky, with shoulder-length hair, and when I met him, he was wearing all black clothes, as if dressed for a videogaming event. He has immediate presence. His business card— black, of course—lists his title as "Janitor of OOPS." I asked him, "Why are you the janitor if you are the founder of the company and a millionaire?" He tells me that their project is translating OCW courses into Chinese, and he must clean up any messes that are made. This is quite different from the job titles of most young Internet entrepreneurs, especially those I came into contact with during the dot-com boom. They always had loftier and more esoteric titles, such as Internet Evangelist, Learning Architect, Internet Presence Crusader, Chief People Officer, Cyberdog Engineer, Web Advertising Traffic Cop, Kung Fu Designer, or Samurai Programmer. Lucifer Chu is none of those. He emphatically is the OOPS janitor in charge of cleaning up online messes and spills.

What Lucifer's business card tells me is that he remains unassuming despite having invested hundreds of thousands of dollars of his own money to better the world. He is interested in giving to the world instead of just taking from it. Such volunteerism endows him with meaning and purpose. Lucifer, which is Latin for "light bearer," is a name he innocently took on as a teenager. It was a magnificent choice because he is now bringing some light and educational opportunities to Chinese people located anywhere. He wants others to take advantage of the goodwill gestures of MIT and other organizations to share their knowledge. In return, naturally, there is some recognition, status, and attention.

Once breakfast was over, Lucifer took time to show me some of the facts and figures of OOPS in an informal presentation that I am sure he had given more formally dozens, if not hundreds, of times previously. In the slides, there is mention that "perfect translations do not exist" and that "collective minds are better than a single translator." At the time, his volunteer core of OOPS translators totaled more than twenty-two hundred and were located in more than twenty-two countries. Collectively, they had adopted more than eleven hundred of the MIT courses to translate. Of these courses, more than half were near completion as of January 1, 2007.[19] By early 2009, this had increased to thirteen hundred adopted courses and nearly eight hundred complete.

Needless to say, I walked away from our initial meeting extremely impressed and hopeful that this project would continue to find success and long-term funding. I also began to wonder how many other Lucifer Chus were out there spearheading similar projects with worldwide educational ramifications.

Our association did not end with that breakfast in July 2005. A few months later, I forwarded him some initial ideas I had for this book and a notice of my first formal presentation of them at the international E-Learn Conference that October in Vancouver. Lucifer immediately ordered a plane ticket and attended the conference. He even joined me on stage at the end of my keynote speech to explain OCW and OOPS to the packed room and enlisted their support. Several times since then, we have met at similar events and forums in Asia and North America. Each time I hear him, I find this famous yet unpretentious young janitor inspiring.

A prime example of what a global education network like OOPS can accomplish occurred in the wake of the devastating earthquake on May 12, 2008 in the Sichuan province of China. Weeks later, there were estimates of eighty-seven thousand people dead or missing.[20] In response, the OOPS people quickly sifted through OCW archives, found courses from MIT and the Johns Hopkins Bloomberg School of Public Health related to how to survive a catastrophe, and immediately began translating them. To let people know what they were up to, they also wrote about their efforts in the OOPS blog. Next, they located more Open Educational Resources (OER) from Taiwan's 921 Earthquake Relief Foundation that were even simpler to share because they were already written in Chinese. These efforts of the OOPS volunteers all occurred within a week of the calamity.

As Lucifer put it, "We couldn't really go in the place where it was hit most severely. So, as a group of volunteers who shared knowledge, we tried to do what we do best." The OER that they found in Taiwan were quite propitious because they had information on how to rebuild homes and communities, how to take care of children who had been through a deadly earthquake, how to acquire loans, and so on. The OOPS staff even helped bring the CEO of the 921 Foundation to China to present at a seminar about earthquake rebuilding and to visit with other key people.[21] OER not only provides educational benefits but can help with relations between countries. Education mends fences and rebuilds communities.

There are several differences between Lucifer's OOPS project and what is happening on the mainland of China with the Chinese Resources in Education (CORE) project. CORE is translating exemplary Chinese courses into English for the benefit of others around the world. It is a government-backed initiative that also has funding from the well-regarded Hewlett Foundation. OOPS, in contrast, received money from Hewlett only after showing much success using Lucifer's self-funding approach. And instead of relying on prestigious universities, he has assembled a legion of volunteer translators akin to the open source movement mentioned in Chapter Four. Whereas open source software projects such as Linux involve a network of unpaid individuals generating and maintaining computer code, OOPS is an open source model of text translation.

When you examine the inner workings of OOPS, you start to see Wikipedia. Like those who generate pages in Wikipedia, OOPS translators make their course translations available for anyone else to change or edit. Somewhat like expert Wikipedians, OOPS translators not only create content, but they also help with editing the work of other translators. In addition, they lend support for proofreading, technical services and support, administrative matters, and marketing and promotions. As Friedman expressed in *The World Is Flat*, with online collaboration and productivity tools, as well as the many social networking tools, today our work colleagues can come from anywhere. There is an underlying community of practice and global spirit. Though most OOPS volunteers are from Taiwan and mainland China, many are from other countries spanning the globe, including Singapore, the United States, the United Kingdom, Canada, and parts of Europe.

That OOPS relies on volunteers, and not translations commissioned from high-ranking universities and institutes, is a common criticism and source of tension. But it is the same argument used against Wikipedia and other community-generated resources. Though society wrestles with such quality and conformity issues, charismatic young leaders like Lucifer keep marching along and providing additional educational resources for us. Through his talents and energy, the OOPS project has become one of the more novel and successful educational projects ever designed. There is a popular Chinese proverb that says, "May you live in interesting times." Well, for educators and learners who are creating, translating, or using OCW, such as OOPS, these are interesting times indeed.

As the OOPS project indicates, there are millions of people accessing higher education course materials from some of the best universities in the world. What if such access increased literacy rates of people in China, India, or Africa, by just some small percentage? What if it encouraged more students to complete their secondary educations and pursue college study? What if this resulted in communities of scholars in different fields sharing their course content? What will happen when pieces of courses are translated from different places—one part coming from MIT, one part from Harvard, one part from Oxford, another from National Chiao Tung University, and still another from Beijing Normal University? I am not sure what the results will be, but I cannot wait to see the reaction from users as well as critics.

OCW OFFSPRING

MIT may be the flag bearer, but there are countless people and projects lining up in this magnificent OCW parade. By February 2008, there were more than one hundred universities placing their content on display for millions of spectators without charging any admission fees.[22] Lining up behind them were more than five thousand online classes that had been added to the pageantry.[23]

There were many familiar names and figures marching in this parade. OCW projects that followed on the heels of the MIT announcement included those from the Johns Hopkins Bloomberg School of Public Health, Utah State University, and Tufts University. Among the notable international initiatives are the Japan OpenCourseWare Consortium, the Vietnam Fulbright Economics OCW, and the Rai Foundation Colleges OCW project in India. Exploring these further, one finds that the Japanese OCW Consortium now has seventeen member institutions that have placed more than one thousand courses online in English and other languages.[24]

Back in the United States, Tufts University was among the first to jump in. Many people have been affected by that decision. Testimonials posted by Tufts, for instance, include a Colombian nephrologist, a tuberculosis and HIV researcher from El Salvador, a Spanish instructor of law and diplomacy, a physiology professor from Iraq, and a Brazilian faculty member interested in infectious diseases. The Brazilian professor is sharing the content he finds in the Tufts OCW with other medical schools in Brazil. His online testimonial says that, "With the tremendous changes that we are seeing in medicine, we need to have a network to discuss and share experiences." A learning technology instructor from Turkey praised Tufts's social responsibility and concern for the people of the world. As he put it, "I think OCW and online learning are key for the world's peace."

As hoped, there are also many self-learners using the materials. Such use includes someone from Greece interested in dentistry, a person from Mexico interested in veterinary medicine, and an eighty-five-year-old American man in the United States who recommended the site to other senior citizens as well as his granddaughter. Parents and students use the site too. One parent stated, "I feel that there is much valuable information here, and it can be of great benefit. . . . High school home educating gets tricky for a lot of us as suitable materials become harder to find." Such materials encourage people to think about the relevance of knowledge outside their primary disciplines and about how they might exchange information with others. They also provide examples of teaching approaches, which might foster reflection on better ways to deliver instruction.

Another notable OCW entry came in late 2007 when Yale University placed complete courses online in areas such as physics, psychology, religious studies, and political science in a project called Open Yale Courses, through which content from Yale is now available in streaming video or audio. In addressing the educational needs of developing countries, Yale officials have contracted to have their courses broadcast over Chinese television as well as a satellite network in India.[25] In addition, three hundred libraries around the world will have the Yale lectures available for viewing. For anyone not familiar with OCW or open educational resources, such figures are eye-opening.

A few months after Yale jumped into the fray, seven institutes in India, collectively known as the Indian Institutes of Technology or IITs, began posting a cornucopia of free lecture content in English to YouTube in early 2008. This is no announcement to yawn about. The IITs are known for training world-leading scientists and engineers and now that training is free for anyone. This project, called the National Programme on Technology Enhanced Learning or NPTEL, was intended to increase the quality of engineering education by providing supplemental Web content for more than one hundred courses. By late May 2008, more than eighteen hundred such video lectures were posted on topics including computer science and mechanical, electrical, and civil engineering. You can find courses in air pollution, basic electronics, computer graphics, tidal energy, quantum physics, fluid mechanics, and so much more.

In his blog, OpenCulture, Dan Colman, director and associate dean of Stanford University's continuing studies program, notes that with this announcement, MIT is no longer the only technology powerhouse that has placed its content online free to the world.[26] Colman is right, though I doubt the press related to MIT's OCW efforts will subside anytime soon. However, this does inspire ideas about how MIT and IIT courses might be combined or remixed in interesting ways. Just how will other universities that lack such experts employ the videos? And what happens when similar types of institutional powerhouses from countries such as Germany, Singapore, France, or Australia jump in?

OPEN ACCESS IS A HUMAN RIGHT

When it comes to the sharing and dissemination of educational content, we are witnessing one of the most exciting periods in human history. One can feel the exhilaration and boundless energy of this era. But this is just the start. We can all see that entry into the world of higher education, whether as an individual, department, organization, or community, just became easier. However, this content is typically not credentialed and often is simply lecture material or associated content to review. As such, it is what I call Level One Knowledge—

basic facts. Though not graded, it brings one to a base of learning that is often needed to survive in higher education. Anyone can dip their toes in these vast pools of open educational resources and find unknown talents, new interests, and possible careers.

There are many other OCW projects I could highlight, but suffice it to say, the opencourseware arena is no longer a one-man show. Not only are hundreds of universities pushing hard in the area of OCW, but similar activities are also underway in K–12 education. For instance, there are countless lesson plan sites for K–12 teachers as well as sites offering online mentoring and exchange portals and programs for their students. As the OCW gains momentum, anyone's course information may eventually be accessed by anybody around the world and potentially translated into any language. The possibility of anyone influencing the learning of anyone else is a sure sign that the education world is more open than ever before.

This is the initial wave in the quest for universal access to education. Self-service and customized online learning is a reality. The next step is governmental and organizational support, indexing, and marketing of such courses. Currently, too few people are aware of what is available and possible. As opencourseware access and awareness increases, we inch closer to fulfilling Article 26 of the Universal Declaration of Human Rights from sixty years ago that stated, "Everyone has a right to education. Education should be free, at least in the elementary and fundamental stages."[27] Knowledge in mathematics, physics, art, photography, history, and literature lies at our fingertips. Open distance education has made this possible. Humans are paving the way for other humans to learn. We are learning creatures. And the sooner we all come to fully comprehend that truth, the sooner we will push ahead and celebrate agendas such as OER and OCW.

Grand plans for open access to education and open educational resources that were christened with the announcement from Charles Vest and added to by many others have created an atmosphere of openness in education not previously felt. Open-access journal articles, open courses, and open books make information more freely available to a public that craves still more information.

Organizations are springing up to help organize and market this content. For instance, the OpenCourseWare Consortium involves more than one hundred higher education institutions involved in the OCW movement. They plan to extend the reach of freely open content. Emerging at roughly the same time was the OER Commons, a free teaching and learning resource for K–12 as well as college courseware that anyone can use, tag, rate, and evaluate.

Perhaps landing in OER and OCW is like finding yourself sipping free cocktails at happy hour. Would you like some hors d'oeuvres to go with those cocktails? OERderves is a popular blog from the Hewlett Foundation that has funded many OER initiatives and meetings. Besides such OERderves, the Open Knowledge Foundation promotes this opening of free educational content at the national and international level so as to foster far-reaching social and technological benefits and thus an educational transformation. According to their Web site, they want "knowledge which anyone is free to use, re-use and redistribute without legal, social or technological restriction."[28]

For those looking to advance their education, the Online Education Database has compiled a list of the top one hundred open courseware projects for self-learners.[29] There are courses in such areas as visual quantum mechanics, plant biology, Mandarin Chinese, and electrical networks. Someday you or your children might be scanning and selecting from among these courses and self-designing a program of studies or degree. More recently, the OED generated a boldly titled article, "Skip the Tuition: 100 Free Podcasts from the Best Colleges in the World." This megalist includes top-tier institutions such as Duke, Harvard, Berkeley, and the University of Glasgow.[30] Not to be outdone, OpenCulture also boasts a Web site with a listing of 225 free online courses from great universities. If higher education is no longer affordable for you or your children, you might look here. Such free course resources could also be used in training busy employees who lack time, money, or the patience needed for traditional university classes.

Today these course contents might appeal to casual or informal learners. Want to hear an expert at Stanford give you the lowdown on stem cell research? Anyone can now listen to Christopher Scott, the executive director of Stanford's program on stem cells in society, lecture on his course, "Straight Talk about Stem Cells." This course, designed with the general public in mind, exposes the world to numerous ethical issues, political concerns, and scientific and technological possibilities.

And this is just one course! Podcasted courses are also available on business ethics, Kant, human emotion, and the future of the Internet.

Imagine learners who want a college degree gaining access to just these two lists from OED and OpenCulture. They could improvise a college education of their choice from some of the best institutions in the world. Whether they could legitimately note such a degree on their resumés is certainly highly debatable and controversial today. I predict that such practices will be more frequent and accepted in a decade or two as such courses become increasingly comprehensive, authentic, and interactive.

It will not be long now before such listings get turned into a repackaged curriculum as self-determined certificates or degrees. For this to happen, a consortium of OCW providers will likely have to approve of any remixing or repackaging of that content. And the degrees offered would more than likely have to be free. Still, it could happen. Perhaps within the coming decade such content will find accreditation and have approved reseller lists.

As a sign of things to come, in January 2009, Peer-to-Peer University (P2PU) was launched as a community of open study groups for short online courses lasting about six weeks. P2PU combines "sense-makers" who structure the online courses with "tutors" who then combine or facilitate them. And they will apparently do all this for free. Among its first courses are those on alternative energy, media in developing countries, nonfiction writing, and open economics. In an attempt to provide more personalized attention and community feel, P2PU classes range in size from eight to fourteen students. It may take a few years before we know whether this approach is successful, but there undoubtedly will be many innovative uses of all the free course content made available today.

More organizations and institutions will come on the scene during the next decade. Some of these will quickly turn into leading organizations of the twenty-first century. Others will not find needed traction and just as quickly cease to exist. Whether they find success or failure, they will all have global educational aspirations and goals. For Richard Smith, board member of the Public Library of Science, it has become a human rights issue in which academics have been enslaved for too long by traditional book publishers and others who attempt to hang on to the keys to knowledge.[31] In the twenty-first century such exclusive control over knowledge rights is being abolished. And the abolitionists are the advocates of open access, open source, and open educational resources.

There are many volunteer soldiers in this teaching and learning revolution. I can just point to a few of them—Yue, Vest, and Chu—in this chapter. For a minute, however, try to envision the thousands of such soldiers involved in these projects who are providing or translating the content to realize their respective learning nirvanas. They believe that knowledge is a public good, and when it is made freely and openly available, it is good for the public. The continued widening access to knowledge invites more people into the learning community instead of locking them out.

John Willinsky, author of *The Access Principle: The Case for Open Access to Research and Scholarship,* argues that access to knowledge is a basic human right. Open access has most certainly arrived.[32] We have extensive access to high-level scholarship and rich portals of knowledge. As will be shown in the next chapter, one can now learn online from past or present scholars from Cambridge, Princeton, MIT, and thousands of other educational organizations and institutions. And this learning can take place without having to spend years taking exams, applying for visas, and registering for the requisite programs. As the world of learning continues to open up, many leading thinkers will, fortunately or unfortunately, fade into the background—but new leaders will emerge to continue to debate, use, and reshape the valuable resources freely provided by others.

Such are the tensions and opportunities of the twenty-first century that have been made possible by new learning technologies. Open access is one of the key ingredients now helping all people to learn. It is a movement that is gaining ground and attention throughout the world. Many scholars no longer contribute their research and ideas in books and journal articles unless it is made openly available. They have made a stand. Publishers have been put on notice. Many are certainly on edge. How this plays out during the coming years will be interesting. I place my bet on the learners as the ultimate winners here. We are all learners for life. Open access to information will make technology-enabled knowledge sharing ubiquitous and help us all to learn.

Portals for the People

OPENER #5: LEARNING OBJECT REPOSITORIES AND PORTALS

THAT'S A LOT OF CALAMARI!

Opening the newspaper on April 30, 2008, I saw a picture of a colossal squid that was accidentally caught in Antarctica's Ross Sea in February 2007. At 495 kilograms, or 1,089 pounds, it was the largest such squid ever caught.[1] Certainly not something I would like to encounter under the sea. For more than a year, it baffled scientists who tried to figure out a way to safely thaw and examine it. So, this creature remained on ice at the Museum of New Zealand Te Papa Tongarewa in Wellington, New Zealand.[2] It was the first colossal squid ever to be examined whole. As the best preserved such specimen to date, the scientists were examining it live on the Internet, some of which was captured and posted by National Geographic News.[3] The Discovery Channel produced a live documentary of the thawing process and ongoing scientific investigation.[4]

This is a freaky moment in science. The colossal squid is the biggest of 100,000 different species of mollusk (including snails, octopus, clams, mussels, slugs, and so forth), and yet science knows hardly anything about it. It was caught by mistake by a fisherman and put on ice for later thawing and examination live on the Internet. How many species have gone from being relatively unknown to having worldwide exposure in a matter of seconds? That is what the Web offers. Pictures and news of exciting events give scientific research worldwide exposure.

Now throw in live video coverage of the historic event on the Internet as it unfolds, and it is a news item not just for a single day or week but for decades and perhaps centuries to come. What did they find? Initial reports tell us it is female. Not impressed? Okay, then, scientists discover that she has eyes nearly the size of soccer balls.[5] Still not impressed? How about the finding that it has light-emitting organs that may serve as a type of underwater cloaking device? Not every species can claim to have a translucent body! Live Internet documentation of these findings as well as continual updates in the daily news entice young learners and hobbyists into the realm of science.

Not every scientific finding is such an anomaly. You can only catch the largest, ugliest, or oldest creature once. Still, learners from young to old need on-demand access to information about different species. In the past, the way in which they accessed such information was from books and reference materials such as encyclopedias. Today those reference materials might be found in free online portals. As an example, I might look up the colossal squid in Wikispecies from the Wikimedia Foundation to find out more about its anatomy, range, and ecology.[6]

If one is concerned about the quality of information in a community-created site such as Wikipedia or Wikispecies, there are other options. For instance, there is now the Encyclopedia of Life (EOL) portal. EOL intends to be a source of information for all 1.77 million species of known life on Earth. EOL partners and affiliates want to index everything: all known types of trees, birds, mammals, insects, viruses, and fungi. EOL is a collaborative global effort involving natural history museums, research institutions, botanical gardens, and many highly dedicated individuals. EOL officials not only hope to inspire school-children to become interested in science, but also to make EOL a key resource for scientists, educators, academics, amateurs, and interested visitors. Armed with $50 million, EOL officials have amassed the equivalent of roughly five years of funding. Should such funding continue, this wonderful project is estimated to be completed in roughly ten years. As new species are discovered, more information will be added.

Wikispecies and EOL are attempts to provide instant access to all the species found on Earth. Other portals focus on particular types of species and, therefore, can foster depth or focus within an area. For instance, Audubon's Birds of America offers pictures and text of all the birds of America. Here, one can learn about the wild turkey, the mockingbird, the barn owl, and the Tennessee warbler. Some 435 different birds are organized and indexed online for anyone to learn from. Naturalist John James Audubon set out to paint every known species of bird he could find in North America in the early part of the nineteenth century, but he ran out of resources. Two centuries later, his dreams have nearly come to life for anyone with an Internet connection. And people can go back in time and purchase his engraved works online based on the original paintings.

Now imagine history, geography, or science projects that might tap into such information. Everywhere we turn, further information on a topic is available. The more that people can access and learn about different species of life, the greater the chance that the species can be protected. At the same time, as more factual information is made available to everyone, notions of what expertise is and what one needs to do to become an expert in a discipline will need serious rethinking and debate.

SEND ME TO THE MOOM

Are you are a fan of museums or museum education but short on time or money for travel? Have you been to the Vincent van Gogh Gallery in Amsterdam? How about the Museum of the History of Science in Oxford? And what about the Smithsonian Art Museum or one of the other Smithsonians in Washington, D.C.? Maybe you spent a day or two in New York and strolled through the Museum of Modern Art. Perhaps by chance you have traveled to Switzerland and seen the Museum of Design in Zurich.

You have done none of that, you say? No worries. Just mosey down to the Museum of Online Museums (MoOM) where you can instantaneously travel to online museums around the planet through links to online exhibits, collections, and galleries, all for free. At the MoOM Web site you can browse the finest in art, history, culture, and science. All of the above museums are there for you. The image libraries, current exhibits and events, and catalogues are all there. And many of these are now enhanced with downloadable podcasts and blogs about different resources on display.

These are exciting times for museums. The Smithsonian Institution has pushed museum education further with the announcement of its newest museum, The National Museum of African American History and Culture. This is not a traditional museum by any stretch of the imagination; in fact, for now it is online only. Items of interest include photographs, stories, and audio recordings of famous people in African American history. As a sign of the times, Smithsonian officials are taking advantage of the Web 2.0 by allowing site visitors to upload their own memories in the form of stories, pictures, and audio recordings.[7] They have also built in an interesting Web-like navigation tool, allowing the user to quickly view and access terms, people, and events that might be related to the resource she is currently viewing.

The actual groundbreaking for the physical museum will not begin until 2012. In the interim, the Web offers a way to learn about a key aspect of American history years before the commonly experienced learning environment—the museum—can be prepared. When someone asks what the Web can do that is different or unique, just think about this project. With such ingenuity, museum learning is opened up in a quicker and perhaps more interactive manner than what was possible before the Web.

Those wishing to travel deeper into African American history now have many cyber-avenues for their pursuits. The Amistad Digital Resource from Columbia University contains information on key people, rare photographs, captivating audio and video recordings, and relevant news clips. Extending the multimedia components further are informative time lines, interactive maps, excerpts of oral interviews, and expert commentaries. If that is not enough, there are links to still other Web resources. Amistad even embeds FBI documents and maps linked to recorded marches, speeches, and rallies. With such a rich multimedia resource, students can do more in-depth research, reading, and reflection. The first module of Amistad highlights 1954 to 1975 and the civil rights and Black Power movements of 1954 to 1975; the long-term intent is to provide a resource for African American history from the time of slavery to the twenty-first century.

Another site documenting the struggle for racial equality was launched by the University of Georgia in 2008. This site, too, contains the voices and images of a critical time period in American history. There is a video from September 1957 of the conflict surrounding the desegregation of Central High School in Little Rock, Arkansas. Other videos include Attorney General Robert F. Kennedy reporting in May 1963 on racial conflict in Birmingham, Alabama; Dr. Martin Luther King Jr. speaking to reporters in October 1964 after finding out he has won the Nobel Peace Prize; and Jimmy Carter, then governor of Georgia, discussing the unrest occurring in Columbus, Georgia, back in 1971. Such videos might be played in succession to recount history or to compare perspectives or leadership qualities. Or perhaps an innovative teacher might show some of them in reverse or somewhat randomly. So much is now possible!

Learning media abound in this site, including newspapers, diaries, reports, and financial and judicial records, to name a few. For educators, there are also instructional materials including teaching guides, worksheets, quizzes, timelines, and lesson plans. Such content is available by searching for specific events, people, or topics. The dozens of organizations and institutions that helped develop this content should be commended. What happens when other countries create similar portals related to periods of civil unrest, citizen protests, and rallies for freedom? Comparing and contrasting such content might nurture new and deeper levels of understanding among students. Richer ways of expressing one's learned competencies will emerge.

Across the Atlantic, the British Library, holder of more than 13 million books, 920,000 journal and newspaper titles, and 3 million sound recordings, is digitalizing some of its more illustrious contents. Turning the Pages, a project launched in 2004, includes digitalized reproductions of the actual works of prominent people. Among these are Leonardo da Vinci's notebook, Jane Austen's early works, Mozart's musical diary, and the first atlas of Europe. The oldest printed book, the *Diamond Sutra* from China in AD 868, can be thumbed through by anyone with an Internet connection. Other famous documents, such as the Magna Carta from England, the Gutenberg Bible from Germany, and the Rámáyana from India, are also available.

With Turning the Pages, you can read actual texts or hear audio versions of them. Studying the Renaissance? You can view the actual handwritten notes of da Vinci himself, and, if desired, magnify them or listen to an audio explanation of the items of interest on a particular page. At the Mozart site, you can listen to musical instruments from his time as well as hear stories of their import. You might also read a letter written by Florence Nightingale in 1855 or hear her voice from 1890. If that is not enough, interactive maps and timelines are provided for different time periods and religions so users can explore books and information pertinent to their interests or needs. Sacred texts from the ninth century might be compared to others from the thirteenth or fourteenth centuries.

This is an interactive experience where the learner can actually simulate grabbing and turning pages. With this one innovation, an explosion of self-study is possible. When resources such as Turning the Pages and two-leaf e-books become mainstream, self-study could morph into an apprenticeship from the master long after that person has passed away. As it exists, teachers of geography, history, religion, music, language, literature, politics, and science will find this site beneficial.[8] In the future, British Library officials expect individuals to post their observations and insights related to these materials to an archived online discussion forum and repository. Additionally, such resources will allow users to engage in discussions and debates with others exploring the same materials located anywhere in the world. Already, there are featured sites such as the one on the Rámáyana with podcasts, videos, reviews, and even associated sets of pictures using Flickr. For now, Turning the Pages sits as one of the more intriguing library sites ever created.

As other organizations adopt and extend this technology, information archiving will take on new meaning. That is only part of the learning potential here. When the original notes and ideas of the great minds of history are called up and juxtaposed or used to support an argument a student is making today regarding someone from centuries long ago, this is where learning and new knowledge will be elevated to new heights. New trains of thought or theories may be uncorked. No longer must learning pursuits immediately be relegated to second-class status with secondary sources. Now we have pages to turn from the original thinkers, authors, musicians, and history makers—turn a few and feel the power of primary data sources!

Though some might question the prominence of Western culture and male scientists, musicians, and writers displayed in this site and the limited artifacts from Eastern culture and women's history, Turning the Pages remains a highly significant venture. This, of course, is a work in progress. The vast collections of the British Library will continue to provide diverse cultural and historical examples. One thing that should be clear from leafing through its different resources is that each century we humans design new vehicles for learning. At times we inch our way into these learning avenues. In this early part of the twenty-first century, however, learning progress is no longer measured in inches but in miles. As the history of the known world is placed into our hands and within our eyes and ears, we owe a huge thank-you to British Library officials and librarians in all corners of this planet who launch such efforts.

When these endeavors are successful, learners can interact with vast stores of political, religious, and educational documents. They also come into contact with Darwin, Shakespeare, Mozart, Einstein, and da Vinci as if they were the first to stumble upon their letters, notes, and ideas. In some cases, they may witness the creative process in action and notice that inspiration is not always divine but takes many failed efforts, extended rethinking, and thousands of hours of perspiration. Real people from another time and place spring to life in an instant as role models and leaders of a field or invention. Such digital artifacts might inspire the next generation of Florence Nightingales, William Blakes, and Jane Austens.

DIGITIZING DARWIN

Perhaps you are interested in explorers or biologists instead of artists, musicians, psychologists, and politicians. There are plenty of free online resources for you as well. Though Google and the OCA may be in the process of scanning Darwin's *The Origin of the Species*, on April 17, 2008, Cambridge University Library announced a new site with the first draft of that famous book, which had never previously been made public.

Cambridge officials also have created a momentous resource titled, The Complete Works of Charles Darwin Online. This portal is intended for anyone wanting to access Darwin's private notes, field notes, experiments, publications, and research. Darwin changed the world with his thoughts and ideas and now, some two hundred years after his birth, anyone can delve deep into his thinking. There are also family pictures, newspaper clippings, and his wife's cookbook. Some twenty thousand content items and ninety thousand images are available at this one site; imagine the tasks and activities that teachers could assign or students might select.

Dr. John van Wyhe, director of the site and a historian of science at the University of Cambridge, noted that for the first time ever the general public will be able to see just how meticulous Darwin's research endeavors were. Dr. van Wyhe believes the release of all these works in one accessible site is a revolution in public access to information. He is right. As shown in this chapter, there is quite a revolution going on and we are all taking part in it each time we enter the Web.

As I explored the Darwin site, I was reminded of a similar site I chanced upon a couple of years before from another equally prominent scientist. This one, the Einstein Archives Online, provides access to forty-three thousand records of Albert Einstein as well as related documents. In addition, high-quality digitized images exist for three thousand examples of his writings. The Einstein portal includes his scientific as well as nonscientific writings, professional and personal correspondence, notebooks of his research, travel diaries, and personal documents. A healthy portion of these are digital documents in his original German handwriting. To boost its utility, English language translations exist for many of the documents. Once again, it is exciting to be able to encounter such thinking and life work so directly and expediently.

You might wonder about copyright claims on the works of these scientific geniuses. Free access to the historical works of scientists from the 1800s such as Darwin is not too surprising because copyright lapses seventy years after death. Darwin passed away in 1882. While seventy years have not yet elapsed since Einstein's death in 1955, many of his works no longer have copyright attached to them either. Those seeking more clarity related to copyright for online materials might browse the Center for Intellectual Property at the University of Maryland University College as well as Creative Commons.

These are but two brief examples of what is available in a Web portal devoted to scientific thinkers. What happens when the Web makes digital documents of billions of people available? How will it be archived, used, and discussed? Can the archiving process be made so effortless and storage costs so low that in a decade or two we might all have digital archives of our own lives for others to browse? With personal homepages, this is already happening. Will anyone be listening to your voice recordings a hundred or a thousand years from now? And what might they do with such information?

Looking for other materials from the times of Darwin and Einstein? In late 2007, the journal *Nature* announced a complete digital archive of its first eighty years, from 1869 to 1949. It had already made the issues since that time available online. That amounts to 417,000 articles from 6,617 issues in 384 volumes. This adds up to a lot of free science from the past 140 years to be searched, read, and reused. In these volumes, you can explore scientific breakthroughs and interesting forecasts. You might read about inventors such as Alexander Graham Bell and his creation of the telephone. You can also read about Australian anatomist and anthropologist Raymond Dart, who discovered a key fossil of Australopithecus in northwestern South Africa.[9] Science, history, or entrepreneurship classes might spend entire semesters exploring *Nature* online and yet only scratch the surface of what is there.

The Darwin and Einstein sites are highly impressive, but *Nature* grants the user a noticeably broader picture of science during the past two centuries. Given that there are few Darwins and Einsteins in the world, the figures and events found in the *Nature* site are more representative of science and more broadly display the issues of importance across the past fourteen decades.

For those who simply want to explore the history of science, technology, and industry, there is much, much more. Do you hear the ECHO? Exploring and Collecting History Online, or ECHO, contains links to more than five thousand Web sites. Mathematics, life sciences, medical and behavioral sciences, business and industry— the history of these fields and more is indexed there.

ECHO is coordinated by the Center for History and New Media at George Mason University. You can browse content by historic period from ancient to more modern times. You can also dive right into a particular domain such as aviation and space exploration and visit the Goddard Space Flight Center. Alternatively, you can learn about early aviation including the history of hot air ballooning or helicopters. ECHO organizers have designed this not just to be a referatory or a set of Web links. Instead, they provide annotations of what you will find before you launch off into a site. Deciding your path in computers and information technology can lead you to extensive information on Alan Turing, the man known for helping crack secret Nazi codes during World War II as well as for proposing the Turing Test of machine (now computer) intelligence. ECHO can also be searched by the type of content, such as images, audios, videos, exhibits, and biographies.

When in ECHO, there is a sense that the history of much of the world is in one's hands. Learning opportunities are supercharged!

ECHO creators want multiple voices to come through so that history is accessible and relevant to multiple audiences. As stated on their Web site, ECHO's mission at the broadest perspective is "to fulfill the potential of digital media and networks to create a more democratic history." When you have thousands of sites of free historical content, it becomes more possible to achieve such goals.

THE PLOS FACTOR: OPEN ACCESS SCIENCE JOURNALS

Portals to Darwin and Einstein and macro portals such as ECHO embody the rich history of science and humankind. Now what of current cutting-edge science? The costs of accessing such work from the books and journals of traditional scientific publishing houses reached ridiculous levels in the last few decades. In response to this problem came the Public Library of Science (PLOS). PLOS is a nonprofit organization of scientists and physicians who are committed to providing freely available scientific and medical literature and research. There are PLOS journals in the areas of genetics, biology, medicine, pathogens, and neglected tropical diseases. Accessing and reading published articles is free, but PLOS receives fairly hefty fees (around $2,000 to $2,500) from those who publish in their journals. Such fees can be waived, however, for those who lack sufficient financial resources.

The goal of PLOS is to open the doors to scientific knowledge by giving it away. Now students, instructors, patients, scientists, and physicians can have access to the latest knowledge in a field and use, share, and discuss it in highly innovative ways. No longer are biology and medical journals too costly for the average person. Anyone with access to the Web can find, scan, outline, and debate research findings and new initiatives. As the PLOS Web site indicates, the doors are now open to scientific knowledge.

I'm Connexing You

Portals provide access to information, typically through links. Portals, also called referatories, hyperlink educators and learners directly to content and resources. One exciting portal that is used by tens of thousands of educators in higher education is MERLOT. This site contains links to peer-reviewed resources from nearly any discipline imaginable. Each one is available with a simple mouse click. Add to that an annual conference, newsletter, journal, and discipline-specific communities, and MERLOT is one of the finest and richest-tasting resources of the shared Internet. In the past, newly hired college instructors could only dream about a resource like MERLOT. Not anymore.

Beyond referatories such as MERLOT are repositories of learning-related content and objects. They are like refrigerators of assorted foods that you can grab and enjoy when needed. Once a needed learning object is located in such a repository, it can be viewed, remixed, and repeatedly tasted. In such a system, the user can take different ingredients and put them together to form whatever meal they want.

Different pieces of educational content, such as a PowerPoint slide show, an audio clip, a video, a picture, or a text document, can be tagged and reused by anyone with access to the repository. You can use and combine the items where it makes sense given your instructional goals. If carefully and creatively designed, the final product will be easily updated with fresh contents as they become available. It will also be reusable across learning environments and platforms should your organization decide to employ a new delivery system.

One repository that was popular at the start of the century came from Canada. It was called the Campus Alberta Repository of Educational Objects or CAREO. More recently, people seem to be heading to Houston, Texas, albeit virtually. Houston is home to a fast-growing repository of academic scholarly materials and resources called Connexions, which was launched in 1999 by Rice University.

Not only is Connexions a global open-access repository of information, but it also contains a powerful set of free software tools to help authors publish and collaborate. The ultimate goal is for anyone on this planet to have access to high-quality educational content at any time and from any location. Learners around the planet can use Connexions to create, download, share, mix, and burn educational content including course modules, textbooks, documents, simulations, animations, and other learning materials.

Richard Baraniuk is the founder and one of the chief architects of Connexions. Baraniuk has engineering degrees from the University of Manitoba, the University of Wisconsin, and the University of Illinois;

was named one of *Edutopia Magazine's* "Daring Dozen" educators in 2007; and is a NATO postdoctoral fellow.[10] He spoke at the famous TED (Technology, Entertainment, Design) Conference in Monterey, California, in 2006 where he opened up for Peter Gabriel. Baraniuk also is the recipient of countless awards and honors.

According to Baraniuk, by September 2006 Connexions had 17 million user hits, 1.2 million page views, and 520,000 unique users from 157 different countries. He remarked that the course collections had grown 30 percent over the preceding six months. In early January 2009, Baraniuk informed me that Connexions contained 425 collections (including courses and books) and nearly 8,000 course modules. Given that by October 2008 there were over 45 million user hits, two million page views, and over one million unique users representing more than two hundred different countries, it was clear that these contents were highly popular. These course modules spanned such areas as engineering, physics, computer science, botany, and statistics. Many of the modules were for highly specialized domains such as nanotechnology, biodiversity, and bioinformatics. There were many resources for history, mathematics, and music instructors. Using these assorted resources and tools, instructors can more effectively build and share custom courses. More than that, any curious onlooker can download and use them.

The philosophy behind Connexions is one of collaborative development, free and open sharing, and publishing on the Web. The content contained there is intended for everyone from young children to college students to working professionals. The small modules that one might find in Connexions can be reorganized into larger collections, modules, or courses. All materials it contains are free and open to reuse by anyone under the "attribution" license from Creative Commons. The developers suggest that content supplied to Connexions be nonlinear and modular, thereby offering more opportunities for learners to discover their own connections across it and build their own relationships. Instead of learning isolated knowledge fragments from books or classes, learners can explore multiple resource nuggets and generate their own meanings.

The basic motto for Connexions, as with all sites mentioned in this chapter, is that "Sharing is good." In addition, the Connexions philosophy is one of collaboration between those creating content so as to generate still more content. And all content in Connexions is stored in XML so that it is accessible across computer platforms.

Back in 1999 when it was launched, Connexions was originally called the "Secret Web Initiative." Some secret! It grew from just two hundred modules during this hush-hush phase in 2000 to nine hundred in 2002, from twenty-three hundred in 2004 to more than five thousand by January 2008, and a year after that to some seventy-seven hundred modules. And it is not limited to English-speaking countries or users from North America. Connexions users come from around the planet. By 2005, it had content in Chinese, English, Japanese, Portuguese, Spanish, and Thai. Clearly, it is no longer a clandestine effort.

This extensive growth indicates that Connexions is on to something. Educators have always wanted to share. Today they are sharing thousands of free educational items with unlimited access. And millions of people on planet Earth are browsing, using, and repurposing the content that they have shared. When thousands of course materials are accessed by millions of users, it is a sure sign of a learning revolution. Baraniuk's own materials on signal processing in Connexions have been viewed by more than two million users. That is more people than most engineering professors could ever hope to reach in their entire careers. And translations of his work to Spanish extend its global audience even further.[11] Clearly, online access is becoming the platform for textbooks and most educational materials of the twenty-first century.

As with any popular online resource where educational content is shared, there are people whose careers have been affected in a highly positive way. One such person is Catherine (aka Kitty) Schmidt-Jones. By November 2007, Kitty had contributed 174 music and music-theory modules and twelve courses to Connexions. The impact has been enormous. Her online music courses have been used by thousands of people and her teaching materials have been viewed more than seven million times.[12] Kitty undoubtedly never dreamed of teaching so many people when she got her teaching license. Unlike much of the higher education content at Connexions, her work is intended for a K–12 audience.

Kitty's content currently averages six hundred thousand visits per month.[13] With the Web, she has become a global K–12 music teacher. She has been contacted by parents helping their children in the United

States as well as by teachers in Uganda, Scotland, Canada, Japan, and India. Inquiries come from self-learners of music as well as those enrolled in high school or college music courses. Kitty is now considering publishing hard-copy versions of some of her content. The popularity of her virtual content has given her a platform and status in the physical world. She envisions the day when a site like Connexions might have enough curriculum materials to design a complete K–12 music curriculum. An e-mail from Kitty in February 2008, noted:

> When I first started publishing lessons in Connexions, it never occurred to me that my materials would have such a large impact. I imagined at most that they would do what I was hoping they would do: encourage other teachers who are not professors to also get involved with Connexions. I envision a time, not too far off, maybe when my grandkids (who don't exist yet) are in school, when teachers automatically go to the Web not only to design an up-to-date, affordable text that is precisely tailored to their syllabus and teaching methods, but also to get extra materials for students who need extra challenges or extra help. When that's not enough, the students themselves can get on the Web and look at a half-dozen different explanations of the concept they are having trouble with, many of which will include helpful movies, animations, and games as well as more examples, problems, pictures and diagrams. And of course, lots of it will be in Connexions.

The possible uses of Connexions are endless. A decade ago, there was no such repository. Times have changed. The human species as a whole has shifted from learning in silos to learning with others and readily sharing what one has learned. When people share by using tools like Connexions, we have entered a golden age of learning. The education world is more open and rich with learning opportunities for everyone connected to the Web. And it no longer needs to be a secret!

A Wiki of a Curriki

Sites like PLOS, and to some extent Connexions, are highly valuable for instructors in higher education who are searching for content or looking to share their ideas. But what about content for K–12 students? A few years ago, one of the cofounders of Sun Microsystems, Scott McNealy, discovered that no such sharing site existed that was devoted to K–12 content. When helping one of his sons on a third-grade science project, he spent many hours combing the Web for content that might provide an engaging explanation of basic electricity. Unfortunately, the only valuable resource he could find was geared to welders, not youth. McNealy soon realized how unorganized online content was for K–12 teachers and students and set out to do something about it. He also realized that kids today rely on technologies like iPods, cell phones, and laptops for their information needs, not on traditional hardcover books.

As the CEO and chairman of a company committed to online education and open source software, his next step, though quite bold, was plain for him to see. In 2004, he led Sun's effort to create the Global Education and Learning Community (GELC). Two years later, GELC became an independent nonprofit company renamed as Curriki.

Curriki represents the unique combination of two names, "wiki" and "curriculum." As a wiki curriculum, Curriki is Web-based, self-paced, open source, and free.[14] With those four attributes, it easily passes any litmus test that might be designed for the WE-ALL-LEARN model. Curriki intends to provide universal access to free K–12 curricula and associated instructional materials and assessments. With an open source approach to educational content, others can use, tag, change, and remix the educational materials contributed by members. The overriding focus is not on the children of Silicon Valley technology executives; instead, Curriki intends to reduce the digital divide in the United States and around the world. If successful, Curriki can break down many key barriers to education for kids around the globe.

On Monday, March 26, 2007, I sat next to Dr. Bobbi Kurshan, executive director of Curriki, during dinner at an open educational resources institute at Rice University. Dr. Kurshan informed me that Curriki provides a practical alternative to the traditional publishing industry. And it struck a chord with educators as it had attracted more than fifteen thousand users in just a few months. She explained to me that, like Wikipedia, the content at Curriki can grow organically as users edit and update the material provided there. If interested, individuals can join existing groups that are creating materials on a particular topic, or they can form their own groups or topic areas. A three-tier system is used to help users browse existing content, ranging from that which has yet to be reviewed by the Curriki team to that which has been reviewed and deemed "premiere."[15] Both master teachers and the Curriki community review posted content. As is evident, there are many quality controls embedded in this system.

When I checked in with Bobbi again some fourteen months later in late May 2008, the numbers she provided confirmed that Curriki had been welcomed by the global community. Since its launch, more than forty thousand teachers, parents, and students had registered at the site. There were thirteen thousand learning assets or courses already uploaded to the Curriki repository and another ten thousand coming up the pipeline. Curriki was a hit in places like India, South Africa, Indonesia, and the United Kingdom. The site had been translated into Hindi, French, Bahasa (Indonesian), and Spanish. It is becoming quite international. In fact, thirty-five of the top forty cities where it was in use were places outside the United States. McNealy pointed out that those in other countries are excited because they cannot afford to build such a site, at least not at this time.[16] Curriki training evaluations indicate that it leads to greater use of information and communications technology in schools. Curriki also fostered school reflections on technology infrastructure, collaborative professional development, and new technology programs.

When I talked to Bobbi about this book and the WE-ALL-LEARN model, she told me: "Curriki is now actively building a community that is providing content that can be customized to meet the needs of the learner and the teacher. Curriki is truly a transformative idea that leverages the strength of the network and the multiplier effect of the community where WE-ALL-LEARN. It is a powerful resource for students, parents, and teachers globally that will significantly change the way we think about teaching and learning."

There is much hope for resources like Curriki. They can provide a role in regions of the world lacking qualified instructors and high-quality content in key disciplines, or in places where the cost of obtaining that content (that is, textbooks) has gotten out of reach. They can provide the triggering mechanism for educators in different locations to collaboratively build content that is more enriching than what they might be able to accomplish individually. Many creative talents can be shared and coalesced and then reshared with others. These sites also provide curriculum standards that can be judged, discussed, compared, and negotiated. And they allow students to grasp the work required to master a set of skills or competencies.

For those with Internet connections or the capability to access content downloaded to a CD, memory stick, or some other computer storage device, learning is no longer deemed available only in a secret club for the privileged elite. Contents for math, science, foreign language, health, and many other areas can potentially help anyone whether they are in Bahrain, Belarus, or Bhutan.

In mid-June 2008, Scott McNealy told me:

> Sharing creates greater economic opportunity, and it's a strategy that my company, Sun Microsystems, has employed for 26 years to spread adoption of our technology. We realized that, while it's one thing to share, or "open source" our operating systems, productivity suites and spreadsheets, we should be applying this sharing strategy to something much more important—K–12 education. Just like the written and spoken language of computing, knowledge should not be proprietary.
>
> Wikipedia killed the encyclopedia. Google made the card catalog obsolete. We believe Curriki can have the same impact on textbooks and other K–12 learning materials, the cost of which is the single biggest barrier for poor communities trying to provide children with a basic education. In the U.S. alone, we spend more than \$4B every year just on K–12 textbooks. Our goal is to get that cost as close as possible to zero, around the world, so those funds can be redirected to programs and resources that help every teacher, student and parent succeed.

People such as Scott McNealy and organizations such as Sun Microsystems are not alone in reaching out to education from the corporate space. Intel and Cisco, for instance, are each well known for their education-related initiatives benefiting teacher training and technology integration ideas on many continents. Cisco even has a global education initiative geared toward the eventual world of Education 3.0 that will be enabled by technology and systemic school reform efforts. At the same time, IBM is attempting to address the critical shortage of math and science teachers with a program to help experienced employees who decide to leave IBM to transition to jobs as accredited teachers. And as many are aware, the Bill and Melinda Gates Foundation funds a wide range of exciting and important school-related projects for underserved populations and neighborhoods in the United States, as well as global libraries and enhanced technology access for those in many developing countries.

These are but a few brief examples. The point is that corporate giving to education is a key component of any success from models such as WE-ALL-LEARN. And such giving will likely increase over time as technology-related companies help schools and institutions ramp up more quickly than they could on their own.

STILL IN A STATE OF CONFUSION?

We have woven our way through a number of useful Web resources as well as fascinating learning portals, referatories, and repositories. We have traveled through just a few of the countless educational resources available today, many of which did not exist a decade ago, or in some cases, even a month ago. The soaring use of Web sites such as MERLOT, Connexions, and Curriki is a testament to the importance of creating high-quality online resources that are accessible, sharable, and reusable.

Certainly this is just a start. For all of us to learn, we need these types of free online educational content and resources for learners across the world—resources for any age group, any educational level, any race or ethnic group, and any language. Such resources provide the pages to be delivered in the pipes of a new participatory learning culture. What exists so far is evidence of the turbocharged speed in which educational contents have been made available to the learners of this planet. It has only been a little more than a decade since most educators paid notice to what the Web can offer. Think about the landscape of possibilities that might be available a decade from now.

With all the free and open source content available, it gets complex and confusing to know where to go online and what to do. When I first outlined the ideas for this book, my colleague Dr. Grace Lin confirmed this confusion. According to Grace's research, each of these portals and resources has a different mission, set of contributors, funding plan, audience, and distinguishing features. For instance, some resource developers have explicit goals to simply provide links to resources or searchable databases. Others want to transform education by creating a community of like-minded educators who freely share their educational content. Some resources target needs in higher education, whereas others are designed for K–12 schools, government organizations, or corporate training. It takes a lot of time to sort all this out. This chapter covers less than one-half percent of what is out there to use.

Quality is also an issue. Some sites rely on expert reviews and prestigious universities, whereas others use volunteers who may not have any credentials or degrees. Although some online content goes through rigorous review processes and criteria, far too many resources are a hodgepodge of links that someone found and decided to index. At the same time, there always seem to be resources you happen to stumble upon that are exciting and dynamic and that might help you in the production of new knowledge as well as the creative remixing of it. Still others are locked down, static sites that exist solely for personal consumption. Naturally, there are also different languages, cultural norms, and licenses for the uses of the content.

Of course, funding is always an issue. Some of the sites outlined in this chapter have corporate, government, or higher education sponsors. Others, like OOPS, mentioned in the previous chapter, are primarily funded through personal monies.

It is quite a chaotic mix. And there is no one magical formula to success. Given these differences, it is difficult to draw definitive conclusions about what does or does not work. But I can offer questions to guide your thinking about this area. For instance, who will maintain or update these sites? Will learning objects and portals created today still find use in another decade or century? How can alternative uses not imagined by the designers be planned for or worked into existing knowledge-sharing sites and tools? And who will coordinate such planning? It is also vital to consider how far knowledge-sharing tools will advance in the coming decades. Can they bridge the extensive digital divide that still exists around the globe? And will sharing of such content become part of every professional educator's job description?

Even more complex are the collaborations and partnerships that are derived from these knowledge-sharing resources. Might projects and organizations such as OOPS, CORE, the IITs, and other institutions offering OCW mentioned in the previous chapter, collaborate and share content with referatories and repositories such as Connexions and Curriki? If free is free, what is stopping them?

At the most basic level, one must ask, "For what purpose will people share?" Will community-sharing trends that we presently see in You-Tube, Wikipedia, Current TV, and MySpace continue? If they do, how will different countries and regions of the world deal with copyright issues as such sites evolve and push the boundaries of intellectual property rights? And what happens when someone did not mean to share an educational resource or content, but thousands of people find it in an online Web site and start sending thank-you letters or recommendations for improvement?

Although so many questions remain to be asked and answered, this particular opener has in many ways already transformed learning possibilities across educational sectors with an enormous wealth of learning resources and materials. The learning portals, referatories, and repositories are far too extensive to document in any one chapter. As such, one must really look to other books and resources to become better acquainted with such educational resources. Or one might simply explore the Web.

Making a Contribution

OPENER #6: LEARNER PARTICIPATION IN OPEN INFORMATION COMMUNITIES

AN HOUR IN SAN FRANCISCO

On March 7, 2008, at 3:30 AM I reached over to turn off my alarm. Time for a quick morning run before heading to the Indianapolis airport with my son, Alex. In a few hours, we would be getting off our plane and jumping in a taxi for a visit to a nonprofit organization that was new to San Francisco but hardly new to the world.

This organization exemplified much of what this book is about—the creation of free and open access educational materials by anyone. No limits on access, use, sharing, or contributions. There was room for everyone. Speak Polish or Hindi? No problem! This is one company that would surely accommodate you. Need to find subway schedules in San Francisco? This place had that information as well. We were headed to 39 Stillman Street—the new headquarters of Jimmy Wales and the Wikimedia Foundation. For those who do not realize it, the Wikimedia Foundation includes Wikipedia and a series of other wiki-related projects.

Wikimedia had recently moved its offices from St. Petersburg, Florida, to San Francisco, which had won out over such places as Boston, New York, Washington, D.C., and London. The talent pool and investment dollars of the Bay Area were too attractive. Besides, the free and open culture of San Francisco was the same one that online communities like Wikipedia were tapping into.

What we did not realize is that we would be just the third outsiders to visit their new nerve center in the South of Market or SoMa district of San Francisco. This is the area where many dot-coms had been located during the boom of the late 1990s. Wikimedia's office space was nothing spectacular. There were ten people working there with talk of expansion to a grand total of twelve soon. This is clearly not Boeing, GE, Ford, or Lilly. For online learning organizations that rely on users donating their time and talents without remuneration, expansion often comes in ones and twos rather than hundreds or thousands of people at a time. Life at a nonprofit foundation providing free wiki-related resources appeared to be extremely exciting, yet at the same time, relatively quiet. The scene reminded me of a typical start-up technology company in a business incubator.

During our hour with Mike Godwin, general counsel for Wikimedia, and Sue Gardner, their recently hired executive director, we discussed various topics including alternative revenue streams, the Wikimedia community, future directions, employee growth, and the upcoming Wikimania conference in Alexandria, Egypt. A time line on the wall showed the peak moments in Wikipedia history from initial ideas to the founding, the first Wikimania Conference, and the recent move. But none of that really mattered to us. What mattered was that, for that one hour, we stepped into an organization that had revolutionized ideas related to access to information, the permanence of ideas, expertise, quality standards for information, knowledge authority, information sharing, and the ownership of knowledge. They were rebels in the knowledge industry, though, it seemed, somewhat quiet rebels. Satisfied that we had made the pilgrimage to this holy land of knowledge sharing, we were off.

2.0 DOWNES TO GO

Organizations such as the Wikimedia Foundation and the work that they do illustrate that the times are changing. As my friend Stephen Downes at the National Research Council of Canada observed: "E-learning as we know it has been around for ten years or so. During that time, it has emerged from being a radical idea—the effectiveness of which was yet to be proven—to something that is widely regarded as mainstream. It's the core to numerous business plans and a service offered by most colleges and universities. And now, e-learning is evolving with the World Wide Web as a whole and it's changing to a degree significant enough to warrant a new name: E-learning 2.0."[1]

According to Downes, the Internet has been transformed during the current decade. It has evolved from a highly popular medium for information transmission and consumption to a platform through which content is created, shared, remixed, repurposed, and passed along by its participants to potential users. This is the age of the Web 2.0. Learners finally have a voice in their own learning activities. In line with John Dewey's ideas, Downes notes that this is often referred to as learner-centered or student-centered design.[2] And he cautions that such approaches do not simply appease a student's learning preferences or give her control over the screen layout or font size, but instead actually empower her by placing learning in her hands.

Ten years ago, most of the action in e-learning was centered around the posting of content. One might take a traditional course and shovel it to the Internet. According to Michael Jensen, director of strategic Web communications for the National Academies, content was king during the heyday of the Web 1.0, roughly 1992 to 2002, in part because there was an assumed scarcity of it.[3] It was vital that authorities create and endorse the quality of such content, which was used in learning or course management systems in higher education and corporate training. Today, instead of these information transmission and consumption models, learners can find, design, mix and remix, repurpose, and select content to share. In contrast to the information scarcity of previous ages, the Web 2.0 harnesses the collective intelligence of individuals to situate us in a time of endless information abundance—the participatory learning age.

As Downes noted, learners no longer just passively read books or listen to a TV or radio program.[4] In this age, they create their own wikibooks; they produce their own news with Current TV; and they generate their own radio programs with syndicated podcasts. Learners also post comments about the books, news, and others' podcasts in their personal blogs or online discussion groups. Today, you may discuss a new book with a group of people who have also read it. And they might come from cities, villages, and regions of the world that you may never visit. It is people like

John Dewey and Seymour Papert who have paved the way for educators to understand and embrace the power of these tools and capabilities.

A decade ago, e-learning was words, words, and still more words. As folks like Downes are quick to point out, human learning is no longer just text. Since Plato first began to write down his ideas and offer them as a tool for learning, we have been in the throes of a text-centered world. Until the advent of the printing press, much of this textual world was only for the privileged.

WEB 2.0 OVERFLOW

I am constantly bombarded with e-mails from friends telling me of yet some other new Web 2.0 tool or Web site to check out. For example, there is Chinswing, which exploits online audio. Instead of narrating pictures, it is a tool for online language use and having conversations with people about different topics. Chinswing is a global message board for topic discussions in areas of personal interest; people can contribute information, debate ideas, and find answers to questions or issues that they are dealing with. It has the feel of a podcast, but is a more interactive one and includes some text forums. It is promoted as an entirely new way to talk and discuss issues, and it is.

The aims of Chinswing are noble—to serve as a mechanism or bridge to bring about social change. People from different races, cultures, religions, educational backgrounds, political climates, and geographic settings can come together to discuss topics of interest. It is an environment for constructive conversations on key issues facing us daily. As stated on the Chinswing Web site, "We all know that the world needs more communication between people of differing social, political and religious contexts—and Chinswing aims to provide that kind of bridge to bring about social change. So . . . let's change the world!"

Chinswing was developed in Melbourne, Australia, by Dean Worth. With this one invention, Worth did his part to change the world. When I chatted with Worth in February 2008, he noted that there were thousands of people using it for free, and that it was in the process of becoming more group oriented.

Tools such as Chinswing increase the throughput of learning. Instead of a mere 50 words per minute in a typical text forum post, Worth says that most people can speak 160 words in a minute. And because the words are recorded and can be replayed, it is time independent. Traditional discussion forums have a permanency of text that can be revisited, reused, and reviewed. Voice message board systems can also be revisited, but there is something unique here. There is an instant sense that you know the person with whom you are communicating that comes from the personal voice message and a small picture next to the recording. People address each other by first names and come back to explain their points or to answer new questions or issues that have arisen in the conversation. It is quick, simple, rich, and meaningful. Tools like this give hope that the people of this world will one day understand each other better. Anyone is a teacher, tutor, friend, debater, or conversational partner in Chinswing.

At present, people can insert comments and questions on a vast range of Chinswing topics such as computer networking, religion, health, business and finance, science and nature, society and culture, recreation, and arts and entertainment. In the "Education" category, there are audio threads related to teaching online, teaching in virtual worlds, and the Classroom 2.0. One thread on poetry has people reading different poems that they or others have written. The conversations may be intense for a day or spread out over several days, weeks, or months.

Another example is dotSUB, which is a tool for adding subtitles in any language to online videos. If you happen to be teaching students in another country whose first language is not English, you can now create subtitles in their native tongue with this tool. Alternatively, you might experiment with having students create the subtitles. Even those whose first language is English can benefit from seeing the text, as well as hearing the video.

Then there is something called YackPack. With YackPack you can send out audiofiles via e-mail. YackPack notices might be sent to particular people or to entire groups. Such a tool might be used for practicing new language skills and abilities. It might also be employed for course announcements, small group work updates, and expert commentary on educational products.

These are exciting times to be a learner or a teacher. All of these tools are essentially asynchronous, allowing the learner to use them when time and energy permit. Equally important, those who do not perform well in a synchronous classroom setting, where they might be put on the spot, have a chance to perform at a higher level here, as they are allowed more time to reflect and think about what they might say or add. With many of these tools, teams can interact and negotiate ideas across time and space. Further, such activities are typically more engaging and appealing to learners; spontaneous bursts of informal learning can transpire at any time. Learners can be united by interesting events or shared histories as well as by topics and ideas of common interest. Geographical distances and time zone differences no longer constrain their interactions.

YOU CAN YOUTUBE TOO!

Like many Web 2.0 tools and resources, YouTube is a highly interesting social phenomenon. Created in mid-February 2005, it soon attracted millions of daily visitors. On October 9, 2006, it was bought by Google for a mere $1.65 billion in stock. It currently ranks fourth in Web traffic on Alexa, behind only Yahoo!, MSN, and Google. YouTube demonstrates the need for tools that allow individuals to generate content rather than simply passively browse content online. That leads us to the "LEARN" portion of WE-ALL-LEARN.

Some caution that systems such as YouTube can bring down the Internet unless capacity is expanded and compression technology is more frequently employed. There is little doubt that YouTube is sucking up Internet bandwidth like a high-powered Hoover vacuum cleaner; in fact, it has grown from twenty thousand video downloads per day at the start of 2006 to sixty-five thousand daily in January 2007.[5] One six-minute video called *The Evolution of Dance* had more than 57 million downloads between April 2006 and September 2007. By late February 2009, this video had been viewed over 115 million times.

In 2008, YouTube became even more of a bandwidth hog. Approximately one-third of Internet users in the United States, some seventy-nine million people, watched more than three billion YouTube videos in the month of January alone.[6] This equates to some thousand gigabytes of data each second from YouTube, or nearly three hundred billion gigabytes each month. By April 9, 2008, Stephen Downes noted that it had over eighty-three million videos and 3.75 million channels.[7] According to a July 2008 article in *Newsweek* that likened the Internet to a gargantuan, virtual sweatshop, ten hours of content is uploaded to YouTube each minute, or roughly the equivalent of fifty-seven thousand full-length videos each week.[8] When I conducted a Google search on "YouTube" on July 4, 2008, I got more than 1.1 billion hits. Small wonder some refer to YouTube as the "King Kong" of online video.[9]

Video is a heavy user of Internet resources. According to Professor Michael Kleeman, senior fellow at the USC Annenberg Center for Communication, one minute of video downloading takes up ten times the bandwidth of voice.[10] To put this in perspective, Kleeman points out that in July 2007 alone, *The Evolution of Dance* video generated the equivalent of one month of the entire data network traffic on the Internet in 2000.[11] What happens if five, ten, or a hundred such videos become equally popular in YouTube or some other system? Will the government come in and shut down YouTube as well as similar online video vendors? Will citizens be given online traffic warnings or tickets for causing such accidents and chokepoints? And what happens as millions or perhaps billions of additional citizens of the Earth are granted Internet access that enables them to cruise that information superhighway? As such individuals create, watch, share, subscribe to, or comment on YouTube videos, what will happen to the quality of service? What happens when one billion Internet users becomes two or three billion, or perhaps even more?

Will YouTube interfere with business and government use of the Internet and thereby slow economic growth? As Kleeman notes, the Internet used to simply complement business and education. Today it is the principal vehicle in which business and education operate; they depend on it to survive. Just watch the frustrations of a business person or a student lacking Internet access for an hour, a day, or a week. Sales and marketing departments in many businesses generate their revenues online. And in the medical field, doctors often remotely access patient medical records and X-rays and may even correspond online with doctors in other countries for diagnoses and advice. What happens when social activities on YouTube and similar media constrain these vital activities in government, business, medicine, and education? Should silly dances and pirated snippets from soccer matches interfere with important business transactions and perhaps one day your own personal health?

Despite these concerns, many YouTube videos have real-world value. For example, shared online videos are finding uses in accounting firms where the demand for a high-quality workforce has never been greater.[12] Faced with huge talent shortages in 2007, the remaining "Big Four" accounting firms began to use shared online video as a way of recruiting new employees as well as a way to share their work culture and create social relations across global offices. Deloitte, for instance, had an employee film festival where teams of one to seven people created short videoclips that responded to the question, "What's your Deloitte?"[13] Amazingly, more than two thousand people participated in the filming process, and the best ones were selected for posting to YouTube. After watching a few of these (for example, *Is This Heaven? No, It's Deloitte*; *Dude, Where's My Proposal*; *Food for Thought*; and *He Doesn't Look Like an Accountant!*), I started to believe that even accountants can be creative. There is energy, passion, originality, thoughtfulness, and spontaneity reflected in each one of these. To further motivate Deloitte employees, there is even a designated "film festival guy" who appears in a "behind-the-scenes" YouTube video.

Posting these videos online, in effect, shares information about what is happening within Deloitte across different geographic regions and time zones. These short videos help create a sense of the work life of those in this company. YouTube enabled that to happen. One competition brought together nearly forty thousand Deloitte employees from across seventy-five of its offices on two continents. Another Big Four firm, Ernst & Young, ran a similar contest asking accounting students to explain why people should become accountants.[14] Beyond shared online video, firms such as Deloitte and KPMG are using Facebook as a means to get new hires to create social networks within the company. The rationale for this is quite simple. If employees feel a connection to others at work, it is less likely that they will leave the firm. In this way, Facebook and YouTube serve as employee retention and recruitment tools. At the same time, they are powerful vehicles for learning.

Although the news media often highlight the use of YouTube for entertainment, politics, sports, and self-promotion, there are an increasing number of educational, informational, and technological videos posted to the site. Such videos might be used directly in face-to-face class instruction as well as in supplemental activities after class. Moreover, as an empowering mechanism, students might be assigned to create a YouTube video as a class project.

Some create YouTube videos for simple information-sharing purposes or to experiment with the technology, whereas others want to contribute to the global education of the people of this planet. Just how much is the YouTube environment a part of people's daily lives? Some examples provided below might help in the explanation.

YOUTUBE: A COMMON CRAFT

In one set of YouTube videos designed by Lee and Sachi LeFever at Common Craft in Seattle, Lee explains emerging and complex technology in extremely simple ways using hand gestures, cute sayings, metaphors, and easily understood steps. For instance, one video compares creating a wiki to going on a camping trip. Another makes the connection between asking someone what they are currently doing and the goals and functions of Twitter. Want to know more about podcasting, wikis, social networking, RSS feeds, blogs, Twitter, or social bookmarking? Common Craft has free online videos on all of these topics and more—in plain English. Hundreds of thousands of people have viewed their *Wikis in Plain English* and *RSS in Plain English* videos through YouTube. Lee LeFever is their free online instructor available at a moment's notice. And he is using the Web 2.0 to teach about the Web 2.0.

When I spoke to Lee in late May 2008, he mentioned that the feedback on these videos has been amazing. In fact, people have used the dotSUB tool, mentioned earlier in this chapter, to subtitle Common Craft videos in twenty-seven different languages, including Arabic, Farsi, Greek, Indonesian, Maltese, and Vietnamese. While watching *Podcasting in Plain English*, for instance, you can switch from Turkish to French to Thai within seconds. One could conceivably play such a video in an international or multicultural class, and have it displayed on a large screen with multiple windows playing the same video with different subtitles below for the different nationalities represented in the room. Everyone could be on the same page and feel respected with such personalized learning. To date, more than half a million people have watched Common Craft's videos through dotSUB.

Nancy White from Full Circle Associates uses Common Craft videos in her international development work in places such as Ethiopia. During one such training event, Ethiopian students reacted extremely positively to them, even simulating Lee's fun-filled "Boo!" and "Yay!" lines from the Common Craft training videos.

With the emergence of freely shared educational videos such as these, "instructional materials" are no longer the province of certified teachers, instructional designers, and e-learning content vendors. Thoughtful and engaging educational content can come from anyone with time, technology access, and creative talent. As this happens, a wealth of educational content is available. For Lee, this translates into "an always-on always-new always-free resource for educators." Despite this optimism, he recognizes that several key problems remain to be solved before schools and teachers can safely allow students to access online video content on a broad scale. Despite these concerns, Lee expects online educational video content, such as that from Common Craft, to soon spread to mobile devices, which will expand their use even more widely.

DANCING MATT: FROM TECHIE TO TRAVELER TO TUBER TO TEACHER

Deans of schools of education across the United States currently worry about the drop in pre-service teacher enrollments and the upcoming dramatic teacher shortages we will face. What many fail to realize is that there is no shortage of teachers. As the *In Plain English* videos from Lee LeFever and Common Craft reveal, resources like YouTube enable people who normally would not be considered teachers to become teachers on the Web. And they are not just teaching small classes but tens of thousands or even millions of people within months or, in some cases, days. There is an explosion of creative teaching talent on display in YouTube. The next set of YouTube videos took this idea to the extreme.

Imagine you are sitting in Brisbane, Australia, working for a company that makes video games. Day after day, going through the motions at work and in your spare time, pretty much any of it, you are playing such video games. Life is just a bunch of bubbles for you; same old bubbles each day—the car bubble, the work bubble, the lunch bubble, the grocery store bubble, the video game playing bubble—and nothing unique or exciting happens to you. Worse still, market research has caused the company you work for to change its mission from socially responsible family games to much more violent ones. They even fund a sham proposal you sent company officials to create a game called *Destroy All Humans* in which aliens visit planet Earth to wipe out all forms of human civilization. Life just does not taste right for you. In fact, there is no life.

So one day you wake up at age twenty-six and decide to quit that job and all the bubbles that go along with it and see as much of the world as you can using all your savings. Well that is where this particular YouTube story begins. It is February 2003 and Matt Harding, born in Connecticut and working in Australia, decides to quit his video game development job and travel the world. Now that takes some courage!

For starters, he visited well-known cities such as Delhi, Hanoi, Seattle, Bangkok, Prague, Moscow, Los Angeles, and New York. Matt also saw interesting places in Tanzania, Siberia, Kenya, India, Cambodia, Uganda, Mexico, and Mongolia, as well as many other countries. More recently, he has been to Sydney, Dubai, Tokyo, Seattle, Guam, and Singapore. Perhaps more important than where he has been is what he has been doing in all of these places. Dancing! In fact, he is probably the only person to ever dance at the pyramids in Egypt, Times Square, the Parthenon, the Berlin Wall, Easter Island, Antarctica, Area 51, Siberia, Machu Picchu, Buckingham Palace, the Grand Canyon, and the Golden Gate Bridge. Matt has even danced underwater in Chuuk, Micronesia, as well as the at Rock Islands in Palau. He has danced, not with wolves, but with elephants, penguins, seals, dogs, and giraffes.

When in Hanoi a few months into that 2003 trip (which involved a total of seventeen countries in six or seven months), a friend suggested that he perform the silly dance he used to do at work whenever it was time for lunch or a break and film this dance ritual at each stop in his world journey. It would be a little memento of everywhere he went. He could then post his videos to the Internet, along with a blog summary of his adventures so that friends and family could keep track of him. Though YouTube did not exist when Matt originally quit his job to travel the world, he was able to post a YouTube video of his initial trip on January 13, 2005. Yes, I said "initial"; Matt was certainly not done traveling!

Readers of this book who might argue that the WE-ALL-LEARN model is unrealistic because a majority of the world lacks Internet access should take notice of the case of Matt Harding. Despite many stops in Third World countries and continents, including Rwanda, Tanzania, Borneo, and Cambodia, Matt told me that Internet access was never much of a problem for him during these escapades. On his Web site, Matt describes the Internet as his lifeline. He has been to more than fifty countries and Internet access was available nearly everywhere. It's significant that much of the Internet access was via free Wi-Fi in cities spanning the globe. For instance, Borneo offered near ubiquitous access in all their Internet cafés. Matt could even send e-mail when in Antarctica using his ship's satellite system. He accurately noted that "the world has changed very quickly."

Matt admittedly dances very badly, but people do not seem to care. In fact, his unusual and carefree dancing is perhaps part of the intrigue associated with his video blog (that is, vlog) posts. A plethora of bloggers started noticing his videos or windows on the world, and they were sharing them with each other. Perhaps these bloggers also dance badly and were glad to see someone rewarded for it. Video site aggregators also were noticing Matt's videos and including them in their syndicated video blog lists.

Soon there were millions of online viewers, including many communities of self-proclaimed computer geeks and nerds. At that point, Matt's server was getting twenty to thirty thousand hits per day. Now television shows were contacting Matt to show the video, including Good Morning America, which had him dance in Times Square as part of one of their shows. Even Walter Cronkite sent Matt an e-mail that he too liked the video. Another one of those happy viewers was Stride®— a brand known for its "ridiculously long-lasting gum." And Stride wanted to sponsor his next trip.

As with the first trip, the second one was filled to the brim with adventure. Setting off in late 2005, Matt visited thirty-nine countries and seven continents. The final video product of the trip, which was three minutes and forty-three seconds long, was posted to YouTube on June 21, 2006, and was seen and eventually downloaded by millions of individuals around the globe. Amazingly, by January 2009, this short video recapping his second journey was viewed by more than 12.4 million people worldwide. Even his video commentary and school lectures regarding these journeys have drawn hundreds of thousands of viewers.

The opportunity to post personal videos to the Web and to use YouTube has changed Matt's life. As he told me in late July 2007, "Well, it's offered me a pseudo-career path that I never would've imagined. And some pseudo-celebrity. Pseudo—a lot of things." Matt then referred to YouTube as "democratized entertainment, where people watch what they want to watch instead of what the TV thrusts upon us." He also noted that YouTube was changing, with the most-watched videos—which are featured on the front page—increasingly receiving corporate sponsorship of some kind. Nevertheless, a vast array of educational opportunities may still lie underneath those top pages. As Matt stated, "YouTube is still a massive storage vault for video content. It can be explored, researched, and referenced, and for that it's a useful tool."

Given all his travel, postings, and fame, he was bound to hear from Google eventually. It was late in the spring of 2007 when Google Earth officials asked him to work on a project with them. They wanted Matt to create a video where he showed the favorite spots he had visited while using Google Earth to navigate through them. According to Matt's blog, "This was not a difficult decision, as Google Earth is pretty much the coolest thing anyone has ever done with a computer."

Matt began reflecting on places to showcase, such as Lemaire Channel, Antarctica; Angkor, Cambodia; Death Valley, California; and Cape Town, South Africa. In this "Where in Google Earth is Matt" video, as Matt clicks on points of interest, he explains what is worth seeing there. For instance, there is the Stratosphere Tower in Las Vegas, which, at 1,149 feet, is the tallest freestanding observation tower in the United States. Next, he might travel to Yaxha, Guatemala, former home of the Mayan culture, and watch old ruins being excavated. He then catapults the viewer across the Pacific Ocean to Chuuk, Micronesia, to discuss World War II and how the U.S. bombers destroyed dozens of Japanese warships in the waters there. In previous YouTube videos, Matt danced among the underwater remains of these ships; this time, he is documenting the historical importance of this place. What an extremely interesting and educationally meaningful use of Google Earth! More than one million people have already watched and benefited from Matt's innovative lessons in geography. Who says YouTube is just used for entertainment?

Matt Harding's story epitomizes this book. Matt has transformed himself from video game designer to dancer and world traveler to online geography teacher. At a higher level, he has created a global movement to connect people through his travels and dancing. In his most recent video, posted on June 20, 2008, people from around the world join him for one of his famous dances. It does not matter if he is in Madrid, Brisbane, Dublin, Istanbul, Tokyo, or Buenos Aires; they want to be part of the experience. They come in the pouring rain or on hot sunny days. They come in the early morning or late at night. But they continue to come. As they do, his viewing community snowballs. Within six months, this latest video has more than sixteen million viewers. That is more than two million people per month. As these dancing Matt videos have revealed, shared online video can show us how similar we all are. We all want to be happy and enjoy life and connect to others while we do so. And Matt has definitely connected us all. He has found a way to foster a sense of global harmony and individual uniqueness through online video. His creation represents the immense possibilities of the Web.

In July of 2008, the United Nations asked Matt to participate in a mission to Africa. YouTube, Stride, and the One Laptop per Child group are also involved. His mission is to help train teachers in how to use the laptop in a millennium village in Rwanda. In addition to laptop training, Matt was asked to create a documentary of the process, which he intends to post to YouTube for the world to see; thus his creativity and video documentary skills will find more new uses.

FISCHING FOR DATA

For Karl Fisch, YouTube changed his life literally overnight. His adventure started in the summer of 2006 at Arapahoe High School in Centennial, Colorado, a suburb of Denver, where Fisch is the technology coordinator. During that particular summer, administrators at Arapahoe asked Fisch to speak at one of the traditional beginning-of-the-year faculty meetings. You all know the type—let's see what's new here and decide how we can get everyone excited about it. According to Fisch, rather than run through a list of all the technology-related improvements in the building as he had done in past years, he decided to try something different. And was it different! Fisch was on a mission not just to showcase the new technologies of his building and run through copyright laws or guidelines for effective use, but also to provide a vision for their use that meshed with the needs of twenty-first-century digital learners.

Drawing on information and themes from books written by the likes of Thomas Friedman and Ray Kurzweil, as well as presentations and blog entry posts by David Warlick, Ian Jukes, and others, Fisch put together a PowerPoint presentation called *Did You Know?* This video included many extremely thought-provoking ideas, projections, comparison data, and mini-stories of global changes. Fisch was hoping that by providing such data with a subtle storyline related to the rise and fall of nations, he could start discussions among his faculty regarding the world that their students were entering. He hoped to get them to think deeply about what their students were going to need to be successful in the twenty-first century and how that might affect what they do in their classrooms. He then creatively mixed in music from three different songs from the soundtrack of *The Last of the Mohicans* to accompany the data he would present.

In this presentation, Fisch spotlighted a wealth of interesting facts that American educators needed to contemplate, debate, and discuss, including statistics related to the emerging economies of China and India. For instance, China and India likely have more honor students than there are students in the entire United States. Additionally, China will soon become the top English-speaking country in the world. He also noted interesting U.S. business and industry statistics, such as that 25 percent of workers had been employed at their company for less than one year and 50 percent had been at their firm less than five years. As many of us realize, it is likely that the top ten jobs most in demand in 2010 will not have existed in 2004. Perhaps more eye-opening is Fisch's statement that we are preparing students for jobs that do not currently exist and that will require them to be savvy about technologies that have yet to be invented. In terms of existing technologies, Fisch noted that as of September 2006, there were 106 million registered users of MySpace, which, if it were a country, would rank as the eleventh largest country in the world, sandwiched between Japan and Mexico.

Fisch intended that such data would help faculty and staff at his school contemplate what a twenty-first-century school would need. He felt that personnel at Arapahoe needed professional development to quickly join the conversation about what a twenty-first-century school should look like. Fortunately, Fisch is not the lone voice at Arapahoe. In his blog, "The Fischbowl," forty-seven teachers contribute their insights into weighty educational issues, technology trends, and reform efforts of the early part of the twenty-first century. Equally important, Arapahoe students contribute to The Fischbowl with their comments as well.

Not only did Fisch get his staff thinking, he also got the world thinking. Several prominent bloggers in the education space—most noticeably, David Warlick, Will Richardson, and Bud Hunt—picked up on his blog post that discussed the *Did You Know?* presentation and spread the word to all their faithful blog post readers and subscribers. These were no ordinary bloggers; between them, they have untold thousands of readers. As edublogging mavens, Richardson, Warlick, and Hunt attract attention from around the globe on everything they write. They are three of the top six names that appear in a Wikispaces list of popular edubloggers. Their blogs were so powerful that Fisch's presentation was shown that fall at thousands of other faculty meetings in North America and in other parts of the world.

This story captures the essence of the Web 2.0. The power of an idea or creative product no longer resides in silos of individual departments, schools, or school districts. Instead one school district or even one individual within a school can rethink what it means to be educated and prompt neighboring schools as well as distant ones to reflect on those same issues. One-to-many soon becomes many-to-many, and the idea virus takes off in multiple directions.

Though lacking hard statistical data on the number of downloads of his presentation, Fisch estimates that between 50,000 and 100,000 people (mostly educators) had viewed the presentation by winter break of the year it first appeared, and some of these people had remixed the video for their own purposes and locales. Then, in late January of 2007, Scott McLeod, a professor at the University of Minnesota, asked Fisch's permission to formally remix the *Did You Know?* presentation and posted the updated version on his blog.

At this point, Fisch's work was about to receive even more attention thanks to the participatory nature of the Web 2.0. In late January someone downloaded McLeod's remix and decided to upload it to YouTube. The title, however, was expanded to *Did You Know; Shift Happens—Globalization; Information Age*. Next, someone else, most likely a connector or a maven type of person discussed by Malcolm Gladwell, started one of those infamous chain e-mails with a link to a downloadable version of the presentation that got forwarded to some friends.[15] However, as often happens if the link or resource is highly engaging, it gets forwarded and forwarded—and forwarded still more. Of course, many people get the same link from multiple friends and watch the video a second or even a third time.

And that is what happened to Fisch's presentation. While all this was transpiring, still other people uploaded the presentation to a variety of video sharing sites. By September 2007, Fisch told me that his best estimate was that more than 10 million people had seen that presentation that was intended for his staff of 150. In YouTube alone, there were more than 4.4 million viewers by January 2009, making it one of the most viewed educational videos in YouTube history. With the participatory power of the Web 2.0, one person in a high school setting in Colorado could now spark global thinking as related to school change—not from a book or series of speeches, but from a compelling six-minute video posted to the Internet documenting changes confronting all schools, educational institutions, and organizations. Without a doubt, leading U.S. competitors in China, Russia, and India were likely watching the video and learning from it as well.

On March 27, 2007, *Did You Know; Shift Happens—Globalization; Information Age* opened a Hewlett Foundation grantees' meeting. The video was shown to get people to think about changes in higher education, and in education in general, and how open educational resources might be a key part of those changes. The room was packed with scholars and special guests from Carnegie Mellon, the Open University, the University of Notre Dame, Curriki, the National Science Teachers Association, and the Wikimedia Foundation. Among the attendees were John Seely Brown, Candice Thille, Marshall Smith,

David Wiley, Tom Carey, Lucifer Chu, Graham Atwell, and Richard Baraniuk—many of whom are featured in other chapters of this book.

This was a meeting among the foremost authorities in the world on free and open educational software and open courseware. Yet, here we all were watching a souped-up PowerPoint presentation (now YouTube video) created by a technology coordinator from Centennial, Colorado. The very people who were creating, enhancing, testing, and promoting the Web 2.0 were the ones who were now being influenced by it and not one-by-one at their convenience back home, but as a group at the start of an important summit. When done, they had had a common experience that could springboard conversations about Fisch's ideas at lunch, throughout the following two days of the conference, and well beyond it.

The Hewlett meeting is just one instance of how this presentation was used. Special versions of it have been shown by a host of companies, organizations, and government agencies, from the National School Boards Association to NASA, Microsoft, and various chambers of commerce. You name the firm or organization, and there's a pretty good chance they've seen it, shown it, or at least heard about it. What is even more amazing is that many of them have created their own remixes of the presentation. One person, Karl Fisch, and one technology, YouTube, helped rethink the purpose and goals of education in the United States and around the world.

WESCH-LING WITH YOUTUBE

A similar type of video, *Web 2.0 . . . The Machine Is Us/ing Us*, was created and posted by Dr. Michael Wesch at Kansas State University on Wednesday, January 31, 2007. With nearly eight million viewers two years later, this is the most-watched education-related video that my research team found. Wesch, who teaches cultural anthropology, demonstrates the power of digital text in this four-and-a-half-minute video. While writing a paper on social networking and other interactive tools, Wesch was stuck in one of those odd moments where the traditional media for explaining your story are inadequate or no longer appropriate.

As in aspects of this very book, he was frustrated when attempting to describe the exciting world of digital media by using only paper. And so began his journey into YouTube celebrity status. Using catchy music along with quite captivating editing techniques displaying an assortment of Web 2.0 possibilities, he uploaded his creation to YouTube. Within just a few short hours, his video had more than a hundred hits. Five days later, it had been viewed thirty thousand times and sixty thousand more times by the following morning.[16] Wesch himself was amazed. As he stated in an interview in *InfoWorld*: "I was ecstatic when I realized that 100 people had watched it. Now that almost 2 million people have seen it, it's all just surreal. I'm geeky, so I'm into this stuff. I thought there couldn't be that many other people who would be into it, too."[17]

As Wesch discovered, there were many geeks and bloggers just like him. He also found out that fame can happen overnight in YouTube. One day you're teaching classes at Kansas State and the next fielding questions from personnel at *Wired* magazine, *The New York Times*, *InfoWorld*, ABC News, and the *Chronicle of Higher Education*, as well as from bloggers and scores of people who downloaded the video around the world. He already knew that the Web 2.0 offers new ways to share and exchange information as well as to link people who previously would never have crossed paths. But when he actually experienced it, the realities of this medium hit him squarely between the eyes.

According to his blog, after sharing an initial version of his video with his Digital Ethnography class, Wesch was hoping to get feedback on a second draft of the Web 2.0 video that he posted to YouTube for ten of his friends to see. However, he did not anticipate that in just a few short days it would become the most discussed video in the blogosphere. As he noted in his March 8, 2007, blog post—a mere thirty-seven days after his video upload—"It is hard to believe that a little video I created in my basement in St. George, Kansas could be seen by over 1.7 million people, be translated into (at least) 5 languages, and be shown to large audiences at major conferences on 6 continents within just one month of its creation." He posted an updated version of the video that same day. By September the original version reached nearly 3.4 million downloads with another quarter million from the updated video. And by mid-April 2008 it had eclipsed the five million viewer mark.

That is 1.7 million potential new viewers (and potential fans) of one's research and ideas in just thirty-seven days, or around 45,000 new viewers of one's creative ideas per day. It is likely that a lifetime of creative works by a scholar in academia seldom generates a million interested readers or viewers; and Wesch's video was a product that took just three days to produce. It is unheard of, therefore, to have millions of people peering into an academic's research just thirty-seven days after its creation. Previously this might have been possible with timely spots on television shows and articles in popular magazines showcasing an unusual or stellar research finding, but YouTube-like distribution outlets are different. With YouTube and the Web 2.0, people who are directed to a video, or who simply stumble upon it, can now share it with friends, post it as a favorite, and revisit it at will. They can also comment on it so that the producer can update his work. At the same time, they can subscribe to still more from the same person or channel.

In addition to comments that viewers might leave on YouTube or on his blog, Wesch has viewers go to a site in Mojiti where they can review and comment on the video in their own words. They can add "spots" or text, shapes, images, freehand drawings, Flash art, audio, or other video in response to his ideas. And these are not general comments but specific ones on any interesting aspect of the video that are also seen by others. Wesch then uses these comments to create an enhanced video. Such is the world of the Web 2.0—a place where dynamic feedback from myriad people you will likely never meet in person can help enhance your products and ideas.

Wesch is not done with his personal YouTube production. When "teaching" cultural anthropology to undergraduates, Wesch uses a self-described "anti-teaching" philosophy—perhaps akin to Jay Cross's notion of an "unconference" or "unbook."[18] For example, in some of his classes Wesch requires students to create their own YouTube videos. His undergraduate students not only post video blogs, or vlogs, of their thoughts and feelings, but most of them also post their video products to YouTube. As Don Tapscott points out in his new book, *Grown Up Digital: How the Net Generation Is Changing Your World*, college students no longer expect or want predigested information and prestructured learning events.[19] Instead, they want to collaborate, share, and explore in technology-rich environments. In the twenty-first century, student learning must be highly personalized and meaningful, not a one-size-fits-all variety.

The Web 2.0 is not for the faint of heart. There are many risks that instructors assume in letting students control much of their own learning. It is not easy for the students either. And Wesch seems to push his students to their limits. In one class in the spring of 2007, in fact, he required hundreds of students to collaboratively create a twenty-two-minute video to represent six hundred years of world history from colonization to the current times of corporate globalization. That's yet another idea from Wesch that is brilliant!

Used in project-based learning, YouTube becomes the platform for a world audience about world history—in effect, a reflection of itself. Given that there are thousands of experts on different aspects of the video who will later watch the final product on YouTube and critique it, this activity involves extensive risk. But whom or what are they critiquing? As Wesch's simulation project evolves and grows from semester to semester, ownership over it becomes amorphous. There is no author or owner. Perhaps the Web 2.0 finally dispels the belief that the instructor is the expert and the student's job is to learn what she can from him. In the end, Wesch and his students watch the video together and then reflect on macro topics of how the world works, including issues related to food production, disparities in income levels, and the potential roles of students in the world.

For Wesch, the current generation of online technologies affords an opportunity for the human species to see the different ways in which the world is connected. His intent is to kindle a conversation on the power of such technology for relationship building. Or as he puts it: "It might help us create a truly global view that can spark the kind of empathy we need to create a better world for all of humankind. I'm not being overly utopian and naively saying that the Web will make this happen. In fact, if we don't understand our digital technology and its effects, it can actually make humans and human needs even more invisible than ever before. But the technology also creates a remarkable opportunity for us to make a profound difference in the world."[20]

Wesch has clearly reached one of his goals—he has sparked a conversation related to Web 2.0 technologies not only among his anthropology colleagues, but also among techies, librarians, business and government leaders, and training departments, as well as among those in language and literature and beyond. And this conversation is nowhere close to done. In fact, as noted throughout this chapter, it is expanding!

TEACHERTUBE?

With the success of YouTube, many spin-offs have arrived. Take, for example, TeacherTube. TeacherTube was launched March 6, 2007, by fourteen-year veteran educator Jason Smith. This site is a place for teachers to explain or demonstrate concepts, principles, or topics in a unique fashion. Thanks to TeacherTube, if a fifth-grade student was ill and missed out on a lecture on geometric transformations, he can catch up with a video explanation of it. A high school student looking for a video lecture on the cerebellum for his class report can find one in TeacherTube. There are TeacherTube videos on neural nets, the use of microscopes, the history of Berlin, the Bill of Rights, beginning volley-ball, New Media, Pearl Harbor, and hundreds of miscellaneous topics.

Stephen Downes notes that TeacherTube is much tinier than its cousin, YouTube.[21] With around twenty thousand education-related videos by early 2008, however, it contains plenty of programming content for instructors to browse and choose. Already there are K–12 as well as college-level videos in reading, math, science, social studies, and many other areas. Some TeacherTube videos been viewed more than half a million times. In the midst of all this attention, several teacher celebrities have emerged including one who raps about mathematics.

Now when teachers around the globe begin to share videos showing their teaching examples and ideas, others can learn from them, discuss and critique them, and perhaps post similar videos. Aspiring teachers can see concepts and principles in action via short video bursts, instead of relying strictly on textbooks and associated course resources. Teacher-Tube offers a rich, global repository of teaching and learning ideas. And as with YouTube, this is a Web 2.0 system in which users can create video groups; subscribe to channels and member videos; upload, tag, and share videos worldwide; create playlists; and connect with people who share similar interests.

A similar resource is SchoolTube, which, in partnership with the Student Television Network, provides engaging media sharing and journalism opportunities for students and teachers across the United

States. There are even Student Video Choice contests to motivate students to participate in SchoolTube and therefore in participatory learning. Many other video production and sharing sites now exist for K–12 students and schools. Clearly, shared online video is a unique form of learning that will be interesting to monitor in the coming years. With it, the world has become much more open for students to learn, and to share their learning with others.

PROFESSOR CELEBRITIES

Shared online video sites such as YouTube and TeacherTube are places where teachers, researchers, and other educators can share their ideas and activities and put them up on display for their world. Some refer to this as "coursecasting" or "Webcasting." Coursecasting is so popular that some universities have started their own YouTube channels in an effort to attract attention from students, donors, and media as well as to promote education. Among some of these trailblazers are the University of Southern California, the University of New South Wales in Australia, Northwestern University, and the University of California at Berkeley. The newest member of this club is the American University of Beirut.[22]

Many in education are excited by the possibilities of content that can be viewed beyond small classes of just a few dozen students to the entire world. As one example, a consortium of universities in the Socrates Project, led by Carnegie Mellon University, are creating a free technology called Panopto to simplify the coursecasting process.[23] For those wishing to pay for coursecasted software, there are vendor products like Tegrity, Apreso from Anystream, or MediaSite Live from Sonic Foundry.

Having used some of these coursecasts, I can attest that they are highly professional and energizing to watch. Still it does require some courage to create publicly accessible Webcasts as well as to watch oneself teach. However, sharing online video content opens doors for students to potentially learn from teachers in hundreds of countries and thousands of schools, universities, corporate training sites, and other educational institutions. Adam Hochman, project manager at Berkeley's Learning Systems Group, notes that with YouTube, "Professors in a sense are rock stars."[24]

Other online video content sites are springing up. One Web site appearing in early January 2008, Big Think, claimed to be a YouTube-like site for people to generate, learn about, and discuss ideas. Videos recently featured on Big Think included Angelina Jolie and a panel of experts talking about displaced children in Iraq and their right for an education; U.S. Presidential nominee John McCain discussing how he would "fix Iraq"; and venture capitalist Esther Dyson reflecting on opportunities from space exploration. Also spotlighted on the home-page is a videoclip from November 17, 2007, in which Sir Richard Branson, chairman of Virgin Group, discusses the topic "Why do you give back?" Authors, corporate leaders, senators, economists, actresses, magazine editors, among others, can be seen and heard in Big Think. The ramifications are indeed big, and they are making us all think.

These are all relatively short videos, but with enough content to foster thinking, reflection, and perhaps even debate. And like YouTube, they are readily accessible and free. But can such a site ever be as widely used as YouTube? To date, Big Think is not.[25] Perhaps someday it will have a wide audience that can quickly identify and converse with like-minded thinkers as well as those who wish to debate.

Big Think, TeacherTube, and YouTube are just a few examples of online video content sharing sites. Many other such sites have tried to follow their lead. A nonprofit consortium of colleges and universities has created the "Research Channel," which reaches more than thirty million homes in the United States alone. As with Glenn Jones's Mind Extension University, discussed earlier, with this one channel, the research of world-class institutions can find its way into homes. Programs such as *Discovering a Link between Fish and Limbed Animals* and *Conservative Management of Lower Back Pain* can be found there. The user can view, download, or share the video. However, resources like the Research Channel are caught in a drift between being examples of a portal of content and pure participatory learning. Unlike YouTube, those at the Research Channel cannot upload content, rate it, or save it as their favorites.

For academics and professionals in the workplace, there is now a site for scientists to not only upload their technical papers but also to post videos and form communities around their research. It is called SciVee. This site was created by National Science Foundation, the

Public Library of Science (PLoS), and the San Diego Supercomputing Center. At SciVee, scientists deliver video lectures or presentations that link to their open access articles in biomedical journals.[26] A key goal is widespread dissemination of scientific content. Not only are text documents and videos available for observers but also podcasts.[27] When you get to SciVee, there are channels you can subscribe to in biology, genetics, medicine, neglected tropical diseases, pathogens, and other science areas.

With the advent of SciVee, researchers, students, or the general public can not only read cutting-edge research, they can also watch the researcher involved in the study present the rationale for the study and the findings. When you mix publications with video content you get what's known as a "pubcast." Like YouTube, anyone with a Web link can view a particular video, share it, and make it her favorite. Options exist to watch, view, or listen. In effect, you can watch the pubcast, listen to the pubcast, or read the paper. With such options, scientists are given opportunities to present their ideas to new audiences and in unique ways. In addition, these options provide solutions for those with visual or auditory impairments. There is power not only in the distribution of such content, but also in greater understanding of one's research.

CHASING JACK BUT FINDING GODWIN

Remember those UCLA students discussed in our Introduction who were reflecting in their blogs while doing archaeological digs around the world? Another quite fun and engaging example of participatory learning taking place while students are spread out in different locales was a sociology class called Jack Kerouac Wrote Here, Crisscrossing America Chasing Cool at the State University of New York at Potsdam from January 3–14, 2007.[28] Here thirty-five students traveled for twelve days across the United States recording sounds and taking pictures in the spirit of Jack Kerouac, who had traveled the country in the 1950s and wrote about it in his novel On the Road.[29] Student pictures, sounds, words, and ethnographic maps were uploaded to this collaborative documentary project. SUNY Potsdam students traveled across the country from New York to San Francisco by plane, bus, train, and on foot to record their sounds and images. Along the way, they captured what they heard when in or near jazz clubs, harbors, graveyards, trains, cafés, and waterfalls in national parks. In the process, they become a community of writers, observers, and researchers.

Imagine the excitement of retracing someone's steps half a century later, as well as the collective experience of thirty-five individuals traversing the country. Clearly, we are no longer confined to a four-walled classroom of learning. The collected images and audio clips can be used and expanded on by others in that particular course, as well as those outside the course who want to feel America, not simply read about it in a book or watch yet another movie or television program. Pushing the uses of technology further still, with the assistance of the Freesound Project, the sounds were "geo-tagged." This means that future students and interested parties can listen to a sound by clicking on a map where it was recorded. With such creative mash-ups of technology—online audio and online maps—everyone's learning experience is enhanced. Most people will not have the opportunity to retrace the steps of Jack Kerouac the way that these students did, but they can appreciate it through these multiple forms of media and hypermedia linkages to them. This is authentic learning in action.

Perhaps that is why resources and media such as Current TV and SplashCast are so popular. As briefly mentioned earlier, Current TV enables individuals to gather news about the world and share it with others for free. No longer does mass media mean we must limit ourselves to watching what some executive or manager decides is worth showing. Adding to the richness of the event, content that is posted might be rated or put into viewer competitions, thus enabling the cream to come to the top.

One short video on Current TV called *African School Dream* was the top rated "pod"—a short video that tells a story, profiles a character, or shares an idea—from among the three thousand available on the day I found it in July 2007. It tells the story of Godwin Agudey, who in 2002 founded New Era School with 16 children in Sega, Ghana, West Africa. This school grew to 250 students in 2006 and now has over 300. Some classes are held outside, because New Era is lacking in physical building space—it has only six classrooms. To make matters more difficult for Godwin, some parents need their kids to herd cattle to make money instead of going to school. Resources at the school are in short supply, but the school is succeeding and growing. This is real life! This is an example of how learning success can be documented and shared.

This particular pod was uploaded by Yan Chun Su or "Ysu" as she goes by in Current TV. When I contacted her I found out that she is an information technology systems designer and consultant. Interestingly, this was not the original version of her pod; Yan had uploaded a new version based on feedback she was given by the Current TV pod community about her editing, professional approach, and emotional content. Like Wikipedia, YouTube, and TeacherTube, Current TV is a highly crowdsourced environment where the most watched or highest-rated content rises to the top. In contrast to traditional media, the best work of amateurs floats to the top. According to Jeff Howe, contributing editor at *Wired Magazine* and author of the book *Crowdsourcing: Why the Power of the Crowd Is Driving the Future of Business*, Current TV crowdsources its content creation, programming decisions, and even its ratings.[30] In browsing through the comments Yan has received, it is clear that she has greatly benefited from the crowd.

Born and raised in China, Yan attended Virginia Tech University where she obtained a master's degree in computer science. After several years of working in financial institutions in Boston, Yan now resides in Boulder, Colorado, where she works independently and has ventured out into the world of documentary filmmaking. Early in 2006, during a two-month stint as a volunteer teacher in Ghana, she ended up at Godwin's school. Yan told me that she was "quite moved by what he did. I interviewed him and filmed other scenes of the school and around the village. The main purpose of that for me is to show the outside world their situation." She was hopeful that Godwin's school could get some support if she could showcase it somehow. So when Current TV arrived, it was a natural fit. As she put it, "No other ways that I know of provide such a platform for independent filmmakers to showcase their work on TV."

Through the educational openings introduced by the Web, Yan has become an independent short filmmaker. *African School Dream* has won her several recognitions and invitations to film festivals. Current TV even picked up her pod for broadcast. She has also developed a couple of other emotionally stirring documentaries about life in Tibet and Western China and went back to China in February 2009 for a month of additional filming. Suffice to say, Current TV has provided her with a new career and perhaps even changed her life purpose.

In the late spring of 2008, Yan connected me to Godwin, who informed me via e-mail that New Era is now Anmchara International School and has doubled its classrooms to twelve—three for a nursery school and three more for a junior high school. On top of those responsibilities, the local chiefs and parents have come to him with a petition. In it, they say, "Godwin, we believe in what you are doing and we want you to add a high school to the school we now have." Although this places a heavy demand on Godwin, he marches on to try to meet their request. Fortunately, these same chiefs and parents donated some available land to make it happen.

The comments he has personally received as a result of Yan's video have been highly encouraging. As he put it, "To be in this boat alone is not that easy so words of encouragement are doing me a lot of good." Godwin feels that the message of Yan's video was loud and clear and helps in such efforts. However, the speed of access to the Internet in Ghana was so slow when Yan first uploaded her video to Current TV that he did not see it until volunteer workers from Belgium brought a copy on a CD and showed it to him personally. In the past couple of years, life in Sega has markedly improved. According to Godwin, there is not only a new school, but also access to electricity and water, which were mere dreams in the past. In May 2008, they obtained a computer with Internet access from a local service provider at 100 mbps. Godwin's school now even includes a compulsory course on information and communications technology. He hopes that this will soon translate into the use of computers out in the real world beyond his school.

An e-mail from Godwin on July 19, 2008 indicated that his hopes had turned up a notch when he was able to parlay a $250 donation into four additional computers. Still, with all the children in his school, he envisions a hundred computers someday. When I asked him how, he responded:

> One of my philosophies in life is to start everything small and to give it my best. I once had a walk in the bush; while I was walking I came across a huge ant hill. I was amazed at this edifice and thought these animals might be so great to have built this hill. I then took a close look and saw little

creatures busily working, carrying small chunks of dirt over a distance. I wondered how small the dirt they carried looked and yet they were able to build such an edifice. A question quickly came to mind, how long did it take these animals to build this? It could be 5, 10 or even more years. These creatures have taught me great lesson that gives me resilience in the face of difficulties. I believe in starting every endeavor of life and it will grow as I add more daily.

After that e-mail, I connected Godwin to my Ghanaian doctoral student, Kwame Dakwa, who is CEO of Novel Solutions, an offshore outsourcing company for business processes and information and communication technology in Accra, Ghana.[31] Perhaps Godwin will soon be closer to his dream of a hundred computers. Let's hope so! Two days later, this story took another fateful twist as I personally met Yan Chun Su in Denver, Colorado, and we discussed my *World Is Open* book manuscript, which she had read. She shared the notes she had taken about the book and offered candid feedback. Such is life in this Internet world. Someone whom you stumble upon when browsing the Web one year becomes a friend and confidante in the next. And often it does not take a year, but just brief moments in time.

Godwin's story is among the thousands found in Current TV. There are also videos on how Generation Y uses iPods, the Brighton Hip Hop Festival, the adoption of highways in America, and yet another on education in Ghana. As I have found, many pods in Current TV are educational stories embedded in real-world settings. Educators, parents, and politicians must think about how they will use this potentially powerful learning resource. Will it become simply another online resource to browse and watch, or will learners become video producers for Current TV as well as YouTube and other shared online video sites?

INTERACTIVE VIDEOCONFERENCING

With Internet Protocol videoconferencing, schools are also involved in global education and sharing whenever they want. IP-based videoconferencing became available in the 1990s just as more efficient video-compression techniques were developed. It allows two or more locations to interact for free using two-way audio and video transmissions.[32] For instance, there is Global Nomads Group (GNG) where students learn about world cultures through videoconferencing.[33] GNG has existed since the late 1990s as an organization dedicated to helping children become more aware of other cultures and people. The goals include fostering critical thinking, global awareness, cultural understandings, communication skills, and geography skills. If successful, the children of the world will have enhanced empathy and understanding of global issues and will take on greater social responsibility. Through videoconferencing, diverse international cultures enter classrooms, board rooms, and front rooms. To foster such insights, GNG is creating an encyclopedia of misconceptions.

Shirley Herrin is a social studies teacher at ALPHA Academy in Magnolia, Texas, located just outside Houston.[34] Using videoconferencing from GNG, her students find out about the cultures of countries such as China, Honduras, Jordan, and Vietnam. When interacting with students from those countries, they learn about geography, politics, cultures, religions, the military, and the government. More specifically, they might learn about the lives of Sudanese refugees in Chad who fled Darfur or those who survived the Rwandan genocide. Alternatively, they might hear about AIDS in Brazil, food in Japan, and life in Iraq from the perspective of teenage students living there. There is an amazing wealth of events and possibilities that can take students out of their textbooks and situate them immediately in the real world.

Among the goals of GNG are to reduce ignorance, misconceptions, and perhaps even hatred among the people of different countries, while increasing learner curiosity, self-esteem, and knowledge. Shirley Herrin notes that it is "the highest high you can get as a teacher, seeing your kids want to know more, asking thought-provoking questions, and then wanting to know even *more*."[35]

GNG is certainly not the only such program. My colleague Deb Hutton at Indiana University has run a similar videoconferencing program at IU for more than a dozen years. This program, which is called ISIS, or International Studies for Indiana Schools, creates programs on topics such as:

- What Do You Want to Know About Iraq?

- East European Origins: Focus on Hungary

- Islam in Africa: Niger

- Meet the Mongolian Throat Singers

- Daily Life in the Netherlands

- Burmese Students: Perspectives of Refugees

Deb and her colleague, Professor Mimi Miyoung Lee, now at the University of Houston, note that the goals of ISIS are to respect and appreciate differences, learn about different cultures, understand the issues of equality in society, and foster a sense of tolerance and openness.[36] There is little doubt that this is where education should be focused today. Deb and Mimi believe that these goals can lead toward the development and empowerment of individuals as thoughtful and active participants of the twenty-first century—toward the goal of educating all people of this planet. Mimi's research has shown how free Web technologies such as IP-based videoconferencing can bring rural teachers and students in predominantly White southern Indiana a step closer to the cultures of the world.[37] Much more is possible.

When I contacted Mimi in July 2008 and asked her about whether she saw the world opening up with technology, she responded:

> This question is not as easy as it first seems. In many ways, yes, technology will help the world open up more. Plenty of evidence could be found in present and past instances of Internet uses and its advancements. Examples such as open source, wikis, and YouTube, all come to mind when we think of "opening up" as sharing and interacting with the rest of the world. We can reach so much further than before, both chronologically and geographically. However, because so many of us now take such wide sharing for granted, it is easier to forget and marginalize (however unintentionally) the population who doesn't have access to this ubiquitous technology. Anybody who relies on traditional modes of interaction not involving technology would be at a disadvantage in accessing the information. How many of us haven't experienced the customer service phone line where it "kindly" urges us to use the online service:)? So again, yes, the technology will certainly open up the world but it will be more difficult for us to realize who we are leaving behind if we believe in it too firmly without continuous reflection.

Mimi is absolutely right. We must be cautious about overgeneralizing from GNG and ISIS. Most schools and teachers lack access to such technology today. And when they do, reflection on what works and what does not is too seldom a key ingredient. Thoughtful use of these global sharing technologies is crucial. Spontaneous use of emergent technology, or the inclusion of a new tool just because it is a sexy thing to do, will not bring about positive change in learning.

Perhaps it is time for such reflection. What if every social studies class in the United States (or the world, for that matter) had access to such videoconferencing technology, thereby enabling students to socially interact with peers in distant regions? Imagine the sense of social responsibility that might ensue. Imagine the healing possible between people of different nations that were previously at war, or in the midst of a major disagreement. Imagine the education, respect, and better understanding that such technology can bring. Mimi herself acknowledged to me that she did not fully appreciate the principles of ISIS until she participated in it as a researcher, program developer, and Korean instructor in one of the programs. It wasn't until she interacted with ISIS students about her own native country that she better appreciated the possible impact. As she put it, "[M]y own assumptions and understanding on the issues of multicultural/cross-cultural education grew significantly." Perhaps we all need such experiences.

In programs like GNG and ISIS, the videoconferencing event is live, thereby enabling interactive questioning, demonstrations, and changes in content presentation based on participant interests and demands. It is live synchronous learning as opposed to the asynchronous participation in YouTube and Current TV.

But the key point is that video—both canned content put up in places like Current TV and YouTube as well as synchronous videoconferencing experiences in GNG and ISIS—is becoming an increasingly popular and effective means for international and global education and awareness. And it is about time! What's more, anyone can participate in this global education revolution.

LET'S WRAP UP THIS VIDEO

As the different stories of this section illustrate, the proliferation and accelerating use of sites like YouTube, GNG, Big Think, and Current

TV satisfy a need to shift the Internet from a tool for text to one for video. Online video has become ubiquitous. Questions arise in the midst of this pervasiveness. Chief among them is whether shared online video traffic pushes the Web to a choking point at which business and industry, governments, and educational institutions and organizations are stymied? Let's definitely hope not; the WE-ALL-LEARN model is admittedly dependent on relatively quick access to the Web.

In discussing the impact of ubiquitous computing, Stephen Downes argues that it is leading to a "world of learning" where "learning is available no matter what you are doing"[38] For some this refers to learning nuggets or episodes that are made available when needed at work as part of a workflow learning process. Downes further notes that such workflow is not restricted to the workplace. Instead, such learning opportunities will be meshed with every part of our lives—political, social, cultural, economic, and educational. If Downes is right, life will be equated with learning. As he noted, "Learning and living, it could be said, will eventually merge. The challenge will not be in how to learn, but in how to use learning to create something more, to communicate."[39]

WIKIWIKI

For all of us to learn and participate in that learning process, we need tools to learn with. However, these tools must no longer be one-directional tutors in the learning process. Participatory tools give learners power and control. As Thomas Jefferson would have encouraged, such tools grant learners a voice in the educational process. Enter Wikipedia.

Between 1994 and 1995, Ward Cunningham designed a Web site that allowed for quick collaboration on a document by people around the world. Originally, Cunningham intended to call it the QuickWeb. However, on a chance visit to Honolulu, Hawaii, he was told by a counter employee to take the WikiWiki shuttle bus between the airport's terminals. When Cunningham asked, "What is the WikiWiki?" he was told that "wiki" was the Hawaiian word for fast, so "wikiwiki" implied really fast. Upon hearing that explanation, he decided to change the name of the QuickWeb to the "wiki."[40] Some affectionately also refer to a wiki as "What I know is" because it captures the role of a wiki in knowledge creation and participation—in effect, saying "I know this and can share it or exchange it with you." No matter the origins or the ultimate name used, Ward Cunningham created something that people had been desperately seeking—a means for work teams to collaboratively write documents online.

It is vital to point out that though anyone can edit or change a wiki, each modification is recorded in the history of a particular document. Anyone can decide to roll the document back to a previous status if an earlier version is deemed more accurate or appropriate. There are automatic recordings of when such changes were made, who made the changes, and the changes that were made. A wiki, therefore, contains an open window into the idea-generation process and how knowledge becomes suggested, endorsed, and potentially changed. Different versions of knowledge or "the truth" can be compared and contrasted by anyone. With a public wiki, learners can now view the knowledge negotiation process in full light. Wikipedia entries exemplify the social constructivist nature of knowledge itself.

Wikipedia was founded by Jimmy Wales, one of the one hundred most influential people of 2006, according to a special edition of *Time* magazine.[41] Wales, who has a master's degree in finance from the University of Alabama, enrolled in the PhD program in finance at Indiana University, but never completed it.[42] Instead of graduating from IU, he became a research director at Chicago Options Associates. His speculations on the fluctuations of interest rates and different foreign currencies were successful enough to give Wales sufficient financial resources to support him and his family for the rest of their lives.

After investing in a male-oriented search engine called Bomis during the dot-com era, Wales began designing a multilingual encyclopedia Web site in 1999. Unfortunately, the design was far too slow to be worthwhile. The following year, Wales announced a peer-reviewed, open content encyclopedia called Nupedia. Larry Sanger, editor-in-chief of Nupedia, came up with the Wikipedia name on January 10, 2001. However, he left in March 2002 when his position was no longer funded. Part of the reason Sanger departed was that he personally preferred encyclopedias that were reviewed by experts.

Wikipedia was actually a side project for Nupedia. Wikipedia was supposed to provide collaboratively written content that might be submitted to Nupedia. As fate would have it, however, Wikipedia quickly became the more viable and sustainable product. Nupedia was stuck in the old world of a prepublication review process. The old approach too often resulted in elaborate and often elongated procedures for coordinating article submission, review, and negotiation. The new approach, like the WikiWiki, was quick!

Wikipedia empowered contributors from all walks of life to pass on their knowledge for the greater good by relying on post-publication peer-review procedures among volunteer collaborators. Think of an idea or story and post it for others to review, change, comment on, expand, or delete, all in real time. Wikipedia is a community-built learning resource—the inherent motto is to let the people who use it build it. Anyone can make a significant contribution to a particular page or resource. And that page might be read by anyone else online at any time.

On March 26, 2008, a Wikimedia press release boasted that Wikipedia had more than ten million pages of content in more than 250 languages.[43] The number of articles in English alone was approaching 2.5 million. I guess no one at 39 Stillman Street is sitting around longing for the good old days of Nupedia. It is likely that Wales is the only one there today who remembers them.

Wikipedia has over seventy-five thousand active contributors creating that content.[44] That means seventy-five thousand workers providing time, talent, and content without remuneration! And if you ignore the revision history pages for each article posted, contributors' names are not even attached to the article. But what these freelance writers and editors have is an audience, and a gigantic one at that. According to the Wikipedia statistics pages, each day there are hundreds of thousands of visitors to the site. At present, Wikipedia accounts for a staggering one out of every two hundred page views on the Internet.[45] There are nearly 7 million registered users worldwide, of which 4.6 million are English speakers, and countless others are unregistered. Such visitors do not need passwords or memberships to access the content, nor do they need special knowledge, experience, or background to make a contribution.

These visitors make edits to tens of thousands of Wikipedia articles while also generating thousands of new ones each day.[46] This lack of prescreening allows many contributors to freely check over work posted. As Linus Torvalds knows, if you have enough eyeballs, you can do wondrous things online. However, the many eyeballs approach also draws extensive criticism.

A large number of those who edit Wikipedia articles—especially those on breaking news—are teenage males. Witness Matthew Gruen, who on May 8, 2007 edited an article on the terror plot against Fort Knox some fifty-nine times, before needing to go to bed. According to a *New York Times* article, this sixteen-year-old from Poughkeepsie, New York, whose Wikipedia username is Gracenotes, had to get up early for high school the next day.[47] As a result of Matthew's exceptional work on this entry, he was considered for admin status in Wikipedia. Such a project is not unusual for him. In fact, after completing his homework and any church-related responsibilities, Matthew typically spends six or so hours each night cleaning up entries in Wikipedia.[48] His parents much prefer him working in Wikipedia than in another online community he had been spending time in.

Matthew Gruen is part of a culture that is opening up education, albeit at a very basic or factual level, to anyone. No elitism here; this is quickly generated and accessible educational content created for the masses by the masses. It is a nontraditional learner's paradise. A decade ago such a learning resource could not be imagined. Millions of people across the planet contributing to one resource that could be used by anyone? A free encyclopedia of knowledge? Who could have predicted it?

Unlike the free encyclopedias and many other free online resources mentioned in the previous chapters, Wikipedia is not a static document or portal. In contrast, it is part of a growing participatory learning culture. Contributions, enhancements, and edits can come from anywhere. And the corpus called Wikipedia is closely guarded by a group of highly involved volunteers called Wikipedians. Wikipedians are immediately notified when a "watch page" has been altered. So when someone attempts to sabotage someone else's reputation by making slanderous comments on his Wikipedia page, it can be changed with minutes. And it is; I know this from experience and it has been documented elsewhere.

Another form of quality control comes from WikiTrust. Researchers at the University of California at Santa Cruz have designed a system to highlight Wikipedia text that comes from less-than-stellar people. For instance, if your contributed text is constantly changed or deleted, you would not have a good reputation.[49] That will show up visually with

tools from WikiTrust. Other such quality indices for wikis will undoubtedly emerge as well.

It is not too surprising that the old world is struggling with this new
one. Despite research showing that the quality of Wikipedia is on par
with *Encyclopedia Britannica*, at least for science content, many criticize
content created by commoners in the Wikipedia community.[50] But
given the daily usage statistics of Wikipedia compared with Britannica,
the commoners must be doing a pretty decent job!

Not so fast. Starting in the spring of 2007, the history department at
Middlebury College added disclaimers on their syllabi that Wikipedia,
though fine for gathering background information, could not be cited
as a primary source. This decision came on the heels of a unanimous
vote of the department effectively banning students from citing from
open source encyclopedias for their essays and examinations. As
reported by Brock Read of the *Chronicle of Higher Education*, the
statement reads: "Whereas Wikipedia is extraordinarily convenient
and, for some general purposes, extremely useful, it nonetheless suffers
inevitably from inaccuracies deriving in large measure from its unique
manner of compilation . . . Students are responsible for the accuracy
of information they provide, and they cannot point to Wikipedia or
any similar source that may appear in the future to escape the
consequences of errors."[51]

Middlebury College has drawn a line in the sand. Jimmy Wales
himself has gone on record to agree that college students should not be
citing from encyclopedias as primary resources for term papers. For Wales,
Wikipedia is an attempt at objective reporting of facts and information.
There is talk of marking articles identified as accurate and reliable as
"stable" pages—those that cannot be automatically changed by anyone.[52] What might be next? More advanced wiki tools might offer
intelligent tutoring advice in systems such as Wikipedia, perhaps by
adding some type of quality index or ranking. The coming generations of
Wikipedia might entail greater personalization and customization so that
one obtains the appropriate resources where and when needed.

Quality debates aside, wikis are highly unique and intriguing learning
tools. Students can work in small groups to finish assignments while
seated anywhere in the world. I have seen students from China,
Malaysia, Taiwan, and the United States collaborate on writing entire

books and make them available for others to use, change, or edit at the Wikibooks Web site, a sister site of Wikipedia. With access to a wiki, students can negotiate course requirements and meeting agendas, generate or edit course content, such as an online glossary, a set of guidelines, or a how-to manual, and even edit Wikipedia itself. This is a new world—a more open world where learners have a voice in their own learning. Wikis exemplify what is possible perhaps as much as any other technology tool or resource available today.

PARTICIPATORY E-BOOKS

YouTube, Current TV, and Wikipedia have not cornered the market on participatory learning and crowdsourcing. You might be surprised to discover that the first opener discussed in Chapter Two, e-books, also offers people an opportunity to engage in participatory learning activities.

Recently, a bit of spice has been added to the digitized book market. For instance, the outside world can now place personal comments beside the text, and, in some cases, actually change the book content altogether. With the emergence of wikis and other online text resources and tools, the e-book field is experiencing yet another upward spiral after years of fickleness. A few very courageous higher education scholars are posting preprints of new books electronically so that they can receive line-by-line critiques on their drafts from hundreds of interested parties around the world.[53] Such comments are used to revise their books, which are later published in print. Some, however, skip the printing process altogether and simply post their work online and submit it to continual refinement. Even more bold, using online resources like WEbook, writers ask the outside world not only for feedback but also for actual help in writing a book on a particular topic. Anyone can launch a book idea or project at WEbook. Anyone can collaboratively help write it. And anyone can offer feedback on it. As an incentive to help, those who successfully complete a book share in book royalties with WEbook fifty-fifty.

This is the age when ideas are exposed to the world as they are still in formative stages of development. Think of an idea and write it down in your blog. It does not matter if these ideas are half-baked or overcooked.

You post them. Today, professional writers and academics commonly ask for feedback on project or article ideas even when still formulating them. With the speed of Internet publishing, a publication is often listed on one's resume and reviewed in online magazines and journals years before it is actually published. With tools such as wikis and blogs, the pace of publishing has become so frantic, I jokingly tell my students that soon they will be listing publications before they think of them.

Publishers such as Yale University Press and MIT Press have been experimenting with several innovative electronic book formats. In the fall of 2008, MIT released a book called *Opening Up Education: The Collective Advancement of Education through Open Technology, Open Content, and Open Knowledge*, edited by Toru Iiyoshi and M. S. Vijay Kumar.[54] The chapters were written by dozens of individuals out in the trenches of this open learning world. As a sign of how open things really were getting, *Opening Up Education* was available as a free PDF document or as a set of free documents (that is, as individual chapters). Exploring openness still further, there were YouTube videos from some of the authors explaining unique aspects of their chapters, an online forum to discuss the book with the other readers as well as chapter authors, Webcast interviews with the editors as well as John Seely Brown, who wrote the book foreword, and numerous blog postings about this book. *Opening Up Education* had truly lived up to its name!

Such tactics are not entirely new. In 2006, Yale University Press also took some bold steps with Yochai Benkler's book, *The Wealth of Networks: How Social Production Transforms Markets and Freedom*. Benkler's book was made available online in several document formats. As expected, one could buy it outright from Amazon or Yale.[55] But what about those who could not afford it or who were not sure if they wanted to buy it? Benkler, then a Yale University law professor, had a solution. With Yale's permission, he would provide many free viewing options. One could download it as a PDF document, view it online in HTML, or browse it in an online wiki. The wiki was not just for viewing the book in another format, but also allowed readers to add resources related to the book.

Those were apparently not enough options for Benkler, who has since taken up shop at Harvard. He attached a Creative Commons license to the document that allowed others to share or remix the work with proper attribution and for noncommercial use only. With that one move, this site drew a wide audience of sharers and remixers, and with their actions, still other fans and entirely new audiences for his work. As proof, various remixes of the book were created, including narrations of the entire book. These narrations were also available in different formats (for example, WAVE, FLAC, or MP3). Equally impressive, a full translation of the book into Italian was completed by the user community, and different parts of the book have been translated into Russian, Brazilian Portuguese, and Spanish. Reviews, blog comments, discussions, interviews, and video resources can be found linked from the main Web site for the e-book.

What is perhaps the most interesting story here is that Benkler's e-book epitomizes the economy of free and open source cultures, such as Wikipedia, which he outlines in his book. He is showing the world what is possible. Benkler seems happy with the results. When I spoke with him in late May 2008, he indicated that between fifty and sixty thousand full downloads of the book had been made in just two years, or about fifteen hundred to two thousand downloads per month. He highly recommends this form of publishing, though he cautions others to think carefully about the teaching platform in which the e-book is presented. Some systems are more interactive and enriching than others.

Benkler is among the fans of the interactive e-book features offered by the Institute for the Future of the Book. After exploring the digital version of Jonathan Zittrain's book, *The Future of the Internet—And How to Stop It*, also from Yale University Press, I quickly understand what Benkler is saying. The e-book version allows readers to add personal annotations or comments on any section of this book; the annotations feel more interactive and provide a better way to track conversations and suggestions about the book. The homepage from the Institute for the Future of the Book argues that "the printed page is giving way to the networked screen." The site adds that the "network book is not bound by time or space." No longer is learning from a book tethered to a reading room when one is awake. Now anyone can chance upon a digital book and read, annotate, discuss, and share it when time permits.

What might happen if such sharing practices went from novelty to mainstream? Naturally, there would be countless resources at our disposal to open the learning world with. Resources for any age learner on any topic. Books, articles, white papers, thought papers, and other flavors of the month will be placed there in an ever-expanding knowledge pool. Someone will need to coordinate all these digital documents. But who? And what would such a site look like? First, it would contain the knowledge access possibilities of Wikipedia and its sister project, Wikibooks. Second, it might also have the commenting, sharing, rating, and subscribing features of YouTube. Third, it would be a portal of learning resources much like Curriki and Connexions. In contrast to those content-sharing sites, such a site would be a resource portal for free books, documents, and papers. After thinking about this, I was on the lookout for such a learning resource or site. I did not envision, however, that I would literally "trip" into it.

TRIPPING INTO SCRIBD

Soon after writing the above section, I discovered that such a site actually exists. It is called Scribd. I looked up Scribd and found that it was located in downtown San Francisco. So after my visit to the Wikimedia offices on March 7, 2008, I took a short break and walked a few blocks from my hotel room to the headquarters of Scribd at 211 Sutter Street, just on the edge of Chinatown. The lobby entrance was filled with balloons, banners, squirt guns, and skateboards. Not exactly what I expected to see, but I soon found out that they were remnants of the one-year anniversary party held at Scribd the day before. Though I did not have an appointment, the receptionist told me that they were willing to accommodate me in less than an hour. When I came back, I met with Scribd CEO and cofounder, Trip Adler.

Trip Adler was just twenty-three years old, full of energy, and open to new ideas. Trip was born and raised in the Silicon Valley, and the valley's entrepreneurial spirit was clearly in his bones.

The idea for Scribd was developed by Trip and his friends about the time Trip was graduating from Harvard. He had experienced all too often the numbing sensation that students at any level feel when they pour their heart and soul into a product that is read by just one person, the professor, for perhaps thirty minutes and then is hurriedly graded and quickly forgotten or thrown into the bin. When it happens repeatedly over a span of four or five years, you start to feel that your ideas do not matter, and Trip developed an antidote for this. The solution, Scribd, is a paper-sharing site similar to YouTube. But instead of recording and sharing videos online, Scribd users post lecture notes, poems, letters, funny stories, magazines, newsletters, and many other documents, including legal documents, maps, and recipes. Whereas college students might share marked-up papers in Scribd, their professors are uploading thought papers and high-level research documents they have written and then discussing them. Educators also share course syllabi, curriculum lessons, and entire books in Scribd.

Suppose you are not a student or a professor; of what use is Scribd to you then? Well, Trip has also heard of people from different countries sharing genealogical records and finding ancestors that they could not have discovered without collaborating in Scribd. When I asked him about copyright problems for some of the documents uploaded to the site, he admitted it was an issue and then cited their compliance with known copyright rules.[56] He added that they attempted to deal with all potential copyright issues within twenty-four hours.

Scribd allows people to upload and share documents using a Flash-based document reader called iPaper. According to Trip Adler, their Web document system is what makes Scribd unique. iPaper is a new and easy way to view, upload, and share Web documents. When I tried it out, I was amazed at the rapid speed in which two of my longest Word documents were converted to iPaper. More impressively, these papers were quickly being viewed by others.

Trip is quite proud that within the first week of going live, Scribd was a top 1,500 Web site and is now in the top 600, according to Alexa. With the immediate popularity came a slew of phone calls about potential funding. He also told me that those who use their system will experience less anxiety when they fall victim to computer theft or a hard-disk crash because their documents will be saved on Scribd. As with YouTube, articles can be found on many topics—history, government, health, sports, science, business, computers, and culture. The most viewed document I found when browsing through Scribd in February 2008 was a music list written in Spanish that had over 400,000 viewers. The most popular article that day was one about the "Top 10 Weird Anomalies in Medicine," which had been posted fully nine months prior and which more than 76,000 people had browsed.

Scribd can be thought of as being in the knowledge matchmaking business. As Trip Adler noted, "[W]e are the organizers of a huge messy library of content." What gets him excited is when "somebody in India is looking for a very specific piece of information and can now find it in a Scribd document." There is a new audience and purpose for one's writing. And that audience keeps expanding!

For example, you might write a paper on computer security systems for a computer science class that is read and cited in a report by a businessperson in Paris a year or two after your college instructor has graded it. Therein lies the power of such a system. The world opens up and creative sparks now have a huge potential audience and therefore meaning. As John Dewey would have hoped, education becomes purposeful. And as his Pedagogic Creed reminds us, it is the social aspects of learning that are just as important as the individual cognitive ones, if not more so.[57]

Given the wealth of resources already found at this site and the traffic it handles, there is no doubt that Scribd, or a site like it, has found a niche and will be highly popular in the years to come. There are countless uses for Scribd. You can find needed documents that are no longer available at the original Web site, publish articles that were rejected elsewhere, post press releases and background information for books and other documents, get knowledge out to those who need it, and ask for feedback on ideas. *Opening Up Education*, MIT's book mentioned earlier, was a featured document in Scribd in the fall of 2008 and is still there for anyone wanting to find, flag, download, tag, share, comment on, or read it.

The community and groups features of Scribd provide another means for fostering online collaboration and the sharing of ideas. As in Yahoo! Groups, there are public and private groups in Scribd on topics such as Google, Entrepreneurship, Indian Vegetarian Cooking, Adobe Photoshop, and Sheet Music. Prestigious organizations are using Scribd, including the National Science Foundation, which has uploaded over 11,000 documents, the Internal Revenue Service with 12,000 documents, the Securities and Exchange Commission with some 82,000 documents, and the Federal Register that can boast a whooping 200,000 documents in Scribd. Document sharing by government agencies is clearly a popular activity in Scribd. Former FBI Director J. Edgar Hoover must be rolling over in his grave. Without a doubt, Trip Adler is a twenty-something technology superstar who, like Lucifer Chu, Jimmy Wales, Richard Baraniuk, and Cory Doctorow, is truly a revolutionary of the shared Internet. Such people are just as needed in the twenty-first century as John Adams, Paul Revere, John Hancock, and Alexander Hamilton were in the latter half of the eighteenth.

All these features and options bring heaps of users to the revolution in document sharing that Scribd has instigated. According to a video interview of Trip Adler, in late 2007 there were approximately 250,000 Scribd visitors per day or 7.5 million visitors per month. When I met him in March 2008, he said this had already jumped to thirteen million visitors per month and two months later in May, it stood at twenty-one million unique visitors. At 20 percent growth per month, there is clearly a thirst for document sharing that they are helping to quench. Such expansion has led to much outside interest, including a healthy $3.9 million of venture capital. By the late fall of 2008, Scribd had become the largest social publishing company in the world with over fifty million readers every month and over fifty thousand new documents uploaded each day. Not too surprising, it was being compared to the early growth phases of YouTube and Facebook. In December 2008, Scribd received $9 million of additional venture capital. At the same time, George Consagra, the chief operating officer of Bebo, a popular social networking software company, was made president of Scribd.[58]

Will Scribd become the YouTube of the document world? That is difficult to predict. What is certain is that most anyone writing or reading electronic documents will soon be a user of Scribd or some similar type of service. Scribd makes free documents available to educators and students around the world. How they are utilized, repackaged, and shared will be highly interesting to watch unfold. *Viva la revolution* called Scribd!

IT'S A LIBRARY THING

Communities not only form around shared online documents such as those found in Scribd but around the books one reads. Remember the assigned quest of Aaron Swartz from the Internet Archive to create a card catalog for all the books of planet Earth? It seems Tim Spalding from

Portland, Maine, has a different approach. He has created a Web site called "LibraryThing" where anyone can be a librarian or "thingamab-rarian" of their own personal library of books. No longer are the masses of books that some people have acquired through the years a secret or knowable only through a personal home or office visit. With Library-Thing, anyone on the Web can quickly catalog her books, join groups with similar reading interests and discuss them, or simply read the discussions of others. Users can join book clubs on hundreds of topics from "Existentialism" to "Youth Writers" to "Making Money" to "Teachers Who LibraryThing." They can also take note of the criticisms as well as the acclaims related to the books from Friedman, Florida, Toffler, and Cross mentioned in Chapter One.

Less than three years after its creation in August 2005, LibraryThing had more than 400,000 users and twenty-six million books in the system. With such growth, LibraryThing argues that it is the world's largest book club where one can find other members with "eerily similar tastes." When I browsed the site early in the summer of 2008, I found such claims hard to argue with.

The LibraryThing process is nearly effortless and is free for the first two hundred books. It took mere minutes to catalog fifteen of my books and become a thingamabrarian. The ease of use makes the posting of more books addictive. When done, I could quickly connect to con-versations that other thingamabrarians were having on the books I had listed. Through this site, one can tag books, rate books, review books, talk about books, swap books, borrow books, and of course, buy more books. It is a book lover's paradise! And it is participatory. Knowledge and ideas were meant to be read and discussed. LibraryThing should be everybody's thing.

TIME TO PARTICIPATE

The tools for participating in learning have never been more plentiful. The Web 2.0 has seen to that. Some will prefer to participate using shared online video. Others will want to contribute text or edit the text of others. Some will be YouTubers and others Wikipedians. It really does not matter the type of content or the tool, platform, or resource. What is vital to note is that, as John Dewey, Seymour Papert, Stephen Downes, and others have hoped, everyone can now actively participate in learning. Schools, colleges, universities, and training departments can no longer hold back. The tide is coming at them full force, and it is not letting up at any time soon.

As we take advantage of participatory learning, we all learn. This typically requires an Internet connection, or, at the very least, access to computer technology and associated resources. It also necessitates that those trained by traditional read-and-recite methods undergo drastic philosophical reflections and changes. But those Internet connections and associated training sessions would be for naught without leadership among technology directors and administrators. However, as this chapter should make clear, there are no more excuses.

Yochai Benkler argues that networked information environments have placed us in a more democratic age. We can now critically review, debate, and question what we view in popular media as well as what arrives via RSS feeds, blog posts, and e-mail distribution lists. As he puts it: "Ideal citizens . . . are no longer constrained to occupy the role of mere readers, viewers, and listeners. They can be, instead, participants in a conversation. Practices that begin to take advantage of these new capabilities shift the locus of content creation from the few professional journalists trolling society for issues and observations, to the people who make up that society . . . The agenda thus can be rooted in the life and experience of individual participants of society—in their observations, experiences, and obsessions."[59]

Benkler's basic message is that we now all have a voice. We have many voices, in fact. And we can use these voices as well as our fingers to share learning-related ideas and experiences with others on similar pilgrimages. On this new participatory learning planet where the world of education is open to everyone, WE-ALL-LEARN. Let's not simply make that a goal or learning creed, but a habit or expression of reality. Contribute! Participate! Enjoy!

Collaborate or Die!

OPENER #7: ELECTRONIC COLLABORATION AND INTERACTION

INSPIRATION FOR COLLABORATION

There is no mistaking the societal trend over the past couple of decades from a highly competitive focus, in schools and in industry, toward the need for greater collaboration and teamwork skills. This does not mean that competitiveness is no longer valued. However, as we emerged from working in silos to collaborative work teams, a gap in such skills was highly apparent. For a couple of decades, educators have been promoting computer-supported collaboration as one solution to this challenge. Recent Web technologies have expanded these solutions and made them more salient. Virtual teaming among remotely located workers is more the norm than the exception.

This transition to an emphasis on teamwork is perhaps most noticeable because online learning success is often dependent on such skills as communication, collaboration, and conversation. The late management guru Peter Drucker often argued that society needed knowledge workers who were adept at problem solving, collaboration, and learning in general. They learned how to learn. It is vital then, that training and education provide tools and activities that adequately prepare workers for these environments. Workers without such skills might as well stay home.

As Friedman documented, with the emergence of Globalization 3.0, individuals from all corners of the globe can participate in a world economy. Collaborative tools bring their ideas, talents, resources, networks, and products together for sharing and innovation. Collaboration could turn a fledgling company into one that dominates a particular niche or market or at least fashions it into a true going concern.

In each revised version of *The World Is Flat*, Friedman has consistently alluded to the fact that collaboration is a key reason why more individuals can compete economically. There are masses of people competing and collaborating in the business world today who did not have a chance to do so previously. With the tools that he points to as key drivers of that collaboration—mobile phones, e-mail, Web conferencing, Voice over Internet Protocol, and, of course, ubiquitous access to the Internet—we can generally enhance work productivity and team collaboration.

Anyone teaching or learning with online support is confronted with a daily barrage of tools for collaboration and interaction. In one project, you might rely heavily on discussion forums. In one with a shorter time line, videoconferencing may be needed. Still other times you will use e-mail. There are also specific collaborative work tools for annotating and sharing documents, syncing team calendars, project planning, presenting, and discussing. Each of these can enhance team effectiveness. Those who have access to such tools—many of which are free—can share knowledge and generate ideas faster. Such individuals can deftly address problems when they arise. And these tools foster a sense of community and loyalty within the organization and work team.

In their book, *Wikinomics: How Mass Collaboration Changes Everything*, Don Tapscott and Anthony D. Williams offer an extraordinary compilation of the societal changes brought on by powerful collaborative technologies such as wikis.[1] They detail many eye-opening stories of the powerful forces of massive online collaboration and open source software in a range of business, education, and consumer settings and situations. These stories show that collaboration can situate a company on the cutting edge of change and innovation. With online collaboration, any individual or organization can discover new partners, procedures, and problem-solving strategies. Tapscott and Williams describe how thousands or perhaps millions of connected individuals can work together on documents such as Wikipedia to create new products or enhance the value of existing ones. Such collaboratively designed products not only impact business and industry, but can advance scientific achievements, educational possibilities, artistic expression, government functioning, and culture and society as a whole. As technology access expands, so too do the forms and outcomes of such collaborations.

One fascinating story that Tapscott and Williams highlight in their book is that of InnoCentive. Started in 2001 by pharmaceutical giant Eli Lilly, by September 2007 InnoCentive had created a network of over 120,000 scientists and engineers from over seventy countries to collaborate on solving complex problems and challenges that could develop into new products and services.[2] Tapscott and Williams liken it to an eBay for science or an online matchmaking system between the global scientific talent pool and companies that have problems to be solved. Problems posted include those in the life sciences, chemistry, business, engineering and design, and math and physical sciences. Those involved receive cash prizes ranging from $10 thousand to $1 million for submitting the winning solution.

InnoCentive is the ultimate in collaborative systems for the advancement of humankind. Scientists are paid for their talents and ideas while being freed up to work with people who they might not have otherwise met. At base level, InnoCentive involves humans meeting humans in an online collaboration and sharing environment with the goals of creativity, innovation, and problem solving. As they exchange ideas, some of the foremost minds on the planet learn from each other, thus amplifying and extending scientific knowledge beyond anything possible for a single human. The coming decade will see many such forms of networked science that are only now possible through cyber infrastructures and collaborative technologies.

Tapscott and Williams point out that the past decade has brought a series of overlapping trends and technologies that feed off each other and escalate changes occurring in business, government, and educational sectors. Such disruptive types of technologies have fundamentally changed culture and society in the past. They contend, however, that the collaborative technologies of the Web bring vastly different changes from those seen before. As Tapscott and Williams observe, "The new Web—which is really an internetworked constellation of disruptive technologies—is the most robust platform yet for facilitating and accelerating creative disruptions."[3] These disruptive technologies for global knowledge sharing include massive online libraries of searchable and reusable data, vast numbers of online courses, and online portals of digital information. And there are innovative and far less expensive tools for collaboration than what was available a decade or two ago. The convergence of these factors allows for greater human participation, interaction, and knowledge sharing.

Given the exponential growth in the number of connection points, the networks that Tapscott and Williams point to can spawn innovation and perhaps even social movements. And this can seemingly happen overnight. When a viral message is distributed and takes hold among millions of connected people, new trends and preferences emerge within a few days, if not a few hours. Innovation is happening so quickly that companies have scant time to delay development of a product for their competitive advantage. The authors go on to argue, "Though we are just beginning a profound economic and institutional adjustment, incumbents should not expect a grace period."[4] Point well taken.

Throughout their book, Tapscott and Williams provide many examples of how collaboration is adding value to companies and helping individuals as well as institutions and organizations form new kinds of relationships. Scientific collaboration can lead to innovative biomedical research and drug developments. Collaboration among geologists in sifting through open source geological data of a gold mining company can harness the power of thousands of talented people to zero in on where gold mining would prove highly advantageous. A form of collaboration also occurs through the use of RSS ("really simple syndication," which allows people to keep up with blogs, podcasts, and news in an automated manner) to aggregate content from different blogs on the same topic or issue. With RSS, bloggers share their insights, talents, and expertise with people searching for it; there is an intellectual talent match taking place online. Similar events occur when social networking tools such as Facebook or LinkedIn are employed to share expertise and interests. If an expert is needed, one can quickly be found and contacted in LinkedIn.

Online collaboration can take the form of audio as well as text or visuals. With Voice over IP, for instance, the expression that someone is just a phone call away is now a reality for those who could not afford long distance calls. The collaborative possibilities of tools such as Skype and

GoogleTalk for free online peer-to-peer voice collaboration join people together for research, writing, thinking, training, and education in ways not previously possible. Tapscott in Toronto and Williams in London used Skype to discuss ideas and exchange critical documents and resources for their book. In addition to team collaboration and research, tools like Skype have found use in language training that brings in fluent or native speakers of such languages as Arabic, Chinese, Portuguese, and so on to train students anywhere with an Internet connection.[5]

As Tapscott and Williams document, online collaboration is also exemplified in the free and open source community as well as the OER movement mentioned in previous chapters. The open source software community is replete with individuals interested in sharing their discoveries and insights. There is reciprocal sharing of new software code and evolving forms of collaboration. And such collaborations bring unique human resources and intellectual capital to bear on the problem.

As implied in the title of Tapscott and Williams's book, wikis are excellent tools for companies, schools, and educational institutions to accumulate, store, and reuse experts' knowledge on different topics. So enthralled are the authors with massive online collaboration possibilities that they left the final chapter of *Wikinomics* empty. They then boldly asked the readers for their input into what they billed on their wiki site as the "first peer-produced guide to business in the twenty-first century." In a post-beta version of this chapter, readers will find sections on models for collaboration, the pros and cons of wikis, collaboration tools, adoption strategies, and collaboration and culture.

PURCHASING PENGUIN PALS

There has been some obsession with social networking software and learning communities during the past few years. They are popular in part because they provide a socially shared space where people can mingle, learn, interact, have fun, and get to know virtual friends or maybe some real friends. This is true for adults as well as young children. Club Penguin is one of many popular social networking sites where kids ages six to fourteen take on an avatar—yes, a penguin of different colors—in a virtual world. In Club Penguin, they can interact with other kids, negotiate the etiquette of how to play games with people they have never met in real life, and learn how to earn and save up enough "coins" to buy virtual things they want.

Like most tools of this kind, initial registration in Club Penguin is free. However, the free version lacks many popular functions such as decorating a virtual igloo, buying clothes and accessories for one's penguin, and adopting and taking care of two or more puffles. As might be expected of a social networking tool, a youngster can also open up his igloo on the map so that he can meet more friends. Given that more than seven hundred thousand subscribers pay $5 per month for those additional features, such add-ons are apparently highly important to children. Unlikely as this may sound, parading around as a penguin is highly popular these days. It is so trendy, in fact, that on August 2, 2007, Disney paid $350 million to acquire Club Penguin with another $350 million possible if performance goals were met.[6] Disney is not foolishly acquiring virtual penguins for its next movie. It realized that half of the kids on the Internet may be members of one or more of these virtual worlds by 2012, doubling the present rate.[7] Perhaps the Google Generation will give way to the Penguin Pals.

JUST 1KG MORE!

Virtual experiences like Club Penguin are highly popular in North America and countries with extensive Internet access. But let's move the landscape to rural China. What do kids there between the ages of six and fourteen like to do? Do they like to make new friends? Would they be excited to see the world beyond their immediate surroundings? Do they enjoy imagining, creating, and sharing? You bet they do. But how? Unfortunately, they do not have access to tools and resources like Club Penguin. Many schools do not have electricity, let alone Internet access and laptop computers. Club Penguin and programs like it are simply not practical there. But what if the core concepts of the Club Penguin community—sharing, imagining, interacting, creating, designing, and discovering—could be created without most of the technological components? What do you get? Well, if you are in rural China, you get 1kg.org!

1kg.org is short for "1 kilogram more in your travel pack." It is a cross between charity and travel. According to its Web site, 1kg asks travelers to bring 1kg of inexpensive educational materials to give away along their travel paths. To participate in 1kg, one follows three easy steps: (1) carry, (2) communicate, and (3) share. First, travelers check the 1kg project Web site for schools along their travel paths. They see what educational materials the schools need and they carry them in their backpack. Second, once they arrive, travelers communicate and interact with the kids, playing games, giving lessons, and bringing information from the outside world to them. Third, travelers then share their stories and pictures on the 1kg project forum when they return. This is where online collaborative technology can have a direct impact on learning in rural communities that may lack access. Unlike Club Penguin, where technology is pervasive throughout the process, in 1kg, online technology starts the process and ends it. In reality, however, 1kg activities never truly end.

Critics of this more open world should take note—though technology is typically not available in these schools in China, collaborative online technology makes 1kg possible. Thus, we can all get access to education resources found on the Web without actually having Web access. This is where the nearly six billion people without Web access can be Web participants.

Andrew Yu, the founder of 1kg, initiated this idea in April 2004 when he heard the story of two volunteer teachers who were teaching in a remote village in Yunnan Province. After spending one year being volunteer teachers, these two teachers encouraged all the other volunteer teachers to remember only two things: "You are not alone" and "You will be successful." Yu was immediately touched by the story and started contemplating how he could help teachers and students in rural China. Soon Yu was talking to one volunteer teacher who told him, "Material deprivation can be overcome. What we need most is the chance to communicate with the outside world." Yu believed a reciprocal sharing experience between the travelers and the kids was the solution. Travelers could bring their experiences from the city into remote villages, and the villagers could invite the travelers into their captivating landscape of untouched beauty and serenity. In August 2004, just four months after hearing about the work of two volunteer teachers, the 1kg organization was formed. The very next month, the first activity was carried out in Chengdu, a city in the Xichuan province.

Yu himself made his first trip to Anhui Province in October 2004. He spent two days in a remote village and played chess, swam, and held a field trip with the kids. That experience made him rethink his views on "charity." He realized that we assume poor people are not happy people. However, as he put it, "Each child has a happy childhood. Such happiness is not affected by them being poor or rich. To help them move toward a fuller life, we should discover and enjoy their happiness and should not uncover and feel sorry for their poorness."[8]

During the past few years, Mr. Yu has continued to refine his idea of 1kg as he experienced more firsthand trips to remote villages. In May 2005, he spent three days in two schools in a village next to the Yellow River in the Shanxi Province. During this trip, Mr. Yu and his team started a conversation where they asked the children to introduce themselves and say what they liked and dreamed of. After some prompting and a lot of patience, the kids started to open up. The girls might like little bunnies and small deer, whereas the boys might prefer tigers and lions. They all liked to go to school. However, when asked what they wanted to do when they grew up, most kids did not seem to have any thoughts or dreams about the distant future. Some wanted to be farmers. Such comments were not unexpected given that all the kids had seen farmers. Some wanted to find employment with the local police because the policeman catches bad people. One kid wanted to be a doctor, and her dream was likely related to her father's early death.

Such exercises encourage the enormous imagination and creativity of these children while helping them understand their family life and situation. During the May 2005 visit, Mr. Yu also witnessed an important conversation between his teammate and the children.[9] The teammate asked them if they had heard of Beijing or Qin Hua University. He also asked them, "What does Qin Hua University have?" The kids imagined Qin Hua University being a place with buildings, trees, and lakes. The teammate asked, "Maybe Qin Hua University has buildings, trees, and lakes. Do you think it has Yellow River?"

"No."
"Do you think it has beautiful mountains like you do here?"
"No."
"Do you think it has beautiful architecture like you do here?"

"No."

"So you see, Beijing might be a great city, but your hometown is wonderful too. So do you think you all should love your hometown?"

"Yes."

Upon reflection, Mr. Yu realized the true message that 1kg was trying to convey to the kids. As he put it, "First we need to inspire their imagination, letting them know that there are many other ways of living. . . . We need to let the kids believe that if they keep dreaming and work hard, they too can choose their destiny." But before the children can reach out to that destiny, they need to develop an appreciation of what they already have, and they should be "very proud of their hometown."

Mr. Yu and many other volunteers have made innumerable trips to many remote villages since 2004. The faces might be different, the locations might vary, but they all share one similar story—as often the case in such experiences, the travelers gain as much as they have given, if not more. Andrew Yu's blog details all the trips, including the children who cannot wait to show him their two pigs, one cow, and a herd of ducks. There is a note about a young girl who exclaimed that she will one day learn how to use a computer. Another post tells of a boy who wrote, "I want to go to Guangzhou to study and go visit Andrew on the weekends." Mr. Yu remembered this child. He cried when Andrew left the village. As he noted: "They will not remember how many pencils you brought or how many that they wanted you to bring next time. They remember the time you spent with them and that is more precious than the extra 1 kilogram you carried with you."

According to the official report in early 2007, 1kg has attracted more than five thousand volunteers who have visited 150 schools, with the potential to reach millions of kids. What is innovative about 1kg is its creative combination of Internet technology and face-to-face communications. WE-ALL-LEARN through such collaboration. The Internet has kicked open another learning door. The 1kg Web site provides a wide array of resources and information for travelers. It has information about schools, instructions for the journey, suggested curriculum activities, and an online discussion forum to ask questions and share experiences. So the Web helps 1kg travelers gather all the necessary information prior to their travel and to later share their stories with others who might be inspired to take part. Technology also becomes an enabler in finding volunteers, coordinating travel schedules, and facilitating projects. Combined with actual face-to-face engagement with local kids, 1kg provides an exemplary case of how technology can play a role in bridging the gap between rural China and the rest of the world.

1kg's Twin Project

In September 2007, 1kg started yet another innovative project called TwinBooks. The basic idea of this project is simple—a child in a city buys one of the TwinBooks, and the other book is donated to a kid in a remote village. Through the TwinBooks Web site, after entering the "twin code" from the purchased book, the child who bought the book can specify where the other book should be donated. The Web site also has contact information about how to write to children in the designated school.

How can they afford this? Simple. The book costs are low. Second, the book that is sold in the city in China has a slightly higher price. Third, as with most such projects, TwinBooks has sponsors. Fourth, all transactions and communications take place via the Internet. That, too, reduces the costs.

Each storybook delivered comes with letterhead, an envelope, a bookmark, a sticker, and a twin card. In addition, TwinBooks children are encouraged to write to each other often or even visit one another someday. With the TwinBooks project, the 1kg people have found another innovative way of making a contribution to rural education in China with an influx of resources in the form of books. As with the 1kg project, the Web sets the stage for learning and resource sharing. It is an outlet for those with fewer resources. Simple collaborative tools for sharing books or for signing up to take resources to schools and children in need are all that is required to get such a program going. Collaborative tools, therefore, are fantastic outlets for educating learners who have fewer resources available. Web-based collaboration is a first step in equalizing access to valuable learning resources.

RAISING GLOBAL ePALS

Advances in Web technology during the past decade have created thousands of ways for teachers and students to collaborate across international boundaries. There are projects related to the environment such as the GLOBE project, Kids as Global Scientists, and the Journey North. Students in such programs might collect and share locally collected data with peers around the world. Their real-world scientific data might be related to barometric pressure in different cities, waterway pollution, or traffic patterns. What is important is that, like real scientists, the students are collecting and sharing information that can be studied, categorized, and then reported. To add meat to the apprenticeship process, scientists in industry, government, or higher education often serve as advisors along the way or as evaluators of final projects.

Some of these resources take the form of "Ask the Expert" forums or similar types of exchanges. Individual students or groups might ask questions of Dr. Math, Dr. Universe, or a Mad Scientist. Such questioning of experts on the Web is a way of engaging students and getting feedback to them on something that truly matters to them. They might also search the Web site for their answers. In the process, students learn that educational resources, including human ones, exist beyond their classroom. They also begin to realize that expertise in an area is vital. These resources are part of a number of approaches to get students interested in math and science.

In addition to online science, there are many other types of international exchanges and mentoring projects on the Web. Projects such as ePals and International Education and Resource Network (iEARN) are well-known to thousands of international participants. With a start in 1988, iEARN predates the Web. It began as a relatively small project between schools in New York State and Moscow; it now boasts the involvement of more than twenty thousand schools and youth organizations from over 120 countries spanning the globe.[10] Through the network established by iEARN, more than one million students each day solve global education problems in an exciting, interactive, and collaborative way. Young people from Australia, Korea, Taiwan, Mongolia, Uzbekistan, and the Solomon Islands might form a single learning circle to share ideas, complete curriculum tasks, and solve problems.

In this crazy digital world, iEARN is a "nonprofit" organization that requires a small fee to participate. In contrast, ePals is a "for-profit" company but is free for anyone to use. Though ePals is geared toward K–12 teachers, students, and schools, there are many posts from instructors in higher education, parents, and local community educators. Requests for collaboration, in fact, might come from any of these sources.

ePals was founded in 1996 and later merged with In2Books in 2006. In2Books is an online service that enables adult pen pals to respond to online letters and summaries about the curriculum books that students read in schools. As with ePals, having an authentic audience for one's work inspires students to achieve at higher levels.

If a student or teacher is interested in working with those from Hong Kong, Namibia, Ethiopia, or Venezuela, that is accomplished by clicking on the ePals map and finding a grade level and interest match. Here are a couple of examples. The first request is from Amod R., who works with kids ten to twelve years old in Hong Kong.

> Tung Koon primary school is a government designated school for Non-Chinese Students, who are from the Ethnic minorities communities of Hong Kong. Most of the children are Nepalese, Pakistani and Pilipino. The curriculum of school is based on local curriculum in English medium of instruction, beside they learn Cantonese and Nepalese language. I want my students to collaborate in different project work to share knowledge to develop multi culture and global awareness.

This post starts the collaboration process. Any member of ePals can then contact Amod R. to set up a cross-class collaborative project.

Clicking on Africa and then Namibia might lead you to the following note from Christine H.:

> I am teaching Internet, email, and web development skills to a group of 10th and 11th graders in Rehoboth, Namibia. The learners are very bright and are eager to expand their computer knowledge. We would love to be able to use our new email addresses to communicate with learners in other countries.

With tools like ePals, Africa and other seemingly far-off lands are now open for global collaboration.

According to Rita Oates, vice president of education markets at ePals, the ePals network includes more than thirteen million students, 325,000 classrooms, and two hundred different countries and territories. Now that is a lot of choice and flexibility in learning! And there are many ways to find a match. In addition to the interactive map search tool, a teacher or student can also search for collaborators by project. Anyone who is a member can post a project need or wish. It is like an international "Make a Wish" foundation for global educators where the Web acts as the matchmaking and coordination service. If you seek global collaborative partners, ePals is the place where your dreams can come true.

As Dewey, Papert, and other learner-centered educators would have hoped, the focus of ePals is on meaningful projects, rich in social interaction, data collection, and information exchange. Interclass collaboration might include projects on topics such as natural disasters, global warming, water, and people and culture. For those needing structure, ePals projects list essential questions, objectives, culminating activities, project elements, and standards to be met. If you do not need the structure, then you can creatively design and advertise your own project.

According to an article from Steve Lohr of *The New York Times*, ePals is a great example of a socially responsible company.[11] Students in this unique program simultaneously upgrade their writing skills and increase their sensitivity to different cultures and regions of the world. An authentic audience—a network of millions of peers—is available every day. Curiosity for other people grows as well as the motivation to attend and complete school.

To help in international exchanges, ePals offers a means to instantly translate e-mail exchanges into different languages. Although only six languages are currently translated, there are some 136 different languages spoken among those classrooms. Overall, ePals is easy to use, collaborative, and safe.

These types of global transactions and communication incubate new patterns of interaction. In ePals, student sharing of knowledge occurs regardless of their geographical locations, cultural backgrounds, religious preferences, intelligence quotients, gender, or economic status. When these same students are later found in global corporations, agencies, or schools, they will more handily adapt to teamwork and productivity expectations, and hopefully, treat each other as equal human beings.

Ice Stories

There are many other sites like iEARN and ePals, in which students exchange ideas with peers from other schools and countries as well as with scientists and others who might be working anywhere in the world. From January to March 2008, for instance, educators at the Exploratorium in San Francisco could access a series of Webcasts from scientists at McMurdo Station near the South Pole as well as scientists in the South Shetland Islands and other remote southern locations. The project, partially funded by the National Science Foundation, was called "Ice Stories: Dispatches from Polar Scientists."[12] In the Ice Stories project, students can read about experiments related to Antarctica's sheet ice dynamics, climate change, penguin breeding behaviors, and the responses of the polar marine ecosystem to the effects of global warming.

One scientist involved in the Ice Stories was Cassandra Brooks. At the time, Cassandra was a master's student in marine science at Moss Landing Marine Laboratories (MLML) in California. Cassandra's work focuses on the life history and population of Antarctic toothfish. It was her second trip to Antarctica. In 2006, she was able to study krill and Antarctic finfish, including her beloved toothfish. This time she returned again as part of a zooplankton survey focusing on the krill.

In a February 23, 2008, blog post, she notes, "I stepped out on deck this morning to find the sea fog had finally lifted, revealing an immense ocean of ice: the world of Antarctica." Cassandra goes on to say:

> As far as I could see in every direction there were icebergs of every shape and size imaginable. There is something incredibly captivating about icebergs. Perhaps it is the reminder that I am very far from home, or the blatant message that I am on the coldest ocean on earth. Their sheer size is enough to impress anyone, especially knowing that 80% of their mass lies beneath the surface. Some icebergs stretch hundreds of kilometers long, so big they alter ocean currents and weather and can be tracked by satellites. Over the course of many years they melt down, becoming part of the ocean.

To help the reader better appreciate her situation, Cassandra in-cluded stunning pictures of Antarctic ice and the coastline of Antarctica with her blog post.

Two weeks later on March 10, 2008, she discussed her research in her Ice Story blog and what drew her down to Antarctica:

> Within ten years local population declines and stock closures ensued. Consequently, fishing boats pushed into the southernmost reaches of the Antarctic waters in pursuit of the Patagonian toothfish's cousin species, the Antarctic toothfish. Toothfish are more commonly known by their snazzy market name "Chilean Seabass." And they are an incredibly expensive and gourmet fish—prices are well over $20 per pound—which is the main reason why the fishery plunders on, despite stock depletions and the potential vulnerability of these fish.

Two months after the post, on May 6, 2008 at 5:30 PM, Naicy from the Philippines posts a reply that says:

> DEAR CASSANDRA,
> HELLO FROM THE PHILIPPINES!!!!!!!!!!HOW I WISH TO SEE THE PLACE YOUR POSE IS GREAT MY MOM IS A AQUACULTURIST AND I LOVE TO KNOW ABOUT THE FISH IF EVER YOU VISIT MY COUNTRY CALL ME OR JUST SEND ME EMAILS I WILL TOUR YOU AROUND MY PLACE IS SURROUNDED BY WATER AND HAS A LOTS OF BEACHES HERE TOO LOVE TO HEAR FROM YOU SOON . . . . . . ITS ME NAICY

A few hours later, Cassandra replies:

> Hi Naicy! Thanks for your enthusiastic email! I would love to hear more about the work that your mom does and to chat with you! I would also be more than happy to tell you more about the toothfish!
>   Best,
>   Cassandra

Here Naicy is getting a personalized response from a scientist. And it is nearly immediate. What a great opportunity for apprenticeship and personal friendship.

Another person comments:

I am only 12 years old but i am soooooooo glad that you had fun! I want to be a vet when I get older so that will be fun! Im glad you had a great time tell us more about it in greater detail please!?!?!?!?!!!!!!!!!!

Cassandra also receives a reply to her post from someone named Nadine who is also a scientist and has also been to Antarctica. Moreover, she lives near Cassandra in the Santa Cruz area of California. Nadine tells her, "What a great post! It summarizes the background for your work very well, and it's very engaging." Cassandra replies that she appreciates the reply and has read of Nadine's adventures in Antarctica, including one involving a "toilet tent." She ends with "It's amazing to me that we can be doing work in Antarctica from Santa Cruz. . . . We should share pics and stories." That is the Web today. People living near each other first get to know of each other's work from reading blog postings about their similar experiences in a far-off land.

A month after that May 2008 post, she told me that when in Antarctica, she wanted to communicate her findings with real kids in real classrooms. After making a few inquiries, she was able to connect with the Exploratorium people coordinating the Ice Stories project. Cassandra informed me that her blog posts were written during free time in what were twelve-hour work shifts. She blogged from her research vessel using satellite e-mail, which limited her connection time to twice per day. She told me that these posts can help teach kids in schools about Antarctica as scientists use multimedia tools such as pictures combined with audio and video to show what this rugged climate is like. As she put it, "I think it's a great interactive learning tool. Moreover, students can follow the scientists along in their trip and look forward to new posts; meanwhile they are learning about this incredible and extreme environment." Cassandra feels extremely fortunate to have ventured to Antarctica twice, and she is hopeful that her blog can educate and inspire others about this beautiful spot on this planet. Her closing words as she was headed to her master's commencement that June were quite poignant, "I cannot stress how important I think it is to educate the public, especially in today's world when all our human actions are having such a growing impact on the world, including Antarctica."

What an amazing experience for Cassandra and all those who choose to track her movements by reading her blog! She is simultaneously a teacher and a student. Such adventure learning projects not only expose students to the real world of science, but they also enable students to share in the scientists' passion for their occupations. Students can watch live Webcam events in addition to reading scientists' blogs. Equally important, this is just not passive reception learning; instead, young learners can directly ask questions of the scientists and read their responses. Such educational activities are a 180-degree departure from listening to a lecture and reading static textbooks that are likely out of date. Now students can observe and talk to those who are conducting primary research on topics crucial to the future of human-kind. Few events in school can be as exciting and interactive.

Web technology provides opportunities for kids to be mentored by adults and older students. They might ask space shuttle astronauts or explorers at the geographic North Pole questions about their experiences and experiments. Frank answers from these experts can bring to life content that might otherwise be deemed too abstract or trivial.

With these resources, young people around the world are collabo-rating with online technologies. They might be collecting and recording real-world data, such as on bird or butterfly migration, and sharing it in an online global database of such information for large-scale analyses. They might also be involved in smaller-scale school exchange projects like the one detailed next.

FLAT CLASSROOMS

Remember Cool Cat Teacher, Vicki Davis, who Ustreamed me in Atlanta? Well, for the past few years, her students at Westwood Schools in Camilla, Georgia, have been collaborating with students from Julie Lindsay's classes in Dhaka, Bangladesh, and more recently, Doha, Qatar, where Lindsay is head of information technology. Inspired by Friedman's *The World Is Flat* book, their collaboration is named the "Flat Classroom Project." With these efforts, Davis and Lindsay reveal some of the ways in which the education world is affected by the flatter world that has resulted from Web technologies. The Flat Classroom project creates unique curriculum projects, friendships, and understandings.

Davis and Lindsay take a pragmatic approach to technology use. Name a Web technology, and they have likely experimented with it.

Their students and teachers have used e-mail; Skype; wikis; shared online video, such as YouTube and Google Video; and audio exchange using various tools, such as Evoca, Podomatic, and Odeo. Social networking tools such as Ning provide them with a means for creating educational networks that incorporate blogs, subgroup creation and interaction, discussion forums, photo sharing, video sharing, and much more. With their constant concern for academic excellence, such interactions do not simply happen; a great deal of planning goes into each interschool event. For others who wish to attempt similar projects, they have designed a seven-step model for creating a flat classroom that focuses on connections, communications, citizenship, contributions, collaborations, creations, and celebrations. Pivotal to the success of a project like Flat Classroom are the initial connections between sites and then later the virtual handshakes between collaborative team members.

As high-end risk takers, Davis and Lindsay are inspired by the potential for a global transformation of education brought about by the Web 2.0 and other learning technologies. Such technologies connect students in the urban capital of Dhaka, Bangladesh, which has a population of twelve million people, to students in rural Camilla, Georgia, a town of under six thousand people. Despite such vast population differences, for each school technology represents a chance to participate in educational events that traditionally were impossible due to cost, timing, and lack of access.

In their first Flat Classroom attempt, students were matched with peers from the other school to explore one of the ten flatteners that Friedman documented. Davis and Lindsay wanted to see if online collaborative activities could be so pervasive and powerful as to make it seem like their two classes were acting as one. They were not content with mere appreciation of Friedman's flatteners. As in the philosophy of John Dewey, they wanted their students to experience them in practice. Given significant time-zone differences, student conversations typically took place asynchronously.

In taking this radically different approach to education, Davis and Lindsay did not allow a lecture-and-test philosophy to drive this curriculum. Instead, collaborative, project-oriented activities would give students a taste of the work-related professionalism and teamwork needed later in life. Their students would now experience the tension of looming deadlines, international relationships, personal accountability to others, and product quality standards. And they had to monitor these concerns not just for their own class situation but for peers in another country. As we all know, when the audience for our work expands, it raises expectations and pushes us to excel. Setting the bar even higher, Davis and Lindsay incorporate international judges from such places as China, the United Kingdom, Australia, and Canada to lend feedback on student work and offer ideas for future projects.

Due to all the preplanning and extensive blogging, this project soon gathered a high profile. Davis told me that she and Julie viewed it as a professional responsibility to share their best practices through these same Web technologies so that others could learn from them and hopefully delve more deeply into the new learning possibilities. Despite being separated by eleven hours of time, these two highly dedicated instructors responded to all students as if they were their own.

Davis and Lindsay have received awards and much attention for their efforts. As a testament to their creativity, there are now many other classrooms pursuing similar types of "flat classroom" projects. As this occurs, they continue to push ahead. A sister project that they have designed is the Horizon Project. This new venture involves senior high school students from Spain, the United States, Australia, Japan, Austria, and Qatar who explore higher-education technology trends that have been forecast for the next one to five years in the annual *Horizon Report* from Educause. And they're not done yet; they have also initiated the Digiteen Project in which their ninth- and tenth-grade students explore digital citizenship along with students from an international school in Vienna.

As they expand their efforts, questions about scalability, efficiency, productivity, and integrated curricula emerge. For Davis and Lindsay, these are much more exciting questions to ponder than those about classroom management, attendance, and time on task, which are definitely not problems in the Flat Classroom. Perhaps Flat Classroom projects are one solution for the drop-out crisis highly evident in the United States and many other countries today.

What is interesting is that Friedman's notions of economic flatness have become a driving metaphor for collaboration among students from vastly different regions of the world. As they connect and find their commonalities as well as their differences, they also discover innovative ways to create joint learning productions. Whereas the concept of an "open classroom" has existed since the 1970s, with Web technology trends today this term may take on new meaning. And perhaps students participating in flat classroom projects will interact with those in more open ones. In addition to such programs 1kg, iEARN, ePals, Ice Stories, and Flat Classrooms that include collaborative features, there are technologies specifically designed for collaboration. In the following section are a few examples.

Microsoft Is Groovy

Unlike many of the other educational openers, online collaboration is often not free. Collaboration can occur at many levels and with many types of formats. Teamwork tools include Microsoft products such as Groove and Sharepoint.

Both of these programs have features for document sharing and asynchronous discussion. Groove also has online sticky notes, project management tools, concept mapping tools, a calendar tool, Web browsing, chat, and more. The user is also able to work offline and sync up later. As a result, Groove enables work teams to collaborate on a document where changes are automatically synched to everyone's workspace, thereby sparing the time and energy needed when relying on e-mail to exchange updated documents.

A single customized workspace is favored over multiple ones. Efficient and effective team and organizational collaboration is the goal here—share, revise, and publish documents as a united team. Updates occur at the office or at home as well as when on the road, on vacation, or anywhere else. Everyone can help on a document, even when temporarily lacking an Internet connection.

With both Sharepoint and Groove, the composition of work teams continues to be expanded. Those using them in a corporate setting might see their colleagues continually change as teams rotate or people move.

Worried about the price of collaborative software or seeking to avoid Microsoft products? No problem. Enter Collanos. Collanos Workplace is a free peer-to-peer teamwork tool for collaboration among team members. It provides an online way for teams to keep track of and organize documents among members. When in San Francisco in early August 2007, my son Alex and I had a chance to visit Gil Heiman, who was in charge of customer development and sales for Collanos in North America. Heiman explained that Collanos Workplace software was more Spartan or basic than Microsoft's Groove. However, most people do not need all of the features of Groove.

Collanos's Swiss founders focused on the key functions of most work teams. The tools and features of Collanos Workplace include icons to alert team members to changes or modifications and the ability to post notes within the document to highlight the changes. Users can also send instant messages and engage in online discussion forums. With Collanos Workplace, team members can stay focused on the latest versions of the documents that they are working on and draw each other's attention to specific areas of concern. No servers are required; instead, team members can access shared workspaces locally on their own machines. At the same time, team collaboration and communication is secure. A beta version of Collanos Phone includes voice, video, and instant messaging features.

Collanos is exactly the type of tool that the WE-ALL-LEARN framework advocates—simple, safe, practical, and collaborative learning. It is also free and open to anyone on the Internet (at least for now). People can work anywhere and at any time, both online and offline, using Windows, Mac, or Linux operating systems. Imaginative teachers and trainers might think of the powerful cross-institutional and global collaborative learning that Collanos offers. In the coming years, such tools will be common across educational settings. Instructors might assign a task and immediately expect students to be working in teams.

Suppose you want to organize an online group. In addition to Collanos, sites such as Yahoo! Groups, MSN Groups, and Google Groups are available for communities to form around issues that are important to them (for example, public health, endangered species, corporate leadership, or bird flu). Individuals in these groups can discuss topics, post documents and pictures, set schedules for meetings, conduct and answer polls, share Web links, search member databases, and ask and answer questions.

Go to the groups on "cars" and you have classic cars, muscle cars, custom cars, dune buggies, station wagons, exotic cars, and so forth. Those into dancing can find groups on salsa, tango, ballroom, folk, swing, tap, and square dance, among many others. Yahoo! Groups alone has 534 different tango groups you can join. If you have an interest or hobby, you will likely find others with similar interests online. Though much of this is informal learning, not academic, it nonetheless opens learning to the masses and connects people to one another. Unlike the one-way informal communications channels that society has relied on in the past for learning, such as books, magazines, and newsletters, today people can comment, talk back, and interact. In these online groups or communities, you can more actively participate and find others with similar interests. What all this means is that learning pursuits need not be lonely endeavors anymore. Everyone can help, and you can help everyone else!

Many companies are strategically positioning themselves in the online collaboration space. In the spring of 2006, Google wisely acquired the popular collaborative word processing tool called "Writely" and later renamed it Google Docs.[13] With this tool, Word documents can be uploaded to the Web for colleagues to edit and approve. No special software is required.

Two years later, Microsoft fought back with the announcement of Microsoft Office Live Workspace beta. This tool seems to be a collaborator's dream. Activity panels in Live Workspace can tell students who has worked on a document, spreadsheet, contact list, or database. Unlike Google Docs, it offers both synchronous and asynchronous possibilities.

The name Microsoft carries a lot of weight in the online collaboration business. Within two short months, more than one hundred thousand users had signed up for Live Workspace.[14] This tool is embedded in Microsoft Live@edu with free e-mail and calendar tools. If successful, millions will soon be savvy with this tool and will once again pay homage to Microsoft products. Now all Microsoft Word, Excel, and PowerPoint files can be opened, saved, shared, and changed online. Using Microsoft, work applications will no longer be a solitary endeavor. Instead, the caffeine-fueled college student working at 3:00 AM in the dorms will now have numerous people to collaborate with in the wee hours of the morning. And students who become adept with these collaborative tools will be more employable and globally and interpersonally aware.

If you want to talk to someone in the twenty-first century you have a host of options. You could rely on synchronous conferencing tools and systems such as Adobe Connect Pro, Elluminate, WebEx, and Centra. Maybe the best and perhaps only option is to chat online or to text message with your phone. Or perhaps you might try an online phone call. Extremely popular today are free VoIP systems such as iChat, Skype, and Google Talk. iChat, for instance, which takes advantage of the built-in video capabilities of Macintosh laptop computers, allows four people to simultaneously engage in a video conference. These free online services are increasingly moving into fully functional collaborative exchanges or courses. For instance, Dimdim extends beyond the free online phone or chat business to allow people to share pictures, PowerPoint slides, PDF files, videos, or their desktops. More impressive, nothing needs to be downloaded to your computer to get started. As these open source Web conferencing tools appear, so too, will additional features. Soon perhaps you will be a dum-dum if you do not use Dimdim.

In educational settings, such tools are used for online team collaboration and class interactions. They are also used by universities to interview potential students or for them to ask questions of the admissions office. In the wake of Hurricane Katrina in August 2005, for instance, the University of New Orleans (UNO) lost most of its recruitment, mailing, and communications operations.[15] UNO administrators turned to online chat management systems. They relied on a tool called LivePerson for students to talk to someone online after completing a quick sign-up form.

A COLLABORATIVE PATH

This opener is somewhat different from the others in several ways. First, it can be costly. Some synchronous tools, in particular, cost more than educational institutions and organizations typically have budgeted. But the costs are coming down, and many such tools are being made open source. Second, collaboration is not just a highly acclaimed social phenomena, it is a vital learning principle. Discussions and negotiations with others typically deepen learning outcomes well beyond what is possible individually. Third, it is difficult to pinpoint what online collaboration is because there are so many forms of it. And fourth, many of the other openers directly or indirectly rely on collaboration and collaborative tools. Other chapters of this book, in fact, are loaded with discussions of collaborative technologies that might just as effectively have been placed in this chapter.

Online collaboration initially took place using text. In particular, there were a variety of discussion forum tools that arose throughout the 1990s. These often attempted to replicate what occurred in face-to-face discussions. But instructors soon became aware that online collaboration could include visual, audio, and interactive animations. Video-based collaboration is perhaps the most salient now that IP-based videoconferencing among two or more people is pervasive and quite economical, as in FREE!

There will be still more advances in online collaborative learning during the coming decades. As these occur, they will affect everyone, or, at least, everyone attempting to learn online. Though many advances will relate to improvements of particular tools or technology features, these will pale in importance to how such tools can foster new forms of learning interaction and engagement. Given the types of interactions already possible with one's peers, instructors, expert mentors, and online intelligent agents, there will be no shortage of ideas related to how collaborative tools and learning opportunities can seep into education.

It is clear that we are living and working in times of increasing collaborative focus. The push is toward global networking, sharing, and idea exchange. Collaborative tools have brought Globalization 3.0 to the business marketplace. As shown here, these same tools, as well as many others, have dramatically revamped educational possibilities. When we step into a school, university, or corporate training setting, we are not simply walking in the footsteps of others from decades ago. Instead, we find ourselves walking abreast with learners from many locations and learning situations. And the experts who teach or mentor us are not the only instructors walking into that building with us. Our training and mentoring can come from anywhere. Collaboration is changing everything.

Collaborative tools are yet another indicator that the lockstep factory model of education is out of sync with current learning possibilities and viewpoints. With effective design and use of collaborative tools, WE-ALL-LEARN. We all learn from our peers. We all learn from experts whom we have never met. We all learn from resources generated in another country or culture. And we all learn from archival records of online learning activities completed recently or long ago. If learning stems from engagement with others on a social plane, then it is collaborative tools that catapult learning to new heights. Collaborative tools and social constructivist theory are complementary evolutions of the learning culture of this century.

Just where we are headed as a learning culture may hinge on refinements in the use of collaborative tools. Our learning futures rest not only on the realization that collaboration is not simply an empowering engine for economic expansion made possible by Globalization 3.0, but also on the gains in education that underpin the economic ones. There are many who want answers—what can and should we do next to fix this huge education crisis in front of us? It is clear that there are huge payoffs from online collaboration. Such payoffs seem especially attractive in the difficult economic times currently experienced around the globe. Further inroads into the use of collaborative educational learning tools during the coming decades will lead to even more powerful tool designs and learning environments. This is a space in which many of us will meet in ways we cannot yet know. I hope to see you there.

Who Are You?

OPENER #8: ALTERNATIVE REALITY LEARNING

A LEARNING BEST BUY

Without a doubt, each year we encounter tidal waves of consumer technologies that find their way into educational settings. If you are from North America, you have likely visited Best Buy, Radio Shack, or some other electronics store during the past few years. Or perhaps you've been to PC World in the United Kingdom, Media Markt in Germany, TK 3C in Taiwan, Harvey Norman in Singapore, Best Denki in Japan, or Electronics R Us in Australia. No matter what the store, you would have seen signs of it with your every move: smartphones, miniature laptops, flat-screen televisions, interactive games, digital cameras, Web cameras, graphing calculators, and perhaps even a few digital books on the side counter. So much to gaze at and wonder if now is the right time to jump in and buy.

Educational technologies are pervasive, but may not be obvious. You may not equate a phone, camera, television, or game with learning. Part of the problem is that your parents and teachers never took you to such stores to show you the learning possibilities there. Your mind-set was formed when you were a youngster that electronics stores were places of play and enjoyment, and schools were for completing boring sets of drills and worksheets. Learning cannot be fun! And fun cannot be learning! And, with such notions, Best Buy, Comet, and Radio Shack cannot be learning companies. But I have a little secret for you. Best Buy *is* a learning company and learning *can* be fun—highly effortful, but still fun.

The next time your niece or daughter asks to go to Circuit City or some other electronics store, do not spoil the fun by telling her you are accompanying her on a momentous event in her learning career. Wait until you have returned. The technologies found there can quickly take you on journeys to fascinating learning worlds and activities. Grab some gaming headgear and explore new civilizations as well as those from the distant past. With games and simulations, you can become whoever or whatever you want to be whenever you want.

What you need to realize is that our entertainment and communications technologies have become our learning technologies—witness the educational opportunities now possible with podcasts playing on your iPod or MP3 players, computer simulations like SimCity and Civilization, car stereos with USB ports for electronic books, and short text messages or Web browsing on your mobile phone. Mobile and wireless technologies will be addressed in the next chapter; in this one we will enter the fascinating topic of virtual worlds, which are part of a movement transforming education and training environments, and, ultimately, our lives. Everywhere you turn, there is an announcement related to alternative educational worlds or a new simulation. The medical field, fitness training, education, and business are all increasing their use of simulations. And, of course, there is Second Life, which provides one with alternative personas, creative life pursuits, and even opportunities to make a living.

Such virtual worlds, games, and simulations exist on a continuum from real-life situations to augmented and virtual reality. Once these can be developed on a scale large enough to reduce the costs and technical requirements, the digital divide might be bridged so that more individuals could have the opportunity to participate in these virtual experiences, thereby affecting education and training around the planet.

We often hear cynical critics of gaming argue, "I do not want my surgeon, pilot, or dentist trained by games and simulations." Well, in many cases, you actually do. Medical and aviation simulators are expensive but can build the hand-eye coordination needed to increase effectiveness in surgery or in an air emergency. Skills for minimally invasive surgery, such as laparoscopic surgery, can be honed through playing video games. One study by Dr. James Clarence Rosser Jr. and his colleagues from Beth Israel Medical Center in Manhattan showed that surgeons who engaged in at least three hours of video game playing per week were 27 percent faster and made 37 percent fewer mistakes than those who did not play such games.[1] The coming decade will see extensive inroads to areas where simulations and gaming make a difference. As this occurs, educational simulations will increasingly become part of being human.

It seems that everyone wants a dose of reality these days. We all crave to experience or do the real thing rather than listen to someone tell us about the supposed real thing. Most people realize that they perform best when learning by doing in the real world. Whenever possible and available, they want to do it now—not some time much later. And, of course, it must be fun. What's more, millions of people are willing to take on a different persona, sometimes multiple ones, in order to experience alternative versions of reality that are different from what they tend to experience each day. Often such experiences are simultaneously sought after by thousands of people worldwide, if not hundreds of thousands.

We have entered an age of alternative reality learning, in which real worlds are approximated or entirely new ones are created, as in simulations. Highly popular in business and educational settings, simulations provide learners with a model of reality and strategies and skills that they can later use when facing similar live situations. Games, too, are part of an emerging learning culture. Members of the Net Generation (also called Generations X and Y) grew up with ever-changing new technologies and became adept at playing games with handheld devices, computers, and television consoles. Educational games, therefore, have a motivational energy about them that other learning delivery mechanisms simply do not have. Still, that is not a blanket statement. Games lacking interactivity and engaging design features will almost certainly fail to tap into such energies and will bore students mightily.

GET A (SECOND) LIFE!

In addition to games and simulations, there are also virtual worlds that learners can enter to discover or share information, make new friends, discuss ideas, and conduct transactions. Some people are understandably hesitant to enter because there are so many worlds to pick from. You should not choose a life or a world lightly. Should you join There.com, SmallWorld, Kaneva, or Second Life? Second Life is among the latest crazes for learning professionals in both business and education. Participation in Second Life escalated from 500,000 to 5 million people in just two years.[2]

As of January 2009, Second Life had more than 16,700,000 residents (up nearly 4 million in eight months) and approximately 1,400,000 of them had logged in during the previous sixty days. Stated another way, one in twelve were steady members of Second Life. More than a quarter million people had logged in during the previous week. Also in January 2009, over US$2.5 million was spent in the preceding twenty-four hours. Not money into the pockets of Linden Lab, the developers of Second Life, but financial exchanges between the people of this world, such as someone making a T-shirt for an avatar and someone else buying it in-world with Linden dollars (L$). A profit made in L$ can be cashed out for a real check in U.S. dollars. Some people make their living in Second Life buying and selling real estate, virtual consumer goods, and consulting services. Islands can be purchased in Second Life for residents to build and create businesses, special projects, educational activities, and political forums, just to name a few options.

Technology companies like Dell, Sun Microsystems, and IBM have been among the more prominent corporate entities in Second Life. Dell initially set up their space to show customers the manufacturing process as well as key moments in the history of the company, including a mockup of the dorm room of Michael Dell when he was at the University of Texas at Austin.[3] It was in that tiny room that he started his multibillion-dollar company with just $1,000. Though customers in Second Life can now create virtual Dell PCs, the eventual intent is to have Dell customers order customized products from within Second Life for their first lives.

When it comes to Second Life, IBM is exploring and exploring and exploring some more. IBM has even started a Second Life business group. As with Linux before it, IBM executives see tons of business opportunities in Second Life. Per Irving Wladawsky-Berger, former vice president of technical strategy and innovation at IBM, the company views it as a tool for collaboration, visualization, and social networking.[4] Employees seem to agree. By the end of 2006, more than a thousand IBM employees were active in Second Life. When the chief executive officer of IBM, Sam Palmisano, made a major announcement in Beijing to spend $100 million to incubate new businesses, he was able to fly into Second Life and announce it there as well.[5]

By the fall of 2007, IBM had expanded its presence in Second Life to some fifty virtual facilities used for research, company meetings, and recruitment and induction of new employees. By jumping in early with conferences, white papers, and announcements in Second Life as well as the ownership of many islands where specific IBM-endorsed activities can take place, IBM has become a leader in the field of virtual learning. The opportunity to assemble people from across the world in an inexpensive way also opened IBM up to other types of employee communications and events. As an example, IBM workers in Italy staged a peaceful demonstration at each of the IBM buildings in Second Life to show their disgust for the loss of their performance bonuses during a time of high profits.[6] Protest T-shirts and demonstration signs were available to anyone from a virtual information booth. A whooping 1,850 avatars showed up in support. They also obtained cheap publicity for their grievances.[7] Corporate protests aside, it is the learning opportunities of Second Life that remain most intriguing.

In the spring of 2008, IBM and Linden Labs announced plans to run Second Life on servers inside IBM firewalls.[8] In this way, employee protests would now be more privately conducted. With this added control, IBM can also offer special conferences, training events, and meetings that are dedicated to its employees and invited guests. According to Jim Spohrer, who helped bring us online learning portals like MERLOT, mentioned in Chapter Six, back when he was at Apple Computer, IBM uses virtual worlds for simulating project management and customer interactions. These virtual "rehearsals" equip employees with skills that they would not otherwise have, while saving huge amounts of training time and money. And these virtual worlds are much more flexible than face-to-face ones. According to Spohrer, "You can experiment with a lot of alternatives and designs. . . . Also, as you start developing these rehearsal services, you can start reusing the components from one service to another."[9] It will be exciting to watch how IBM employee training changes or transforms during the next few years as a result of virtual worlds such as Second Life.

A Second Life at Harvard

At the same time Dell and IBM were picking up media attention for their Second Life initiatives, universities such as Harvard, Stanford, and MIT were among the first to buy islands there and integrate this world into instruction. Widely advertised by Harvard in the fall of 2006, for instance, was a virtual law course called CyberOne: Law in the Court of Public Opinion, which was jointly taught by Professor Charles Nesson and his daughter, Rebecca Nesson, a computer scientist, doctoral candidate, and 2001 Harvard Law School graduate.[10] To add to the uniqueness, the general public as well as students from other universities were allowed to enroll in the course. Extension students took the course in Second Life while those on campus attended a face-to-face version. In reference to Harvard's Berkman Center for Internet & Society, a center that Professor Nesson founded, class lectures, videos, discussions, and office hours were all conducted on Berkman Island within Second Life. They even created a replica of Harvard's Ames Courtroom in Second Life. For those who needed to meet the instructor, Professor Nesson was available for face-to-face office hours, whereas Rebecca Nesson held her office hours directly in Second Life.

Across all components of this class, they offered students options on how to learn. As shown previously, in a world where WE-ALL-LEARN, people increasingly want options. According to Professor Nesson, his students might learn from blogs, wikis, podcasts, Webcasts, discussions, debates, and online community television. Using Second Life as the platform allows the general public to peer into a Harvard class and participate in a course for free, while perhaps bringing real-world experiences and ideas that raise the level of the course quality for enrolled students. The synchronous or real-time interactions in Second Life provide a sense of a personal touch or presence that is not felt with online discussion forums and blogs. Synchronous technologies encourage immediate interaction, collaboration, and information on demand that connects students more deeply to a course.[11]

Assorted Web 2.0 technologies have meshed well with the use of Second Life for the Nessons. For instance, as a means to promote the class and its various delivery formats, Professor Nesson created a YouTube video for under $1,000. In this video, Nesson's avatar, Eon, arrives at Harvard on his motorcycle. After taking off his helmet, Eon discusses aspects of the course while introducing you to his daughter's avatar and her role. The video was a way to market the course to people who ordinarily would not be exposed to Harvard law classes.

Professor Nesson explained in a follow-up debate and discussion posted to YouTube in December 2006 that while there are concerns about Second Life as a course delivery platform, "It is an extraordinary time in which to reimagine education." In yet another YouTube video with Rebecca, he makes the argument for the openness of higher education content. In fact, the law discussed in their class and the core ingredient he wished to introduce and amplify within the Berkman Center was the focus on openness. Professor Nesson wants to expand higher education far beyond traditional face-to-face course activities. Educational options might include community television, the Internet, and any other learning outlets. More is better. I think he is spot-on!

When I corresponded with Rebecca Nesson in May 2008, she said, "We are now at a point at which it is possible to imagine making the content of higher education available widely and in high quality." However, she noted that availability of content is not enough. For education to be elevated, rich conversations between students and instructors need to occur around that content. She further admitted that limited access continues to impair visions of what is possible. As Rebecca reminds us: "Access is limited in so many ways, from lack of computers and software to lack of sufficient Internet access and band-width, to challenges posed by language barriers and lack of literacy. We are not yet close to overcoming these problems, so it is important to remain realistic about the actual promise that the technology offers." Still, she claimed that once these various access barriers are removed, serious questions related to effective education will remain.

Other universities have attracted attention for more general uses of Second Life, such as for student orientation and alumni updates. Ohio University and San Jose State University, for instance, both made heavy splashes in the news for their campus tours in Second Life. Now hundreds of universities are using it for various reasons though it remains exploratory, and many educators remain highly skeptical and reluctant. In response to such resistance, college faculty members who need support can go to a special support island made available by creative folks at Georgia State University.[12]

A Date with Intellagirl

A couple of months after the Nessons initiated their Second Life course experiment, who pops into my Web 2.0 class for a visit on a late Monday night but the famed "Intellagirl," Sarah Robbins, and her partner, Mark Bell. Intellagirl is a celebrity in Second Life, and Mark is a self-proclaimed "Storygeek" who assumes the name "Typewriter Tackleberry" when in-world. Sarah and Mark arrive fresh from the completion of their *Second Life for Dummies* book and a speaking engagement in the United Kingdom. Though they look tired, they quickly spring into action and generate much enthusiasm within my class, which for weeks had been grappling with the educational uses of Second Life. Sarah demonstrates how to fly, buy, explore, communicate, and build in it.

Sarah and Mark did not just happen to stumble into my class. They found their way to Bloomington a few months earlier so that Mark could enroll in a doctoral program in telecommunications. Sarah, about to complete her doctoral degree from Ball State University, teaches freshman composition courses. Her students are not found in traditional classrooms but on Second Life islands. Only fifteen to twenty students are allowed to enroll in Sarah's academic writing and research course, yet more than three hundred students sign up for it each semester. As this suggests, most of the names remain on the dreaded waiting list. Perhaps she gets more attention because of her distinctive name as well as her trademark hot pink bangs. Her hair color is so radiant that the first time I saw her speak at a large conference room in Chicago, from my seat near the back I thought she was wearing a Chicago Cubs baseball cap. The hair may be the attention grabber, but it is the content and refreshingly frank and engaging delivery of that content that sets Sarah apart.

Of course, not every English instructor is willing or able to do what Sarah does with technology. She has her feet firmly planted in many traditional occupational roles while creating fully unique virtual roles at the same time. Straddling the academic and business worlds, Sarah admits to being part geek, part researcher, part marketing guru, part academic, and part writer and speaker. She is also an avid blogger with an extensive readership base. Her celebrity status in Second Life has brought press coverage in *The New York Times*, *USA Today*, and the *Chronicle of Higher Education*. If that is not enough, the pink-haired Intellagirl is mom to six-year-old triplet girls. Perhaps there is nowhere else but the Web 2.0 that can enable her to accomplish all this.

YouTube videos on the educational uses of Second Life describe how it could be used in teaching history by having students walk around re-creations of ancient Roman or Greek buildings as well as similar uses in architecture courses. Learners might also enter into worlds where they become actors in Shakespearean plays. Just as easily they might explore the inside of an iPod or iPhone from Apple Computer and view its manufacturing processes. With Linden dollar transactions, Second Life can readily be used in economics, business marketing, retail trade, and finance courses.

Some educators are naturally concerned about sex in Second Life. The University of Plymouth in the United Kingdom is attacking this concern head on by using Second Life to educate students about sexual health and contraception issues. Free virtual condoms can be obtained from a virtual dispensing machine at the site. Visitors can also find sex education materials, watch presentations by experts on the topic as well as movies about HIV/AIDS, read articles from a newsstand with sexual health stories from Yahoo!, and participate in one-to-one sex counseling in a "sky box."[13] Compared to real-world equivalents, such a site is extremely inexpensive to design and use. It also allows for greater choice and more meaningful learning when teaching about sex, enabling the student to hear different viewpoints. And for many students, it is much more fun than sitting through a dull or intimidating sex education lecture given by a high school instructor or parent. Goals of the site include promoting healthy sexual lifestyles and the prevention of STDs and unwanted pregnancies. This is clearly a highly creative and noteworthy educational use of Second Life. Of course, the University of Plymouth is not the first nor will it be the last to offer sex education online, but it is more formal and reputable than most such sites.

Second Life is a highly visual instructional platform. Those teaching art appreciation can have their learners walk into and become part of a famous van Gogh painting. Some give virtual tours of sculptures that become more colorful and vivid as one approaches them.[14] Indeed, any course where visual forms of learning are central can find Second Life applications. Such courses naturally would include history, geography, geology, aeronautics, automobile design, anthropology, and archeology. At the high school level, civics classes might use Second Life to display maps of political districts and help understand gerrymandering.[15] Such approaches could also spur volunteer activism.

Writing and communicating are key parts of online education. Second Life environments are no different. One should not be surprised, therefore, that both journalism and field research courses are highly popular in Second Life. Such uses do not have to be solitary events, either. Collaborative explorations, meetings, and activities are definitively possible.

Intellagirl Sarah noted that at the root level, the tools within Second Life enhance the learning possibilities and the overall meaningfulness of an activity. Flexible and creative use of avatars could offer role-play, debate, and self-exploration opportunities. She added that students who are learning at a distance could feel as if they are in more of a community with their instructors and other students. Sarah contended that this sense of community was a "big bonus for distance ed." Typewriter Mark had a different angle. He felt that educational research was about to explode in Second Life with possibilities for large-scale surveys, designing and testing innovative simulations, and "building spaces in which experiments can be conducted in ways that are cost-prohibitive in real life."[16] When I pressed them about digital divide issues—Second Life effectively separating the "haves" from the "have nots"—they made the following argument: "[Although] Second Life's hardware requirements [and frequent updates] prevent it from being the 'perfect' virtual world, its popularity certainly opens the door for other less demanding spaces and for educational theory to be developed that will help students who might not have access to a good school environment."

According to Sarah and Mark, "Second Life itself isn't helping to narrow the digital divide but the idea of it is." If true, other spaces will soon appear that have more far-reaching educational implications. Let's hope so.

SERIOUS GAMING?

Though not yet heavily utilized, virtual worlds can be found in all levels of education and business training settings. While this opener will quickly resonate with many gamers and Second Lifers, I often sense much tension and see countless smirks when introducing it. The naysayers ask how learning can be fun. What exactly are the learning outcomes of playing a game? They will state that worlds such as Second Life and There.com are far too complex for most learners. Can we afford to spend the type of money required to build a quality simulation or game? And can we take money from traditional learning delivery methods for tools that do not map directly onto learning goals and required outcomes? Undoubtedly students love these things, but who can tell me how to teach with them or assess the learning?

Among the most pressing concerns is that games cannot be taken seriously. To combat such fears, conferences, institutes, and forums have sprung up around the world on "Serious Gaming" that explore and promote the learning possibilities and results of playing games. Higher education institutions and foundations are dedicating massive resources to serious gaming. The first serious gaming institute in the United Kingdom, located in the West Midlands, is Coventry University (CU), which has invested heavily in a Serious Games Institute. How serious? Seven million pounds serious!

Based at the Coventry University Technology Park, this institute will not target the entertainment market but will instead focus on education, training, and simulations. Within a few months of the initial announcement, a press release from Cisco revealed that it is now working with Giunti Labs and the Serious Gaming Institute on a project to uniquely blend mobile learning and virtual world learning. This blending of technologies will enable Coventry University to push out learning content to students according to their location and the type of computing device they are using.[17] And this particular collaborative partnership is part of a much larger plan to create a "smart campus" by 2010. I have presented at Coventry University on several occasions over the past few years, and each time I walk away with a sense of excitement for their embrace of e-learning, emerging technologies, and change.

Coventry is not alone. Back in the United States, the MacArthur Foundation has a $50 million, five-year effort called the Digital Media and Learning initiative.[18] Fittingly, the announcement was simultaneously streamed into Second Life. With such presentations, the MacArthur people show their commitment to new media for learning, as well as their awareness that the way that humans on this planet learn is shifting.

MacArthur funding is not earmarked for just one discipline; rather, progress is to be interdisciplinary. Fundable projects are coming from a variety of sources: humanities fields such as philosophy, history, and political science at Duke University; telecommunications at Indiana University; the Exploratorium in San Francisco; the MIT Media Lab; and the Advanced Distributed Learning Lab at Wisconsin. Results can have an impact on educational and social institutions. Among Mac-Arthur's initial awards was one for $450,000 to help Parsons School of Design in New York City create a lab devoted to studying serious games.[19] Games about the environment, financial planning, and immigration are being discussed.

MacArthur also funded Global Kids, a nonprofit youth organization in New York City. Founded in 1989, the mission of Global Kids is to provide transformative experiences for urban youth that will help them become global and community leaders. In addition to addressing more than seventeen thousand youth in person, this program affects millions of them in online spaces. Part of the funding is being used to design online essay forums for kids to discuss how they use digital media.

According to Barry Joseph, Global Kids's online leadership program director, the funding is also earmarked for exploring how teens might use Second Life for social and educational purposes. Global Kids is the first nonprofit organization that has bought designated space in Second Life devoted to teen-related issues and programming. The "Teens Second Life" (TSL) island is restricted to thirteen- to seventeen-year-olds. Already tens of thousands of young people use TSL.[20] In TSL, we will begin to understand how virtual worlds can be used for youth development and learning around major global issues. There are broadcasted and streamed events in TSL as well as after-school programs on film production, civic engagement, digital media literacy, and global education. Summer camps are also held in TSL on topics from the rights of children to the Holocaust.

Organizations like the MacArthur Foundation and Global Kids recognize that we live in a fast-changing world. In such a world, kids need to know how to quickly adapt to these changes and locate the new knowledge, wherever and whatever it might be. Discrete data points or facts that were once thought to be truths, in reality, often are changed or modified. We have moved from "what" knowledge as the pinnacle learning achievement to "where" knowledge. At the same time, the platforms for learning engagement are in the midst of a metamorphosis from a control-centered approach to one that is more varied, informal, and individualized. We are in a transformation that is putting us on a path, albeit one that is still somewhat muddy and with much brush in the way, to support everyone in learning.

As new media centers, institutes, and projects spring up, we will better understand how virtual worlds change human capacity for collaboration, communication, interaction, and learning. We are in the midst of a major shift in how people learn. The interest in virtual worlds and serious gaming makes this evident. By understanding how younger generations of learners engage in learning, play, and socialization, as well as how they generally participate in life, projects funded by MacArthur such as Global Kids are helping cultivate future generations of successful learners.

Massive Multiplayer Online Games

The interest in alternative worlds is seen in the explosion of massive multiplayer online gaming (MMOG) around the planet and the associated research and development funding from the MacArthur Foundation. In the game Lineage in Korea, when a player is a prince or princess, the status is often equated with that of a Hollywood movie star. Millions of people around the globe are playing in virtual worlds such as World of Warcraft, Final Fantasy XI, EverQuest, The Sims Online, Call of Duty, Halo, Ultima Online, and Star Wars Galaxies. More than ten million were playing World of Warcraft alone![21] Working in virtual teams when playing MMOGs, learners acquire effective communication skills while building trusting relationships. And these games are so lifelike that EVE Online recently announced the hiring of economist Eyjolfur Gudmundsson from Iceland to monitor inflation and trends, as well as publish economic information related to the EVE Online community.[22] His quarterly reports should prove interesting for players as well as outsiders.

The U.S. military is among those taking notice of the trends. A few years ago, my colleague Vanessa Dennen and I were commissioned by the Department of Defense to write a technical report on where the research in massive multiplayer online gaming was headed.[23] We found it intriguing that the U.S. military was interested in how such games might be used to teach leadership, management, problem-solving, decision-making, and planning skills. Certainly perceptual and fine motor skills were still needed in the military, as seen in the free online game, America's Army, but now the critical skills are those that involve higher-order thinking. The military is not alone. Today, businesses are also seeking clues as to how leadership and quick decision making within massive online games might transfer to job settings.[24] Can leadership skills be nurtured in online labs where failure is more acceptable than in real-world business situations?

Military organizations as well as the film and entertainment industries often develop technologies that find unique applications in education, training, and performance support. A few years back, computer gaming obtained similar status with the film and music industries in terms of revenues, customers, and employees.[25] Many computer games became so popular that films were later made about them (for example, *Lara Croft Tomb Raider*, *Super Mario Brothers*, *Mortal Combat*, and *Final Fantasy: The Spirits Within*).[26] In 2002, the commercial computer gaming industry was estimated at $7 billion in the United States and globally at $27 billion.[27] By 2007, the game industry in the United States had jumped to nearly $19 billion, with software sales representing nearly half of that total.[28] Though game sales were projected to surpass both the record industry and the home video markets, the lines demarcating each industry continue to blur and make comparison statistics somewhat meaningless.

Computer games are ubiquitously available from one's hotel room television, mobile phone, iPod or MP3 player, or laptop. Kirriemuir noted that more than 60 percent of the American population plays video games—for teenage boys it is 75 percent.[29] The average age of these massive gamers is twenty-eight.[30] The Entertainment Software Association paints a different picture of the average gamer.[31] Their statistics peg the average age at thirty-five and the most frequent gamer at forty years old. Setting aside age for a moment, wireless gaming is now the hot market. This market will intensify as mobile devices such as cell phones, watches, iPods, and Internet phones permeate society.

Gaming is basically a part of life. A September 2008 report from the Pew Internet and American Life Project found that nearly all teenage boys and girls play video games at 99 and 94 percent, respectively.

Racing, sports, action, and adventure were not the only types of games played, but also puzzle, dancing, and strategy games. This is much higher than an earlier study which found that 70 percent of college students played computer, video, or online games at least once and 65 percent were deemed regular players.[32] It is interesting to note that most of those studied felt that online gaming environments were a positive aspect of their lives. Whereas gaming was once a solitary or single-player type of activity—picture a teenage boy sitting alone in his bedroom after school playing Nintendo—today it is a highly collaborative one. Such a turn toward socially shared gaming has been intentional on the part of game designers as well as game researchers and theorists.[33]

There are many types of games, of course. Some are strategy games or puzzles, which are more educational. There are also war games, quests, role-playing games, sports games, and simulation games. Games can foster a sense of strategic thinking among the players. Pervasive learner experiences with gaming have repercussions for school and training environments. For example, as gaming experiences grow, today's learners are seeking richer and more engaging educational experiences. Expectations for authenticity or a sense of reality in these games are simultaneously on the rise. And with MMOGs, such experiences can be shared with hundreds, thousands, or even millions of game players around the world.

WHAT'S NEXT?

Games, simulations, and virtual worlds add turbo power to the WE-ALL-LEARN model because they are replicable, and hence quickly sprinkled among the corners of the planet. The sense of personal empowerment one learner feels can conceivably be duplicated for millions of others. This opener simultaneously takes human learning to a deeper and richer place that engages and retains learners, rather than allowing them to walk in the front door and out the back door as my Grandpa George did.

There is certainly much excitement in virtual learning. Questions fill the air as well. Will virtual worlds replace classroom instruction? Will meeting instructors and classmates in virtual worlds prior to signing up be a common experience? Can one's thoughts control virtual characters? Don't laugh! Researchers at Keio University Biomedical Engineering

Laboratory, in fact, have already developed a system for the user to control characters in Second Life with their thoughts.[34] Using specially designed headgear, electrodes can monitor thoughts in the region of the human brain that controls physical movement. Think about moving the feet of the on-screen character and he will go forward. With this one advance, wondrous possibilities await those who could not previously gain admission to online worlds such as Second Life and other virtual worlds because they suffer from spinal cord injuries or other physical disabilities.

Research groups also are now working on ways for avatars or virtual presences to walk in and out of different virtual worlds.[35] If successful, this would speed acceptance and ultimately lead to the mass population of virtual worlds. Philip Rosedale, the inventor of Second Life, argues that "within ten years, virtual worlds will be bigger than the Web itself."[36] He also expects that access to virtual worlds will be more pervasive than access to the Web. In raw numbers, he notes that Google presently requires 100,000 machines for its operations, whereas a decade from now, virtual worlds may require "hundreds of millions of machines." The predictions he makes are of mammoth proportions. One thing is certain: if there are huge numbers anywhere on the Web, Google cannot be far behind. Sure enough, Google announced its entry into the virtual world race in July 2008 with a world called "Lively."[37] Apparently, it was not lively enough, as Google quickly disbanded the project less than six month later on the final day of 2008. No explanation was given. Perhaps the world is not yet ready. Or perhaps Google has other virtual world plans involving its Google Earth project, which enables visitors to explore ancient Rome and the art masterpieces of Madrid's Prado museum. Whatever the reason, you can bet that Google has not completely or permanently left this space.

The degree of authenticity and believability keeps growing in online scenarios, simulations, and virtual worlds. We are entering a time that continues to push the envelope of what is possible. But these same envelopes have been pushed before. Will this lead to higher levels of expertise in shorter time bursts? Will simulations or alternative worlds created in one culture be readily transferred to another? How authentic must a virtual world be for educational payoff of some kind? And just who will determine the payoffs?

Authenticity, of course, is enhanced by the portability and mobility of learning. In the next chapter, we explore the ninth opener, which in fact has turned the world of e-learning into m-learning. Now we are no longer prisoner to a particular office, desk, or computer lab. We can be a passenger in a car, waiting for a plane, snacking at a mall, or visiting a zoo—and still be learning! The learning pursuits now possible on this planet have widened a thousandfold in just the past few years. Our species has never before had so many ways to learn, as well as so many ways to put so much learning on display for others to view.

U-Learning?

OPENER #9: REAL-TIME MOBILITY AND PORTABILITY

YES, U CAN LEARN; I M LEARNING 2!

For the learning world to be truly opened, educational activities must be possible wherever any single human being steps foot. Enter the ninth opener—the world of mobile and portable learning. After a decade of mad human scrambling to attempt to understand e-learning and blended learning, we now are confronted with mobile or m-learning, and ubiquitous or u-learning. M-learning has sprung up in recent years with the escalating use of handheld, portable, and wireless devices by learners on the move. Kids come to the classroom equipped with cell phones, iPods, and other mobile technology. With such devices in hand, m-learning technology costs are often quite lower than educators in K–12 schools realize. In underfunded schools and learning centers, m-learning is practically a no-brainer. It is difficult to name a technology that better fits the currently troublesome economic times.[1]

Mobile technology is pervasive today. Whether you are a soldier in Iraq under intense attack or walking the streets of a dangerous neighborhood, standard equipment these days seems to be an iPod.[2] You can even get your iPods equipped with an attached Taser so you can learn in safety while walking the streets![3]

With mobile devices, the educational event or activity follows the learner, instead of the learner having to arrive at a designated place in which to acquire it. Access, access, and more access is demanded everywhere one travels. The calls for access ring out from airport lounges to shopping malls to convention centers. Internet access is now the top hotel amenity for business travelers.[4] Stuck with a few extra hours on your hands in Singapore's Changi Airport or nearby Kuala Lumpur (KL) International Airport? No problem, wireless (Wi-Fi) Internet access is provided free of charge in KL and there are well-placed, free Internet terminals in Singapore.

What happens when you leave the terminal and enter the plane? In the past, if you needed to work or learn while in flight, you were stuck working on whatever documents you downloaded before hopping onboard. Today, Virgin America, Delta, American Airlines, and others are beginning to offer Wi-Fi services to passengers.[5] This effectively makes air flight no different from going to the library or bookstore café. In addition, those flying first class can access all-important iPod connections to power and charge learning and listening devices when in flight.[6] Instead of wasting endless hours watching mind-numbing movies, you can be learning during the entire air travel experience. To add still more value, you can download an audiobook and listen to it on the way to and from the airport, as well as when waiting for your bags or even in your taxi. You can be learning all the time.

Today's travelers want it all. Laptops, iPods, and mobile phones with Internet access. Many of them even have mobile phones with prepaid daily newspaper services. Frequent business travelers, in particular, want their technology small and light.[7]

Not content? Still waiting for that chip in the brain instead? For the time being you should try Internet-enabled wristwatches that make Web access more convenient and handy. New devices to create content for the Internet are also increasingly lighter and more widely available.

Technology enthusiasts wanting to take quick videos when on the run now have the Flip, an easy-to-use video recorder the size of a digital camera. Just point and shoot; then pop out the USB connector, stick it into your laptop, and upload to YouTube. Small, sturdy, cheap, colorful, and simple—one button creates a product that David Pogue calls "the Zen of Flip."[8] Now add high-quality video to that list, and it will soon be a standard travel item. Those on the move increasingly crave such light mobile devices that enable them to multitask and access the Web while on the go. It is now seamless and simple! No slowing down of this trend is in sight as the costs, sizes, and weights of such devices continue to plummet.

I NEED MY CHUMBY

In early 2008, the Chumby appeared. This little wireless device looks like a small bedside radio and alarm clock. In actuality, for anyone with a wireless network, the Chumby provides an array of data and information from the Web. You can view newsfeeds, weather reports, Webcam feeds, stock reports, course announcements, informational videos, and updates to your e-mail accounts.[9] You can even get a short language lesson from the Chumby when placed on hold during a phone call. In some respects, it is a gap-filler. I think of it as a learning tool. As Elliott Masie notes, the Chumby is a type of "learning appliance" that we can come to expect in this century. This chapter will highlight a few such other learning appliances that push us in u-learning directions.

Wireless and mobile technologies have made u-learning possible. And when there is u-learning, WE-ALL-LEARN. U-learning takes advantage of the capabilities of mobile and wireless technologies to support a seamless and pervasive connection to learning without explicit awareness of the technologies being relied upon. Simply put, if you are using technology to learn without reflecting on it, you are likely experiencing u-learning. With the increasing mobility, connectivity, and versatility of educational technologies, there is the potential to devise environments where learning is taking place all the time and for anybody seeking it. And when options for learner participation—not just learning consumption—are added in, learning becomes a more personalized and customized 24/7 experience.

The emergence of mobile and wireless technologies for learning— which place educational opportunities literally in the learner's hands and allow him to schedule learning when he wants it—has paralleled the growing acceptance of a more learner-centered educational philosophy. Such m-learning and u-learning technologies are deemed ripe for learner-centered activities because they provide for more flexibility and choice in the learning process. And like the virtual worlds of the previous opener, the ninth opener adds yet another layer of fun and authentic learning, collaboration, and engagement. This opener alters the traditional teacher-student relationship by encouraging learners to be more active in their learning pursuits. And m-learning and u-learning nurture the digital learning skills required of twenty-first century learners.

iPODDING ALONG

Most likely, you have directly experienced the benefits of portable learning when listening to audiobooks or podcasts in a car, bus, or train. If not, then perhaps you have listened to your iPod or MP3 device when exercising, wirelessly accessed the Internet with a laptop computer, or used your mobile phone to text message, check e-mail, or browse the Web for information. These events represent just a few of the ways that learning, both formal and informal, has become more mobile. Mobile devices such as phones, laptops, PDAs, and clickers or student response devices are increasingly being used in corporate training and on college and university campuses as well as most other educational settings. In the midst of this m-learning explosion, many primary and secondary education schools have held up temporary flags of resistance to such opportunities. Soon most of those flags and signs will come tumbling down.

There is little doubt that nearly all mobile learners are connected in some way. Walk across a college campus today, and what will you observe? You undoubtedly will make note of many young people socializing. At the same time, you will also see students learning through their mobile phones, laptop computers, ubiquitous Internet hot spots, and handheld devices such as iPods and MP3 players. And these are field entry devices. Soon MP4 players will offer us additional video, audio, and text formats. Who knows how MP5 or even MP10 technology might transform the campus setting in a decade or two? Whatever the result, it is certain that we will have greater access to multimedia forms of learning wherever we are. The question is what types of information and learning will be preferred and selected, and what will be the results.

The image of a secondary or higher education student today is someone engaged in multiple activities at one time. Some might access the Web from their mobile phones to answer practice examinations. They might use laptop computers to download lecture notes or supplemental materials. Laptops and mobile phones are increasingly expected, desired, and warranted in higher education. If you do not possess a laptop and a mobile phone on a college campus in North America, and many other regions of the world, you are using old technology.

These same tools offer more formal learning possibilities. For instance, video iPods are used to teach sign language, as well as help hearing-impaired students to learn more richly from text and video. As is happening in many countries, Kaplan Test Prep and Admissions is now offering U.S. teens SAT preparation lessons from an iPod.[10] Currently, there are three interactive lessons in critical reading, writing, and mathematics, each costing US$4.99. Kaplan officials note that they might create similar programs for Microsoft and Cisco certification training. With such tools, learning can happen in more places than ever imagined.

Education is on the go. The percentage of teenagers with iPods, mobile phones, and other mobile devices in the United States continues to escalate.[11] Some schools keep cracking down on mobile phone and iPod use, but many educators prefer to focus on the educational potential of mobile devices. For instance, electronic flash cards can test students' knowledge. Images with commentary and video snippets stored in an MP3 device or mobile phone are also possible. Mobile phones can be used for text-based surveys and other communications between students and instructors that can enhance course interactivity. Text messages might prompt students to attend a special event related to a sociology or political science course, such as a protest in a human rights class or an unplanned appearance from a political leader such as Barack Obama, as happened to my son six months before Obama became president.

ZIPPING INTO AN iPHONE

The signs are all around us—smartphones, laptops, iPods and MP3 players, and hot spots. This is the age of the mobile learner. In *The World Is Flat*, Friedman talks about the upwardly mobile youth in India who walk with a "zip in their step."[12] Sure sounds mobile to me! They are described as quite young—often ages fifteen to twenty-five. They are also confident, creative, and seeking professional challenges. The Zippies are destination driven or goal oriented, and, therefore, feel little guilt or remorse about making money or taking someone's job. Given that half of the population of India was under age twenty-five at the time of Friedman's writing, this is a huge trend that cannot be ignored.

Mobile phone numbers attest to the ongoing transformation in India today. In 1980, India had seven hundred million people and only 2.5 million telephones. Most people, in fact, had to wait years to get one, if ever.[13] Fast forward three or four decades and India is the fastest-growing telecommunications market in the world with over a million new mobile phone subscriptions sold each month. That translates into one million additional tools for learning and teaching each month.

Similarly, young people around the planet are expressing themselves in more mobile ways. Today's students are increasingly wired as well as unwired. Entering an unfamiliar building on a college campus, the Net Generation will immediately search for the computer lab or an Internet hot spot.[14] Between classes such students are elated when finding a connection to the Internet in a café, a bookstore, or an empty room, or even while sitting on an outdoor bench during the summer. Of course, their jubilation is maximized if they quickly receive a response from someone located far away.

We live in a time when access rules the day and learners are perpetually online or attempting to be. While some are communicating with friends and family, others are ordering online concert or movie tickets, checking the weather, or reading headline news or sports scores. Those with more academic intentions might be downloading lecture notes or podcasts for the week, uploading completed assignments, or trying to determine their grades in a particular class. And you could be engaged in many of these pursuits simultaneously as your professional and personal lives seamlessly intertwine as a result of the mobile and wireless world we navigate today.

A July 2007 report from the *New York Times* indicated that there were 230 million Americans with mobile phones. However, just 32 million used them to access and browse the Web.[15] Though this particular article was focused on potential revenues that e-commerce companies might reap from mobile advertising, mobile phones also open up myriad educational opportunities. What if mobile phone consumers start demanding access to free and open educational resources instead of games, sports, weather, news, and entertainment? Broaden this out to a world where more than 3.3 billion people have mobile phones and potentially 4 billion by 2010, and mobile education and training solutions become increasingly scalable and cost justifiable.[16] Now that roughly half of the world has mobile phones and over 80 percent live in areas accessible by mobile devices, educators need to think of effective and innovative ways to design and deliver education with mobile devices.

For decades, Apple Computer has been at the forefront of efforts to educate the world. Apple made a huge splash in January 2007 with the iPhone.[17] Here is yet another device that will add steroids to human mobility. You can check e-mail, text message friends, browse, collect, and share information and pictures online, and handle phone calls. Within days of the release of the iPhone, I received an e-mail with an associated five-minute video from learning and training guru Elliott Masie explaining some of its learning implications.[18] Masie notes that sharing and collaboration as well as personal browsing will be a vital aspect of using the iPhone for learning.

Of course, with such a hit on their hands, Apple was not done. On June 9, 2008, the same day that IBM announced the fastest computer in the world, Apple announced one of the best mobile phone deals ever made at its Worldwide Developers Conference in San Francisco, the iPhone 3G.[19] Those in much of Europe, Japan, and Korea may yawn, but 3G is a big deal here in the United States where people who travel have been screaming to seemingly deaf ears for more advanced phone services and faster Internet access speeds from their mobile phones. In addition to Internet speed boosts, the new iPhone also includes Global Positioning System (GPS) capabilities and enhanced battery life. Most important, these phones are cheaper than the first line of iPhones that appeared just seventeen months earlier.

There is also an "App Store" to add nifty games and other applications to your iPhone. Apple officials apparently caught sight of the growth experienced by Facebook when it allowed developers to create mini-applications for its device. This action makes so-called "smartphones" even smarter and, of course, more cool and productive devices.[20] Pioneering teachers will look at this as a means to create interesting applications for their classes. Smartphones now include things like quick guides for chemistry, the human nervous system, cell biology, and other important science areas as well as religious topics ranging from the Qur'an to the Bible to the gods of ancient Greece. Dictionaries embedded within smartphones might also help a student learn a foreign language as well as enhance the use of her own native language.

The iPhone and other smartphones represent a portable learning device that is a key driver for the current learning revolution. According to Elliot Soloway, Arthur F. Thurnau Professor at the University of

Michigan and cofounder of GoKnow, Inc., a company focused on mobile technology in K–12 schools, "There are different versions of the venerable, but tired 'flash card' app available for the iPhone; but school curriculum-centered iPhone apps can't be high priorities for developers since schools currently ban mobile devices from the classroom. That will change shortly, however. When—not if—all the kids in the class took out their cell phone computer, laid it on their desk, and looked up at the teacher, a quiet revolution would occur. It will happen sooner than later."

Apple had hoped that by the end of 2008 iPhone sales would total ten million units and would expand to seventy countries from a mere six at the time of the announcement.[21] However, Apple underestimated the potential of this mobile learning and communications device as nearly seven million iPhones were sold in the third quarter of 2008 alone.[22] Small wonder that Samsung quickly came out with the Instinct available through Sprint and LG was offering the Voyager via Verizon.[23] Next came the LG Dare. Will the Double Dare be next?

Advertisers are trained to project what the proliferation of mobile technology means in revenues, but educators must start thinking about how such smartphones might affect learning and the delivery of education. Business pundits speak in terms of $700 million in revenues today becoming $2.2 billion by 2012.[24] That is a mere tripling effect. In learning, the potential multipliers are much higher because the base figures are so low. And as voice recognition is integrated, storage capacity is expanded, and screen displays become crisper, bendable, expandable, and foldable, there will be few learning limits. School policies banning these devices will be laughable in ten years if not less.

TWITTER CRITTERS

We are a highly mobile species engaged in enormous social networking. In June 2007, *Wired Magazine* featured an article on Twitter technology.[25] As noted in Chapter One, Twitter is a tool for you to post notes to the Web from your mobile devices about your current activities, moods, perspectives, and day's agenda. You might note, "I'm having a bad day," and people can get your updates via the Web, IM, or a cell phone. With a maximum of 140 characters, those who use Twitter need to learn to be pithy. In addition to Twitter, many young people use a system called "Dodgeball" to indicate their current location. With Dodgeball, friends can perhaps find them and catch up.

David Parry, an assistant professor at the University of Texas at Dallas, argues that his use of Twitter has changed his class dynamics to a greater degree than anything he has attempted before.[26] He can communicate with his students while sitting in a restaurant, standing in line at grocery store, or when walking on campus. Life inside and outside the classroom walls is more seamless, according to Parry.[27]

Educational applications of Twitter are many. Students might receive course announcements and reminders in Twitter. They might also get instant feedback on their work.[28] Instructors might require students to track the movements of a well-known researcher in the field who uses Twitter. Such an activity gives them a close-up view into the life of the expert. It is a quasi-virtual apprenticeship or shadowing experience. Professor Parry also notes that creative thoughts and ideas might be recorded in a public notepad, thereby allowing groups using Twitter to write continuous stories with each person adding interesting twists or elements to it. Such a novel task might motivate everyone in the class to read along. Students could also track conference events and activities in someone's Twitter postings. All of these types of ideas create a sense of classroom community.

In addition to the academic uses, there are a range of social purposes for these micro-blogging tools—such as determining the mood of someone you might have lunch or dinner with. These seemingly narcissistic technologies could potentially help groups function better and give small teams a sense of identity or community. In effect, there is a shared social space or collective understanding that can enhance the ability of teams to solve problems and to interrelate with each other. With a few added group collaboration or communication features, tools such as Twitter and Dodgeball may evolve into successful workgroup productivity tools instead of simply filling a social need to be connected.

A LIVE SCRIBE

Mobile devices are proliferating. Apparently, it is smart to be mobile. Witness the emergence of smartpens such as the Pulse from Livescribe. With the Pulse, the learner can jot down notes and transfer them to a computer as well as record lectures in a minirecorder.[29] Created by Jim Marggraff, an inventor of talking books and other educational toys, the Pulse smartpen includes two microphones for recording sound, a speaker for playback, a small display to denote what you are doing, and a hidden computer chip. A tiny camera near the tip of the pen records what is written, thereby linking the writing to the audio. Tap the pen on a word written down and any conversations that transpired while that word was being written are immediately played back.

A student possessing such a smartpen can place it in a docking station of a computer and upload his written notes as well as the associated audio files. Such notes can then be organized, searched, played back, and shared. In this way, paper products become more interactive and potentially collaborative. It is interactive paper! More importantly, perhaps, thoughts are portable. Ideas can be brainstormed anywhere—even right on your hands—and then uploaded to a computer or server.

Eventually, the learner will be able to write down things that he wants the computer to do, such as search a database, buy a book online, send an e-mail message, or call up a document. Eventually, a whole series of transactions and online learning quests might be stored in such penlike devices and, when uploaded, are carried out by intelligent agents while you are on break or holiday. I am not advocating for lazy learners; quite the contrary, I am pushing for engaged learners and learning round the clock, or should I say, around the pen. Of course, there would be timely breaks for refreshing your batteries.

This is not a dream. It is part of the learning revolution taking place today in mobile learning. I witnessed this revolution firsthand in late July 2008 when giving a series of talks at an accelerated learning institute in Denver. James Moore from DePaul University, seated just to my left, had recently bought one of these nifty pens and asked me if he could record my presentations with it. "No problem," I said. Within hours of the close of this two-day event, Moore posted all three of my talks to the Web. With that, everyone attending the institute as well as those who could not attend are able to listen to these Livescribe recordings any time they want. And, as they listen, they can view the notes James took that relate to different sections of these talks.

Perpetual recording of all that you see, hear, and do is simply part of life today. Jim Marggraff contends that writing notes down indicates that the learner eventually wants to access them. He further states, "We are giving a way for people to essentially forget about forgetting."[30] Socrates might have a field day with such notions, but it begs the question of what memory really is, and what it means to know or to forget something. At $200, it is much cheaper than an elephant, but it still may be a while before this techno-pen catches on. As someone with quite cryptic handwriting, however, I see immediate uses for the Pulse for doctors, who are notorious for their poor handwriting, as well as for students working multiple jobs, engaged in several extracurricular activities, or coping with long-winded or boring professors.

MOBILE GIVEAWAYS IN NORTH AMERICA

Despite many schools not knowing what to do with cell phones or iPods in school and those that have outright banned them, some K–12 schools have decided to embrace such devices or, at least, experiment with them. In 2008, for instance, the North Carolina Department of Public Instruction launched Project K-Nect, which provided a repository of math and science problems aligned to state standards that students could solve through their mobile devices.[31] With this one decision, student mobile phones came out of their lockers and into the classrooms for instruction. As the sophistication of features increases and convergence across mobile devices unfolds, mobile technologies will move front and center as K–12 learning tools of choice. Smartphones can offer students voice communication, multimedia, e-mail, messaging, and Web browsing functions. As with graphing calculators, electronic planners, and note-taking devices, supplemental learning support is available on demand.

The integration of mobile technology in K–12 schools sets the stage for their use in colleges and universities. Given the amount of money being spent on college-related technology purchases, students and parents are surely anticipating this trend. Laptops are no longer a luxury item but a needed commodity. Between 2006 and 2007, desktop computer usage among undergraduates in the United States dropped from 69 to 58 percent, whereas ownership of a personal laptop rose from 68 to 76 percent during the same time.[32]

In 2006–07, students were projected to spend 27.5 percent more on electronic purchases than students the previous year. That is more than

$10 billion in a category that includes flat-panel TVs, video game consoles, laptops, and, of course, digital music players.[33] These college freshman often show up on campus unpacking new laptops and other technology that are better than what will be soon found in their college classrooms and computer labs.

With hard disks and other parts dramatically reduced in size, students no longer have nightmares of lugging their laptops around campus. In January of 2008 at Macworld, Apple CEO Steve Jobs unveiled and effortlessly held up the MacBook Air.[34] Less than an inch thick and weighing under three pounds, it comes with an amazing array of hardware and learning potential. Students also show up on campus with mobile phones as well as video iPods, each of which can be considered learning tools.

In five or ten years, we will witness another dramatic bumping up along the learning technology evolutionary scale. Soon learners will be carrying thumb drives with up to a terabyte of data. Researchers at Arizona State University have already developed a form of low-cost, low-power computer memory that will someday do just that.[35] Such nanotechnology would quickly find its way into other portable technologies including cell phones, thereby dramatically increasing their storage as well as their multimedia capabilities.[36]

With this one advancement, many of the barriers to technology-enhanced learning that have existed for decades may finally be cast aside. Complaints have been leveled at each new generation of technology for being too slow, too expensive, or too small in scale to matter. With inexpensive terabytes of data that are quickly accessed from portable devices, such arguments will be more difficult to sustain. There are enormous learning implications for developing countries and thus for society, from this one invention. With increased memory, storage, and access speeds, the learning infrastructure will be transformed with enhanced simulations, extensive database searching, and elaborately designed interactive virtual worlds.

It is difficult for schools and corporations to keep their learning technologies up to date. What is current today is passé tomorrow. Today, e-mail is considered "old school" or just for adults, whereas social networking and chatting is the province of teenage learners and young adults.[37] Instead of e-mail, younger learners dominate in such areas as text messaging, instant messaging, blogging, Twittering, and Internet surfing.[38]

Postsecondary institutions and corporations are pushing strategic initiatives to take advantage of such trends—they are providing services to students' phones and handheld devices. For example, Pennsylvania State University offers mobile phone alerts for campus emergencies and sports-related information. Emergency mobile information is now considered critical to campus administrators.[39] Witness the problems caused by not getting the word out to students during the April 16, 2007, massacre at Virginia Tech University when officials thought an initial murder scene was an isolated event.[40] Less than two months after the horrible tragedy at Virginia Tech, thousands of students had signed up for the university's new emergency alert system, which includes text messaging to cell phones, instant messaging to users of IM in Yahoo!, MSN, or America Online, and the use of automated phone calls and e-mail.[41] Talk about technology options!

Have you ever talked to your clothes? Perhaps you have, but I doubt there was much of a response. Places like MIT, Carnegie Mellon University, and Boston College are using their technology know-how to give students the capability to check on available laundry machines in their dorms without having to go up and down stairs. While waiting for their clothes to dry, students at universities in the D.C. area, such as Georgetown and George Washington, can order late-night snacks and other needed commodities electronically.

Some mobile announcements are more academic in nature. With noticeable fanfare, institutions such as Arizona State University, Temple University, and the University of Massachusetts–Lowell now offer students the chance to download every lecture in every classroom to their iPods or computers. They can then listen whenever and wherever they want. Many universities, including the University of California at Berkeley and Stanford University, were leaders in posting their podcasted lectures in iTunes for anyone in the world to download. Stanford also has created a campus activity wiki that anyone can populate.[42] The applications that universities offer continue to proliferate. Students at Montclair State University, for instance, can check their grades, bus schedules, and dining hall menus using a cell phone. These students can be mobile and still access a host of personally relevant information and resources.

Mobility pushes on. On February 27, 2008, I purchased a new stereo for my car that has inputs in the front for both my iPod and a USB flash drive. Given that I have a passion for listening to audiobooks in my car, with this one purchase the mobility of my book-related learning has kicked into high gear. Many of us no longer can afford the time to sit down and read a book cover to cover. Those days ended perhaps a decade ago if not longer.

The same week I bought my new car stereo, Abilene Christian University (ACU) in Texas, located about 185 miles west of the Dallas-Fort Worth area, announced it would give all nine hundred incoming freshman in the fall of 2008 a choice of an iPhone or an iPod Touch.[43] (The Touch has most of the same features as the iPhone, but is not a mobile phone.) Now there is a marketing tool for a university: giving technology away. In these difficult budgetary times, it categorically signals changes in the air for teaching and learning on college campuses.

This is no small-scale effort. ACU has also created a two-part YouTube video documenting a possible day in a life of a college freshman using the iPhone or iPod Touch. The featured student is named Amanda. They show Amanda using her iPhone as she negotiates the activities of the first two days as an ACU student. Using the iPhone, she receives text messages from her professors, checks on friends in Facebook who recently updated their account with pictures from a vacation in Europe, and changes her class schedule to more convenient times. This is just in the first few hours of the day.

Later on, she accesses course syllabi while her roommate mentions that she can download class podcasts from iTunes U. The iPhone also comes in handy for day-to-day life, such as checking the weather, receiving thunderstorm warnings, and ordering and paying for food. She later uses it to walk through campus and finds campus buildings using an electronic campus map. When in class, she and her classmates send links to the course Web site, take surveys, and vote on class activities. One instructor explains that she can record interviews she is going to do at Habitat for Humanity because the iPhone doubles as a voice recorder. Podcast lectures that they watch or listen to before class help the instructors focus on high-level aspects of the content. Of course, she can talk to her mother on the phone itself and then dock the iPhone and meet her mother in iChat for a free videoconference. Amanda ends the call by claiming that people walk around with no backpacks because everything is in their iPhones. She feels "so connected."

And connected she is. The iPhone has made this possible, in part, because we live in a society that increasingly relies on digital information storage and access. It provides access to what is already there, while also using the iPhone as a recording tool as well as an idea generation and sharing device. It is a learning tool. Amanda learns in the dorms. She learns when walking to class. And she even learns when in class. Amanda learns in many ways—from maps, chats, videoconferences, podcasts, Web explorations, voting, interviewing, sharing information, and talking on the iPhone. We live in the day of the learner. And it is about time!

ACU studied many emerging technologies and came to the conclusion that the iPhone is different. The iPhone is an invention with monumental learning implications because it represents a convergence of technologies. ACU officials have a vision for a twenty-first-century classroom, campus, and university. There have been previous experiments with giving iPods to incoming freshman, such as at Drexel and Duke, as well as giveaways of mobile phones, Blackberries, laptops, and other learning tools. ACU people, however, have taken additional steps beyond simple student giveaway enticements. An exploration of their Web site announcing this project indicates that they have used a highly collaborative and comprehensive approach in planning for the iPhone and iPod Touch. There is a social interaction team, a digital media interaction team, a pedagogy team, a student research team, a living and learning team, a study coordination and invention team, an administrative and infrastructure team, and, of course, an application and programming team. It is refreshing that they are not overly focused on the technology.

ACU is not the only mobile learning option for college students. A week after the ACU announcement, Oklahoma Christian (OC) University said that it planned to offer multiple mobile technologies—both an iPhone (or iPod Touch) and an Apple MacBook laptop—for incoming students.[44] Apparently, the combined price was lower than what OC had been paying for laptop PCs from Dell. Universities wanting to keep up with OC and ACU will certainly need to offer increasing mobile service and technologies.

Such initiatives are ramping up learning for everyone with a mobile device. With expanded mobile phone coverage and lowered prices as well as increasingly smaller devices, those relying on m-learning will soon comprise a large percentage of the planet. But will we be ready?

It seems the Canadians like their giveaways as well. In one project created at Athabasca University in Alberta, students from the Mennonite Centre for Newcomers can learn English from grammar lessons downloaded to their mobile phones.[45] For those needing options, there is also an associated Web site with text, PDF, and Word documents for the different grammar units. Athabasca officials hope that these lessons will be used around the world by anyone with a mobile phone. Now that will be some giveaway!

M-JAPAN: MOBBING AND MIXI-ING

Japan has adopted the "learn as you go" principle to a more significant degree than most other countries. When I saw Howard Rheingold present ideas from his *Smart Mobs* book on my campus in the spring of 2006, he started with a personal story of mobile phone use in Japan.[46] As he highlights in the introduction to his book, what he observed back in the spring of 2000 is that people in Japan tend to learn, share information, and congregate based on the exchange of information in short text messages. By 2003, the Japanese had already figured out how to use mobile devices to operate vending machines, find dates in location-based matchmaking systems, and rapidly organize meetings. More recently, they have begun using their mobile phones as their transportation pass for trains, buses, and subways in the Tokyo areas. This popular service, called "Mobile Suica," is rechargeable from your phone.[47] With it, huge numbers of people can breeze through areas that were previously transportation barriers while on their daily commute—what a wonderful application of mobile technology.

A couple years after Rheingold's widely acclaimed book was published, I was struck by an article that described tens of thousands of Japanese mobile phone users reading full-length novels on their tiny screens.[48] People are reading and, therefore, learning in their spare moments. Reading when at home, reading when waiting on traffic lights to change, and reading when on the subway; it does not matter, they read constantly. Curiously, the largest market for such mobile reading seems not to be mobile learners in the traditional sense of the term but females reading from home. Using her phone, a housewife can search for content by author, genre, and title as well as write reviews or send adoring letters to authors. Small installments of each book are downloaded as needed. And the Japanese keep adapting to mobile learning possibilities as they come up. Mobile reading has gained traction in nearby China and Korea, but it is in Japan where people are hooked on using it as an informal learning device.

Reading from a mobile phone may soon be common for all of us. Sony has apparently created bendable screen technology for mobile devices. Companies such as LG Phillips and Seiko Epson are also hard at work on developing transportable "electronic paper" technology. One of the problems that they are all addressing with such innovations is the screen display size on your mobile phone.

According to a May 2007 announcement from Sony, they have stretched mobile learning with the design of a 2.5-inch display unit for cell phones and similar handheld gadgets that is a mere .01 inch thick and bendable.[49] Not only will mobile phones quickly become adopted as educational devices, but so too might our bodies. We might have these lightweight screens wrapped around our wrists, legs, or waists. Imagine humans as walking entertainment and educational programming while strolling through the streets of Tokyo, Paris, or Rome. Is the screen too small on your mobile phone for casual reading? Perhaps the back of a jacket will someday double as a portable screen and you will be reading books while standing behind others in a subway. Learning. Yes, we are learning all the time.

Some people are now taking online courses from the Cyber University of Japan with their mobile devices.[50] Streaming videos, PowerPoint images, text information, and audio narration from the instructor are part of these courses. The first mobile course announced—one on the pyramids—sounded intriguing and, better still, was free to the public. Some of the hundred other courses from the Cyber University are apparently on the way. With this initial example, the Japanese have shown us that course containers can come in many sizes. Online discussions and social networking wrapped around mobile phone courses are no longer just possibilities, but actualities.

Yayoi Anzai, an instructor in the School of International Politics, Economics and Communication at Aoyama Gakuin University, has spent several years researching podcasting and other mobile forms of learning in Japan. She notes that in Japan they use a social networking system called "Mixi" to keep up with others. The name "Mixi" connotes that the user, "I," can use the service to "mix" with other people.[51] Like a blog, in Mixi people share personal stories or diaries, and they use these diaries to form communities around common interests, hobbies, and personal tastes.

Mixi is exceedingly popular in Japan. It has grown from ten thousand users in 2004 to more than fourteen million in 2007.[52] Not only can Mixi users write their stories when on the go, but reactions to their posts can come from other mobile users instantly from anywhere. Besides blogging, Mixi allows users to upload video content they have created or have found in services such as YouTube. A footprint feature allows the user to see who has visited her page and when they did. In this way, Yayoi explains, "I can know who cares for me."

Some of these same people are learning English through podcasts and other mobile learning techniques. Yayoi has found that podcasts can improve Japanese students' listening as well as writing skills.[53] She has innovatively used online news shows, such as those on CNN.com, to engage her college students in authentic English content. For younger learners, she notes that CNN Student News is geared specifically toward middle and high school students. Included in these news shows are supplemental curriculum materials such as short quizzes, discussion questions, maps, and transcripts. She adds that Voice of America also has a "Special English" Web site targeted to people whose primary language is not English. The program, which is read at a slower than normal speed and relies on short and simple sentences, has a core vocabulary of roughly fifteen hundred words.

Though such free online resources are increasingly utilized by Japanese ESL instructors, Yayoi has walked down a road few in Japan have traveled by having her students produce their own English podcasts.[54] She is fascinated with such possibilities for empowering students and accelerating their learning of English. Yayoi is not alone. One resource currently being tested, Kinjo Podwalk, has Japanese students introduce their hometowns through online podcast shows. More such innovations are likely on the way.

These are just a few brief examples that reveal that the Japanese have ushered in a new era of learning. Without a doubt, cultures around the world will continue to monitor and adapt many mobile learning trends started by the Japanese. I am quite certain the coming decade will see a flood of mobile learning applications with easily recognizable Japanese footprints.

M-KOREA: IT'S A CYWORLD AFTER ALL

Japan is not the only place on this planet to find millions of technology-crazed and highly mobile people. Their neighbors to the west love their technology just as much. With services such as "Moneta," many Koreans use their mobile phones for banking and other transactions. In fact, such devices are often referred to as "wallet phones."[55] As technologies converge toward smartphones, these mobile wallets will grow in popularity. In some countries, mobile wallets allow the owner to not only get through transportation terminals and pay for coffee, but to enter office buildings, open homes, and access key personal data, such as passport and insurance information. As this technology proliferates, standard hand-bags and wallets may end up slimmer or perhaps become nonexistent.

Inexpensive and highly accessible bandwidth is a key reason the Korean populace is so mobile. More than 90 percent of households in Korea are already connected to cheap, broadband Internet.[56] It is normal for young people here to have a social life that revolves around the cyber cafés or "PC bangs" that dot nearly every street corner.[57] For many in Korea, Internet access is essential to life.

Several personal visits to Korea during the past decade have confirmed the love affair that Koreans have with technology. Glossy government reports from places such as the KERIS (Korean Education and Research Information Services) on e-learning and ICT in Korean schools and universities weighted down my luggage each time I traveled back from there. Annual reports of the International Telecommunications Union (ITU) confirm that Korea has ranked at the top of its Digital Opportunity Index.[58] Countries such as Japan, Denmark, Iceland, and several others are closing the gap, yet Korea has maintained top-dog status for the past several years. What this ultimately means is that government officials, educators, and corporate trainers will increasingly look to Korea for trends in learning-related technologies. Interestingly, the United Kingdom ranked tenth, Canada seventeenth, and the United States twentieth in the 2007 report. In raw numbers, South Korea has thirty-four million Internet users, below only the United States, China, Japan, India, and Germany, all of which had substantially larger populations.[59]

Funding to strengthen the Internet infrastructure throughout Korea is as much an economic decision as it is an educational one. For instance, such connectivity gives Koreans the edge in research and development efforts from smart clothes to electronic textbooks to massive multiplayer online games (MMOGs). In March 2007 the Ministry of Education and Human Resource Development (now the Ministry of Education, Science, and Technology) announced that it would be developing a sophisticated digital textbook that can be inexpensively and quickly revised.[60] It will also allow students to interact with their teachers at any time or location. In addition, sick children will be able to attend class, and those from low-income brackets will connect with supplemental online resources and materials such as online videos, animations, and virtual worlds. Textbook, workbook, dictionary, and communication possibilities are all being designed into the system.

Digital books are but one initiative in Korea. Smart clothing embedded with digital music players, computer chips, and other devices is projected to reach $14 billion USD market by 2014, and Korea expects to gain over 20 percent of the smart clothing market.[61] If successful, and there is no reason to believe that they will not be, we could soon find ourselves walking around at work and home with sensors or memory chips inserted into the clothes we wear.

Korea is a country filled with learners who love their mobility. Today Korean students can download their lecture notes, college test preparation programs, music, pictures, and videos to their portable multimedia players or PMPs.[62] Using these PMPs, Korean teens can watch high-quality broadcasting of college entrance TV programs from the Educational Broadcasting System (EBS). And these are free! Koreans operate in a highly competitive system in which gaining access to the highest tier colleges and universities is the ultimate goal. Therefore, providing equitable access to such exam preparation programs in Korea is a monumental announcement. With such video-on-the-go possibilities, learning in Korea is highly mobile and ubiquitous. Perhaps in a few years it will be quite common for the education departments and public broadcasting companies of different countries to provide similar types of resources for their young learners.

Another South Korean frenzy is blogging and, as in Japan, many Koreans update their blogs using mobile devices. Given that most phones come with cameras and video capabilities, mobile bloggers are more likely than computer bloggers to upload pictures and videos with their posts. South Korea is home to three of the ten most popular blog hosting services: Cyworld, Planet Weblog, and Yahoo! Blog.[63]

Cyworld is often the tool of choice. In Korea, maintaining a Cyworld Web site has become a national pastime. Owned by SK Telecom, Korea's largest wireless service provider, Cyworld combines aspects of social networking services like MySpace and Facebook as well as personal homepages, blogging, e-portfolios, and photo sharing. As an added enticement, basic services are free, though cyber currency called "dotori" (meaning "acorns") is highly popular. When reading an interesting post or comment on a picture, you can click on the name of the person who posted that comment and immediately be transported to his digital room.

With the emphasis on building, creating, designing, connecting, and sharing, Cyworld is right in tune with the participatory learning culture that has emerged with the proliferation of the Web 2.0. In perhaps no other place on this planet is there a culture more ready for this than Korea. Cyworld has found a gold mine with the South Korean populace, which has the access, throughput, and digital savvy to take advantage of emerging technologies that connect people in ways previously impossible or unheard of. Interest groups, friendships, marriages, and small businesses blossom from activities in Cyworld. And one can enter Cyworld from a mobile phone or PMP.

Those who spend inordinate time enhancing or updating their Cyworld site are said to be in "Cy-jil" (as in "zeal") or a "Cy-holic."[64] Though decreasing in recent years, many Koreans have been known to spend three to four hours per day decorating and updating their Cyworld mini-homepage.[65] And with the extensive broadband infrastructure in Korea, they can access it wherever they happen to be. As with most such spaces, Cyworld has developed its own lingo. One's homepage is referred to as a "mini-hompy" and groups of them are called "hompies." Akin to the diminutive character in the popular movie, *Austin Powers*, one's avatar, which resides in the mini-hompy, is named "Mini-me."

Fortunately, such lingo certainly does not deter people from using it. In fact, by 2005, twenty million individuals or more than 40 percent of South Korea's 49 million people had a membership in Cyworld.[66] More impressively, over 90 percent of those in their twenties with Internet access used Cyworld. I know when I share pictures with my Korean colleagues and students, they soon land somewhere on a Cyworld site. Friends can invite others to meetings in someone else's Cyworld Web site where people can chat with others, reply to posts, and read about recorded events or transactions. In contrast to similar sites in Western countries, Korean Cyworld users are required to provide real names and their Korean resident identification number to register. Such practices obviously limit deception and criminal activities.

There are many cultural reasons why Cyworld is popular in Korea. Such countries as Korea, Japan, and China are known as collective, interdependent, and high-context cultures.[67] It is important to maintain awareness of others in their in-groups through the types of social and contextual cues that Cyworld provides. So it doubles as a means of individualistic expression, as well as a way to express one's status as part of a particular group. As such, the Cyworld phenomenon is not limited to South Korea. It has already expanded to East Asian cultures such as Japan, Taiwan, and China, as well as the United States. South American, European, and Indian Cyworld sites are coming soon.

M-AFRICA: THE LAND OF LEAPFROGGING

Not every interesting mobile learning story comes from Japan and Korea. My friend John Traxler at the University of Wolverhampton in the United Kingdom has studied mobile learning around the world and has written a few books on the subject.[68] Some of his work is in African countries—in particular, Kenya and South Africa. He believes that mobile learning is more flexible, personal, and portable than the static forms of online learning that have dominated the past decade.[69] Traxler told me that the uses of mobile learning in Africa are different from what they are in other countries he has monitored. For many

Africans, m-learning helps overcome problems associated with poor connectivity.

The debates about the benefits of m-learning are vastly different in Africa than in Europe or North America. So are the debates about the challenges. Traxler detailed an array of problems with traditional educational solutions related to computer-based training and online learning in Africa. In many places, Africans lack computers, electricity, secure buildings, appropriate software licenses, and IT support. At the same time, according to Traxler, there is increasing mobile phone ownership, acceptance, and use. This rapid spreading of mobile phone use and associated networks makes it a viable educational option. Those in Europe, the Pacific Rim, and North America point to informal, spontaneous, and personal lifelong learning, as well as the bite-sized nature of m-learning. In contrast, m-learning experiences and needs in Africa, where unique educational traditions and priorities are evident, are much different. In many cases, there is no debate; it might be the only option.

There are many ways that mobile learning in Africa plays out. For example, in Kenya there is a pressing need for the professional development of two hundred thousand primary school teachers. In partial response, a pilot project Traxler is coordinating supports eight thousand of these teachers with supplemental material in the form of text messaging.[70] He also noted that the University of Pretoria is using SMS for administrative support of teachers in their distance learning program. More recently, it expanded m-learning activities by allowing students to phone in their academic questions and receive feedback via SMS. They could also phone in and listen to minilectures specifically designed for them. Students in this project are also using mobile phones for interactive multiple-choice quizzes of their knowledge. It makes perfect sense to package training and education in Africa with the technologies to which people have access.

Traxler is not done. In yet another mobile innovation in Africa, he informs me that there are pilot projects in South Africa to test out a mobile-audio Wikipedia. Another project, the Digital Education Enhancement Project (DEEP), offers professional development for rural primary teachers through illustrated e-books installed on handheld devices. Other mobile resources provided in DEEP include video- and audioclips and associated Web links.

It is clear that those in Africa are in the midst of a game of leapfrog to jump over the technology hurdles of the past. Mobile learning allows more people to join in this game of leapfrog. And jump and join they will! Other countries wishing to have a turn at m-learning should be closely monitoring Africa during the coming decade.

M-LATIN AMERICA: THE POCKET SCHOOL

Africa is not the only country in the midst of leapfrogging with mobile technologies. When my son Alex and I visited San Francisco in early August 2007, we arranged to have dinner with Dr. Paul Kim, chief technology officer in the Stanford School of Education, as well as several others from nearby San Francisco State University and the well-known Exploratorium. Upon exploring his Web site and associated projects, it was clear that Dr. Kim is simultaneously working on perhaps a dozen innovative learning technology projects.

Among his primary pursuits, Kim was searching for an inexpensive way to reach disadvantaged youth through mobile devices. In particular, he was interested in how mobile technology might help the indigenous children of Latin America who are often underserved in education and, consequently, are illiterate. He informed me that there are between fifty and sixty million indigenous people in Latin America, the majority of whom reside in Mexico, Peru, Bolivia, Guatemala, and Ecuador.[71] For a variety of reasons, nonindigenous people have access to vastly superior formal education resources. Paul noted that in places such as Mexico, indigenous people might travel for annual harvests and live in communities too small for a formal school to be built. And in places where there is a school, it is often substandard and its teachers are poorly trained. Worse still, the parents of indigenous youth often lack formal schooling experiences themselves. As a result, there are few books or educational resources found in many of their homes.

When you combine these factors, the educational opportunities for indigenous children in Latin America are at best bleak—while the rest of the world continues to make technological advances and scientific breakthroughs. Unfortunately, these advances require even more sophisticated skills and extensive knowledge to succeed in this global world. This situation is indeed quite dire.

Dr. Kim's solution: the "Pocket School." To illustrate, he pulled out a $19 MP3 player from his shirt pocket. He then showed us a few key features such as the 1.5-inch color screen, six buttons to flip through content, built-in speaker, microphone, camera, USB port, and, of course, a power switch.[72] With between 512 MB and 1 GB of memory, the device has the capability to play books that young kids could listen to, as well as engage them in language-related games and activities. This unique device stores images and records sounds, thereby enabling grammar and spelling lessons. For example, the alphabet, along with corresponding words and images, can be read to the learner.

When you combine these capabilities for words, sounds, and pictures with such a lightweight device, you see decades of learning psychology research on multimedia come to life. This little device is a revolutionary learning tool that will help educate innumerable young people who previously had no access to teachers! Dr. Kim is not acting alone. There are thousands of brilliant minds around the planet conducting research on media, psychology, sociology, reading, computer science, instructional design, human-computer interaction, and computer design and manufacturing. They are the ones who have gotten us to this point. For illiterate people around the world, learning can now be delivered inexpensively and individually with a rich multimedia device that can quickly provide an engaging educational experience.

A study of Dr. Kim's project revealed that children learn to use these devices quite quickly. Given that these indigenous youths have limited educational and play opportunities, it is not surprising that some children listen to the stories over and over without hesitation. As an option to playing the stories from the device, any of the uploaded stories can be printed and read. Once printed, the documents have a bar code that can be identified by the built-in camera of the mobile device and played so that learners can follow along with the audio. Dr. Kim's research has found that children with no literacy skills tend to pay more attention to the audio, whereas those with some literacy might track the words on the paper or simply read the printed text. In effect, the mobile device provides u-learning opportunities and several learning options at a cheap price.

Such multimedia learning tools could help in the education of children of migrant workers in any country. These particular devices are highly affordable through rent-to-buy programs. For now, the devices come with around 350 short stories or 200 long stories that are easy to read and cheap to print because they are only a page or two in length. Price is not the only reason the Pocket School is attractive. More important, many indigenous parents have no literacy skills, so mothers cannot read to their children. The device offers a way to provide for such experiences that most of us take for granted.

Keep in mind that this is a mere start. Chip memory prices will continue to plummet and additional content will be designed. As this happens, students will have gigabytes of exciting educational content at their fingertips not only to improve their reading skills, but also to help them in science, math, health, and other areas. The end result will be Dr. Kim's dreams of a comprehensive pocket school as well as a pocket teacher for personalized learning. Such a program is not focused on replacing schools or teachers but rather on providing them where none exist and perhaps where few can afford to go to help out. With such ingenious m-learning, an enormous education gap can be filled in Latin America and among migrant workers in North America. As it does, the learning world opens up for millions of people previously underserved.[73]

M-WORKERS

Similar m-learning needs exist in the workplace. M-learning alters the nature of work by shifting where job-related learning occurs. Traditional classroom-based training in walled-off rooms no longer suffices. Today, productive workers require performance support on the job. Such changes are especially true for knowledge workers. M-learning is therefore part of the accepted lexicon of the workforce of the twenty-first century. According to John Traxler, "Mobile devices create not only new forms of knowledge and new ways of accessing it, but also create new forms of art and performance, and new ways of accessing them (such as 'pop' videos designed and sold for iPods). Mobile devices are creating new forms of commerce and economic activity as well. So mobile learning is not about 'mobile' as previously understood, or about 'learning' as previously understood, but part of a new mobile conception of society."[74]

There are many workers today accessing training and learning online. Some might download to their iPods or MP3 players information related to customer service training. Others may well need an update on government regulations or mandatory compliance training. Still others might learn about a desktop application or perhaps advanced features that they had not previously used. Listening could take place during break time, when in the midst of a strenuous workout during lunch, or during a daily commute to work; such learning is especially handy when in a time-consuming traffic jam.

Though hard for many to imagine, it is not uncommon for a sales agent staying at a posh international hotel to find himself extremely bored. When such boredom strikes, he might decide to learn about new company products from online tutorials, demonstrations, and product announcements through a wireless connection in the hotel lobby or in his room. Oftentimes, corporate user group Web sites are flush with pertinent information. Such m-learning activities not only provide respite from the monotony of travel, but more important, help the salesperson gain valuable information that might be used in meetings the following day. Learning is on demand and just in time!

Employee training via the iPod is becoming more accepted. For example, thousands of employees at the Hilton-run Homewood Suites are receiving on-the-job training with two-minute video modules delivered via video iPods.[75] As part of this training, the video training was deemed essential because it illustrated different features related to new food and beverage standards. With this program, learning was more flexible, adaptable to worker needs, practical, and easy to apply. For now, this content is supplemental to existing training programs. With greater familiarity and acceptance, such programs may soon be standard practice while other training becomes supplemental.

Ted Hoff, chief learning officer at IBM, noted that the pace of change is so rapid that entire industries change within a decade. In our globalized times, when technologies enable individuals to work together across countries and departments in ways never before imagined, multiple specialties are required, not just one. The learning tools and resources need firepower and responsiveness. As Hoff put it, "IBM has drastically changed as a business in the first decade of the 21st century. And therefore, learning has to respond by enabling more immediacy in how people learn."[76] He recognizes that people learn best in a continual apprenticeship where employees immediately apply what they have learned and get support for such learning in collaborative environments.

One way to ensure such immediacy is to use mobile learning, such as podcasts. At IBM, employee downloads of more than 4.5 million podcasts help workers keep up with change and acquire cutting-edge knowledge. There is no telling the range of forums and times in which such podcasts were enjoyed. One thing is certain—employees at IBM are highly mobile learners.

To boost such mobile learning opportunities, IBM relies on wikis, virtual worlds, social networking exchanges, and various other Web 2.0 applications. For instance, near the end of 2007, IBM officials conducted a four-day virtual conference for two hundred of its top people to discuss and debate how to better leverage virtual worlds. Given the novelty of this type of conference, supports were provided in the form of a Web site, interactive wiki, teleconferencing, collaborative tools, and audio recordings of sessions. The only snag was oversubscription to the event as the intended two hundred attendees became three hundred. With this format, IBM employees in the United States could learn from and interact with others in the organization from Canada, the United Kingdom, India, Brazil, and Australia who participated in different sessions without having to travel. And with audio recordings, attendees could continue to participate after a particular session ended. Such examples indicate the power of combining mobile, virtual, and collaborative tools.

ONE LAPTOP PER CHILD

The final example of current mobile initiatives is perhaps the most ambitious and publicized. As already discussed, laptop computers with wireless access are now a staple of the American college student. They pervade many primary and secondary settings as well.

But what about the poorer countries and regions of the world? Once again, it is the MIT Media Lab taking the lead. Thanks to Nicholas Negroponte, former director of the Media Lab, the One Laptop per Child (OLPC) organization, and many other participants, millions of cheap laptops are being produced for children in places such as

Argentina, Libya, Rwanda, Peru, Brazil, Palestine, Nigeria, Pakistan, and Thailand.[77] This computer, nicknamed the "XO" as well as the "Children's Machine," was originally priced at $100 causing many to refer to it as the $100 laptop. At least initially, however, its price will be closer to $170. Costs are expected to come down over time. Quanta Computer, a computer notebook manufacturer from Taiwan, announced it could ship five to ten million such units in 2007.[78] Quanta, however, faces increasing competition from companies such as Intel with its Classmate PCs and a host of others who rushed in to fill this new market niche of inexpensive mobile learning devices. Adding to this challenge, Quanta and its competitors must attempt to navigate through government bureaucracies as well the cultural and political issues in each country.[79]

Demand does not simply come in ones and twos but in tens of thousands or even hundreds of thousands. By the fall of 2007, Italy was purchasing 50,000 computers for children in Ethiopia.[80] At roughly the same time, an order for more than 270,000 machines was placed in Peru and yet another for 100,000 laptops destined for Uruguay.[81] And in May 2008, Colombia placed an order for 65,000 XO laptops for public school children, of which 50,000 would be delivered in 2009.[82] Such orders demonstrate the need for mobile learning devices around the world. If anything can change the world quickly, it is inexpensive and highly usable technology placed in the hands of young learners.

This technology is making an immediate impact. Remember those 100,000 laptops headed to Uruguay? Darren Murph reported on how hyped up 160 children in the town of Villa Cardal were about their laptops.[83] As he put it: "The relatively small Uruguayan town was thrown into a mild frenzy as a batch of shiny green and white OLPC XOs showed up to give the impressionable kiddos a taste of how learning should really be done. As promised, every child was gifted with their very own machine." This batch of XOs and others like it will undoubtedly generate some rethinking of the curriculum there and elsewhere.

The XO is definitely one of the most unique computers ever designed and perhaps the most ambitious and educationally significant. It is portable, sturdy, wireless, and rechargeable with a hand crank. A kid-friendly case is included. The XO comes with a rugged keyboard intended to resist any buildup of dust or dirt. It will also be configured for the language of the community in which it is used. At two watts of power, it requires just a tenth of what the average laptop requires today. The hand crank will provide power to children using this machine where there is no electricity. In addition, for those without shade or in an open area, the XO, with a super high-definition 7.5-inch screen, also has a display screen with a reconfigurable black-and-white mode option that allows the user to read from it in bright sunlight. The screen on the XO also swivels and closes much like a tablet computer, game machine, or e-book device.

It seems they have thought of many possible uses! In smartly taking advantage of free and open source software, the operating system of the XO is Linux. Instead of a hard disk, it relies on flash memory. In addition, the XO comes with internal wireless devices that allow XO computers to talk to each other and engage in peer-to-peer interaction, such as sharing photos or composing music together. And using the powerful fold-up antennas, such peer networks might be up to one-third of a mile apart. It is also easy to recognize with its bold green and white colors. When used in large numbers, such low-cost access to learning will ignite the use of some of the other openers mentioned in this book, including opportunities for online learning as well as the use of learning portals and learning objects. Perhaps the goal of having these laptops distributed like textbooks will soon be met.

Many of the ideas for the XO come straight from Seymour Papert's ideas about constructionist learning discussed in Chapter Two. Learning should be active, fun, and filled with creative expression. The project homepage mentions goals of exploring, expressing, learning, collaborating, and sharing; learners can find resources, create knowledge, and share what they have found. It is here that the laptop is not just a low-cost, portable learning tool, but one that empowers learners and transforms the entire learning process.

Papert's influence is all over the XO. Its free Web browser, media player, and e-book reader can immerse the user in rich text, video, pictorial, and audio content. Learners can also create their own products. Built-in are many tools children can use for expressing themselves and generating new knowledge. Of course, there are the common tools for writing, but also those for composing music, designing buildings, and critiquing the ideas of others. Plus there is software for debugging computer programs or math problems, imagining new worlds, and collaborating with peers and others around the planet. Though instruction from the many resources found online is important, learners can take new ideas they discover and act on them. The hope is that students will do something with that new knowledge by using the XO to assist in their peers' learning.

I have been in meetings where some people question whether the XO is pushing a particular learning agenda on other countries. But my feeling is that these computers are tools. If it is natural to use them in a constructionist way, then we should let nature run its course. Who is to stop a school system or teacher who wants to use the XO for more traditional learning activities and experiences?

Here is the WE-ALL-LEARN power. With tools like the XO, a student can actively contribute to learning as well as receive learning. And one can be situated in a learning process where the higher-order thinking skills that the human race needs to survive in this millennium can be roused to life and nurtured. Those running the OLPC project view it not simply as a means to get educational resources out to the children and schools who need it, but as a way for these children and schools to use their laptops to contribute back to the world. The Web is a rich and globally shared resource. Student work with the XO is now a highly valuable part of it.

Among the first places that the XO was tested was in Nigeria. An opening quotation on the OCPC Web site is indicative of the transformative powers of just one machine. Mrs. M., a teacher at Galadima School in Abuja, Nigeria, says: "With the laptop we can say that our school is really elevated because the children are really learning more. . . . They see themselves discovering things that they have never been doing before." Consider some of the other openers that might link to this trend—for instance, the free availability of portals of content on nearly any topic, the tools available for online collaboration and interaction, the free and open source software, and the active, participatory forms of learning. Now add the XO in the hands of youth in developing and underdeveloped regions of the world. Imagine that they are holding in their hands the educational power to change and transform the world.

Negroponte and his colleagues at the Media Lab are heroes and revolutionaries of the shared Internet. They have set off on a journey to change the world, and they have made that world more open for learners in many developing countries. Imagine if the new educational possibilities were not just placed in the hands of young children but also their older brothers and sisters, parents, or even grandparents. The goals are definitely educational, but they are also much more than that. As Grace Rubenstein at the George Lucas Educational Foundation (GLEF) observed, "Drop a laptop computer into the hands of a child in a remote Chinese village, and Nicholas Negroponte predicts a cascade of results will unfold: The child will encounter new knowledge and ways to express herself through images, words, and sounds. She may help her parents find markets for their products in other cities via cheap satellite Internet—or even develop a business plan herself. One family's growing prosperity will lift the village's fortunes and expand opportunities for their neighbors."[84]

When Rubenstein asked Negroponte what his one greatest hope was for the One Laptop per Child project, he replied that he had "a three-step hope": "World peace *through* the elimination of poverty *through* education *through* learning. Education is the goal; learning is the means. A lot of learning can happen without teaching. We're banking on that."[85]

For Negroponte, the unique contribution of this project was learning. People learn. Tools such as laptops, which enhance, extend, or transform the learning process, do far more than educate. They offer multiple perspectives and enable new personal dreams. Various converging trends may have flattened the world economically, but tools like the XO open it up educationally.

One has to pause for a second and ask how it is that the MIT can take the leadership on so many issues. It has played an active role in the Sakai project mentioned earlier. It was the first involved in the OCW movement with their grand announcement back in 2001. And now the OLPC. There is much more happening at MIT that space does not allow for here, including the Open Knowledge Initiative, a project creating specifications that enable different components of a software environment to communicate with each other; DSpace, an open source digital archiving system for capturing, managing, and sharing research; and Lrn, open source software for digital communities and e-learning. Of course, many of these projects are supported by university, private foundation, and corporate sponsorship. Through major project initiatives and examples, MIT is leading the world down a path where we all can learn.

MIT's leadership has already sparked many similarly innovative educational technology efforts. For example, in late July 2008, the government of India announced its own plans, not for a $100 laptop, but for a $10 one.[86] Apparently, the Indian government hopes to advance its strength in information and communications technology through distance learning. And if more people can afford a computer, then more people can be educated online. Imagine if this country of 1.13 billion people expands access to education from inexpensive laptops by just a few percentage points. Remember we already discussed the entry into opencourseware by the Indian Institutes of Technology with thousands of YouTube videos. Now imagine those free online contents being put to use to help educate the next generation of engineers, computer scientists, and chemists. Watch out, world, India is on its way!

A week after the India laptop announcement, however, news arrived that the $10 laptop was a mistake and the target price is actually $100. Not to worry. A day or two after that, a student group at MIT announced plans to build a $12 computer. And the race to provide the cheapest, fastest, smallest, and most useful laptop continues!

MOBILE REFLECTIONS

We often hear that we live in a highly mobile society. Today the technologies for learning are adjusting to that fact. At the present time, countries such as Korea or Japan may be making greater use of mobile technologies than other countries or regions of the world. As is evident in those places, this opener pushes the other nine into highly novel environments for learning. This is no time to dillydally, however. It will take some time for humans to become used to all the wireless places where they can now learn. Catching up will be particularly difficult because the standards for wireless and mobile learning will continue to reach new heights.

Second, there is little doubt that the ninth opener allows you to be a learner at any time. There will be learning moments that will cause many people to pause and appreciate these new opportunities to learn. Not that work, entertainment, good health, and significant emotional relationships are unimportant. It is just that now is the time for learning to move to the forefront of our lives.

Third, wireless and mobile learning will bring new partners in one's learning journey. That is perhaps the most exciting aspect of this particular trend. We literally have no idea whom we will meet, learn, and grow with in the coming months and years.

Fourth, mobile and wireless learning devices place our family or personal life more directly into our work and learning life, and vice versa. With such technology as laptops, thumb drives, MP3 players, and iPhones, we can witness each other learning more often. Such overt and yet ubiquitous learning should foster more discussion and reflection on our lives as learners.

We are surely just at the starting position when it comes to m-learning and u-learning. In four or five years, wireless and mobile devices will be more plentiful and associated costs much more reasonable. Can James Bond-like watches be far away? Sony-Ericsson already has a watch that comes equipped with a mobile handset that contains a wireless earpiece and microphone.[87] Incoming calls or text messages are signaled through vibrations on one's wrist. Will communicators akin to those in Star Trek or Star Wars be too far behind? Convenient technologies like watches and phones will increasingly add learning and communication features. We must be prepared to take advantage of them. As we do, the learning will become ubiquitous.

Mobile and wireless devices open up learning to entirely new possibilities. They allow us to be farther away from our instructors and classmates, while at the same time putting us in closer proximity to them in cyberspace. Mobility finally shakes us from our fixation on walled classrooms as places of learning to the passageways and corridors of a new generation of learning tools and environments. Exciting possibilities, to be sure, but it is the tenth opener that personalizes this whole process and expands our learning networks. It is the connecting tissue that makes the other nine openers more meaningful and momentous. I now turn to this quite exciting final learning opener.

Learning at Your Service

OPENER #10: NETWORKS OF PERSONALIZED LEARNING

THE NETWORKED SOCIETY

As Yochai Benkler makes us aware, we are witnessing the emergence of a networked information economy.[1] Signs of this new economy include multiple voices and viewpoints that can be raised, debated, and extended based on personal experiences and observations. Benkler argues, "We are a networked society now—networked individuals connected with each other in a mesh of loosely knit, overlapping, flat connections."[2] Interwoven in this way, individuals can find personally relevant information in more openly accessible communities produced by peers with similar interests. As shown in earlier chapters, such networks produce open information communities, open access software, and learning portals. The watchword, then, is "open."

These networked information environments are not only radically transforming education but business, government, and politics as well. The educational aspect of this transformation significantly alters accepted notions of what it means to learn, visions of where that learning is to come from, and, more important, what it means to be human. We have stepped into a new culture of learning where we assume radically new perspectives of ourselves as learners and what it means to participate in the learning process. The culture is one of participation and personalization.

Clearly, the top-down, expert-driven, and often boring lecture-based forms of learning have given way to learner empowerment and revamped notions of teaching and learning. Today learning no longer is simply consumption driven. Instead, young learners are members of a participatory learning culture.[3] As such, individuals can contribute to the knowledge-building process instead of passively consuming prepackaged knowledge and information. Now anyone with Web access has mammoth opportunities to build, tinker with, and share information that might be of value to a growing knowledge base, community of practice, or open access digital repository.

There is little doubt we live in a culture obsessed with technology. Today the iPhone is the craze. A few years back it was the iPod. Tomorrow, there will undoubtedly be something smaller, faster, cheaper, and more efficient that attracts our attention. The crucial point is that these technologies have vast educational applications that personalize, customize, and individualize learning in its many formats. Technology tools, systems, and resources encompassing the Web 2.0—tools for producing and sharing audio files, creating a live, interactive talk show, uploading personally produced videos or news, or posting one's daily or weekly thoughts and ideas—foster learner exchange, collaboration, and the design of new course content and information.

Learners participate. Passive reception learning is possible, but it is no longer the only game in town. What seems passive, moreover, may not be passive at all. Instead, learners are actively making choices about which Google Video or Current TV episode to watch. Which ones to share. Which ones to comment on. And which channels to subscribe to for more. With millions of hours of video content fully loaded on the Web, the choices are endless.

With the emergence of the Web 2.0, we live in a culture that is accelerating human creations and simultaneously finding new ways for sharing such creations. We can express ourselves in ways not previously possible and share with more people in less time than ever in the recorded history of this planet. And the scales for such sharing are literally astronomical to consider. If you doubt it, spend an afternoon browsing popular educational videos in YouTube or listen to a few podcasts on the Educational Podcast Network. Perhaps your mind will race with ideas.

SAVING "FACE"BOOK

Increasingly more personalized or learner-centered tools and resources are finding their way into the educational landscape. Spending time in Flickr, Furl, Facebook, or whatever new resource pops up is part of many Web user's daily itinerary. Here are some common practices: (1) checking out a particular blog or adding a post to your own blog; (2) monitoring specific pages in Wikipedia or looking for quick facts within it; (3) sending a survey question to friends by using popular social networking software, or adding a new friend to your network; and (4) listening to a podcast detailing an event coming up or summarizing a key event that you could not attend. Such experiences are central to the lives of millions of people on this planet.

Social networking tools are among the most dominant on the Web today. These services bring people together with common interests, experiences, and activities, allowing people to share their commonalities. The tools you use often depend on what country or region of the world you are in. As mentioned before, if you are in Japan, it is Mixi, whereas in Korea, it is Cyworld. If you are from Romania or Cypress, you are more apt to be a member of hi5 than Friendster, which is popular in Southeast Asia. Your friends in the United Kingdom, Ireland, and New Zealand might use Bebo. Those in the corporate world find LinkedIn to be their tool of choice. For photo sharing in North America, you likely use or have seen Flickr or Picasa, whereas those in South America might be savvy with Fotolog. If you are into movies, perhaps try Flixster.[4] And the list goes on and on and on.

Facebook, once the exclusive domain of Harvard college students and then a few other colleges and then all young people, was opened up to the world in April 2006. Adults could now join and monitor their children. Kids across the world were not happy with the thought of parents monitoring their virtually posted movements. For some, making friends in Facebook with anyone over forty was downright "creepy."[5] But Facebook executives were seeking to expand their reach and raise their market share. Adding millions more potential users was one way to make it happen. And they came. During the past few years, Facebook has become highly popular among college professors and other academic professionals.

As of May 1, 2008, Facebook reported membership of some sixty-nine million people, up from a mere seven million in July 2006.[6] Facebook cofounder, twenty-five-year-old Mark Zuckerberg, is predicting $70 million in profits on $140 million in revenues in 2008, and for this to jump to over $6 billion in revenues by 2016.[7] Companies such as Microsoft, Google, Yahoo!, and Viacom were interested in getting a piece or perhaps even all of Facebook. Imagine being twenty-three and worth $1.5 billion—and that is likely the low point for the rest of your life. Imagine saying "No" to Microsoft and Google when they dangle hundreds of thousands of dollars in front of you for just a 5 percent share of your company. That is exactly what Zuckerberg did.

During the late spring of 2007, Facebook opened up its platform to include additional outside applications as part of its open platform initiative. Soon a multitude of applications appeared that allowed users to ask questions of friends, determine who had similar musical tastes, post events, and send specific types of messages to other people. You could send your friends hugs, good karma, zombie bites, and questions you wanted them to answer. A more educational application called "Courses" allowed college students to share notes, start discussion forums, and manage their course activities.[8] The number of Facebook applications quickly became confusing and overwhelming. Worse still, sometimes users got tricked into sharing a Facebook application or some mindless content with their network of friends. In response to this somewhat chaotic state, Facebook altered and simplified its interface during 2008.

One must realize that in less than a year, more than seven thousand software applications were developed for Facebook.[9] Though some users got fed up or overwhelmed by the application options and committed the equivalent of Facebook suicide or simply stopped using the tool, Stanford University jumped on the application rollout bandwagon by offering a course on how to specifically design applications for Facebook.[10] The attention from new features and millions more users increased the value of the company. During July 2007, Facebook jumped up five notches to the thirteenth most visited site in the world according to Alexa and seventh in the United States. Not surprisingly, traffic to nearly any application that was linked to Facebook also exploded.[11] By late February 2009, Facebook was ranked fifth most visited site both in the United States as well as worldwide and was second in the United Kingdom, Greece, Hong Kong, Turkey, Italy, Chile, South Africa, and Nigeria. At the same time, MySpace dropped to eighth internationally and was fourth in the United States.

While all this was shaking out, Zuckerberg became an extremely rich young man. When Zuckerberg eventually caves in and sells part or all of his Facebook holdings, there are many things he can do to save "face" and contribute to the global movement to share free and open educational resources. It will be interesting to see if, in a couple of decades or perhaps sooner, Zuckerberg and other young technology mavericks adopt the philosophy of Bill Gates and make solid attempts to improve the life and educational opportunities of the citizens of this planet.

WILLIAM PENN HAD A BLOG

Some instructors and schools are experimenting with student use of social networking tools such as Facebook as well as video-sharing sites, text messaging, and blogging in their classrooms, because such services open up students' work to expanded audiences. Mark Franek, a former English teacher and dean of students at Philadelphia's William Penn Charter School, established by William Penn himself in 1689, reflected on his use of emerging technologies for writing, reflecting, and sharing in the September 10, 2007, issue of the *Christian Science Monitor*. Franek pointed out that when teachers incorporate Web 2.0 technologies in their classes, students begin to pay more attention to their thinking and their work. As he puts it: "When students know that anyone in the school with an Internet connection—or around the world, for that matter—can read what they have written or created, it is remarkable how quickly their thinking improves, not to mention the final product."[12] He argues that such tools are a means to prepare for the flatter world that Thomas Friedman talks about. They can foster reflection, perspective taking, and higher-order thinking.

When I talked to Franek, he told me that when he taught at William Penn High School, he had each of his students design and maintain their own blog using the free WordPress blog site. With this tool, they could upload their papers and projects from all subject areas and present them in a more user-friendly way that anyone could access and comment on. Students were also able to digitally connect to all the other members of the class through a special sidebar feature called the "blogroll." Adding more people to this blogging community for commenting and sharing would simulate many features that teenagers are drawn to in social networking sites.

Such activities are not easy to establish. One problem is that most schools block sites like Facebook and MySpace from their computer systems. Second, even if they were unblocked, most teens would not want their teachers to see their social networking site. Franek ingeniously got around this dilemma by recreating some of the "feel" of MySpace or Facebook and by showing kids that they can create and manage a site that is open to the Internet world. At this site, kids can showcase their academic talents via all kinds of digital posts (papers, pictures, podcasts, some YouTube clips, and so forth). Most of the kids loved the project: "Like a MySpace site dressed up and ready for its first job interview," one student called it. Franek cautions, however, to get permission from principals and headmasters as well as parents before attempting anything like this.

Besides dressing up one's ideas and placing them in these "presentation studios for student work," Franek reminds us that blogs and special interest groups in social networking sites can bring students into expert conversations on a topic. Students can actually have conversations with authors, professors, journalists, critics, other experts, and celebrities. This is where they can find mentors and become excited about further study of a subject area. All they need is an Internet connection. Social networking systems like MySpace and Facebook can be used to find and make those connections.

In his blog, Franek added that if your class was interested in the use of video-sharing resources like YouTube, it is easy to do. Such videos can inspire students and make highly complex ideas more clear. To connect these interests in blogging and video technologies, students or their instructors can simply jump into Facebook, make a relevant group on video blogging, and have hundreds of like-minded souls join their group. College students have some fun groups including, "I learn more from Wikipedia than from my professors," "When I was your age, Pluto was a planet," and "Students Against Professors Who Don't Utilize

Technology." What quickly forms is an audience of both experts and amateurs who have come together virtually to share.

There is a sense of belongingness or identity from social networking sites. We have membership with a group of our close "friends" in one site. We can subscribe to information feeds about their lives. Those with professional interests can join groups, lurk in related groups, share job postings, attend events, and invite others to join such groups and special events. Those with personal interests can share photos and videos, write on each other's walls, send gifts, and receive updates on each other.

In social networking sites, people can chat, share files, discuss ideas, e-mail each other, and send emoticons. These are the standard vehicles of communication for young people. Tools like Facebook and MySpace are the online spaces for such actions. In education, instructors often employ course management systems or virtual learning environments for similar activities. Systems like Moodle, Sakai, and Desire2Learn provide the virtual spaces or class containers. But what happens when the course management systems and the social networking systems merge? Who will oversee it? Where might this lead?

In past centuries, people relied on letters, the telephone, and the telegraph for communicating with friends and family. Today, it is social networking, blogging, and text messaging. But instead of private communications, this sharing is typically much more public and accessible to the world.

As waves of traffic run through the pipes of Web 2.0 companies, even more technologies are invented, celebrated, and passed on to others. The tools for creation and sharing, including podcasts, blogs, social networking software, wikis, and online photo albums, are dramatically changing the educational landscape. Wikipedia, Google, and Facebook are central to our lives. And so is blogging.

NO PEEPS FROM YOU!

We are becoming used to the near-instantaneous connection between online writers and online readers. Now imagine writing a diary and having it show up as a popular blog later on—not a few days, weeks, months, or years later, but centuries afterward. That is what happened to the diary of Samuel Pepys, written in seventeenth-century England.

Born in London on February 23, 1633, Pepys began his diary in 1660, just two years after the death of Oliver Cromwell. Amazingly, he kept on writing every day until May 1669 when his eyesight and health were suffering from overwork. Perhaps few would care except that when Cromwell died, his title of "Protector" (or, in effect, king in all but name) was passed along to his son Richard. And Richard was closely associated with Pepys's employer at the time, Edward Montague. Such events give this particular diary immediate importance for those who wish to understand these turbulent times in England, a period when all of Europe was beginning to transform into our more modern age.

In his diary, one quickly discovers that Pepys loved music, plays, women, and an assortment of alcoholic drinks. Across his posts, it becomes clear that he lived a highly interesting and eventful life during a key historic period for England. Everything is there for one to read—from various jealousies to business dealings to government issues to still other highly trivial matters. Pepys even provides firsthand accounts of the Great Plague of London, the Great Fire of London, and the Second Dutch War.[13]

Pepys's daily reflections now appear on a public blog each day, one by one. For instance, the post from January 4, 1661, starts off with: "Office all the morning, my wife and Pall being gone to my father's to dress dinner for Mr. Honiwood, my mother being gone out of town. Dined at home, and Mr. Moore with me, with whom I had been early this morning at White Hall, at the Jewell Office, to choose a piece of gilt plate for my Lord, in return of his offering to the King (which it seems is usual at this time of year, and an Earl gives twenty pieces in gold in a purse to the King)."

That is but a small remnant of that day. Each account is quite rich. To give the reader a way to read trails of thought and search for themes, underlined words in the blog mark text that are embedded with hyperlinks for further explorations.

As his diaries are made public in a blog, Samuel Pepys becomes a journalistic historian. But unlike his original writings, anyone alive today or born sometime in the future can read his online diary. Pepys's life is on display in full view. One can also peek in on the lives of many of his friends and acquaintances, as well as the daily events of the country in which he so fully lived.

What we have here is the reverse of blogs that later become books such as with Riverbend's *Baghdad Burning: Girl Blog from Iraq*.[14] With Pepys's online diary, we can view thick books that became blogs. Visitors to the blog can also comment on it and read the comments of others. They can click on hyperlinks between blog posts to get some sense of Pepys's relationships and assorted connections. They can travel to places mentioned in the diary through an embedded Google map of the location. There are also contextual pop-ups on different words in the blog as well as "Encyclopedia" entries that include background reading found in Wikipedia. For those who want more in-depth discussion or socializing with potentially like-minded people, there are associated groups such as "pepysdiary" in Yahoo! Groups.

Here we see some of the colossal powers of Web technology in opening up the educational world. The fact that someone can take a static work, like a diary, and put it up on the Web may not be surprising anymore. However, when repurposed with hyperlinks, added context, discussion forums, pictures, and other media, it becomes a more accessible piece of history that can evolve and expand as more and more people visit it. This is what the open educational world is all about. With creative repurposing and enhancements, a diary is no longer someone's private musings but rather a document that comes alive to its audience. It does all this without changing a single word of the author. As a text document, Pepys's detailed account of seventeenth-century England was privately or serially read by a few. Online technology, however, transforms his diary into a rich tapestry of interweaving events that can be personally explored and understood in any order by anyone. No history book has all this. Pepys's diary has become our history book. Such is the power of E!

The developer of this highly inventive and award-winning Web site is Phil Gyford. In his day job, Gyford is a freelance Web developer and consultant. Each day he gets to reveal to the world a day in London from the 1600s. Per Gyford, "Not only will I finally read the diary, I'll do so at the same time as people all over the world. It's like the world's largest book club."[15] People at LibraryThing, mentioned earlier, may contest that, but perhaps he has created the largest book club for seventeenth-century English literature. Gyford was able to establish this unique book club because he found a version of Pepys's diary dating from 1893 that was free of copyright. The text he used was provided by Project Gutenberg, which was started by Michael Hart at the University of Illinois in 1971 to provide copyright-free books. Such is the life of OER; one free resource begets another.

The Pepys site is highly popular. Gyford told me that in March 2008 there were over forty thousand unique visitors and 186,000 page views. In addition to the success evidenced by such computer log data, in late 2008, the Diary of Samuel Pepys Web site was nominated for Best Literature Blog for the 2008 Weblog Awards. Clearly, many people are finding the site worthwhile and engaging. They are learning history from a man never intending to be a history teacher and who passed away centuries ago. There could be more educational power if other diarists' works of the time were also posted. Gyford suggests John Evelyn, who kept a similar diary of the art, culture, and politics of the time and frequently corresponded with Pepys.[16] Imagine the critical thinking skills that might be nurtured by comparing two such treasure troves of history. How might the power of the Web elevate our understanding of England and key aspects of early modern European history?

In some ways, each modern blogger in the blogosphere is not simply a virtual news writer, but also a history teacher and commentator on the twenty-first century. Our teachers and mentors continue to shift and expand beyond people in our present physical spaces to those found living virtually in the present as well as in the past.

The posting of historical blogs such as Pepys's reminds us that the personal human accounts of trivial as well as more momentous events embedded in the Web create a gigantic story. Anytime we contribute to the Web, we are adding to this story. Through Samuel Pepys's diary, we begin to see a rich tapestry of ideas, events, and people that weave together to form culture. We come face-to-face with the life of another and the ways in which ideas and people can coinfluence each other.

Today, with new information and communication technologies, we are bombarded with much more information than Pepys ever had to contend with. This bombardment, however, is a constant reminder of our connections to others. Any bloglike reflections on such information and the connections made in discussion forums resulting from online postings of his thoughts and ideas might be used immediately in the classroom as well as for other virtual learning pursuits. There is even a chance that these postings and hyperlinked connections among them might be rediscovered and innovatively used hundreds of years in the future.

A VIRTUAL WORLD BRIDGE

In addition to blogging, podcasts and Webcasts can provide social commentary on key educational issues. For example, Worldbridges is an online community for individuals and organizations that employ Webcasting and other media delivery formats to connect people in learning forums. Worldbridges is filled with podcasts about a range of issues. Worldbridges also sponsors the popular EdTechTalk show and educational programming related to Korea (Koreabridge) and Tibet (Worldbridges Tibet).

As noted at their Web site, the goals of Worldbridges are relatively simple and straightforward: "Our primary goal is to foster understanding and cooperation amongst the citizens of the world. We value civility and respect, open source collaboration, fair distribution of income, and a sense of world identity." As part of these efforts, Worldbridges seeks to foster positive systemic changes in areas such as education, the environment, and politics. It also supports reliable and fair commerce. And it promotes a "people's forum" for more civilized discussion of problems, issues, and conflicts that pose significant challenges in uniting people. The inherent mission of Worldbridges is to foster discussion, interaction, collaboration, and reflection among the diverse people of this planet.

In 1993, Jeff Lebow began experimenting with the idea for World-bridges (initially called "World Explorer") after a year of teaching English in Thailand. At that time, he enrolled in a master's program in training and learning technologies at the University of New Mexico.[17] Lebow was excited about the possibilities he saw in the convergence of intercultural interaction and collaborative and interactive online technologies. After completing his master's, he returned to Asia—this time to Pusan, Korea—where he taught English at a university and began to experiment with online audio and video. His pilot testing included covering the Nagano Olympics in 1998. After burning out on all his activities and attempting to envision and build a Webcasting network, his life took a significant turn for the better. As he puts it, "I decided to quit my job, shave my head, and go to India for a while to contemplate the next chapter, for me personally and for Worldbridges. After some quality offline time, I decided to give Worldbridges a shot." And the world was significantly improved by his decision.

Lebow wanted Worldbridges to become a means for using Internet technology to create a global Webcasting network of people. Though it has accomplished many of its goals, like innumerable nonprofit ventures, there are struggles with sustainability. Jeff admits that not everyone knows what works so he continues to experiment with online educational formats. A few things have been phenomenal. For instance, he once had what he called a "spacecast" or Webcast with junior high school students in Virginia and a teacher from Iran who participated via Skype. The students got to ask serious questions followed by some concerning sports and music. Those participating soon came to appreciate the teacher in Iran as a real person. Jeff believes that governments of the world have not done a good job appreciating the perspectives of others, solving world problems, and collaborating with each other. Perhaps it would help them to first learn Farsi or some other language. Well, that is possible to do online as well, and for free!

THE LANGUAGES OF THE WEB

Need a Little Mocha?

Social networking tools are morphing into language learning tools and vice versa. Take Livemocha, for instance. Just plop yourself down at a computer with Internet access and sign up for free lessons from experienced Livemocha tutors. It is that simple. Complete a profile page indicating the language you want to learn, and dozens of potential tutors will send you e-mails offering their assistance. You will be turning dozens of people away in no time. While you do that, you can also select a tutor who appears to offer what you need. Millions of such matches have been made within Livemocha since it launched in the fall of 2007.

After a kick-off at the end of September 2007, Livemocha went from a few users to more than one hundred thousand in under three months.

According to Livemocha officials, it is a vibrant community with many of those signing up between the ages of twenty-five and thirty-five. In the initial months of service, the top language demanded was English; more than three-fourths of users were asking for English support and tutoring. French and Spanish were distant second and third choices at roughly one in twenty of the language learners. As the number of languages taught increases and membership from different countries rises, English will likely no longer be as dominant a request. What is quite clear is that the concept of Livemocha, which was brainstormed in the cafés of Seattle, has opened a learning door that cannot be shut.

According to Shirish Nadkarni, CEO, designated "Chief Roaster" and founder of Livemocha: "[W]e did not want people to know what we were working on as we were searching for an alternative name. But people liked it, and, as with the name 'Apple' in the computer industry, it differentiated us from the competition."

Nadkarni was born in India. At the age of twenty, he moved to the United States and finished his undergraduate degree in electrical engineering with a focus on computer engineering at the University of Michigan. He later obtained an MBA from Harvard. Degrees in hand, Nadkarni tasted a series of successes in previous business start-ups such as leading a team to develop the consumer wireless e-mail platform for popular BlackBerry devices. He also was central to Microsoft's acquisition of Hotmail and partnership with Inktomi. Simply put, Nadkarni is a man who can spot opportunities. He saw a pressing need for Livemocha after viewing the ineffective online resources his own children had access to when learning a language. They had learned Spanish vocabulary in school but could not effectively converse in it.[18] As he told me,

My kids have been learning Spanish for a number of years at school. However, while they were able to get good grades they couldn't really carry out a conversation. It struck home to me once while we were in Spain and we got lost. No one around us could speak English and my kids were of no help to me in conversing with the local population. I quickly came to the realization that the only way to really learn a language is to practice it with native language speakers. I know from personal experience with my own native language which grows rusty when I am in the

US but am quickly able to pick it up every time I travel to India and am "forced" to speak my native language.

The Internet can really help solve this problem without requiring us to travel to another country to converse with native speakers. With broadband and VoIP penetration and social networking trends, the time was "ripe" to introduce a solution that combined structured online learning with an integrated community to encourage people to practice the language. Our success in building a fairly large community suggests that we may be on to something here.

Nadkarni was on to something. It grew so fast, in fact, that the secret codename for the project, "Livemocha," stuck. There was something brewing at Livemocha that definitely was worth sipping. What is unusual is that Livemocha is immediately commanding so much attention from venture capitalists as well as users. It has no expensive advertising campaigns or premium paid marketing departments. No hoopla. The first wave of 130,000 registered users from more than two hundred countries was principally created through word of mouth and online viral marketing. In the early months, most members were naturally coming from the United States, but many others were from Egypt, Brazil, China, India, and Italy. Livemocha started with 160 hours of content for six key languages: English, French, Spanish, German, Mandarin Chinese, and Hindi.[19] By April 2008, beginner language lessons had been added in Brazilian Portuguese, Italian, Japanese, Icelandic, and Russian. These ten languages represent the majority of the languages spoken today. Undoubtedly, other languages such as Korean, Dutch, Arabic, and Polish will soon be added. In September 2008, just one year after launching, the Livemocha user base had crossed the one million mark. By March 2009, Shirish informed me that it had doubled to two million users. This adds up to a huge amount of new online language learners!

Livemocha is designed for those just dipping their toes in the water of a new language as well as those seeking more advanced lessons. Such lessons include exercises in reading, writing, listening, and speaking: the four staples of language learning. The lessons are meant to immerse and engage the learner in the sounds of a new language. Scan the site, however, and you will see that it contains much more than that.

According to Nadkarni, the learning technologies used by Live-mocha, such as podcasts or instructional content, are not what is interesting and engaging. What is vastly more important is people. The community-based approach of Livemocha, which seems half educational, half social, is what distinguishes it from other online language systems and most first-generation online education approaches. The inclusion of content at the site, moreover, distinguishes it from social networking sites such as Spanish or German language learning groups in Facebook that lack content. With the acceleration of broadband access, the timing is right for virtual language learning among friends.

Livemocha members can learn by chatting online (in text) as well as by talking to each other using headsets, or via video if they own a Webcam. Emblematic of this tenth opener, it is highly localized and personalized language instruction. Now anyone with access to the Internet can find an experienced language tutor through a quick online request. Instead of hiring a tutor who perhaps has a few years of training in a given language, as in many university settings and language institutes, you can interact with native speakers of that language as well as your peers in the same learning situation. And you can make international friends at the same time. At Livemocha, you can have conversations, fun, and the opportunity to meet great people—things you could never experience by simply carrying around CDs, books, or audiotapes. Friendships build connections and learning motivation.

Livemocha encourages people to help each other learn. This is the new age of learning in which WE-ALL-LEARN. It is an age of shared learning resources that include people as much as, if not more than, content. With Livemocha, another door has been opened to learning—a personalized network of learning.

Livemocha represents the educational power of social networking. People naturally want evidence of the power beyond the advertising dollars that sites like Facebook, Friendster, and MySpace bring in. As Nadkarni himself noted in his blog post on February 19, 2008:

> The fact that we have been able to quickly build up a user base of 200,000 users from over 200 countries demonstrates the tremendous need that people have to utilize foreign language learning to improve their lives. In many countries, people can literally double their income by learning

English. What is also very interesting, I believe, to the press is the perfect confluence of this global need with the emerging phenomena of social networking allowing people all over the world to leverage their native languages' proficiency to help each other. They are also excited by the possibility that social networking concepts can be applied to "more productive" endeavors such as learning language as opposed to enabling people to engage in "food fights" on sites like Facebook.[20]

With the huge number of people already using Livemocha, it will be a difficult animal to slow down. Who will police it? How might educational institutions and organizations use it and certify it? Nadkarni informed me that he intends to work with schools and universities to make them more comfortable and confident in granting credit for courses or modules completed at Livemocha. It is plausible that Livemocha may evolve into an online language institution and organization. We soon could be referring to Livemocha for all of our language learning needs.

Clearly, Livemocha is different. It pushes the Web 2.0 ahead by combining several of its most significant technologies. Livemocha has harnessed the power of social networks plus that of open educational resources and internal human needs or motivations to learn and to teach. Forming friendships while learning is the motto. And instead of traveling abroad to become immersed in a language, Livemocha users stay home and do it for free, without the need for paperwork or immunizations. And, in answering potential critics, Livemocha users still participate in real-world experiences with actual people instead of negotiating contrived lessons and lectures. Motivating? Yes! A revolution? Most definitely! The way to go? The jury is still out.

ADDING FLAVORS FROM YOUR FRIENDS ABROAD

Livemocha is not the only language brewhouse in town. One can just as easily sign up for language tutoring lessons at Mixxer, FriendsAbroad, and Languagelab. Communities of learners and future friends await anyone visiting any of these sites.

Let's start with Mixxer. Mixxer is a free educational community for language learners developed by Todd Bryant, an academic technology liaison to the foreign language department at Dickinson College in Carlisle, Pennsylvania. By early 2009, Mixxer had roughly twenty-five thousand users. With Mixxer you can participate in public chats and Skypcasts, submit documents, ask for help from native speakers, and attend events hosted by language teachers around the world. Bryant told me that "among my first goals at Dickinson when arriving was to use some kind of messenger to allow our students to have tandem language exchanges with native speakers abroad." Quality connections helped Skype quickly win out over Yahoo! and MSN. A journal article from the summer of 2005 on emerging technologies for language learning briefly mentioned Mixxer and brought it the necessary traction.[21]

Bryant told me, "Skype is always looking to integrate itself into other social networking services and devices (e.g., MySpace)." He further stated that students in European universities, such as in Germany, have the luxury of learning language directly from someone else due to the large numbers of international students and the large percentage of students in Europe who speak multiple languages. But in the United States it is different, especially for students in small colleges and less populated areas. Mixxer opens up new language learning possibilities to such students—and by using Skype for online interactions, it's free.

Bryant also stated that inexpensive tutoring services using video-conferencing are increasingly common. He believes that textbook companies will eventually become major players when they put two and two together and see that they can offer professional tutoring services via tools like Skype to connect students in various countries using their language textbooks. With a Webcam, Skype users can see and hear their language instructor and more quickly understand the nuances of the language. The immediacy and specificity of the feedback is a key reason why users find it engaging.

In contrast to the nonprofit Mixxer community, there are online language learning companies like LiveMocha and FriendsAbroad. By November 2008, FriendsAbroad, headquartered near London, had in excess of a half-million users from more than two hundred countries speaking over eighty languages. In early 2008, one of the first profiles I found was from "Mystii," a twenty-two-year-old woman from Venezuela who had just joined FriendsAbroad an hour earlier. Here is what she stated: "Hi, I'm from Venezuela. Spanish is my native language. I'm here because I want to speak perfectly ENGLISH and to learn a lot of FRENCH. I like the good music as metal, cl ic rock, cl ic music, dark ambient, metal/industrial and many others styles, the art, drawing, reading . . . I CAN HELP YOU WITH THE SPANISH = D."

Clearly Mystii's English was not quite as perfect as she hoped it would be. If Mystii is not a match for you, there is Jorge, age twenty-four, also from Venezuela, who speaks Spanish and wants to learn English, or perhaps Tawab, a thirty-two-year-old male from Afghanistan who speaks Persian (or Farsi) and wants to learn English. FriendsAbroad became so popular that Babbel, a Berlin-based language learning company, acquired the company late in 2008.[22]

For those with a penchant for virtual worlds and avatars, Languagelab is available. Languagelab utilizes the voice system in Second Life. As of early 2009, courses at the Languagelab were available only for English instruction, though there were options including courses geared for business, academics, casual conversation, and more general English practice. Students from more than forty countries were meeting at this online language lab. As in "real life," one could learn English in Second Life bars, clubs, parks, and restaurants. Most classes contained six to eight students and were held for one or two hours. In addition to general discussion, vocabulary and grammar lessons and tests were available.

For those wanting more solitary experiences, there also is the heavily used language learning site, About.com. About.com is owned by *The New York Times*. It offers free language learning lessons and resources to independent learners in Italian, Japanese, German, Mandarin Chinese, French, Spanish, and English as a Second Language. Each of these seven individual sites is run by an expert guide who is charged with creating original materials including language lessons, practice exercises, audio files, study aids, lesson plans, and, of course, tests and quizzes. There are also items to promote a learning community such as blogs, practice forums, and newsletters. Every item there is available to explore at will.

CAN I HAVE A REFILL AND A CHINESEPOD?

There are many questions that surround ambitious efforts such as FriendsAbroad, Mixxer, and Livemocha. There are also a variety of alternatives to such systems. Among them are podcasting and mobile learning.

Imagine that you have decades of experience with language education in Asia and have built many successful language learning centers in Shanghai. Things are going very well. Then someone floats a business opportunity by you—the idea of franchising your pedagogical talents and ideas via the Web. What would you do? This is what happened to Ken Carroll in February 2005. His Canadian business partner, Hank Horkoff, had keenly predicted that podcasts and other Web 2.0 tools would lay the basis for a revolution in language learning. As my British friends might say, he was "spot-on, brilliant"!

The hit product was ChinesePod from Praxis Language. ChinesePod is part of a learning revolution that millions of people now personally participate in each month. "Are you surprised?" I asked him. "No, not really. Happy, yes!" Carroll replied. These numbers are not too surprising given that more than thirty million people worldwide are currently studying Chinese as a foreign language. An article in the *China Daily* indicates that the Ministry of Education in China is estimating an increase to one hundred million in the not-too-distant future.[23] Lending credibility to such lofty predictions, enrollments in learning Chinese in college settings have grown more than 50 percent since 2002.[24] Given that university courses cannot keep up with these demands, alternatives such as podcasts and other forms of online content quickly draw attention. Interest in Mandarin is also apparent in K–12 schools with between thirty and fifty thousand students in the United States studying it.[25] As noted earlier, in the United States, places such as Michigan and Florida have received much press about their Chinese language initiatives. Other states will likely follow in their footsteps.

ChinesePod was developed to teach Mandarin Chinese through online podcasts, which are so popular that hundreds of thousands of people visit the Web site each month to browse, listen to, or download them. The podcasts are free, but additional premium and supplemental language services, such as the podcast transcripts, language learning exercises, and other services cost between nine and thirty dollars per month. At present, thousands of people subscribe to such add-ons, but as they scale up, it is conceivable that this could grow to hundreds of thousands or perhaps even millions of subscribers. For high-end users willing to pay more, ChinesePod can provide daily conversations and language lessons with native-speaking teachers using Skype.

The podcast shows are produced for individuals ranging from newbies to those at the elementary, upper elementary, and intermediate levels, and advanced members. Users can listen to sessions in many wide-ranging areas including entertainment, sports, people, weather, business, relationships, and food. In ChinesePod, specific topics cover content such as tea, dating, getting your hair done, studying abroad, to love or be loved, and restaurants with bad service. Carroll told me that he believes in the power of conversation and dialogue for language learning, which the podcasts can provide.

A voracious reader, Carroll is constantly on the lookout for new tools, theories, and resources for fostering language learning. If there are opportunities for language learning from cell phones and other mobile devices as well as from online video and animations, Carroll will have read and likely blogged on them already.

Carroll is one of just a handful of people I have talked to during the past few years who truly understands the Web 2.0 as a transformative pedagogical device. Not only has he seen the learning world become more open, he has fashioned a few of the more attractive doors and windows. Carroll knows the importance of emerging technology plus innovations in instruction.

Then there is Jenny Zhu, who many perceive as the voice and image of ChinesePod. Back home in Shanghai after obtaining a master's degree in public policy in Sydney in 2004, Jenny was hoping to be a diplomat or perform community-related work. Instead, within a couple of months she found herself employed by one of Carroll's language learning institutes. Recognized as a highly skilled teacher of Chinese, her verbal and interpersonal talents instantly came into full view when placed in the recording studio. Her engaging voice, flexible personality, and air of confidence are immediately apparent in each podcast show. This appeal quickly resulted in an extensive fan base and thousands of loyal listeners.

When I spoke with Jenny in March 2008, she said that she did not know what to expect when agreeing to work for ChinesePod. At the same time, she realized that this program was embarking on pioneering efforts. She was literally stunned by the attention the site mustered in its first few months. As regular visitors flocked to ChinesePod and began commenting on a daily basis, Jenny felt a "lovely affirmation" that she had made the right choice. An appearance on CNN online was next. With all the attention and accolades, it was clear that online education would trump a career in public policy, at least for now.

Though public policy may be on hold, her public speaking has increased substantially. For example, in late October 2007, Jenny was flown to the United States to keynote the Learning 2007 conference in Orlando, run by Elliott Masie. Over two thousand learning professionals from twenty-nine countries were stunned by her live demonstration that revealed how easy and engaging ChinesePod was. As she said, it "shattered the conventional perception of learning Chinese."

From her viewpoint, what makes ChinesePod successful is that it is highly accessible and learner focused. According to Jenny, online technology liberates potential Chinese learners from the traditional "physical, time, and teacher constraints." She then stated that the strength of ChinesePod is that it "constructs learning around the learner's needs, giving real-life practical language that's authentically designed to teach Chinese as a second language, and building and sustaining a very vibrant community that energizes and motivates learners." No wonder it is successful! Not fully satisfied, Jenny hopes to keep building and expanding ChinesePod. In her closing comments to me, she mentioned, "The beauty of ChinesePod is that it is a live learning event, one that keeps going. There are so many fresh topics and dimensions that I am eager to try out. My wish is to age gracefully on ChinesePod." Her fan base undoubtedly hopes so too.

As Carroll notes in his personal blog, Networks, Languages, and Learning 2.0, "Things are going to be different three years from now. Mark my words!" Carroll is undoubtedly on to something, and it will probably not take three years for the rest of the world to discover it. Carroll and Praxis march on with SpanishPod, FrenchPod, and Italian-Pod.[26] FrenchPod and ItalianPod both rest on a personalized learning system (PLS), which gives users a chance to learn a language on one's own terms.

Portable products from Praxis fit this opener on personalized learning quite well. Although Carroll admits that there is a fine line between autonomous learning and system guidance, he believes that they have found a learner-centered philosophy and suite of tools that can help balance it. In each language they teach, they have a large database of lessons that can be listened to over and over to reinforce the learning. The lesson transcript is available to follow along with each lesson. In addition, there are opportunities to practice a language with an online counselor as well as with the ChinesePod community.

SO EC TO SHOW YOU THE COFFEE

Whereas podcast-based systems like ChinesePod are highly valuable for mobile and auditory learners, some start-ups are adding video and other features. David Liu, director of curriculum development at start-up KanTalk in Ann Arbor, Michigan, reported that as of mid-January 2009, this network had 19,317 registered members—of which 1,048 were language teachers—from forty-seven countries. According to the numbers, the highest usage of KanTalk has been by individuals in Brazil, the United States, China, India, and South Korea. KanTalk allows non-native speakers to improve their spoken English by practicing as well as listening to and watching native speakers.

Like many online language systems of the twenty-first century, KanTalk integrates an assortment of technologies—Skype, digital recorders, and YouTube. With KanTalk, you can make recordings of your voice, listen to others, watch English videos, and have Skype discussions or mentoring sessions. It has features akin to popular social networking sites where members can share common interests. As in YouTube, video lessons can be shared, rated, or saved as favorites. Watching such context-based videos of live events is exciting and enhances language learning by providing video to go with the text. Some include transcripts. Other video lessons provide questions that can be discussed.

KanTalk is not the only system relying on contextualized video for language learning. Though it is limited to English and Mandarin, ECpod is another. Take for example, Mr. Shou-Bing Fu. He rides his bike daily to the high school in his village to access ECpod language learning sites from computers in the school library. Shou-Bing, a high school chemistry teacher, is from the First High School of Tunxi in Huangshan City in the southern Anhui province in Eastern China. He learns English daily using ECpod. When I clicked on his name in ECpod, I learned that he was a semiretired forty-two-year-old chemistry instructor who had joined ECpod in May 2007. Shou-Bing cycles back home twenty-five miles for a simple lunch of rice and stir-fried vegetables with salted fish but will return in the evening to learn more. This is his life now: to learn. And learn he does!

Shou-Bing was quite happy to tell me his story via e-mail and practice his English at the same time. I soon found out that health problems caused him to retire from teaching at a young age back in 2001. Now he works in the lab at the high school. Shou-Bing is learning English as a hobby, but also so he can teach others using ECpod. When he taught high school, there was no opportunity to teach using English; only the English teacher could do that. As he told me, "I learn a lot from the action of teaching. My English is improved each day."

Similar to Wikipedia, there is a worldwide community in ECpod helping each other learn. As on YouTube, there are free online videos available on a range of topics. And much like Livemocha and ChinesePod, conversation is the key, instead of simple drills and practice lessons. What is unusual about ECpod is that members often film each other in everyday activities to help people learn the nuances of the language and the cultural innuendos that do not make it into textbooks. Members participate! They decide the content of the film and how it is shot. In this way, learning is personalized in a growing online social network.

When exploring their videos, you observe tiny dirt roads and remote villages in the Chinese countryside not typically seen by those studying Mandarin in the West. There are videos on cooking, makeup, traditional Chinese games, going for a haircut, and tiger swimming contests. Key words in English and Chinese text often flash on the screen as reinforcement.

With these shared videos in ECpod, cross-border friendships and contacts emerge where none were previously possible. People are also exposed to different Chinese dialects without having to travel to another city or province. On ECpod, anyone can be a teacher or learner, from those in the rural streets of China or Vietnam to those in more urban settings.

Shou-Bing himself has posted many videos for those learning Mandarin, such as "Computer-Basic," "Fitness Equipment," and "A tennis court." This man is dedicated and highly prolific. In the tennis video, he shows features of a tennis court in China and pronounces the names of these in Chinese as well as English.

The learning world is opened more widely for people like Shou-Bing, whereas just a few years prior, it was tightly shut. At the same time, Shou-Bing and many others at ECpod are opening the world of mainland China and many other countries for the rest of us. This is the vision we need as a human race: one where we all revel in the fact that now anyone can learn. When one person finds success, we all do, even if it was with someone else's product, invention, or idea. We are now a global sharing culture.

THE DELHI TUTOR

Paralleling the explosion of online language learning is the emergence of online tutoring and mentoring to personalize learning. Those dipping their toes into the water include elementary school principals, school counselors, nutrition experts, and park rangers. Online mentors might soon be available for every person in every step of education. Mentor-Net, for instance, is a nonprofit organization that matches female and minority college and university students with professionals in scientific and technical fields, in the hopes that more such students will enter these fields. It includes one-to-one online mentoring as well as Web-based discussion forums and resources.

Online homework tutoring is perhaps more prevalent than mentoring. AskOnline uses online formats to help tutor middle school students through adult learners. Similarly, Tutor.com offers support, for a fee, in science, math, history, and English. The State of New Jersey picked up the tab for tutoring in their "Homework Help NJ" program to aid students in grades 4–12 with personalized learning supports.[27] New Jersey kids have plenty of opportunities and choices when it comes to mentoring. In fact, there are more than two thousand tutors in Tutor.com who are available twenty-four hours per day, seven days per week to help with such subjects as calculus, algebra, physics, chemistry, and history research. And no appointment is necessary. To ease the concerns of parents, every session is recorded and available for review. Talk about personalized service!

Other companies include SMARTHINKING, TutorVista, and Growing Stars. In most of these services, the tutors may come from seven or eight thousand miles away in places such as Bombay and Bangalore, whereas in other cases, the mentors are located down the block.[28] Of course, the hourly rates for outsourced tutors are much more reasonable than paying for local services.

These companies have found a niche and are steamrolling ahead. Based on the immense success they found in providing tutors for someone else's courses—and realizing that college costs were out of hand—SMARTHINKING had an ingenious idea. In May 2008, it launched a new line of online services called StraighterLine. With StraighterLine, students could enroll in inexpensive introductory college courses such as Economics 101 or English composition ($399) developed by McGraw-Hill. They could start and end the courses at any time.[29] As an added enticement, ten hours of tutoring would be available from SMAR-THINKING during each course experience. Some higher education institutes quickly agreed to grant credit for such courses.

Initial reactions from higher education instructors were understandable. One commented, "Poor students; they don't know what they've lost." Another said, "Obviously, according to the article everything can be outsourced except the issuance of the diploma. Here it is. We've finally arrived. We don't educate anymore. We are officially a credentialing service." A third offered his perspective, "An 'education' continues to give way to 'job training.' We can expect to see more of this as well as relaxed standards in general." Implicit in this news is that the courses StraighterLine could make available online, and the tutors—ten hours worth—would come from India. Yes, these courses would be highly affordable, flexible, and individualized, but the individualization would come from people not trained or hired in the United States. Their credentials were not the only thing in question, but also whether a major book publisher could create quality classes and offer them online. These concerns, however, seem to bypass the fact that many self-paced courses now exist for college credit and are widely accepted. StraighterLine is actually adding a layer of additional support.

What is going on here? A decade ago, we were outsourcing our Y2K problem and then other programming needs to India. Next up was customer service. That was at the corporate level. Soon individuals were getting in on the act. They could hire someone from India to schedule them a haircut, book a reservation in a restaurant, buy tickets, or make travel arrangements.[30] Today we are farming out our education. We can get a tutor from Delhi more easily than one from next door. What's next? Outsourcing our pension plans?

MENTOR AND TUTOR REFLECTIONS

Through such online mentoring and tutoring programs, anyone can assist in the learning of anyone else. The underlying story is that the doors to learning success swing further open with such personalized attention. We all can now learn and we all can be provided support in whatever educational pursuit we seek. With the Web, companies and agencies can offer mentoring and expert guidance to young children wanting to become engineers, scientists, and astronauts. Electronic mentoring programs extend to all ages and in a way bring us back a few centuries to the days when apprentices expected to learn a trade such as tanning, soap making, or printing, from the masters. Today young people enter into tele-apprenticeships to become meteorologists, counselors, and game developers.

Direct one-to-one mentoring is perhaps the most powerful form of learning in human history. Think Socrates to Plato to Aristotle. With today's online communication tools and resources there are innumerable ways to automate, legitimate, and facilitate the process. Mentoring in the time of the ancient Greeks was highly circumscribed. Assuming you were not Philip of Macedon, it was unlikely that you could get Aristotle to personally mentor you or your family members anywhere outside of Athens. You were limited by your physical location. Today, those limits to mentoring no longer apply. The eradication of such a requirement makes expert support available to the commoner. Every human being with an Internet connection can now have a mentor. In fact, there are literally dozens of individuals—if not hundreds—in your chosen field or newfound interest area to select from. If the first one proves inadequate, ill prepared, or unresponsive, don't fret; there are many more available.

Increased human connections, mentoring, and networking are not just apparent in this particular learning opener, they are *the* trend! *The* opener! If there is one thing that is salient across the ten openers, it is this very notion—that more humans, as well as more resources, are now fully loaded in the teaching and learning loop. As this happens, the odds that all of us can learn through the Web just got exceedingly better.

THIS IS GETTING PERSONAL!

Personalization elevates human learning to new heights while encouraging everyone involved to seek more. The tools and ideas for such personalization are highly apparent today. The most obvious perhaps is the use of social networking software to build a collaborative network of people to share life events with. Did anyone a decade or two ago envision hundreds of thousands, if not millions, of online tutors in most any language at any time that people would like to learn? And if someone did, was the word "free" part of that scenario? How about podcasts to make that learning portable and convenient? As we all know, language learning is just the start. Mentoring and tutoring on nearly any topic are now possible. Need help with managing a team, preparing for a college entrance exam, or completing an algebra assignment? A mentor is within electronic reach. What's more, such expertise is available 24/7.

Are Livemocha and ChinesePod correct in their emphasis on conversations between members as the key to language learning? Given the explosion of users of these systems as well as Facebook and MySpace, it seems that conversations unite people and serve as the foundation of all human experience. There are many signs that the Web is increasingly an oral culture with Twitter, Facebook status updates, blog postings, and mentoring via chat tools and Skype. In a short time, we have gone from pen pals to Skype pals. From online writing to online talking. The experience is synchronous and immediate, rather than asynchronous with long lags between interactions. As this occurs, learning is more personalized, participatory, and interactive. We feel connected to others who care about us. Online friends might show us that they care by joining our Facebook groups, by subscribing to our blog or Twitter posts, or by offering to mentor us in the language we have indicated a desire to learn.

There has been a sudden explosion in providing online mentoring and other supports when and where deemed needed. It requires tools for collaboration as well as expanded piping or bandwidth. Specific personalized learning services are available from an international tutor or mentor. Our teachers can now be anyone. They can be anywhere. And they can be requested anytime. The same can be said for one's peers and colleagues—no longer must they possess the same postal code, experience the same weather patterns, or even speak the same language. It is truly a learner's world.

The next few years will propel us more deeply into such learning options as well as the pedagogical approaches for establishing or pursuing them. An inherent goal is to arrive at a stage where we no longer see personalized learning as the ideal, but as standard and accepted practice. When that occurs, we will be living in a world where WE-ALL-LEARN is not contested or seen as implausible for most, but where the citizens of this planet get their learning needs met in ways that are best suited for them. And perhaps while meeting such needs, they will be generating educational resources for still other learners following, at least momentarily, in their footsteps. Enjoy the road!

The Treasures and Traps of This Open Learning World

DO WE-ALL-LEARN?

In this book, I have employed four distinct tactics to reveal to you the riches of this more open learning world. First, a series of stories is presented in each chapter that bring to life the people who have added to this learning transformation. They are the heroes, gurus, and revolutionaries of the shared Internet that we all now frequent. It should be clear from reading the stories that there is not just one person, one resource, or one innovative idea that is responsible for the immeasurable changes taking place. Together they are intended to provide a convincing tale that now we can all learn.

Second, for those in a perpetual love affair with numbers and statistics, each chapter contains extensive facts and research results as well as associated references. Anyone can go online today and find scholarly research and the stories behind such research that support different learning models and approaches and vice versa. Many popular technology trend books do just that. Stories can make the facts and figures come alive. At the same time, current data help lend credibility to those stories and point to future trends. Taking this to heart, there is a Web site associated with this book—WorldIsOpen.com—where anyone can share similar stories as well as browse through the references cited in the book, the majority of which include hyperlinks to the original article. For those seeking to gather even more statistical information and read additional anecdotes about this new world where WE-ALL-LEARN, there is a companion e-book, which is available at WorldIsOpen.com and also at Scribd. That free e-book, with dozens more stories and hundreds of extra resources and projects, follows the same chapter sequence used here, but with different content, in an attempt to open the learning world to many others.

Third, for those with more pragmatic needs, the Web links for all the projects, tools, and resources referred to in the book are also accessible on the WorldIsOpen Web site. Proof of concept is not just in the research data but in real-world experiences with the learning materials and resources mentioned. I encourage you to dip in and explore the many opportunities described here, as well as any others you may stumble upon.

Fourth, and perhaps most important, there is a model in this book to make sense of the ten converging learning technology trends that are now opening up education, and thus the world, for everyone. The WE-ALL-LEARN model offers a framework to strategically plan for and adapt to technologies for learning.

This framework represents the convergence of three factors: (1) an enhanced Web-based learning infrastructure, (2) billions of pages of free and open content placed within that infrastructure, and (3) a culture of participation and knowledge-sharing that personalizes learning within it. The fact that these three things—pipes, pages, and a participatory culture—have emerged at roughly the same time is fortuitous for all of us learners. In Friedman's terms, this is a triple convergence! However, instead of an economic one with new processes for horizontal collaboration allowing billions of new players to operate on a flatter or more level playing field, this triple convergence opens up the world through electronic education. Each of us is empowered by this learning convergence though as of yet there is no one theory or perspective that can fully explain it.

We are emerging from an age when prevailing theories helped us understand and utilize learning technologies, though often unsuccessfully, to a time when technologies are part of a much more complex learning environment. No longer can technologies be pulled apart, individually observed, and understood from the standpoint of a single theory or perspective. The only way to make sense of them in this age of the Web is with overarching frameworks and models.

When I first drafted and presented the ten openers back in the fall of 2005, I could not help but wonder how people living fifty years ago as well as those fifty years in the future might react to them. Each of these openers offers transformative educational power. How might electronic collaboration or open educational resources have changed my own education? How about that of my parents or Grandpa George's generation of a century ago? We certainly appear to be entering a new age of learning, one that has no starting or ending point. This is a time when there are no set limits on who might enter learning spaces with us or influence our learning when there. It is an era that blends the physical with the virtual. Twenty-first-century learning pivots around choices and opportunities rather than sorting individuals according to previous test scores and personal backgrounds. As the framework for this book tells us, WE-ALL-LEARN.

The WE-ALL-LEARN template is a starter for rethinking and reforming educational practices. With this simple mnemonic, it becomes easier to remind ourselves that education buttresses the economic flatteners that Friedman documented, not the other way around. Without these ten educational openers, the world would not be flat economically or even more spiky. Without collaborative educational experiences, people working in small and large businesses would not have the skill base to take advantage of the knowledge networks now possible with synchronous and asynchronous online conferencing. And they would not have access to the resources to upgrade their skills and competencies as the needs arise.

The Web 2.0 and its associated technology are among the latest fighting tools for change in education. Inevitably, there will be resistance to it. Many will argue that such tools are fads that will soon pass. In the twenty-first century, however, learning technology is hard to ignore. There are stockpiles of Internet technologies that are not simply fashionable but are part of the standard online learning lexicon, including asynchronous discussion forums, streaming video, and real-time chats. There really is no more debate here. Such technologies impact education in a major way today and will continue to do so throughout this century; it is just a matter of figuring out exactly where, when, and how much. When answers emerge, we can put in place a WE-ALL-LEARN type of model. Fortunately, each of the ten openers offers educational hope in accessing information on nearly any topic and subtopic known today and tomorrow and then evaluating, categorizing, synthesizing, and sharing such information.

Everyone benefits from the ten openers—they open windows with majestic views and doorways to new careers. Learners as well as instructors and trainers in primary and secondary schools, colleges and universities, corporate or government training centers, and in other educational situations all can benefit from these ten trends. During the past decade, countless instructors who were once hesitant to place their syllabi or course curricula on display on the Web are now part of complete online programs or are collaboratively teaching online with instructors they never met. New consortia, communities, and collective knowledge-sharing centers of excellence are appearing in an age when, in fact, WE-ALL-LEARN. If singer Bob Dylan were an educator, he might proclaim that "the learning times indeed are a-changing."

THE WEB OF LEARNING AWAITS

The Web accommodates millions of learners. For career advancement goals as well as for lifelong learning, self-esteem, personal fulfillment, and economic reasons, they are signing up for online and blended learning classes in droves. Some are even getting complete degrees and other credentials online rather than stepping foot in a physical class-room or fighting for the last open parking spot on campus. Thousands are browsing and downloading resources from MIT's OpenCourseWare initiative as well as satellite projects such as OOPS, which are trans-lating those courses to Chinese and other languages. A vast array of digital books, many of which are free, as well as library, museum, and university resources are also indexed and categorized at innumerable learning portals.

One might be able to jury-rig an entire college degree with all the free courses found online. Interested in working with the hearing impaired? There are free courses in American Sign Language from Michigan State University. Alternatively, you might spend some time in Carnegie Mellon's Open University Initiative and learn biology, statistics, French, calculus, economics, or empirical research methods. Or perhaps you might explore free courses from MIT on aeronautics, civil engineering, nuclear science, urban studies, or women's studies. And if interested in learning more about bioterrorism, you can check out resources from the North Carolina Center for Public Health Preparedness. If health care is of interest, Johns Hopkins Bloomberg School of Public Health has free online courses in public health, adolescent health, nutrition, mental health, and injury prevention. Or perhaps travel virtually to the West Coast and learn conversational Mandarin Chinese from Dr. Tianwei Xie at California State University Long Beach, or Turkish from the Computer Aided Language Instruction Web site created by the Department of Near Eastern Studies at the University of Arizona. These are but a few free stops you can make online today.

Certainly, courses are great, but so are life experiences. The Web can provide those as well. George Siemens at the University of Manitoba envisions a world without courses but still rich in learning experiences.[1] Such a world might rely more on connections or networks between people and resources as well as the conversations that those people could have using such resources. Siemens has written extensively about a possible learning theory based on technology-enhanced networks called connectivism.[2]

As we enter this highly interconnected world, millions of people are taking time to create personal blogs and comment on the blog postings of others that they bump into when exploring resources online. They are downloading podcasts for later listening as well as generating a few of their own. They are checking out needed facts and information in Wikipedia as well as contributing to entries or corrections to them. To satisfy their learning curiosities, some might even be taking on a persona in a virtual world such as Second Life. Of course, many are also connecting with a broad group of friends using social networking software. It is here that they might be exchanging educational ideas and interests. These learners are increasingly mobile, connected, and interactive, and their learning is wireless, collaborative, ubiquitous, and on demand.

The Web awaits teachers and trainers. Anyone wishing to teach or train other people online can find educational outlets for their knowledge; you do not have to be an educational professional to make a difference. Instructors can find free educational materials in places such as MERLOT, Connexions, and Curriki, and scan through any relevant reviews before deciding to include them in their classes. Portals of additional contents, such as online cases, simulations, and scenarios, might also be indexed for learning activities and explorations. Some of these simply reference online resources through a set of links, whereas others are repositories of the actual objects. And communities are developing ways to share and expand the possibilities of these portals, referenceware, referatories, and repositories. For the first time in the history of education, millions of educators are banding together to share their teaching ideas and approaches with people they may never meet or personally talk to. Now that the knowledge-sharing faucet has been turned on, the resources running through it are serving millions of people who previously lacked access to education.

Once satisfied with what they have discovered, they are using Moodle, Sakai, Drupal, and other online content and course management systems to upload course contents and manage their online classes. Impressive power here! Not only are these containers for courses, but they foster communication with free synchronous chat, discussion forums, wikis, blogs, social networking tools, and other forms of electronic collaboration. In addition to the extensive functionality of these free systems, there are other options. Many, in fact, are not happy being restricted to the functionality of one system; instead, they piece together a set of more lively and exciting Web 2.0 technologies to personalize their learning experience. In this personalization process, some prefer more participatory activities from wikis, blogs, podcasts, online surveys, and other tools.

As personalization and participation increase, the Web is transformed from a tool to replicate eyeball-to-eyeball instruction, to a place where learning innovation is clearly on display. In contrast to initial complaints about the boring nature of most online content, the creative ideas of many instructors have created a swell of energy in online spaces for others to experience and expand on.

The Web has shifted teaching and learning approaches that have been in residence for millennia. Former practices are not abandoned, but rather added to in a smorgasbord of technologies and pedagogical approaches. Thanks to the Web each of us is exposed to a unique blend of learning approaches each day. You might listen to a favorite educational radio or podcast show. While you're doing that, your partner or children might prefer watching a YouTube, Current TV, or Big Think video related to a topic of interest. Your neighbor might no longer subscribe to the newspaper but instead read online news stories and watch video clips from CNN, BBC News, *The New York Times,* Canada.com, or Yahoo! News. Later in the day, you might listen to an audiobook in your car or on the train and then decide to buy a paper version of the book for your home library. Alternatively, you could also listen to a keynote speech from a conference you missed and later e-mail that person for additional resources and articles to read that can be found online.

There is an avalanche of formal and informal learning possibilities. Keep in mind, however, that this is just the warm-up act. Technology innovations in the coming decades will bring unfathomed opportunities. For this reason, it is crucial to remind ourselves continually that human learning remains the primary goal. Technology by itself is often nice to show off to friends, supervisors, and journalists, but without some lingering imprint on the human brain, what is the purpose?

Nearly two decades ago, Gavriel Salomon from the University of Haifa noted that there must be either impacts "of" the technology or impacts "with" it.[3] The choice is between true cognitive gains or residual effects of the technology and the use of technology tools to replace or augment some lower-level brain functions or support one's problem solving. In the latter scenario, one's skills are upgraded with the intellectual partnerships between man and machine. In the former, such partnerships leave lasting cognitive residue within the learner. One is meant to stretch what mankind can do at a particular point in time, whereas the other is much more durable and permanent. This entire book could be written from the standpoint of that one distinction. If I had done so, you would quickly see that the vast majority of the Web-based learning technologies detailed in this book would be in the "with" section, rather than "of." Why? Well, measuring the cognitive impact from technology is never easy. In contrast, showing someone what you can do with a new technology tool or feature is fairly straightforward.

Salomon was not the first to hint at such possibilities. More than half a century ago, Charles Wedemeyer, a distance learning educator and pioneer from the University of Wisconsin, and Vannevar Bush, an engineer and technologist from MIT and the federal government, both attempted to push the envelope of learning technologies. They each envisioned a future in which we are now currently immersed. What might they tell us today?

ENVISIONING A MORE PERSONALIZED AGE OF LEARNING

It's impossible to end a book like this without a few predictions. A decade ago, I was among those discussing possibilities for an inter-planetary Internet.[4] As the Web 2.0 kicks into high gear, we hear similar ideas such as mind-reading computers, intelligent agents or butlers that serve up all one's learning and information needs, and a single personal computer with the ability to store all the knowledge ever created, which you can transport with you in your pocket.[5] Such predictions are always enticing to hear, but I would rather end with fifteen predictions, some of which are fairly certain and immediate as well as several that perhaps are not. And though technological improvements—such as faster search, better access, larger storage capacity, higher-quality video, and more effective language translation—are implicit in these fifteen, the focus here is not on the technology but on what the convergence of many learning technologies is giving rise to.

1. Five Billion "Have-Nots" Have at It!

I agree with Microsoft founder, Bill Gates, who in his five-university farewell tour in the United States in the spring of 2008 suggested that education needs to open up to the poorest two or three billion people on this planet.[6] As curricula and content are increasingly free or cheaply available, those who were left out of education in the past, either fully or in part, will be more and more involved. But they need access. Currently, only one billion of the 6.7 billion people on this planet have Internet access. What happens when a large percentage of the billions of people without Web access begin to acquire it? Where will they go to learn? Imagine the language translation tools needed. Imagine how they might use learning tools and resources from the WE-ALL-LEARN model. If we have additional billions of people with access to free and open education, there will be multiple simultaneous social, economic, and perhaps political revolutions. However, it is the educational revolution that sets the stage for all the others. This is perhaps the most fundamental issue of our age—how to provide increasing access to Web-based educational opportunities, especially free and open educational resources. When successful, the "have-nots" will have at it—they will enter the Internet and engage in learning pursuits perhaps never imagined. Given the learning revolution they will be joining on the Web, instead of labeling them as part of "the haves," we might refer to them as the "have-ins."

2. The Emergence of Lifelong Super E-Mentors and E-Coaches

Howard Gardner, the expert on multiple intelligences from Harvard, is correct in pointing out that with all the information available today, we will continue to need coaches and mentors for our learning pursuits.[7] Anyone attempting to apply the WE-ALL-LEARN model in a strategic way will quickly come to realize this fact. As information access and learning options increase, the role of the educator will be subdivided into different parts. Some will be advisors. Others will be program and course developers or supervisors. Of course, a large percentage will still teach. But it will be those who assume roles of tutors, mentors, coaches, and learning guides who will rise in importance.

Everyone will need and likely have an electronic coach or e-mentor. With fast-growing learning options, opportunities, and societal needs, learning without such a guide, or series of guides, will likely be impossible or incomprehensible. In the past, some looked to heroes, gurus, and religious leaders for ideas, models, and advice. By 2020, there will be access to learning gurus who understand the innumerable learning pathways available on the Web.

These super e-mentors and e-coaches will be knowledgeable in counseling as well as human developmental psychology, providing timely advice about one's learning journeys and future paths. At first, such super e-mentors will spring up in high schools and higher education institutions. But as time goes by, many of them will serve a societal function, not simply an institutional or programmatic role. And they will be available lifelong.

3. Quarter-Century Learning Clubs

The average years of formalized education will continue to lengthen. At some point in the next two or three decades, the standard twelve-year educational obligation will double. As we live longer and have more information requirements to absorb and ultimately master in order to be a specialist or a generalist, we will need to devote more time to learning. Two or three generations from now, ending college at age twenty-eight or thirty will no longer be a luxury for a small percentage of the population; it will be expected of nearly every contributing member of the planet. This elongation of learning will not happen overnight, but will gradually shift year by year in a more subtle and perhaps unnoticeable fashion. At some point, however, the lengthened journey that the human species takes into educational pursuits will be highly evident and applauded. Along with these changes will appear increasingly specialized or unique classifications of degrees. Keep in mind that with the free and open educational resources movement, such learning does not necessarily need to be expensive or even cost more than nominal amounts of money. Given these realities, quarter-century learning clubs will not be uncommon.

4. Terabyte Learning Access Points

Information and knowledge will be pervasive. Within two or three years, most of us will have access to encyclopedias of knowledge on our wristwatches and mobile phones. What will be momentous is when, in the coming decade, we can store most of the knowledge of our respective discipline as well as other disciplines related to it in such mobile devices. Terabytes of information and knowledge off-loaded to a nearby mobile device will free up mental capacity for creative thoughts and collaborations. It also allows learners to participate, if only casually, in an activity on a particular topic or engage in a conversation as needed. Not only is learning ubiquitous, the range and type of learning possible is increasingly amplified. The explosion of storage capacity on mobile learning devices will also lend support to the emerging renaissance of creative expression. This is the age of terabyte learning.

5. The Veneration of Learning

During these societal shifts, learning will become more important than stock market reports, the weather, sports, or the daily news. We are moving toward becoming a learning culture. Reports on new resources or innovative tools from which to learn will become part of daily life. Learning is no longer the boring activity you sat through begrudgingly for a dozen or so years and then thankfully left at age eighteen or perhaps twenty-two. In the twenty-first century, learning is the essence of being human. If current trends continue, this century will be known as the learning century.

6. Personalization + Portfolios

Humankind will come to realize that learning customization and personalization is the norm, not the exception. Learning options will make this increasingly apparent. Web 2.0 technologies and learning plans push us toward the creation of personalized learning environments. Key factors in the success of this movement are the choices and options provided. Visual, hands-on, reflective, and auditory options will be available with just a click of a button. Fairly soon such options will float by and be accessible through simple pointing or voice comments and, perhaps one day soon, by mere thinking. Learner excitement will heighten when learning style options can be juxtaposed so that students can simultaneously see, hear, feel, and perhaps even taste the learning. Along the way, any resulting learning will be captured in individual learning portfolios. The Web 2.0 is just the starting point for this personalization. Individualized learning approaches will be shaping the learning environment to move you toward developmentally challenging goals. Success will not be measured by accomplishing annual goals but by preparing you for goals that were previously impossible. Your learning-related successes, challenges, and reflections will be carried forward each year in your own digital learning portfolio.

7. The Selection of Global Learning Partners

As present technologies such as ePals, Ning, or Facebook have hinted, within a decade every learner on this planet will have a colearner or set of colearners in another part of the planet. Learners will even have a voice in picking partners to share their educational journeys with. These learning partners will be connected in ways never before imagined. Already learners give presentations or write books and papers with those in other parts of the world. They discuss ideas, collect data, and share with international classmates and colleagues. What is different is that as this becomes standard practice, there will be chances to dramatically change how we deliver courses, programs, and education in general. And there will be opportunities to reformulate what and how we think with others thousands of miles away who are interested in similar topics and ideas. Global education will transform the curriculum from K–12 to corporate. As this happens, collaborative projects across the planet will be so pervasive that skills in intercultural communication and collaboration will be among the most prized. Identification with and membership in a particular community will widen. Concepts of what it means to be human will be forever transformed.

8. The Shared Learning Era

The sharing of curricula and educational ideas will be expected of all in education. We are moving from times when we were solitary teachers and learners to a new era when sharing is part of what it means to be an instructor or developer of educational content. Sharing will also be expected of every learner. The world is open, in large part, because we now share it. This sharing culture will be the mark of teaching and learning in the twenty-first century. But will the knowledge-sharing events among rich nations and people, who are among the first with Internet access, be put on a pedestal for others to observe? Will the Bill Gateses and the MITs of the world continue to dominate the headlines? Or might the sharing of educational resources lead to new forms of trust and collaboration among the people of this planet? Can free and open education lead to forms of human kindness and empathy never previously witnessed?

9. Teaching-Learning Perpetuities

When and where we learn and teach will be increasingly undeterminable. We can teach from our homes or cars, the beach, a restaurant, an airport terminal, or the library. We can learn when in our apartments, class-rooms, virtual worlds, or favorite resting spot. Informal and more formal types of learning will meld. As this happens, lines designating the workplace and the learning place will fade. Work time will be learn time and vice versa. Credits, if they continue to matter, will be earned and monitored from any location. The only certainty will be that learning is constant.

10. Teachers, Teachers

Just as learning and teaching will be more apparent and increasingly ubiquitous, the sheer volume and type of teachers at the ready will skyrocket. Teachers and trainers will be available for anyone at any time. The world will never have had so many teachers. Early childhood educators perplexed about a particular situation might text or voice record what the problem or issue is and allow the Web to locate one or more experts with possible solutions. Primary students might arrive at school with no particular teacher assigned to them. Instead, they might enter a code into the Web with their current level and types of tasks and activities as well as their moods and learning preferences. When submitted, a set of teachers will pop up on the screen for them to choose from. Soon any student who is bored with her current teaching situation will be able to select a personalized substitute teacher for the day or week or beyond. This is just a start. Secondary students in a math class in London or New York might have a teacher streamed to their classroom from Manila, Tel Aviv, or Mumbai. School districts might hire such external instructors where and when needed. College-level students studying at night, or at any time for that matter, will be able to access a teaching-learning exchange network to submit questions or receive timely demonstrations from a stockpile of video footage for concepts that they do not fully grasp. If at any point in the process such videos are not sufficient, they could seek additional support from expert tutors from a range of countries and language backgrounds who are on hand 24/7. Teachers would also be available for adults at home. Interested in screenwriting? Dozens of experts will be at the ready via synchronous chat or Webcam tutoring. Some of these teacher resource pools, from K–12 to adult, will include quality rankings to set them apart.

Those you select might first send you to archived presentations and events to see if such resources meet your needs. They might also read your work and give you insightful advice and timely support. And most of these services will be free!

11. The Rise of the Super Blends

Learning will be increasingly blended. There are myriad resources from which to learn: some are physical, others virtual. The mixing or blending of learning contents and technologies will make it difficult to categorize the primary delivery platform. Shared courses, seminars, discussion groups, and degree programs will be made available for students—courses from different schools, institutions, corporate training institutes, and so on will form the blend. There will be super blends of such technologies and teaching ideas that will arise to push learning far beyond what is possible today. These blends will evolve and raise learning standards higher with each wave of technology.

12. Self-Determined Humans

With help from mentors and coaches where needed, learning events, activities, and degrees will be increasingly chosen by the learner. As online learning resources proliferate, learners will make decisions on the type or amount of learning that is appropriate. Unique and self-labeled degrees and programs of study will characterize learning in higher education, especially for those seeking second or third degrees. Given that learning is what it means to be human, we will be self-determined humans. Freedom to pursue and express one's learning will be sacred.

13. Free Learning Zones

In 2009, the cost of higher education is skyrocketing. At the same time, the economic situation around the world is fairly dismal, forcing considerable budget cuts and associated job layoffs across all sectors of the economy. As these events unfold, the financial resources required to obtain a degree in higher education are becoming increasingly beyond the means of millions of younger and older adults in North America, and perhaps beyond the means of billions of potential learners around the world. Because of these worsening conditions, think tanks, government agencies, and foundations will be forced to explore ways to bring costs down. One solution would be to expand the number of free educational resources. The coming decade will see heightened tension between free education and high-cost education. As people become more familiar with online content and comfortable with online courses and degrees, free learning certificates and degrees will emerge. Mentors, tutors, and teachers providing that content might do so free of charge for some initial activities or limited-interaction events. The free learning providers will offer fee-based services over the top of such degrees; they may also sell advertising space and merchandise. In an effort to focus on quality, some educational institutions and government agencies will create designated "free learning zones" and Web resources without advertising and other capitalist schemes. With the wealth of information available, openly accessible content from any provider will be personally structured and delivered in these free learning zones.

14. Authentic Learning Amalgamations

Advances in technologies for simulations, gaming, virtual worlds, and real-time experiences will foster an era of learning authenticity and learning on demand. Of course, there will be various shades of such authenticity depending on the technology and learning path selected. Individuals will scan previews of the learning options before deciding which format is most relevant to them. When done with an activity or lesson, they can immediately review their learning on small roll-out screens or other portable devices. Though a variety of options will be available each time, what is deemed authentic in one situation will not work in another. As learning formats rise, learning will continue to shift from the mastery of instructor-based content to problems to be solved and products to be created.

15. Alexandrian Aristotles

Libraries are structures to preserve, house, and disseminate information when needed. In their book, *Wikinomics*, Tapscott and Williams compare the gigantic book-scanning and digitization projects like Google Book Search and the Internet Archive to the attempt at Alexandria to store all mathematical and scientific knowledge in one building.[8] The proliferation of open-access journals, such as those found at the Public Library of Science, add fuel to such efforts. Unlike Alexandria, digital libraries provide access from any connected location. If anyone could personify the Library of Alexandria, it would likely be Aristotle, who is described as the last person to be learned in all known disciplines. What happens when humans are able to walk this planet with the entire known world of information in their pockets and are able to access, update, and display the content equivalent of Alexandria and Aristotle on demand? And what exactly is memory if everything known or knowable is so close at hand?

If technology trends play out, there will be three forms of Alexandrian Aristotles:

1. Fingertipping Alexandrian Aristotles
2. Frontal Lobe Alexandrian Aristotles
3. Combiners or Fingertipping Frontal Lobers (*note:* these are the most potent of the Alexandrian Aristotles)

"Fingertipping Alexandrian Aristotles" will be those who know where and how to retrieve any information needed. They will likely have browsed or stumbled upon such information previously or been close to it in a learning portal. "Frontal Lobe Alexandrian Aristotles" will actually have learned a good portion of the content and will be able to tell you about it when quizzed. Assuming technology access is allowed, both fingertippers and frontal lobers will be impressive when on problem-solving teams or responding to questions. But it is the third class of Alexandrian Aristotles who conceivably will be the most impressive of all. They will have personal access to the world's knowledge in Flash memory sticks or iPods in their pockets and know how to access it efficiently. On top of that, they will have assimilated much of it in their minds through arduous study. This "superbreed" of learners—Fingertipping Frontal Lobers—will be able to find and solve problems with creative insights and resources that were previously impossible. Imagine situating several such individuals together on collaborative teams to work on huge societal issues, or any kind of problem.

No matter which of the above predictions holds true, there is no doubt that we are entering a new age of learning—in particular of learning at a distance—and along with it, a new age of being human. Unlike the closed-door attitudes and solitary instructor activities of the past, we are finding increased attention on sharing educational materials and activities online as well as making the software to run or display such contents freely accessible and more interactive. As a result, e-learning activities and content are less static and more open for others to use, refine, distribute, and comment on.

With Web 2.0 technologies, learning is a more interactive and shared experience. As evident throughout this book, tools exist for personal publishing of one's ideas such as blogging and writing wikibooks. Now anyone can author new knowledge and make it available for others. No longer must all knowledge come unidirectionally from a teacher or other expert. Previously bored learners can now participate or contribute something. This explosive shift in the flow of information provides the impetus for the tremendous expansion of the content and matter contained in all of the openers because it gives everyone a voice or meaning for learning. It is the Big Bang of education!

In a participatory learning environment, our learning networks are deeply connected to those of others.[9] Web 2.0 tools also help in aggregating and personalizing news and reports, collaborating with others around the globe, and chatting with friends. Still other resources help with scheduling meetings and events. What exciting times these are!

Each opener is a step forward in the process of personalizing learning. As this occurs, we will all feel that learning is touching us in important ways. With intelligent agents personally filtering and highlighting news and resources of interest, learning growth trajectories will be of interest. Personalization will persuade staggering numbers of people to enter deeper chambers of knowledge and expertise than ever before. As this occurs, the speeds at which some obtain a semblance of expertise will be astonishing. At the same time, expertise in any discipline will require more in-depth study than ever in the past.

With such technologies, there are now greater opportunities to create personalized learning environments (PLEs).[10] Ideas surrounding PLEs—increasing learner ownership and control over learning, enhancing interactivity and feedback on your learning, organizing ways for learners to collaborate and interact with each other, and expanding the possible communication channels for your ideas—underpin the tenth opener. Now combine this with the other nine openers and witness an era of educational rejuvenation. No longer will Plato or Rip van Winkle be able to awaken in the modern world and recognize schools. We are in the midst of dramatic change never before seen in education. It is my hope that models like WE-ALL-LEARN can support organizational planning and personal decision making related to such changes.

It is a time when the technologies have evolved beyond prevailing educational theories on how to use them. Learner-centered and constructivist theories do not fully explain learning in the age of the Web 2.0. Stephen Downes argues that the simultaneous use of social networking tools, such as instant messaging, blogging, wikis, and picture sharing, radically redefines the possible community members in our online course journeys.[11] When a student blogs for a particular class, feedback might come from anyone with an Internet connection located anywhere on this planet or circling above it. As this occurs, a network starts to form with those of like interests, not limited to those in one's classroom.

Technologies emerging during the past couple of decades have nurtured new forms of learner interaction and collaboration. Communication tools help teams negotiate ideas, share and annotate documents, and collaboratively build products and reports. Wikis, for instance, transform the one-way communication systems of lecturers and textbooks into a nonlinear, evolving process including multiple authors and authorities of knowledge. In a wiki activity or setting, the focus is on the exploration of knowledge, communicating such knowledge, and building consensus, rather than a set of predefined truths that are presented without argument.

The Web is laden with opportunities, some that replicate those possible in a traditional physical setting, some that extend well beyond it, and others that offer fully new possibilities. Thoughtful leadership, however, is required to create transformative experiences within a range of blended and fully online opportunities. This book is intended to offer unique views into the emerging open learning world. Such windows open rather quickly and in quite unexpected places; learning activities that are possible today were unimaginable just a decade or two ago.

What is clear is that everyone has an expertise of some type, and millions of people are now taking that expertise and sharing it online with others. They are writing it down in Wikipedia and personal blogs, creating and sharing videos of it in YouTube, telling others about it in the form of podcasts and Webcasts, and collecting it all in portals for others to browse and exploit. The sharing and organizing of expertise used to be the province of teachers or professionals in the field. Today such sharing comes from all of us. Are the critics correct in suggesting that better quality controls are needed to filter and shake out the credible and accurate pieces of knowledge and information that have been shared? Sure! But the world of learning is now open—for all of us. There is no doubt about that anymore.

We must find new ways to celebrate this learning epoch, as well as use what has been created, instead of continuing to ignore or resist it. There is certainly a need to further improve the situation as well as debate best practices. However, we can no longer debate whether to dip our toes in or not. That decision has already been rendered moot by the hundreds of learning doors that have opened during the past decade. You do not have to find all these doors advantageous. In many cases, in fact, traditional forms of instruction may prove equally if not more powerful.

No matter which door opens first, the ten trends of WE-ALL-LEARN are just the start. They provide the infrastructure for talking about a whole new learning era for humankind. Learning underpins nearly everything we do as a species, whether it is religion, politics, business, education, medicine, or recreation. We all learn. Today we spend at least some of that learning time online. Those who offer the tools, resources, and materials for us to learn online could now come from Tokyo, Melbourne, Houston, or Bangalore. Oftentimes, we do not even know where they came from.

When my grandfather went to school a century ago, he knew who his teachers and classmates were. Children today can also list their teachers and schoolmates. What they may not realize when they generate such a list, however, is that it will not include most of the people who have actually educated them. One's virtual tutors and teachers are not typically recognized or celebrated. Students do not realize that Kitty Schmidt-Jones is their teacher when they use her music training materials in Connexions. They do not credit Matt Harding for their learning about Easter Island, the Parthenon, or Area 51 after watching him dance in front of each place or later lecture on it in a YouTube video. They may not immediately list peers from ePals or iEARN who helped them complete a final project. And they will not know the names of the developers of the Complete Works of Charles Darwin or other online portals that they explored in a history class.

The field of distance learning has significantly evolved during the past two decades. It has always been concerned with learning access and providing any potential learner with some type of learning opportunity. With the Web, many of the plans and dreams of more than a century of distance learning visionaries are coming to fruition. Without a doubt, the tools, resources, and activities available for blended and fully online learning are proliferating at the exact moment that increased demand for online education across sectors is redefining the meaning of education. As this occurs, there are widespread opportunities to address learners with an assortment of learning needs and preferences. We all have educational alternatives and choices. Fortunately for us active learning participants, such choices have been ratcheted up many notches during the past few years. We can go to learning places each day—places that we never even dreamed of a short while ago.

THE WORLD IS OPEN!

The world is now open. It is open for you. It is open for me. It is open for anybody hoping to learn something new or relearn something acquired long ago and forgotten. It is just as open at 6:00 AM as it is at 6:00 PM. What do we seek when we get there? Knowledge, of course, though we often settle for bare-bones information. The Web of Learning contains riches beyond anything any of us ever envisioned growing up. It is our personal pirate booty. It is a fortune that no one except our local service provider can take from us. Perhaps those learning online can be compared to the alien archaeologists in the 2008 movie *Indiana Jones and the Kingdom of the Crystal Skull*. We are seeking the knowledge nuggets of our planetary past and present. As Indy said, "Their treasure wasn't gold, it was knowledge. Knowledge was their treasure." If that is true for us as well, then today pretty much all the world's known treasures can be found online.

The stories, data, links, and converging technology trends that underlie the WE-ALL-LEARN framework combine to help you realize that there is no turning back. Learning awaits each of us at our every move. Access is pervasive. We can work online from research vessels in Antarctic waters or from the family sailboat in the Caribbean. As the opening story revealed, we can be blogging about our learning adventures from archaeological digs around the globe. Or we can be learning from them as armchair Indiana Joneses. Each of us is now a teacher and a learner. There is no excuse not to take on such roles every single day. It may not appear in the newspapers, but you can help tutor and mentor those on every continent and potentially in every country on this planet. Do it! You will feel immediate rewards.

THE DEADLY DOZEN

Despite their enormous promise, the ten educational openers are not without their problems or concerns. There are at least a dozen issues that we will need to keep in mind as the world of learning opens up. Each of these issues is a deal breaker for thousands, if not millions, of people. If you lack answers for them, any promotion of a more open educational world will abruptly end. I call these the deadly dozen. Certainly, some of these concerns are more pressing and significant than others. You will need to decide which are most pertinent and urgent for your situation.

1. Winners and Losers

As shown throughout this book, some people or organizations are racing to be first in one or more of the openers. Just who will end up graciously opening the door for each of us is uncertain. Some want to be the first to scan in all extant book knowledge or organize all the shared online video content. Many educational organizations want to have the finest or most popular online program or set of courses. Others want to be the preeminent and most used online language system or resource. A few are experimenting with new revenue models by providing free online access to learning and then selling supplemental resources and print materials. Some want to index the most podcast shows, stream the largest quantity of free video programming, or build the largest group of wiki-related users. There is an amazing amount of competition to be the best, biggest, and most well-known. For some, such striving is to appease stockholders. For others it is related to their personal mission to improve education for the people of this planet. Some seek to do both. Unfortunately, there will be many well-intended people or programs who simply do not amass sufficient users or eyeballs to continue their quests. Some are giving up midstream, as Microsoft did in its book digitization project. Each time a winner is apparent, there will likely be dozens of losers whom we quickly forget even though they truly wanted to make an impact on education in a positive way. Try as we might, we typically cannot predict the ultimate winners and losers. And in the present economy, the number of losers will definitely mount. As this happens, it is critical not to lose hope and give up on open education plans and visions.

2. Web Access Limitations

A related and more serious issue is that the majority of people still lack access to the Internet. If Web access is the ticket to these open educational resources, then there is worldwide failure on a massive scale. What is the timeline for expanding access to the majority of the planet, or to everyone? Will an elite class of digitally educated citizens appear? Might there be two distinct forms of humans walking this planet during the coming decades: those with extensive online educational opportunities and the skills to continue learning online, and those without such skills and experiences? If the Web is proven valuable for learning, the first priority of every politician, educator, foundation leader, and philanthropist is to provide access to those who presently do not have it. Remember, we have roughly six billion people still needing access to the Web and its educational treasures.

3. Some Quality Please

Anyone using the Web for learning purposes recognizes that there is the pervasive issue of quality. Wikipedia, for example, is incessantly attacked over such concerns. The images of fingers showing up on pages of the Google book-scanning project have also raised a few red flags. At the same time, free online classes and learning portals from people who are not credentialed elicit alarms from noted scholars and educators. Instead of mining the educational potential of You-Tube, jokes are made about the amount of entertainment and comedy found in it, while educational uses are often ignored. Article after article in the past few years maps out concerns with the quality of online content. Some of the more recent ones point to services that help address this. What seems obvious in wading through all the opinions is that there are few agreements on the metrics for assessing or credentialing quality. Just whose quality will it be? Is quality the same in Finland as it is in Brazil?

Among the more widespread concerns is the quality of online courses and programs. No one wants diploma mills or inferior degrees. A barrage of daily e-mails offering you a degree in a month or less without having to buy books or attend classes forces anyone, at least temporarily, to question all online learning. Worse, there are well-known fake diploma companies where you can order phony high school or college degrees and transcripts that even name the degree-granting institution. Unfortunately, for many people the mere existence of these crafty organizations ends the discussion when it comes to the importance of online learning of any kind even if this represents just a small fraction of what is actually happening online.

4. The Evil House of Cheat

Along these same lines, one of the most serious challenges to the acceptance of Web-based learning of any type is online plagiarism. Scores of online paper sites exist. One of my favorites was originally called "The Evil House of Cheat" but is now simply known as the "CheatHouse." Students using the CheatHouse could pay for papers by the page. Ironically, the CheatHouse used to advertise that their site helped "honest students" with their homework. Similar sites include "AcademicTermPapers.com" and "PinkMonkey." Such services currently charge seven to ten dollars per page for a paper, with extra fees, of course, charged for expedited services.

There are dozens of solutions. Some rely on plagiarism-detection software such as Turnitin for help with finding papers that have been plagiarized. If that is not affordable or available, an organization or institution can rely on educating students about what constitutes plagiarism. They can also post the policies and consequences of cheating. Some rely on an internal code of ethics. Others take the easy route; if they suspect cheating, they cut and paste a section into a Google search engine and see what comes up in terms of a match. A large percentage of organizations offering online classes proctor or supervise their exams while others try to randomize questions within their exams. Other more futuristic solutions such as iris scanning or fingerprint recognition before taking tests will be commonplace in the next decade or two. Despite these methods to reduce plagiarism, as access to information and technology grows, so too do opportunities to deceive instructors and testing. Technology has opened up not only the world of learning, but also the world of cheating.

5. Copyright in a Shared World

Open knowledge also leads to issues of privacy and copyright. Clearly, not all knowledge that is shared was meant to be shared. What if someone shares their courses, papers, or ideas with a limited audience and then someone in that group republishes them without credit to the originator? What if those people do not want their information shared to the world? What legal options do they have without a long litigation process? Or what if they shared it accidentally or even intentionally but then later reconsidered it? Can one retrieve or rescind such knowledge-sharing actions?

There are many more issues. What if people share knowledge that is confidential, improper, or unauthorized? Posting what an instructor confidentially stated to a student is illegal and potentially embarrassing. And today, many students are posting YouTube videos and blog narratives of events taking place in their classrooms. Some are posting their graded papers in Scribd. And there are embarrassing pictures posted to Flickr and other such photo-sharing sites. As is apparent, there are a host of legal concerns surrounding the sharing of online content.

Some of these concerns relate to institutional or organizational policies and practices. Corporations and government agencies are often strictly forbidden to share proprietary information outside of their organization. Such restrictions result in the availability of more reports and educational content from higher education settings than from corporate training settings. Typically, higher education reports are freely obtainable online, whereas corporate reports, if they exist, are highly expensive. Such higher education reports are often shared with millions of people. What happens when people ignore copyright notifications on such documents or fail to ask permission before sharing them?

6. Open Learning for Terrorists?

As Friedman pointed out, when knowledge is free, open, collaboratively shared, and available 24/7, there is a serious problem that the information of the world will get into the wrong hands. What if the educational vault of the world's knowledge was let loose and shared with all people of this planet? Just who decides when and how this information will be shared and with whom? Once the learning is made free, it is always available somewhere on the Internet or on someone's hard disk. Questions need to be raised regarding who are the gatekeepers to the accumulated knowledge of humankind. Should there even be gatekeepers? And how is information archived and made accessible for Internet browsers and other tools?

At the same time, the more optimistic might see the open learning world as a tool for reducing terrorism by lending hope to every person on this planet that he or she can learn. Educational resources are provided now for everyone and by any connected citizen who wishes to provide them. It is possible that the Web might bring to life not only additional educational opportunities but also a more tolerant world. Freely available educational programs might be specifically designed to foster such tolerance, hope, and enhanced abilities to grasp the needs and perspectives of others.

7. The Breeding of Lazy Learners

Some might argue that learners and instructors may become intellectually lazy as they rely on the Web for everything. If all knowledge can be found in five seconds or less online, then why bother to learn? What useful purpose will it serve? And if computer-generated knowledge is an extension of the human species, might we all not begin relying on technology for our factual information and focus more on critically needed analysis, decision-making, and evaluation skills and other higher-order problem-solving abilities? Will we become a lazier species or a more internally motivated one? Or perhaps some aspects of both?

8. An English Monopoly?

The dominance of the English language is the eighth issue. As any person browsing the Web will quickly discover, most online documents are in English despite only 20 to 25 percent of the world's population speaking English as a native or second language. In fact, of the two hundred languages with at least a million or more native speakers, English is the third most used with over 340 million native speakers, and lagging far behind Hindi at 425 million and Chinese at over 870 million native speakers.[12] However, English is often the second language people speak. As a result, it is the language spoken at foreign embassies as well as the lingua franca in mail systems, faxes, and electronic communications. It is the official language of more countries than any other language. What happens to the languages and cultures of hundreds of people around the world, however, as English dominates the Web? If learning is what it means to be human and much of that learning is only available in English, does it force people to absorb not only a language, but an entire culture, in pursuit of their learning and humanness?

9. Is the Web Disabled for the Disabled?

A key issue since Web-based learning was popularized in the mid-to-late 1990s concerns those with special needs. Not only are those without Internet access left behind, but so too, are those with certain disabilities. Those with visual impairments cannot see a Flash animation rolling across the screen or an online video. And deaf individuals as well as many hearing-impaired people cannot hear a podcast or audio file. How do those with different disabilities or impairments negotiate the Web? If the goal is for all of us to learn, no one can be left out.

Though many such challenges remain, the Web offers boundless learning possibilities for nearly all learners with special needs or disabilities. Visually impaired learners can review class activities when the class session is recorded and archived as a podcast. And so can the hearing-impaired learner when the session is captured in a video format that displays the audio transcript through closed captioning. Physically immobile learners and those who are sick or critically injured do not even need to leave their houses to learn. The Web offers those who need more time to learn the opportunity to reflect or revisit the learning activity or turn in assignments at a time and in a format that is convenient. Still, many critical questions and issues need to be resolved.

10. Wherefore Art Thou, Teacher Training?

Although self-paced learning is part of this new age where we all learn, the world will not be open to many learners without sufficient teacher training. Some teachers will need basic training on what the Internet actually is and how to use it for instruction. Other instructors might want assistance in understanding the opportunities of the Web 2.0. Those who remain reluctant or resistant to using the Web may require different types of training programs and opportunities. Governments and educational institutions cannot expect learning to happen simply because there are millions of podcasts, blogs, learning portals, and other types of content resources and materials online. There are many mechanisms for training instructors in the Web—best-practice examples, constant sharing, laptop initiatives, mentoring programs, and awards and recognitions, among other ideas. Innovative strategic plans and visions are typically needed to take advantage of these options.

11. Upskilling Digital Natives?

The coinciding issue to teacher training is student training. For learners to take advantage of online technologies and resources, they too need training and familiarization with what is available. They may think that they know how to use all the latest technologies, but those intended for learning may be different or unfamiliar to them. As detailed in earlier chapters, digital literacy skills are growing in importance. In most cases, students cannot be successful learners without them. As tens of millions of additional people acquire Internet access each year, they will need both online and face-to-face training. Programs will need to be developed and continually refined.[13] Without learner training, most of the possibilities outlined in this book are not possible.

With the escalating reliance on the Internet for learning, there are pervasive concerns related to student information literacy skills. How easy is it for students to weed through all the resources and reports now available to find, read, summarize, and use such information with creative insight as well as critical judgment? What is fool's gold and what are genuine nuggets? Will the new tests created by ETS force teachers and schools to address student information literacy skills? Will such tests actually find extensive application and acceptance?

12. What Is the Question Again?

Finally, how does anyone keep up with all the developments happening everyday online? Can anyone keep up? Every Internet learner wants to be greeted by educational resources that are relevant or meaningful to him or her. But how does the learning environment become more personalized so that a learner does not need to keep up with everything? Can it?

In a debate with Dr. Robert Kozma in the *Economist* about whether new technology and media can add to the quality of education, Sir John Daniel, president and CEO of the Commonwealth of Learning, noted, "[T]here is the quest for the magic medium, the ultimate technology that will revolutionize education. Yesterday it was the Internet; today it is Open Educational Resources. But there is no magic medium and never will be. Each technology has its strengths. The task is to use them to create a world where education of quality is abundantly available."[14]

Sir John Daniel adds that too often we fail to ask what questions or problems the technology is solving before voting to buy and install it. Before that happens, though, we need to think about how or why to use it. From his perspective, truly transformative learning technologies should not simply enhance existing environments or educational systems but should create fully new ones. Educators typically have not shown the vision necessary to take advantage of technology innovations for learning. Consequently, education has been the one area of society that has not been transformed by technology. Not yet anyway. We are beginning to feel it now.

He is absolutely right. There is no one medium that has transformed education. No one technology. On the contrary, today we have at least ten technology trends for learning and education that, when combined in whole or in part, do offer interesting possibilities to transform learning across educational sectors and climates. The Internet is a key part of this transformation. However, the Internet can hardly be labeled as one technology; unlike most previous educational technologies Sir John Daniel lists—the radio, TV, film, programmed instruction, and computers—it is an enticing, ever-present passageway to all types of learning and to fellow learners. With YouTube, the Internet is a television. The Internet is a place for writing film scripts, production, editing, and review. The Internet is home to programmed instruction as well as spontaneous learning. The Internet is a computer waiting to be programmed or accessed. The computer workstation is the printing press. With thousands of daily podcasted shows, it is radio.

It is clear that Sir John Daniel has spoken for yesterday's technologies. Those of today and tomorrow are different—they are not standalone or separate but, instead, are converging in ways that present us with educational machinery to transform education. Still it will require years of additional planning, experimenting, and sharing to truly understand what is now possible.

CONVERGING TECHNOLOGY TRENDS

Technological convergence will enable multiple trends to be more fully exploited in highly ubiquitous ways. Such convergence is already happening. We become aware of this convergence in singular technologies such as James Bond types of watches, smartphones, and $100 laptops. When the ten trends commingle, new forms of learning will arise that are not inherent in the WE-ALL-LEARN model or in the technology examples discussed in this book. And there will likely be no theory to explain the learning impacts of that commingling. That is to be expected as the list of ten trends was not meant to be all-encompassing or eternal. Nonetheless, the model can help in understanding the different ways learning technology might be combined as well as some of the learning-related offshoots of such events.

This convergence need not be just toward multifunction, singular devices, however. It can be found in our everyday actions and interactions with technology. We also see evidence of it when someone with a Second Life account uploads the photos he took of his Second Life activities to Flickr and blogs about them. We notice it when a podcast transcript is posted that contains audio and video downloading options, along with a blog post on what to expect from reading, watching, or listening to it. We become even more aware of these possibilities when a designated "last lecture" is made by Professor Randy Pausch from Carnegie Mellon University, while he was dying from pancreatic cancer, and a copy of it is immediately posted to YouTube for the world to view. The technologies for learning and communication become even clearer when the *Wall Street Journal* writes an article about Pausch's lecture; soon hundreds of known bloggers post opinions about the event, and many millions of people quickly view the entire seventy-five-minute video on YouTube.[15] Such uses of technology to tell personal stories foster intense reflection and inspiration to action. And for those still desiring paper products, a book recapping all these events and suddenly appears titled *The Last Lecture*.[16] Dr. Pausch passed away on July 25, 2008, just a little over three months after the release of his book; but he held on long enough to see it reach the top of the nonfiction bestseller lists.

I have personally witnessed hundreds of examples in which the intersection of emerging learning technologies roused to life a powerful learning environment unlike any I had previously seen. For example, I was a happy participant in early September 2007 when my friend, Dr. Michelle Selinger from Cisco, gave a keynote presentation at the Association for Learning Technology Conference (better known as "ALT-C") in Nottingham in the United Kingdom. I first downloaded her presentation slides to follow along with her talk. I later posted questions through the conference chat window that the session moderator could ask at the conclusion of her talk. And I did all this without even leaving my home office in Bloomington, Indiana.

As one of the opening stories of this book indicates, two months after Michelle's speech, the power of this convergence nearly knocked me unconscious when Jennifer Madrell Ustreamed a Ustream video of a talk I was giving at a conference in Atlanta. Her conference participants could watch the presentation in real-time in New York after receiving a brief notice of it through Twitter. Now there is convergence for you!

That same month, I took part in this technological convergence as a university professor when I instructed my students to read online papers as well as watch associated online videos of famed educational technology guru Dr. David Merrill from Utah State University. My students later discussed and debated the issues they read or observed within an online discussion forum. After that, we brought Dr. Merrill into our class from his home in Utah for a live question-and-answer session using a cheap Webcam connection and Adobe Connect Pro. It worked so powerfully and easily that I had to ask myself why it was not more common.

Wikis can also be a tool for convergence. The Digital Research Tools or DiRT Web site from Rice University is a wiki that is a portal of open source software and other free online contents. DiRT is a collection of software that is intended to help those in the humanities and social science areas conduct their research more effectively. Lisa Spiro, director of the Digital Media Center at Rice, told me that she saw a need for a directory of research tools and decided to do something about it. Within a short time, DiRT had tools for collecting, visualizing, organizing, and analyzing data. Free brainstorming, note taking, blogging, and multimedia authoring are also present. But the site is not static. It is publicly open for viewing as well as contributing, once approved. To entice users, the content found there is typically DiRT cheap—as in free. It is a portal of online content links (Opener #5), much of the content is open source software (Opener #3), and it fosters participation or contributions from users (Opener #6). One site, three openers. No doubt, it is not the last such site.

Given this convergence, we must back up a step to think about how all this is possible. Despite the persistent news headlines about learning-related innovations at MIT, Cambridge, Google, and IBM, there is no one institution, organization, learning venture, or billionaire philanthropist at the center of all these efforts. As shown in this book, there are countless individuals and organizations in Japan, India, Korea, Canada, Ghana, and other countries dramatically changing the world of learning. With one creative idea or useful educational resource, anyone can significantly improve or reshape the world of education, and accomplish it without extensive financial backing or personal risk. That is a key point. Money, though still important, is no longer the prevailing determinant of the players in the educational dance.

HEROES, GURUS, AND REVOLUTIONARIES
OF THE SHARED INTERNET

The world is currently flush with ideas and resources from individuals who are giving their time and talents to change the educational experiences of others. We heard of the passion and commitment of people like Richard Watson from the Global Text Project to bringing about free electronic books and reducing our reliance on costly text-books. Others such as John van Wyhe from the University of Cambridge now offer us the complete works of Charles Darwin at our fingertips. Educational entrepreneurs such as Julie Young and Bruce Colston are working furiously to place courses and programs on the Web for teenagers, while other well-known innovators such as Michael Offerman and Glenn Jones focus on working adults who lack the time, money, motivation, or educational access to learn from more traditional formats. Several high-end risk takers such as Charles and Rebecca Nesson as well as Sarah Robbins are showing the rest of us what is educationally possible in Second Life and other virtual worlds.

Some learning innovations are more informal in nature. For instance, through their innovative YouTube videos, Michael Wesch, Karl Fisch, Lee LeFever, and many others have fostered local, national, and international reflection on what should be taught in schools and universities. In so doing, they have shed some light on how we might effectively use shared online video in education. And their change efforts did not cost millions of dollars or take years to produce and distribute. Equally important, amateur filmographers and video hob-byists create inspiring educational stories when on vacation, which add to educational reform efforts around the globe. Witness the travels of Yan Chun Su to places such as Ghana, Western China, and Tibet to create documentaries freely shared online in Current TV. While Yan is bringing the cultures of the world to us asynchronously, programs such as GNG and ISIS expand student perspectives synchronously as they personally interact with peers around the world and gain new cultural perspectives and appreciation. Thoughtful educators such as Mimi Lee and Deb Hutton are helping us understand the current impact and future potential of such Internet-based videoconferencing programs and systems.

At the same time, John Traxler is expanding the frontiers of mobile technology to foster learning in Kenya and other parts of Africa where such technology-enhanced learning previously was not possible or even considered. Another person relying on relatively inexpensive mobile technology is Dr. Paul Kim from Stanford. Kim has found a way to place literacy teachers in the pockets of underprivileged children in Latin America using MP3 players. Also relying on our emerging mobile learning culture, Ken Carroll and Jenny Zhu are now the teachers in the pockets of hundreds of thousands of people attempting to learn Chinese. Other online language learning innovators like Shirish Nadkarni, Dean Worth, and Todd Bryant have each designed engaging online systems and approaches to learn practically any language you wish; you also have the opportunity to help someone else acquire a language you know. I am talking about one person leading the charge that energizes the lives of thousands or even hundreds of thousands of people. For these technology innovators, informal learning is the preferred learning mode. And for the children of the Pocket School project, informal is their only choice. Informal becomes formal.

This reshaping of the way we learn is occurring at institutional and organizational levels as well. As noted in several places in this book, MIT officials are placing key components of all their courses on the Web for anyone in the world to browse and learn from. Seeing an opportunity to expand these efforts to a population of over a billion people, charismatic individuals such as Lucifer Chu are using personal funds to translate such courses for people who are not native speakers of English. At the same time, leadership from corporate visionaries such as Scott McNealy has resulted in a shared global curriculum resource called Curriki that intends to be universally available, widely used, and, of course, free. This more open world of universally available free educational resources across grade levels that McNealy has embraced is rooted in the work of many educational pioneers including Martin Dougiamas, who with his time and sweat gave the world Moodle, and Richard Stallman, the brains behind GNU and the leadership associated with much of the free software movement itself. Each of these people had key roles in the transformation to the open educational world we are now part of.

These are highly novel and interesting educational times. Educational problems and opportunities are much more globally shared and solved than in decades past. In recognition of the new global consciousness in this era of learning and education, an assortment of people, including Richard Baraniuk from Connexions and Jimmy Wales from the Wikimedia Foundation, are creating and signing declarations that education should be free and open. You can be part of that declaration.

These are some of the heroes, gurus, and revolutionaries of the shared Internet. It is such people who make Friedman's economic world flatter, Florida's innovative world spikier, and Cross's learning world more informal, while powershifting Toffler's business world. If education can change the world, or even just an adventurous individual or two setting foot into it, then the folks documented in this book are world changers. How can one not be excited?

OPENING UP FRIEDMAN'S FLATTER WORLD

Thomas Friedman argued that the world has become flatter, deeper, richer, and more personally empowering for those who want to compete and collaborate economically across countries and continents. He primarily told the monetary side of the story, however. Concurrent with this flattening process, the world is making available a huge percentage of its educational treasures. It is unlocking windows and doors to educational opportunities for the entire world that were previously sealed shut. It is unveiling new visions of what an individual, group, community, country, or region of the world can accomplish. It is opening up hope for education and, hence, for economic opportunities where none existed previously. Such educational hope is not restricted to one topic, area of study, or discipline but to nearly any area of learning that anyone wants to pursue.

There is not just one door being opened. As with ePals and iLearn, there are doors to learning online from instructors located in other regions of the world. With projects like OOPS and CORE, there are doors to content created in one culture that has been translated and localized for another culture. And with MERLOT, Connexions, and Curriki, there are doors to generate educational ideas and curricula that are shared and evaluated by people you will never meet. And people need not restrict themselves to a single path or doorway; they can walk through one or all of them, and if they do not like what they find, they can quickly retrace their steps or branch off on a new learning journey. The intensity of the learning experience and range of options for learning is their choice. There is freedom to learn.

Web 2.0 and numerous other emerging technologies support extremely rapid development of educational collaborations. Visions of the Semantic Web in which intelligent agents find, share, and help us integrate vast stores of information more easily and converse with our various technologies in order to access and use information as needed will create hundreds of other educational openings heretofore not witnessed on this planet. And this teamwork is often on display for others to view and perhaps replicate in still more learning partnerships.

In a wiki, for instance, teams of people who do not know each other can fashion unique documents and resources, including study guides, help systems, meeting agendas, committee summary reports, dictionaries for different disciplines, and entire books. We can now make comments on online documents and interactively respond to each other without personally knowing the other person with whom we are communicating, collaborating, or critiquing. The same is true of many wikibooks that have been developed or are in process today—your writing collaborators are often no longer physical friends and colleagues, but electronic ones. This situates us in an entirely new era of learning.

What will it take for WE-ALL-LEARN to become a reality? Perhaps that is the seminal issue here. Global collaborations have formed during the past decade to provide free access to a wide range of educational resources. Already, thousands of free and open books, scholarly journals, online documents, and audio files, video files, and other media elements are available for learners who have Internet access or a computer with

CDs of downloaded online content. At present, most of us can only make out the tip of the iceberg floating in open educational waters off in the distance. Still more such educational resources will break off from the entrenched grip of the past few millennia and follow in their paths. As they appear, we will study and monitor their movement and potential uses. To help in these observations, giant clearinghouses of learning objects and portals such as Connexions and the Internet Archive will grow in popularity and use, as will online catalogs of free and open source software as well as anything now made available in a digital format for educating the people of this planet.

The ten openers today are not magically going to coalesce, dissolve, or impede other ones from bursting into view. Still, imagine a learner in 2020 who has all of these things—where all ten openers are not only available but are seamlessly integrated into her learning environment. Of course, the scenario includes full translation of any learning resource on demand into any language or context required. It is worth taking a few minutes to simply pause and reflect on such a world. There are nearly seven billion learners on this planet. If we all contribute to the open education movement by providing one resource or learning opportunity or developing a software product that houses or brings to life such opportunities, the impact will be widespread and transformative.

Each of you now has a chance to make a contribution to this opening process. And many of you will hopefully find more than one opportunity to do so. You might create a podcast or an entire podcast show. You might present one or more learning tools or resources such as Second Life or Connexions to someone else. You might also reflect on this book or other related ones in your blog. Those requiring specific applications for their school, higher education community, or training environment might explore books related to online teaching.[17] Individuals in corporate, government, or military training might check out reports from Brandon Hall Research, The eLearning Guild, or the Masie Center. They might also become active members of Elliott Masie's social networking community for learning professionals, "Learning Town!" Educators in primary and secondary schools can find a wealth of resources at the George Lucas Education Foundation (GLEF) and its Edutopia Web site. Given that the ten converging trends documented in the WE-ALL-LEARN model include many sub-trends and events, one can quickly become overwhelmed and discouraged. Models, guidebooks, and frameworks can reduce felt anxiety and frustration.

NOTHING REALLY NEW HERE!

Despite all of the exciting stories and initiatives summarized in this book, some will say that this is really nothing new. People like Ivan Illich, John Dewey, Seymour Papert, and Charles Wedemeyer gave us similar, and perhaps far superior, glimpses of the future decades ago. More recently, Henry Jenkins, George Siemens, John Seely Brown, Elliott Masie, Chris Dede, Jay Cross, and a host of others have extended those visions. For many of them, the ten parts of the WE-ALL-LEARN model are obvious evolutions of the open and distance learning field of the past few decades.

Readers of this book should keep in mind that what was possible in the Web at the time of this writing was scarcely imaginable several years prior. The same will undoubtedly be true a few short years from now. The ten openers will have converged in minor as well as major ways to bring about an educational renaissance in our very lifetimes. The renaissance is already under way. Accurate predictions of the coming decades are always difficult, but it does not take a Nostradamus to see that the world of education in the coming century will be markedly different from what was experienced in previous ones.

There are some things we can be sure of. First, the scanning of books by Google, the Internet Archive, and others will not only continue, it will push ahead at a faster pace due to competition as well as increased familiarity and use of such resources. Second, there will be no shortage of an educational "wow" factor. The Lucifer Chus of the world that personally finance such projects as the translation of MIT courses from English to Chinese will no longer be viewed as curious anomalies. Third, collaborative sharing and remixing of dynamic learning contents such as OOPS will soon be as common as sending e-mail. Such a vibrant sharing community will accelerate as computer scientists and engineers from projects like Connexions and Curriki design new ways for knowledge sharing and interaction. Part of the content shared will be more traditional media such as books, papers, and other documents as seen in Scribd. Part will be nontraditional visual forms of expression that include comments and connections made between and among creators and audience members. Fourth, as these resources evolve, it is likely that services such as Scribd and YouTube will merge or morph into something new altogether.

We are at the first stages of WE-ALL-LEARN for online education. Learner demand for fully online and blended learning formats will not abate in the coming years. The explosion of online learning events, activities, courses, and programs during the past decade has only scratched the surface of what is currently possible while scarcely hinting at the opportunities of tomorrow. The forms of institutional and global collaboration will move from a series of pilot tests to students increasingly receiving secondary and postsecondary diplomas and degrees from joint programs offered by educators and institutions in different regions of the world. For much of that education, if not all of it, they will use handheld and mobile learning devices. And some of these courses and degrees will be completed in virtual worlds such as Second Life instead of the physical one.

I am fairly confident that nearly any technology trend opening the world of learning today will increase its momentum and power tomorrow. Learning is more mobile than ever before. Cell phones, wristwatches, and different types of memory chips will enhance the learning portability of our civilization. And choices and flexibility will be expected by all learners. Options will exist for when, how, and where learning occurs, and what actually takes place. As this happens, addressing learner preferences and needs will be more critical. Taking advantage of these opportunities, learners will increasingly craft their own degrees and programs of study. With such self-selected learning, the learning environment has moved from a boring bowling alley type of approach, where each learner is only allowed one lane or path, to one where the learner can explore as many routes for learning progress as possible.

As sharing and interacting become the norm, the designated times when one is a learner or an instructor will become more difficult to determine or differentiate. Along these same lines, one can be teaching or learning at any time or place. Pinning down teaching times and loads will be next to impossible. What's more, one can be interacting with learners while at remote beaches or nearly any location with an Internet connection.

AUDIENCES OF THE OPEN WORLD

In each chapter, I have tried to speak to humans who learn. That is all 6.7 billion of us. Nevertheless, there are specific messages that I want to convey to more than a dozen potential audiences of this book. I outline some of these below.

Parents

In the opening page of the third edition of *The World Is Flat*, Thomas Friedman points out that a key reason to update his book yet again was to provide answers to parents who wanted to know what to tell their children about the flatter world he describes.[18] I am sure those same parents want to know what to do in this open world as well. Clearly the first thing you should do is find Internet access for you and your children, either at home, at school, at work, in a library, from a Wi-Fi connection, or in a community center. It might even be secondhand access, such as paper printouts from someone else's computer. Second, you might explore the Web resources documented in this book or similar ones and then talk with your children about some of them. Basic cyber safety and security issues are vital today as too often the younger generation reveals information that can later hinder future educational as well as career opportunities.[19] Sit next to your children and discuss the issues surrounding a provocative video in YouTube or picture in Facebook. Check the filtering preferences in Google and other search engines. Help them learn to judge the credibility of different online information sources. At the same time, explore newfound opportunities online. For instance, you might explore the open courses from MIT or other universities with your children to get them to think about a college education. At the same time, you might serve as a role model by learning a language for free online.

Children

Those under the age of twenty-one might get in the habit of sharing new technologies and educational resources with their parents, grandparents, or caregivers. Most parents typically do not have the time to be on top of the latest gadgets or programs. For a more open learning world to work, you must be open to talking to them about it. Browse! You can learn a lot from viewing or listening to snippets of free YouTube lectures or podcasts from colleges and universities. If you stumble upon something educationally interesting, consider writing it down and showing it to your family when time permits. Dig more deeply into subjects that really interest you. You might also show your parents how to edit a Wikipedia page, make a podcast, create a blog or Facebook account, chat in MSN, or navigate through Second Life. If you are bold, you might invite one of them to play Halo, Star Wars Galaxies, World of Warcraft, or some other massive online game with you. Technology can connect families and friends. It is your time to take advantage of it. Do not wait!

Teachers and Trainers

It is an extremely daunting task to try to provide definitive advice to anyone teaching in this brave new open world. It is an unfair expectation to believe that teachers and trainers should attempt to keep up with everything that is happening with educational technology and adjust to it. Of course, you can start by reading and discussing books like this one. Perhaps catalog the books you read in LibraryThing. The model underlying this book is a macro lens for reflecting on emerging learning technologies. Those who want practical, step-by-step examples and advice might consult my recent book with more than a hundred online activities and suggestions.[20] There are other such resources to turn to. Experiment with the ideas you find. Take some risks with global education exchanges and interclass collaborations. Share with your colleagues what works and what does not. Ask students to show you technologies that they have found that relate to your class. Take classes and workshops that are offered. Join professional organizations related to using technology in teaching. Much is possible for the informed.

Bloggers and Podcasters

This book will undoubtedly generate some controversy related to the degree to which the education world has become more open with Web technology. It is not within the direct purview of the book to debate alternative views, theories, frameworks, and models of learning. It is also extremely difficult to keep such a book up to date—or even the companion e-book at WorldIsOpen.com. What could help open educational opportunities and awareness of such opportunities would be for bloggers and podcasters to take different strands of the WE-ALL-LEARN model or one like it and offer updates as creative extensions or applications of them emerge. You have tremendous power to liberate us from more constrained, mainstream media as well as boring and ineffective educational approaches. This is a participatory learning age. Nowhere is this more evident than in the blogosphere and podosphere. I will do my part by posting updates to my TravelinEdMan blog, which will be simultaneously posted to the book Web site at WorldIsOpen.com.

Theorists

There will also be some who wish this book had focused more on learning theory than learning technology. As an educational psychologist, I, too, wish there were learning theories that could serve as magic lamps in this sea of madness. As Gavriel Salomon argued more than a decade ago, for the first time in the history of psychology, novel technologies have taken us to places that learning theory cannot explain.[21] He further contended that we need both technology and theory. I believe it is time to shift from debates about which theory is best to the creation of engaging environments for learning. No one theory explains everything. There are now millions of new learning resources and materials open to anyone online and, hence, millions of new ways to learn. It is incumbent on all psychologists, technologists, educational scholars, and other interested parties to find, evaluate, and promote effective ways to learn with these technologies. What should be clear is that a more participatory and learner-centered style of learning is possible with Web technologies. Learners can explore, design, remix, and share content. We will all learn when the theorists join the party instead of standing at the river banks perpetually waiting for the next boat to arrive or bickering with those standing alongside them.

Technology Administrators

If I could wish for one takeaway for technology administrators, it would be to keep the WE-ALL-LEARN model, or something similar, in mind for technology planning meetings, strategic plans, or new initiatives. Too often "learning" is not the top concern of technology administrators. One year it is computer security, another year it is bandwidth or networking, and in yet another year, the key concern is which technologies to place on the desktops of their bosses. None of those things should ever find its way to the top of the concern list. Foremost on the mind of anyone connected to the field of education, from technology administrator to janitor to bookkeeper, should be learning. Student learning should drive all the other peripheral decisions. It is what you are ultimately hired to do: help the people of your organization—young, old, or in between—to learn. This book highlights hundreds of ways you can do just that right now!

School and University Administrators

The open world is different from the one for which you and your instructional staff were trained. Hold seminars, institutes, and retreats where you and your staff can learn and reflect on this world. Build your infrastructure to take advantage of some of the trends that society is now embracing, such as online and blended learning, wireless access to such learning, and online collaboration across schools and universities. We are in a globalized learning world. It is this world that offers hope for nurturing the next generation of problem solvers who will be needed to address the serious crises related to health care, energy, global warming, and education itself. The WE-ALL-LEARN model and associated disposition toward a more open learning world can guide your efforts.

Technology Companies

As discussed, through philanthropy, research and development, and volunteerism, technology companies are among the leaders of the open learning world. This is not the time to look back and be satisfied with these efforts. You were central to the emergence of technology now lifting us to the discussions and opportunities of the Web 2.0; but in education around the world, we now need to design the Web 3.0 or something far beyond that. Technology companies must foster thinking of what the Web 3.0 might look like and help develop the technologies to make it a reality. Of course, you will be among the chief beneficiaries from educating workers in the Web 3.0 and beyond. In terms of financial support, those in the corporate world might follow the lead of Sun Microsystems with its Curriki project and fund some of the promising new open educational resources projects or those that are still in incubation stages. Such projects might be related to interactive e-books, virtual worlds, online content portals, and wireless educational content. Companies that find ways to embrace, support, and extend the open learning world will not be the ones going out of business but instead will find unique ways to design and market the products of tomorrow.

Government Agencies and Politicians

There is much that those in government settings can provide to open the education world more widely for its citizens. Given all the ways to motivate youth with technology, as well as the many ways in which learning is now free, we should not see a single dropout. Not one. For those in K–12 schooling, new models of what learning is and how to support it are needed. At the same time, there is a serious lack of funding related to the education and training of adult learners. We, the people of this planet, are living and working longer. Yet research, development, and evaluation monies related to the teaching of adults via emerging technologies are almost nonexistent. There has been no time when the opportunities as well as the needs have been greater. Just look at the present international economic crisis and resulting surge in unemployment. Adult learning, and hence economic development around the world, is dependent on your courageous and innovative initiatives and ideas. Government leaders from each country should reflect on how they might open up their educational plans toward a more global vision of education. Significant social change and, potentially, world peace start with education. Such words were never more true than today.

Members of the Media

As this book reveals, the forms and types of media at our fingertips are exploding just as fast as many standard forms of media are imploding. There are dozens of ways to get a message out. However, there are few resources that actually provide a consistent voice and balanced perspective. It is time for media to stop emphasizing the extreme negatives or positives of educational technology. In truth, it is seldom that the scenarios at either end of the pole will exist. There are problems and there are opportunities. The reality today that needs media coverage is that people learn with the support of Web technology, but additional funding from governments, foundations, companies, and individuals is needed to help us advance to a state of unsurpassed educational openness and quality. Though there are controversies related to using technologies such as YouTube, Wikipedia, and iPods in learning, there are also thousands of opportunities that never existed in the past. So much is happening that affects the entire human race that one article here or there in a prominent newspaper or magazine will not suffice. Ideas related to the flattening of the economic world, whether one agrees with them or not, ignited a firestorm of press. Given that education trumps economics in twenty-first century living and survival, the educational opportunities brought about by the world being more open need to be better documented, discussed, debated, and disseminated. You can help.

You

Yes, you. This is the age of YOU. You were *Time* magazine's Person of the Year in 2006 for a reason.[22] You now have technologies within arm's reach that can link you to everything in the Web. With Internet access, you can send an e-mail message to nearly any professor of higher learning in any country. You will also find millions of primary and secondary teachers, corporate and military trainers, and other experts and educators. You do not have to enroll in college to send an e-mail to a professor or noted authority. If you have a question, you can find a range of answers from human as well as nonhuman sources. You can pick anyone in the world to ask to be your mentor. You can browse through any resource found online to assist in your learning. Along the way, peers with similar interests or engaged in comparable learning pursuits can also support your learning. They can confirm what you have uncovered and share still other information that has helped in their learning quests. Every single learning opener documented in this book is an opener for you. Your learning can be wired or unwired, fully online or blended, face-to-face or in virtual worlds, solitary or in a group, and formalized or highly informal. What an extraordinarily exciting time to be a learner!

Librarians, Military Trainers, Businesspeople, Retirees, Informal Learners

Listed above are just some audiences of this book. Many others exist, including the librarian, the military leader, the business person, the retired person, and the informal learner. The librarian, or cybrarian, may have the most to gain from this open learning world: witness e-books, online portals, open access journals, and online video to accompany many publications. And with tools like LibraryThing, we can all become cybrarians! At the same time, the military leader may utilize massive multiplayer online games and highly authentic simulations. As an added bonus, training with such tools might take place just prior to the time of need. In addition, the corporate training director or business executive may realize the need to open up educational resources that her company has developed and decide to share them with others. This book also speaks to the recently retired person who may be starting a new career and needs to find resources available to help in that regard. Such a person might sign up to be a mentor to teenagers or younger adults. Finally, the informal learner might take her shoes off and browse learning resources to her heart's content. The fact that we are all informal learners has never been clearer. No matter our role, this more open learning world affects all of us every day.

EXPECTATIONS MATTER!

As the world opens up for learning, expectations rise. Expectations of learners rise in part due to the learning avenues available—blended, online, classroom-based, television, correspondence, mentoring, and so on. They also rise from the sheer amount of learning materials available. It is difficult to imagine a ten-year-old in the United States of average mental abilities and with adequate care and support at home, including Internet access, who cannot learn the fifty states and capitals or identify the location of Colombia, Algeria, or the Ukraine on a map. There are online maps, flash cards, crossword puzzle games, Webquests, practice exams, audio files, videos, geo-tagged objects, memory aids and mnemonics, activity handouts, free text documents, drag-and-drop exercises, quiz shows, and many other educational choices. And there are millions of possible online learning partners to learn them with.

Expectations also rise for the instructors. Any teacher or trainer with Internet access now has a rich supply of support systems, expert knowledge, indexed learning resources, digital libraries, sample activities from professional colleagues, and archives of prior course records and activities. At no time in the history of this planet have teachers had so much available to them to help them teach. As should be clear by now, these supports are not just for a single teacher here or there but for communities of educational professionals. And each instance of a course can be swiftly advertised, critiqued, shared, and tweaked. Support is instantaneous. Online friendship networks send electronic waves of aid and energy just when you need it.

What we expect from learners and their instructors is only a small part of the vast changes taking place across the educational landscape. We also will demand more from our social institutions and any organization involved in educating the citizens of this planet. We will count on all educational entities, whether they serve young children, college students, workplace learners, or the elderly, to take advantage of the free and open resources that now exist. Such organizations and institutions will need to create new mechanisms for the way knowledge is created, supported, disseminated, and consumed. And instead of continued high-stakes achievement test scores that typically measure factual knowledge and comprehension, they might support conversations around definitions of knowledge and learning and new forms of assessment.

WHAT CAN YOU DO?

Whatever happens, the coming decade will increasingly be one in which learning is more personalized. The Web 2.0 and other emerging technologies will customize the learning process, thereby helping with the huge motivational and dropout problems seen today. The trends comprising WE-ALL-LEARN push us in that direction, but it is clearly only a start. Much more needs to happen in the world of learning and education, and it will. We all have to do more! What will you do to make a contribution toward understanding and using the Web to help all people learn?

Listed below is a reminder of the WE-ALL-LEARN model. Below each technology trend are a few ideas you might consider in contributing to this open learning world. Each of us has a role to play in educating the citizens of the planet. See if you can find an idea or role that works for you.

TEN OPENERS: (WE-ALL-LEARN)

1. Web Searching in the World of E-Books

   You can write books and other documents and make them available for others online. Perhaps lend your services to free book initiatives such as the Global Text Project. You might take a major or minor leadership role in a book-scanning project. You could also donate time, money, energy, and ideas to projects serving those less fortunate who need Internet access or strategic planning for Web-based learning in their schools.

2. E-Learning and Blended Learning

   You might take your expertise and transform it into an online course. Or perhaps you could find and index free online courses in your area of expertise. You might also evaluate such courses. Given the huge need for preparation of both students and teachers for Web-based learning, you could develop training or evaluation programs for online or blended learning.

3. Availability of Open Source and Free Software

   You could locate free software tools that might be useful for a local school or nonprofit agency. If you have technology skills, you might offer your services to help such community agencies adapt free and open source software to their particular needs. Those with extensive computer backgrounds and significant time might design new open source or free software—or provide help in the form of funding or leadership that enables others to fashion such resources.

4. Leveraged Resources and OpenCourseWare

   A single person could lead efforts for an organization to create open-access content. Alternatively, networks with other OCW institutions might be forged. Such work might start with just one sample course or learning module.

5. Learning Object Repositories and Portals

If you teach or design instruction, consider making it available for free to others. You might prescreen online content repositories and write reviews of what you find. For those with expertise in a particular area who enjoy exploring Web resources, you could create a portal or suite of high-quality free Web resources.

6. Learner Participation in Open Information Communities

Anyone can make contributions to educational resources and activities in the Web. You might produce engaging educational videos or documentaries and share them in TeacherTube, or share links that others have created. You can also upload documents to Scribd that have never been published. You might also create or coordinate a wikibook on a topic in which you have interest or expertise. There are many types of wiki resources that you could use to design and form unique collaborations and partnerships.

7. Electronic Collaboration and Interaction

As should be evident by now, there are many ways to collaborate online. You might create online tutoring and mentoring exchange programs. More simply, you might show a local school board or teacher organization the types of online collaboration available to them. You might also design guide sheets, tips, pointers, and overviews for online collaboration. As technology proliferates, you might create field guides or perhaps even an online guide to collaboration. In addition, you might create a group focusing on some aspect of online collaboration in Yahoo! Groups, MSN Groups, or Google Groups.

8. Alternative Reality Learning

Those interested in opening the world of learning might think about wholly new worlds like those found in Second Life. At first, you could experiment with such virtual learning tools and write reviews of them. Once comfortable with such resources, you might help teachers and administrators get a sense of the learning possibilities with them. For those with money or a grant, you might buy an island in Second Life and create some type of education-related theme or activity.

9. **Real-Time Mobility and Portability**
Experiment, experiment, experiment! Technologies for mobile and wireless learning will proliferate in the coming decade. Today mobile phones like the iPhone are relatively new learning devices and much learning experimentation is needed. Ditto the MacBook Air. In a year, there will be many other innovations to consider. You could write grants to acquire such technologies for students or teachers in your organization or community. You might sign up for pilot programs to send course information to your students or employees and conduct formative evaluations of their reactions.

10. **Networks of Personalized Learning**
Think about how the different technologies link together to personalize the learning process. You might attempt to better understand or even model their use with your own blog or social networking site. Anyone can create a group in Ning, Facebook, MySpace, Cyworld, or Yahoo! Groups; try it! You might also attempt to learn a new language online using KanTalk, SpanishPod, or Livemocha and then share your experiences with others.

The model or framework provided by WE-ALL-LEARN can help new as well as experienced users of the Web better grasp what is now possible. It also can be used to plan for what might be possible in the future. No longer must we remain passive browsers and polite connoisseurs of the Web. The WE-ALL-LEARN framework and others like it can move us far beyond that. Today, we can exploit Web 2.0 technologies and beyond, using tools that allow learners to engage in reflective as well as participatory learning as they build, tinker with, and share their learning. WE-ALL-LEARN can provide initial guidance for professional educators wanting their learners to generate ideas online as is possible through wikis, blogs, virtual worlds, and social networking software.

The ten educational openers have changed our very existence on this earth. Individually, they each represent a form of learning that only a few years ago most humans would have deemed extraordinary. Today, however, they are part of the code that makes us uniquely human. Strapped to our hip or placed in our ears, learning technologies are part of the DNA of modern life. When combined, in total or in a more modest way, watch out.

We are on the cusp of massive cognitive, social, and behavioral changes resulting from thoughtful use of technology-enhanced learning. This will set in motion a quantum leap in the evolution in our species. Web browsing and electronic writing of the 1990s were just faint forerunners of where we are now, with technologies for participation, collaboration, and joint problem solving. Individual online learning quests, though still vital for study, have shifted to social bookmarking and collaborative searching as well as collective intelligence initiatives and community-developed novels using wikis. As this occurs, the peers who join us in our learning quests and who know us as learners could have been born and may now live anywhere. Having a baby this week? It is likely that the individuals who will most influence her learning will not be members of your neighborhood, city, or even your country.

THIS IS NOT PLATO'S PLANET

I started this book's Introduction with a commonly told tale in education. In it, Plato and Aristotle would easily recognize the classroom environment of students and teachers, but the settings of other professions would be more difficult to identify. A similar anecdote appeared in Chapter One of Rip van Winkle awakening from a century-long nap to see that schools had not changed much. Such tales are no longer completely true. Unlike education 2,400 years ago, today's learning situations and problems, as well as the resources to solve them, are now more personal, available on demand, and enriched by multimedia. As documented in this book, many schools and corporations are taking advantage of knowledge sharing among learners and instructors in vastly different time zones. There are fascinating opportunities for interactive and collaborative learning among people who have never physically met and perhaps will never meet.

This is no longer Plato's planet. Writing, a new invention then, was cursed by his mentor Socrates who preferred the oral traditions, lest one's memory skills atrophy. But today we see the resurgence of audio. There are free tools and resources to channel audio, such as Skype and GoogleTalk, as well as technologies such as MP3 players and iPods, which facilitate listening to podcasted educational programming and lectures. We also have a wealth of asynchronous conferencing and chat tools for writing. Everywhere one looks on the Internet, there is writing by someone intended for someone else. There are online collaborative writing tools for learners or workers to jointly compose documents and set meeting agendas. Guest experts can log in and participate in online chats on any topic that comes up. Comments can be inserted on online news sites as well as in documents, reports, and announcements.

Reading and writing skills are tested when responding to e-mail as well as contributing to a wiki, blog, chat, or some other type of Web page. Even when out on archaeological digs in remote locations around the planet, as in the opening story of this book, learners can still find ways to write about their experiences and share them with the world. Plato would perhaps be pleased to find so many writing outlets. Of course, within seconds, anyone today with Web access can find and scan through *Plato's Republic* in Scribd. He is a distance educator yet again! But the Web presents us with much more than reading and writing opportunities. Would those learners who relied exclusively on the spoken word in ancient Greece or Rome complain about learning or memory being shortchanged today?

This is not my grandfather's planet either. Learning is not just different from the times of the ancient Greeks and Romans, but also from the times of my Grandpa George who started attending school almost a century ago. The ten openers documented here demonstrate that education is markedly changed today; it is more pervasive and potentially interactive and collaborative than it was in his day. While my grandfather may have walked in one door of his high school and out the other without learning much of anything in that short journey, the doors he could open today would lead him to learning pursuits that he could personally design, engage in, and evaluate. The forms and types of education are exploding before our eyes. With tools such as wikis, blogs, and virtual worlds, along with Web conferencing, videostreaming, and podcasting—just to name a few—my grandfather could participate in his own learning, not one contrived by a teacher or textbook publisher. As a result, I believe, he would be more motivated to learn and would have finished high school. Keep in mind that these learning technologies have emerged at merely the dawn of this new millennium. One hundred or two hundred years into it, there will be even more transformative tools for learners across age levels and competencies. We will finally be living on a continually learning planet. Perhaps we already are and do not realize it.

Without a doubt, there are galaxies of enticing learning possibilities today that were unavailable to our ancestors. Each day there is some announcement or press release about an incredible online news program, biology simulation, virtual campus tour, or portal related to the work of a literary great. So many education and training opportunities lie in front of each of us, whether we are a businessperson, politician, refugee, librarian, teacher, nurse, religious leader, consultant, high school student, university administrator, farmer, retiree, or displaced worker. Educational professionals and decision makers can use the technology trends or openers described in this book as a framework for reflecting on what is now possible online in the Web.

In this book, we have covered much terrain and yet we have only glimpsed a small portion of the Web. There are many learning technology trends that are emerging and coalescing to offer the learners of this planet freedom to learn. If just one of the ten trends in the WE-ALL-LEARN model happened, it would be momentous. If just one person learned from one of those trends, it would be worth writing about. But this is not a story of a single learner or single technology trend. Hundreds of millions of people around the world take advantage of the Web on a daily basis and many of them are doing so at this very moment! Within a decade, we will likely be talking about billions of such motivated people. Of course, no one should be satisfied until everyone has access to the Web of Learning and uses it to accomplish something meaningful.

Those who do have Internet access have information and learning possibilities at their fingertips. Each day, the complex and ever-present Web beckons every one of us down many learning paths and opens countless windows and doors to enhance, transform, and reflect upon our individual learning growth. It does the same for our classmates, colleagues, and global community members. Each of us now has choices regarding our own learning pursuits that we did not have a decade ago. Some of these options are mobile, some virtual, and some individual and exploratory in nature, while still others are embedded in rich social networks and in joint participation with others. The exact form of learning that is pursued may not be the crucial factor in determining the success of a class, a community, or a culture.

For you as an individual, however, it does matter. This is no longer Plato's planet or my grandfather's; this is actually your learning planet now. This book is an attempt to reveal a wide range of learning options in front of you while also offering you a framework to make sense of them. As the Grail Knight said in the 1989 movie *Indiana Jones and the Last Crusade*, "choose wisely." If you do, WE-ALL-LEARN. The world is now open to you!

Acknowledgments

As with any book, and in particular one such as this, there are a host of individuals spanning the globe who helped in its production. First and foremost, Grace Lin, formerly of the University of Houston and now at the University of Hawaii, lent insights into technologies and educational resources that I did not know existed. Without Grace's fantastic encouragement, optimism, and unique perspective, there certainly would be no book here. She helped me formulate many ideas and concepts discussed throughout the book. It was often an e-mail or phone call from her regarding a new tool or innovation that kept the flame glowing on many a long night when the fire inside me was beginning to smolder. She understands the potential of the open educational resource (OER) movement better than anyone I have met. At the same time, she provided a critical eye and sense of balanced perspective when I grew too euphoric over a particular idea, tool, or trend. I thank my fabulous friend and colleague, Dr. Mimi Miyoung Lee from the University of Houston, for nudging me further into the world of open education and the perpetual giving aspects of it, especially as it relates to the needs of those who are less fortunate or underserved, oftentimes with little knowledge she is doing so. It was her casual yet timely introduction to Grace Lin that made this book possible. Thanks so much, Mimi, for opening up my learning world.

Three others who have also significantly opened up my learning world are my longtime colleague and sounding board Tom Reynolds from National University, my former professor and distance-learning mentor Bob Clasen from the University of Wisconsin, and my amazingly creative and caring friend Paul Kim from Stanford University, the king of mobile learning for transformative change. You guys are great!

Charles Graham from Brigham Young University was instrumental in helping me with the initial ideas related to the ten trends that underlie the WE-ALL-LEARN model. In fact, we nearly collaborated on this effort as we had done on a prior book on blended learning. Ideas from Charles enabled this book to come alive, first in his mind and then in my mind, and a few months later on paper. A huge thank-you and hug to Charles! With that said, I must thank Peter Fingar from Meghan-Kiffer Press for suggesting that I do this book by myself instead of as an edited volume, even though this meant Charles and I would not collaborate this time.

Family also got involved. A key assistant on this project was my son, Alex, who found, compiled, and filtered through information as I needed it and traveled with me on some of the journeys documented in this book. He was a key member of my research team. My daughter, Nicole, enthusiastically completed some of the final manuscript reference and Web link checking for me, though any remaining errors are mine alone. Given that Alex and Nicki are both in college now, they are among those to whom I hope I can sell a few copies of this book. No matter the results, they are fabulous young adults of whom a father can be quite proud.

Timely feedback and editing was provided by Brian J. Ford from Cambridge, who suffered through two early drafts of the book, and Sharon Stoerger from Indiana University, who meticulously edited two later versions. Both were saviors! Once they were done, Erica Reichert came to my rescue and copyedited the entire manuscript after moving into town just a few weeks before. After that, the manuscript ended up in the very capable hands of Kate Bradford from Jossey-Bass/Wiley, who helped shape it up further and streamline it. Thanks, Kate, for all your wonderful suggestions and continued support. You took on a huge project and turned potential into reality. Without Kate, this book might not have existed at all and definitely not in this format. And thanks to everyone else at Wiley and Jossey-Bass who rallied around the manuscript, including Debbie Notkin, Pamela Berkman, Carrie Wright, Nana Twumasi, Dimi Berkner, Meredith Stanton, and Karen Warner, as well as to Donna Cohn for her superb copyediting talents. Thanks, also, to Debra Hunter, David Brightman, Erin Null, and Jessica Egbert for their encouragement to submit my manuscript to Jossey-Bass.

I also thank my highly insightful publicist, Meryl Moss, for getting the word out that the world is really open for learners and educators everywhere. Similarly, Paul Sennott, my insightful attorney from Fish and Richardson, was indispensible to this book process. Anyone writing a trade book needs a sharp person like him. Paul, you are great!

Many others influenced the final result. The magnificent people supplying specific comments and insights on different sections of this book include Judith Enriquez from the University of North Texas, Lena Lee from Ohio University, SuJin Son from the University of Illinois, Dazhi Yang from Purdue University, and Yayoi Anzai from Aoyama Gakuin University in Japan. Still other great friends lending manuscript-related support include Lori Teng, Ke Zhang, Chuck Ferguson, Elliot Soloway, Nancy Hays, Kyung Ha Oh, Ying Wang, Jim Hensman, YaTing Teng, Nantana Wongtanasirikul, and Veronica Acosta. Thanks for your quick reads, my friends! Others providing the ideas for the various trends documented here include Jay Cross, Padma Medury, Will Richardson, Mike Wenger, Guohua Pan, Les Watson, Ron Owston, John Savery, Jon Dron, Vanessa Paz Dennen, Gilly Salmon, George Siemens, Kira King, Okhwa Lee, Tom Reeves, and countless friends and colleagues who cannot be thanked individually due to space limitations.

Of course, I want to acknowledge all the individuals with whom I corresponded and interviewed for this project who really are this book— you are the heroes, gurus, and revolutionaries of the shared Internet. You are the ones who have supplied the fuel and resulting optimism for the educational openers detailed here or in the companion e-book. Without any doubt, you have changed the world! In particular, I want to thank Intellagirl (Sarah Robbins), Typewriter Tackleberry (Mark Bell), Kitty Schmidt-Jones, Robert Slater, Thomas Reynolds, Richard Baraniuk, Mark Franek, Terry Anderson, Peter Young, Cassandra Brooks, Lee LeFever, John Traxler, Jeff Lebow, Brian J. Ford, Yayoi Anzai, Lucifer Chu, Andy Carvin, Mike Offerman, Julie Young, Kay Johnson, Laura Francis, Tom McGee, Murray Goldberg, David Wiley, David Thomas, Kathleen Micham, Shauna Mecartea, Lily Henry-Roberts, Jamie Aprile, Glenn R. Jones, Ellen Waterman, Ellen Wagner, Karen Fennell, Bridey Fennell, John Dehlin, Shelley Henson, Marlene Scardamalia, Jennifer Maddrell, Cool Cat Teacher (Vicki Davis), Julie Lindsay, Larry Lessig, Yan Chun Su, Godwin Agudey, Mike Godwin,

Gil Heiman, Todd Bryant, Bruce Colston, Darren Draper, Bobbi Kurshan, Scott McNealy, John Seely Brown, Gerald Kane, Maxim Jean-Louis, Trip Adler, Paul Kim, Richard Stallman, Dick Yue, Jim Hensman, Martin Dougiamas, Mitch Kapor, Mesfin Getachew, James Moore, Steve Carson, Barry Joseph, Chris Anderson, Yong Zhao, Jim Theroux, Sonny Kirkley, Bob Wisher, Shirish Nadkarni, Byran Hurren, Ken Carroll, Jenny Zhu, Shou-Bing Fu, Jason Turgeon, Stephen Downes, James Spohrer, Dwight Allen, Michelle Selinger, Richard Watson, Erik Moeller, Jimmy Wales, Charles Nesson, Rebecca Nesson, Hyo-Jeong So, Rita Oates, Burks Oakley, Ray Schroeder, Cory Doctorow, Wing Lam, Margaret Driscoll, Mike Harris, Jaz Hee-jeong Choi, LiRong Huang, Otto Toews, Christopher Brownell, Richard Wiseman, Matt Harding, Karl Fisch, Bude Su, Ed Gragert, Michelle Eady, Michael Lindeman, Steven Hornik, Alexandra Juhasz, Sanjaya Mishra, Herb Hilderley, Chris McIntyre, Constance Steinkuehler, Kurt Squire, Yochai Benkler, Jonathan Zittrain, Michael Wesch, Mingming Jiang, Andrew Yu, David Liu, Lisa Spiro, and many others for insightful stories, time, and feedback. How cool to know you all! Of course, it is only possible with the Web of Learning.

There are countless others who have attended my talks and presentations on this topic during the past few years and provided timely and insightful feedback as well as their friendship. Thanks for your reactions, testimonials, and far-reaching ideas regarding the framework for this book. I also thank the former students and colleagues who provided candid feedback, comments, advice, encouragement, and inspiration on various chapters or ideas in the book as I completed them. As you know, I think of each of you daily.

I am also blessed with some of the world's best students in instructional technology and educational psychology, many of whom supplied me with their abundant encouragement, plentiful resources, and rich humor, where and when needed. It is your optimism and energy that will push ahead educational opportunities for everyone on this planet and make sure that WE-ALL-LEARN! Please never stop forging ahead and making a personal dent here or adding to the wedge in progressive education! Each of you must continually attempt to make your dents! Thanks to each of you!

May readers of this book find new educational successes in the crucial decades ahead and offer their support for the successes of others in the Web. I thank Mary Bonk and all my family and friends for putting up with me while I wrote this monster. My mother, Joanne Bonk, is the reigning family historian who lent insights into my grandfather, George Goronja, who is mentioned in several key places of this book. Thanks, Mom! I thank my lifelong friend, Stan Lowe, for information related to several historical aspects of this book. In addition, I thank the Twelve Girls Band from China for their mesmerizing CD, *Eastern Energy*, which I listened to over 250 times while writing this book. Thank you all!

Finally, as noted in the Introduction, a Web site has been created with a companion e-book containing hundreds of pages of additional content plus dozens more stories, resources, projects, and ideas that do not appear in this book. To access such information, please visit WorldIsOpen.com. At that site, you will find links to all the Web sites and references mentioned in this book as well as the companion e-book, in addition to many other useful online resources. To extend the themes of this book, I am now working on books related to how people learn and teach in unusual places such as boats, planes, trains, mountaintops, and shopping malls—using Web technology. If you have stories, references, or ideas related to nontraditional learning with technology, I would love to hear about them at the WorldIsOpen.com Web site or via a personal e-mail to curt@worldisopen.com or story@worldisopen.com. Maybe your tale will end up in my next book. Stop by the Web site and enjoy your open learning world.

Postscript: An Open Letter to the Learners of This Planet

When you went to sleep at night in the twentieth century, you were not likely dreaming about your next learning moves or adventures. Today, who can afford not to? Each day is a learning experience that can be enhanced by hundreds of freely shared online video sites, tens of thousands of open access journals, millions of books, and hundreds of millions of bloggers. Locating and checking out similar text, audio, or video resources would have taken days, weeks, or perhaps even months only a decade or two ago. Today they are can be accessed online in mere seconds at the click of a button. And a large percentage have huge educational implications.

You may not see it each time you walk outside or drive down the street, but the educational world is in a state of rapid transition. Part of the reason is that millions of educational resources are being made freely available for the first time in the history of human civilization. Anyone who searches for information on the Web is quickly overwhelmed by the volume of free and open access to learning materials. Members of the media, politicians, educators, students, parents, and others are asking important questions about the quality of such content. Some want to know if personally selected content might lead to school or college credits or even degrees. Organizations, agencies, and institutions are also sorting out what should be free and what should cost money. Interesting ideas and solutions are just starting to emerge.

In the midst of this discussion and debate, human learning is transforming so rapidly that teachers do not know what to do. Schools and colleges are unsure how to react. Corporations are often left with the job of reskilling and testing new learning and evaluation approaches. Unfortunately, such training programs continue to rely too much on formalized training with prepackaged content and preset rooms, chairs, podiums, and times. Instead, they should be training employees with timely and on-demand podcasts, virtual conversations, and online brainstorming in a wiki or synchronous chat. Such tools can support and put into action new management processes and practices eons faster than what can be accomplished in traditional classroom training. And when combined with face-to-face meetings either during or after work in a blended learning approach, it is even more powerful. Traditional learning is integrated into the virtual and informal, and vice versa.

THE LEARNING CENTURY

Let's declare this the "Learning Century." To live up to the name, of course, we need on-demand access to teachers, mentors, tutors, and other learning facilitators. More than a couple of millennia ago, Plato was perhaps the first distance learning educator, as humans across the planet read his works years, decades, or millennia after his instruction had taken place. Today you can call up his books in Scribd, Google Books, and countless other sources. The same will likely be said for each of us millennia from now. Be careful what you say, write, or record!

In this millennium, everyone can be an educator as well as learner at any moment of the day or night. With Web technology and an abundance of open educational resources, we can learn just as effectively at 3 AM as at 3 PM. We can be teaching others when on a Norwegian tanker breaking through whatever ice remains at the North Pole as well as when sipping tea or coffee in our study back home.

Without a doubt, new forms of teaching and learning will emerge in this century. One interesting trend will be the rise of super e-mentors, tutors, and coaches. Such people will understand counseling and human development, the various pathways to learn online, and one or more subject-area disciplines. Of course, more personalized and elevated forms of mentoring were always possible if you could afford it; now mentoring will just be more apparent, accessible, accepted, and affordable.

By the close of the next decade, most learners will have experiences with one or more online mentors or tutors. And well before the close of the century, each learner on Planet Earth will be assigned a super mentor or coach. This will be a person to consult with at critical junctures in your learning process. Such individuals will be critical in helping sort out the myriad ways you can learn today as well as the interesting routes you might take to reach new learning milestones. As learning becomes increasingly essential in our lives, super mentors will continually provide the breath of life by leading us to relevant and meaningful learning paths.

Online environments free learners from the constraints of formal schooling and education while providing them with hundreds of formal learning venues where few or none previously existed. Jay Cross and others remind us that informal learning already comprises more than 80 percent of learning. We Google something. We casually check a fact in Wikipedia or the Encyclopedia of Life. We subscribe to the online writing of experts, such as Jay's insightful Internet Time or Informal Learning blogs. We listen to online audio files of conference keynote speakers months or years after they gave their talk. And we watch professors from Seoul National University, the University of Pretoria, or Stanford University present their lectures in biology, computer science, or business marketing even though we are not students in any of those classes or seeking credit. In this gigantic learning expedition, we are just hyperlinking to the next learning experience, one after another. And we are no longer tethered to a desktop computer. With laptops and devices such as the iPhone, iPod, iPad, and Kindle, learning can go where you go.

Heading further into this century, we will find that informal and more mobile learning will constitute an even greater percentage of our learning experience. That is not to discount formal learning venues. We will be learning longer, faster, and more efficiently than ever before. By 2070, formal education to age thirty will be commonly accepted. Why? Simple math. As knowledge within each discipline continues to explode and lifespans expand, a year will be added to educational requirements during each decade this century. On a yearly basis, such changes in learning milestones are subtle, but they are happening to you as well as all your friends and family members.

Despite formal learning to age thirty and beyond, informal and on-demand learning will dominate educational discussions and policy decisions during this century. When this happens, age may no longer matter. Soon you will be in work teams or committees in which centenarians will be helping you tackle huge global problems while others of this older age group will be in graduate school pursuing their master's and doctoral degrees as well as conducting research in postgraduate study. At the same time, some elementary and middle school youths will be online teachers and mentors to others or graduating from college. Current young phenoms like thirteen-year-old Adora Svitak illustrate how this is already happening. Adora, also known as the "World's Youngest Teacher," already has a couple of books under her belt and uses Web-based technology and SMART boards to teach K–12 educators how to teach writing and other subjects—while simultaneously taking her own classes online from the Washington Virtual Academy. Each day is a unique opportunity to teach and to learn for Adora as well as for her band of followers in her social network.

As humans, we naturally learn. We learn every single day. Ideally, you are learning something right now. Although other creatures do learn, the capability to quickly respond to, reflect upon, and later refine new ways to learn is what distinguishes us from all the others.

YOU LEARN

This is your time to learn and to make a contribution to the evolving Web of Learning. You can generate or add to a Wikipedia entry. You can fashion and update a blog. You can have a weekly podcast about a topic of cultural or scientific significance. You can design and post a video to YouTube that benefits other learners of this planet. You can decide to join a group in social networking spaces such as Facebook, MySpace, or Ning. And you can subscribe to the blog, video, wiki, Twitter, and Facebook posts of others.

This is just a start. With each passing year, such ways to learn will become more integrated and personalized. Each of us will have customized the methods that accelerate and monitor our own learning. Earth will become a learning planet, rather than one known for industrialization, smog, or the endless mismanagement of resources. You need to help push this journey ahead today, not tomorrow. The only way to solve global problems is through thinking, education, discussion, and group collaboration.

Recheck your occupational goals and lifelong aspirations. Your standing as a productive member of the human race in the twenty-first century will not likely be measured by the firm you founded or the legal cases you have won. During the coming decades, learners as well as learning innovators, providers, and supporters will be celebrated. We will learn together as citizens of this more open planet. As we do, we will celebrate the ongoing learning accomplishments in each phase of one's life and perhaps reach new life vistas never before experienced or imagined.

LEARNER RIGHTS AND RESPONSIBILITIES

This is your learning world. You have the right to learn where, when, what, and how you want as well as from the people who fit your learning needs. Throughout history, billions of humans have lived and died on this planet. None of those who left this world prior to the end of 1999 had the learning resources you now possess. Not a soul!

Keep in mind that you do not even need Internet access to benefit from the explosion of Web content and learning technologies. All that is required is for you to live in a community that has an organization or institution that is connected to or touched by the Internet. People from around the world can give their time, talents, and money to it; often making their contributions or commitments from a Web page or link. As this happens, we all learn.

Learner Rights

Learners of any century need rights, but this is especially true for learners of this century. As we push into the technology-rich twenty-first century, you—the learners of this planet—can see your rights crystallizing before your eyes. I suggest that we all have the following ten learner-related rights:

1. The right to learn when and how you want in a learning environment that is personally safe and comfortable.
2. The right to access any content you need at any time you need it.
3. The right to learn from the best educators and learning guides on the planet as well as from as many instructors as you so choose.
4. The right to help others learn.

5. The right to share your learning-related discoveries and ideas with others (such as experts, peers, instructors, friends, and family) for their prompt and candid feedback.

6. The right to self-monitor your learning progress as well as obtain feedback from others on that progress.

7. The right to share content that you create as well as comment on or evaluate the educational resources that you find.

8. The right to form groups of individuals or learning communities with similar learning interests and experiences to discuss, debate, and extend such ideas while finding personal learning identity and meaning.

9. The right to create new tools, materials, and resources to facilitate your own learning as well as that of others.

10. The right to teach, train, tutor, and mentor others using Web tools and resources.

These are the inalienable rights for learners in this century, a time period when we are inundated with seemingly limitless learning opportunities. Each of these rights is easier to visualize, support, and actualize with Web technologies. With these ten rights in place, cultures and people can advance in more harmonious ways and at a much quicker pace than in the past. We can learn whatever we want with whomever we want at the times and places that we want.

Learner Responsibilities

Along with learner rights regarding Web technology, we also have responsibilities. Among these are the following ten learner-related ones:

1. The responsibility to take ownership for our own learning when and where appropriate to do so.

2. The responsibility to seek out the most accurate and credible information while questioning and examining online information and knowledge in a critical and reflective manner.

3. The responsibility to dialogue with children or any other unseasoned learner about how to evaluate the quality of the educational content found online.

4. The responsibility to contribute to the learning of others in a productive and humane way.

5. The responsibility to educate others about the learning potential of the Web—to show them how to contribute to the Web and how to receive learning from it.

6. The responsibility to seek help when online tools and resources are overwhelming or frustrating.

7. The responsibility to respect those who provide meaningful educational content and tools as well as all the teachers, trainers, tutors, mentors, and learning guides you encounter in your online learning quests and queries.

8. The responsibility to test and experiment with new learning resources and discuss and report on their utility with others.

9. The responsibility to report online educational resources that are inappropriate or potentially harmful (as well as the people who placed them there).

10. The responsibility to think about how online educational materials can benefit those beyond your household, neighborhood, community, or region of the world to your global brothers and sisters who have different educational and cultural backgrounds, needs, opportunities, and supports.

THE LEARNING WORLD IS OPEN

The Web has accelerated access to learning. There has never been a time in the history of this planet when so much learning was possible throughout our lifetime. Not only is your access to learning instantaneous, but you can also learn from global partners via technology that is increasingly social, ubiquitous, and inexpensive. Despite persistent complaints about the state of education today, when it comes to opportunities to learn outside as well as inside schools, these are auspicious times.

We can look back to preceding generations within our own families, cultures, and regions of the world. There is likely no other group of learners that has been so fortunate. Of course, billions still cannot afford direct access to the Web and a large percentage of such individuals lack sufficient food, shelter, and clothing. With each passing day, however, tens of thousands more people have the chance to learn from mobile devices and local learning centers equipped with technology that did not exist for their parents and grandparents.

To explicitly demonstrate this open learning world, I continue to work on an e-book extension of *The World Is Open* with the same chapters, just different content (to be made available from http://worldisopen.com/). The e-book extension will be freely available for anyone to download, print, disseminate, and forward to others. At that site, you will also find the references and Web resources to both books as well as several book excerpts and book reviews.

Share any part of this that you want—the world is open to you. And as you do, please write to me about the innovative ways you are participating in the open education movement. I look forward to hearing from each of you.

Enjoy your adventures in this open learning world.

April 2011

The Author

Curt Bonk first entered the business world in his late teens as a production control coordinator in manufacturing plants in Milwaukee. By his early twenties, after obtaining an accounting degree from the University of Wisconsin at Whitewater, Bonk was a CPA and corporate controller in the computer technology and medical supply industries. After becoming sufficiently bored with life as an accountant, he took correspondence and television courses with Dr. Robert Clasen at the University of Wisconsin (UW) Extension and Outreach Department. He received his PhD degree in educational psychology from the UW in 1989. During graduate school, Dr. Clasen further opened Bonk's learning world and passion for distance learning by offering him a job to help create television-based educational programming on critical thinking.

After graduating from the UW, Bonk served on the faculty of West Virginia University from 1989 to 1992. He arrived at Indiana University (IU) in August 1992 just as it was opening a fabulous School of Education building created to demonstrate new technologies in education. Bonk has been experimenting with emerging technologies in that building since that time, first as professor of educational psychology and later in instructional systems technology. He is also an adjunct professor in the IU School of Informatics, an affiliate member of the IU Cognitive Science Program, and visiting professor at the University of Glamorgan in Wales.

Bonk has been a senior research fellow with the Advanced Distributed Learning (ADL) Lab within the Department of Defense as well as the Army Research Institute. He is the recipient of numerous teaching and mentoring awards from IU, including the Burton Gorman Teaching

Award and the Wilbert Hites Mentoring Award. In 2002, he was awarded the CyberStar Award from the Indiana Information Technology Association and in the following year was given the Most Outstanding Achievement Award from the U.S. Distance Learning Association, as well as the Most Innovative Teaching in a Distance Education Program Award from the State of Indiana. More recently, Bonk received an alumni achievement award from the University of Wisconsin. In November 2008, Bonk was program chair for the international E-Learn Conference from the Association for the Advancement of Computing in Education (AACE). He is currently helping AACE develop a new online conference related to technology and learning as well as a live conference in Asia and the Pacific Rim, "Global Learn: Global Conference on Learning and Technology." The first Global Learn conference will be held in April 2010.

Bonk has presented nearly a thousand talks and workshops around the globe on emerging technologies, blended learning, online motivation, e-learning pedagogy, and future technology trends, to K–12, higher education, corporate, government, military, and other audiences. Organizations that have sought Curt for such consulting include Intel, Sun, Cisco, Microsoft, McGraw-Hill, Harvard, Oxford, Samsung, LG, ITT Educational Services, Manchester Business School, Dubai Women's College, Maricopa Community Colleges, the University of Texas Medical School, the National Security Agency, and the eLearning Guild. Among the places he has presented are China, Thailand, Korea, Finland, Ireland, Singapore, Australia, New Zealand, Iceland, and Saudi Arabia. Bonk's TravelinEdMan blog (http://travelinedman.blogspot.com/) provides detailed accounts of what he has witnessed in these journeys, including how some organizations and institutions are leveraging the power of online networks and emerging technologies for e-learning to bolster their competitive advantage, improve people's lives, and open up the world of learning for millions of people around the world.

Bonk has written more than 225 articles and books on topics such as online learning, massive multiplayer online gaming, wikis, blogging, open source software, collaborative technologies, synchronous and asynchronous computer conferencing, and the future of online and blended learning. His books include *Electronic Collaborators*; *The Handbook of*

Blended Learning Environments: Global Perspectives, Local Designs; and *Empowering Online Learning: 100+ Activities for Reading, Reflecting, Displaying, and Doing*. Finally, he is founder and president of CourseShare and SurveyShare and can be contacted via his homepage at http://mypage.iu.edu/~cjbonk/ or through the "World Is Open" book Web site at http://worldisopen.com/.

Endnotes

Introduction

1. Lily Henry Roberts, "Canada: Learning to Use a Machete on a Private Island," *Blog post, UCLA Archaeology Field Program* (July 2, 2008), www.magazine.ucla.edu/summerdigs/?p=78 (accessed Aug. 1, 2008).

2. Ibid.

3. Meg Sullivan, "Dig In, Archaeology Fans! UCLA Blogs to Offer Front-Row Seat at Archaeology Digs," *UCLA Newsrooms* (June 25, 2008), www.magazine.ucla.edu/summerdigs/?page_id=70 (accessed Aug. 1, 2008).

4. Anthony P. Graesch, "Canada: Setting Up Using Machetes, Axes, and Chainsaws," *Blog post, UCLA Archaeology Field Program* (July 2, 2008), www.magazine.ucla.edu/summerdigs/?p=77 (accessed Aug. 1, 2008).

5. Anthony P. Graesch, "Canada: Stó:lō Landscape, History, and Archaeology," *Blog post, UCLA Archaeology Field Program* (July 28, 2008), www.magazine.ucla.edu/summerdigs/?p=110 (accessed Aug. 1, 2008).

6. Jamie Aprile, "Albania: Life in the Field and on a Bus Named Skanderbeg," *Blog post, UCLA Archaeology Field Program* (July 14, 2008), www.magazine.ucla.edu/summerdigs/?p=95 (accessed Aug. 1, 2008).

7. Alison Hewlett, "Hard Work Has Never Been So Much Fun," *UCLA Today/ UCLA Magazine* (2008), www.magazine.ucla.edu/summerdigs/?page_id=67 (accessed Aug. 1, 2008).

8. Ibid., para. 8.

9. Ibid.

10. Dani Cooper, "Scholar Finds New Archaeological Sites by Googling," *Discovery News* (July 21, 2008), http://dsc.discovery.com/news/2008/07/21/archaeology-google.html (accessed Aug. 1, 2008).

11. Thomas L. Friedman, *The World Is Flat: A Brief History of the Twenty-First Century* (New York: Farrar, Straus, & Giroux. 2005).

12. John Naisbitt and Patricia Aburdene, *Megatrends* (New York: William Morrow, 1982); John Naisbitt and Patricia Aburdene, *Megatrends 2000: Ten New Directions for the 1990s* (New York: William Morrow, 1990).

13. Gary Klass, "Plato as Distance Education Pioneer: Status and Quality Threats of Internet Education," *First Monday* 5, no. 7 (2000), www.firstmonday.org/issues/issue5_7/klass/index.html (accessed June 19, 2007).

14. Frederick Bennett, "The Future of Computer Technology in K–12 Education," *Phi Delta Kappan* 83, no. 8 (2002): 621–625.

15. Klass, "Plato as Distance Education Pioneer."

16. Charles A. Wedemeyer, *Learning at the Back Door: Reflections on Non-Traditional Learning in the Lifespan* (Madison: University of Wisconsin Press, 1981).

1. We All Learn

1. Xiaojing Liu, Curtis J. Bonk, Richard J. Magjuka, Seung-hee H. Lee, and Bude Su, "Exploring Four Dimensions of Online Instructor Roles: A Program Level Case Study," *Journal of Asynchronous Learning Networks* 9, no. 4 (2005), www.sloan-c.org/publications/jaln/v9n4/v9n4_liu_member.asp (accessed Aug. 12, 2006).

2. Jay Cross, *Informal Learning Rediscovering Natural Pathways That Inspire Innovation and Performance* (San Francisco: Pfeiffer, 2007).

3. Kyong Jee Kim and Curtis J. Bonk, "The Future of Online Teaching and Learning in Higher Education: The Survey Says . . . ," *EDUCAUSE Quarterly* 29, no. 4 (2006): 22–30, www.educause.edu/ir/library/pdf/eqm0644.pdf or www.educause.edu/apps/eq/eqm06/eqm0644.asp (accessed July 14, 2007).

4. Carl R. Rogers, *Freedom to Learn for the 80s* (Columbus, OH: Charles Merrill, 1983).

5. Curtis J. Bonk and Ke Zhang, *Empowering Online Learning: 100+ Activities for Reading, Reflecting, Displaying, and Doing* (San Francisco: Jossey-Bass, 2008).

6. Thomas L. Friedman, *The World Is Flat: A Brief History of the Twenty-First Century* (New York: Farrar, Straus & Giroux, 2005).

7. Andrew Welsh-Huggins, "It's All About Location: The World Isn't Flat in This View of the Global Economy," *Detroit Free Press* (Apr. 13, 2008), www.freep.com/apps/pbcs.dll/article?AID=/20080413/FEATURES05/804130551/1030/FEATURES (accessed May 25, 2008).

8. Richard Florida, "In Praise of Spikes," *Fast Company* (Mar. 2008), http://creativeclass.com/richard_florida/events/ (accessed May 25, 2008).

9. Richard Florida, "The World Is Spiky," *The Atlantic Monthly* 51 (Oct. 2005), http://creativeclass.com/rfcgdb/articles/other-2005-The%20World%20is%20Spiky.pdf (accessed May 25, 2008).

10. Richard Straub, "Is the World Open?" *Global Focus* 2, no. 10 (Apr. 2008), www.elig.org/files/repository/web_content/elig_contents/5-Resources/2-Articles%20&%20Presentations/GF_4trichardstraub-Open.pdf (accessed May 25, 2008).

11. Alvin Toffler, *Powershift: Knowledge, Wealth, and Violence at the Edge of the 21st Century* (New York: Bantam Books, 1990).

12. Toffler, *Powershift*, 470.

13. Cross, *Informal Learning Rediscovering Natural Pathways That Inspire Innovation and Performance*.

14. Don Tapscott and Anthony Williams, *Wikinomics: How Mass Collaboration Changes Everything* (New York: Penguin, 2006): 37.

15. Campus Technology, "News Update: Stanford Debuts Wiki of All Things Stanford," *Campus Technology* (Oct. 10, 2006), http://campustechnology.com/news_article.asp?id=19384&typeid=150 (accessed Feb. 2, 2007).

16. John Seely Brown, "Relearning Learning—Applying the Long Tail to Learning," presentation (MIT iCampus, Dec. 1, 2006), http://mitworld.mit.edu/video/419/ (accessed Feb. 9, 2007).

17. Claudia Wallis and Sonja Steptoe, "How to Bring Our Schools out of This 20th Century," *Time Magazine* (Dec. 10, 2006), www.time.com/time/printout/0,8816,1568480,00.html (accessed July 9, 2007).

18. Wallis and Steptoe, "How to Bring Our Schools out of This 20th Century," para. 2.

19. "Time Magazine Person of the Year," *Time Magazine* 168, no. 26 (Dec. 25, 2006/Jan. 1, 2007).

20. Lev Grossman, "You," *Time Magazine* 168, no. 26 (Dec. 25, 2006/Jan. 1, 2007): 38–41.

21. Bryan Alexander, "Web 2.0: A New Wave of Innovation for Teaching and Learning?" *EDUCAUSE Review* 41, no. 2 (Mar./Apr. 2006): 32–44, www.educause.edu/apps/er/erm06/erm0621.asp (accessed July 9, 2007).

22. Joseph Ellis, *Founding Brothers: The Revolutionary Generation* (New York: Alfred A. Knopf, 2000).

23. The Cape Town Open Education Declaration, "Cape Town Open Education Declaration: Unlocking the Promise of Open Educational Resources," (Jan. 22,

2008), www.capetowndeclaration.org/read-the-declaration (accessed May 4, 2008).

24. John B. Horrigan, "Adoption Stalls for Low-Income Americans Even as Many Broadband Users Opt for Premium Services That Give Them More Speed," report (Pew Internet & American Life Project, July 2008), www.pewinternet.org/pdfs/PIP_Broadband_2008.pdf (accessed July 13, 2008).

25. Julia Sanchez, "Internet for Everyone Campaign Aims to Bridge Digital Divide," *Ars Technica* (June 24, 2008), http://arstechnica.com/news.ars/post/20080624-internet-for-everyone-campaign-aims-to-bridge-digital-divide.html (accessed June 27, 2008).

26. Jimmy Wales and Richard Baraniuk, "Bringing Open Source Resources to Textbooks and Teaching," *San Francisco Chronicle* (Jan. 22, 2008), www.sfgate.com/cgi-bin/article.cgi?f=/c/a/2008/01/22/EDRTUJ346.DTL (accessed June 28, 2008).

27. Ibid., para. 6.

28. Ibid., para. 8.

29. Ibid., para. 9.

30. Elliott Masie, "#529 Learning and July 4th," *Learning Trends* (July 16, 2008): para. 2, http://trends.masie.com/archives/2008/7/4/529-learning-and-july-4th.html (accessed July 16, 2008).

2. To Search and to Scan

1. Charlie Demerjian, "Tyan Brings Supercomputing to the Desktop," *The Inquirer* (Mar. 13, 2006), www.theinquirer.net/en/inquirer/news/2006/03/13/tyan-brings-supercomputing-to-the-desktop (accessed May 27, 2008).

2. Andy Patrizio, "NASA, SGI Plan Petaflop Computer Breakthrough," *EarthWeb News* (May 8, 2008), http://news.earthweb.com/hardware/article.php/3745856 (accessed May 27, 2008).

3. Hans W. Meuer, "The TOP500 Project: Looking Back Over 15 Years of Supercomputing Experience," *HowStuffWorks.com* (Jan. 19, 2008), www.howstuffworks.com/framed.htm?parent=question54.htm&url=www.top500.org/ (accessed May 28, 2008).

4. Josef H. Herbert, "Scientists Develop Fastest Computer," *Yahoo! News* (June 9, 2008), http://news.yahoo.com/s/ap/20080609/ap_on_hi_te/fastest_computer (accessed June 10, 2008).

5. Jon Brodkin, "IBM and Los Alamos Smash Petaflop Barrier," *TechWorld* (2008), www.techworld.com/news/index.cfm?RSS&NewsID=101717 (accessed June 10, 2008).

6. Chris Anderson, "The Long Tail," *Wired* 12, no. 10 (Oct. 2004), www.wired.com/wired/archive/12.10/tail_pr.html (accessed May 27, 2008).

7. Chris Anderson, *The Long Tail: Why the Future of Business Is Selling Less of More* (New York: Hyperion, 2006).

8. John Seely Brown and Richard P. Adler, "Minds on Fire: Open Education, the Long Tail, and Learning 2.0," *Educause Review* 43, no. 1 (Jan./Feb. 2008): 16–32, http://connect.educause.edu/Library/EDUCAUSE+Review/MindsonFireOpen Educationt/45823 (accessed Feb. 23, 2008).

9. Elliott Masie, "402-Fingertip Knowledge and Lowered Memorization," *Learning TRENDS by Elliott Masie* (Sep. 18, 2006): para. 3, 5, 6, http://trends.masie.com/archives/2006/9/18/402-fingertip-knowledge-and-lowered-memorization.html (accessed June 28, 2008).

10. Time Public Affairs, "Time Magazine and the Oprah Winfrey Show Team Up to Examine the High School Dropout Crisis in America," (Apr. 10, 2006), www.civicenterprises.net/pdfs/timeoprahtrade.pdf (accessed Apr. 17, 2008).

11. Nathan Thornburgh, "Dropout Nation," *Time* (Apr. 9, 2006), www.time.com/time/magazine/article/0,9171,1181646,00.html (accessed Apr. 18, 2008).

12. Christopher B. Swanson, *Cities in Crisis: A Special Analytic Report on High School Graduation* (EPE Research Center with support from America's Promise Alliance and the Bill & Melinda Gates Foundation, Apr. 1, 2008), www.americaspromise.org/uploadedFiles/AmericasPromiseAlliance/Dropout_Crisis/SWANSONCities InCrisis040108.pdf (accessed Apr. 17, 2008).

13. "Report: Many Big City Graduation Rates Below 50%," *CNN.com* (Apr. 1, 2008), www.cnn.com/2008/US/04/01/school.grad.rates.ap/index.html#cnnSTCText (accessed Apr. 9, 2008).

14. Pat Orvis, "A 'Hole in the Wall' Helps Educate India," *Christian Science Monitor* (June 1, 2006), www.csmonitor.com/2006/0601/p13s02-legn.html (accessed Apr. 20, 2008).

15. David W. Gardner, "Taipei Tops Hotspot Survey," *Techweb Network* (June 29, 2006), www.techweb.com/wire/networking/showArticle.jhtml?articleID=189700082 (accessed Apr. 12, 2008).

16. "MIT Figure Struck, Injured in Hanoi," *The Boston Globe, Boston.com* (Dec. 7, 2006), www.boston.com/news/local/articles/2006/12/07/mit_figure_struck_injured_in_hanoi/ (accessed June 29, 2007).

17. Andy Carvin, "Prayers for Papert," *Andy Carvin's Waste of Bandwidth* (Dec. 7, 2006), www.andycarvin.com/archives/2006/12/prayers_for_seymour_papert.html (accessed June 29, 2007).

18. "Seymour Papert," *Wikipedia*, 2007, http://en.wikipedia.org/wiki/Seymour_Papert (accessed June 29, 2007).

19. "Nonscience," *Wikipedia*, 2007, http://en.wikipedia.org/wiki/Nonscience (accessed July 20, 2008).

20. Brian Ford, "Absolute Zeno," *Laboratory News* (Jan. 16, 2007): 16, www .brianjford.com/a-05-ZENO.htm (accessed July 26, 2007).

21. Jay Cross, *Informal Learning Rediscovering Natural Pathways That Inspire Innovation and Performance* (San Francisco: Pfeiffer, 2007).

22. John Ambrose, "On Demand: The Googlization of Learning," *Chief Learning Officer* 7, no. 1 (Jan. 2008): 28–31, www.clomedia.com/features/2008/January/ 2050/index.php (accessed Feb. 21, 2008).

23. Jinger Jarrett, "Are You Googlelized?" *Ezine Articles* (Mar. 2, 2007), http:// ezinearticles.com/?Are-You-Googlelized?&id=480545 (accessed July 25, 2007).

24. Candace Lombardi, "Google Earth Gazes into Space," *USA Today* (Aug. 2007), www.usatoday.com/tech/products/cnet/2007–08–22-google-earth-sky_N.htm (accessed Apr. 13, 2008).

25. Jeffrey R. Young, "Google Plans to Put a Lot More Books Under the Scanner," *Chronicle of Higher Education* 54, no. 27 (Mar. 14, 2008): 13, http://chronicle.com/ wiredcampus/article/2792/google-plans-to-expand-book-scanning-partnerships (accessed Apr. 6, 2008).

26. "Google 'Dominates' World Search," *BBC News* (Oct. 11, 2007), http://news.bbc .co.uk/2/hi/technology/7039114.stm (accessed Oct. 11, 2007).

27. Nicholas Carr, "Is Google Making Us Stupid?" *Atlantic Monthly* (July/Aug. 2008), www.theatlantic.com/doc/200807/google (accessed June 28, 2008).

28. Andrew Orlowski, "Google Founder Dreams of Google Impact in Your Brain," *The Register* (Mar. 2, 2004), www.theregister.co.uk/2004/03/03/google_founder_ dreams_of_google/ (accessed July 25, 2007).

29. Robin Good, "Internet Searching Graduates to Classroom Lecturing Assistant: The Google Jockey," *Robin Good's MasterNewMedia weblog* (May 19, 2006), www .masternewmedia.org/news/2006/05/19/internet_searching_graduates_to_ classroom.htm (accessed Apr. 13, 2008).

30. Dian Schaffhauser, "Google Book Search: The Good, the Bad, and the Ugly," *Campus Technology* 21, no. 5 (Jan. 2008): 32–28, http://campustechnology.com/ articles/57064/ (accessed Apr. 4, 2008).

31. Katie Hafner, "Libraries Shun Deals to Place Books on Web," *New York Times* (Oct. 22, 2007), www.nytimes.com/2007/10/22/technology/22library.html?_r=1& oref=slogin (accessed Apr. 11, 2008).

32. Schaffhauser, "Google Book Search: The Good, the Bad, and the Ugly."

33. Jeffrey R. Young, "A Million Books Scanned at U. of Michigan—and Counting," *Chronicle of Higher Education* (Feb. 4, 2008), http://chronicle.com/wiredcampus/ article/2717/ (accessed Apr. 6, 2008).

34. University Library, University of Michigan, "Million," *University Library, University of Michigan* (2008), www.lib.umich.edu/news/millionth.html (accessed Apr. 6, 2008).

35. Schaffhauser, "Google Book Search: The Good, the Bad, and the Ugly."

36. Barbara Quint, "Search Inside the Book: Full-Text on Amazon," *Information Today* (Nov. 3, 2003), newsbreaks.infotoday.com/nbreader.asp?ArticleID=16587 (accessed July 23, 2007).

37. Elinor Mills, "Amazon, Random House Throw the Book at Google," *CNET News.com* (Nov. 3, 2005), http://news.com.com/Amazon,+Random+House +throw+book+at+Google/2100–1025_3–5931569.html (accessed July 23, 2007).

38. Chief Learning Officer, "SkillSoft's Books24x7 Bolsters Information Access with Chapters to Go," *Chief Learning Officer* (July 18, 2007), www.clomedia.com/ industry_news/2007/July/813/index.php (accessed July 23, 2007).

39. Donald T. Hawkins, "Electronic Books: Reports of Their Death Have Been Exaggerated," *Online* 26, no. 4 (July/Aug. 2002), www.onlinemag.net/jul02/ hawkins.htm (accessed July 23, 2007).

40. Andrea Foster, "Vendor of Educational Materials to Expand E-book Offerings," *Wired Campus: Chronicle of Higher Education* (June 18, 2008), http://chronicle .com/wiredcampus/index.php?id=3098 (accessed June 18, 2008).

41. Andrea L. Foster, "Microsoft's Book Search Project Has a Surprise Ending," *Chronicle of Higher Education* (May 29, 2008), http://chronicle.com/free/2008/05/ 3022n.htm (accessed May 29, 2008).

42. Catherine Rampell, "Microsoft Shuts Book-Digitizing Project," *Wired Campus: Chronicle of Higher Education* (May 23, 2008), http://chronicle.com/wiredcampus/ article/3031/microsoft-shuts-book-digitizing-project?utm_source=at&utm_ medium=en (accessed May 27, 2008).

43. Satya Nadella, "Book Search Winding Down," *Blog: Live Search* (May 23, 2008), http://blogs.msdn.com/livesearch/archive/2008/05/23/book-search-winding-down .aspx (accessed May 27, 2008).

44. Brock Read, "The Open Library Makes Its Online Debut," *Chronicle of Higher Education* (July 19, 2007), http://chronicle.com/wiredcampus/index.php?id=2235 (accessed July 19, 2007).

45. Hafner, "Libraries Shun Deals to Place Books on Web," para. 18.

46. NCSU Libraries News, "TRLN Member Libraries Join Open Content Alliance," *NCSU Libraries Newsletter* 35, no. 8 (Mar. 2008), www.lib.ncsu.edu/publications/NLarchives/NL.vol.35/NL_35_8.pdf (accessed Apr. 10, 2008).

47. Nadella, "Book Search Winding Down."

48. Mills, "Amazon, Random House Throw the Book at Google."

49. Stephanie Olsen, "An Open-Source Rival to Google's Book Project," *CNET News.com* (Oct. 26, 2005), http://news.com.com/An+open-source+rival+to+Googles+book+project/2100–1025_3–5915690.html (accessed July 23, 2007).

50. Joshua Glenn, "Open Library Talk Tomorrow," *Brainiac: Boston.com* (Oct. 22, 2007), www.boston.com/news/globe/ideas/brainiac/2007/10/open_library_ta.html (accessed Apr. 15, 2008).

51. "Aaron Schwartz: A Lifetime of Dubious Accomplishments," *Aaronsw.com* (Apr. 15, 2008), www.aaronsw.com/dubious (accessed Apr. 15, 2008).

52. Andrea Foster, "An Upstart Web Catalog Challenges an Academic-library Giant," *Chronicle of Higher Education* 54, no. 24 (Feb. 22, 2008): A11, http://chronicle.com/weekly/v54/i24/24a01101.htm (accessed Apr. 10, 2008).

53. Scott McLemee, "Open Library," *Inside Higher Education* (Aug. 8, 2007), www.insidehighered.com/views/2007/08/08/mclemee (accessed Apr. 15, 2008).

54. Jay David Bolter, *Writing Space: The Computer, Hypertext, and the History of Writing* (Hillsdale, NJ: Erlbaum, 1991), 1.

55. George P. Landow, "Hypertext and Collaborative Work: The Example of Hypermedia," in *Intellectual Teamwork: Social and Technological Foundations of Cooperative Work*, eds. J. Galegher, R. E. Kraut and C. Egido (Hillsdale, NJ: Erlbaum, 1990).

56. Alexis Garrobo, "No Borders: Global Text Project Digitizes Third World," *Redandblack.com* (Jan. 30, 2007), www.redandblack.com/news/2007/01/30/ (accessed July 10, 2007).

57. Richard T. Watson, "Building the Network," *Global Text Project Weblog* (Apr. 6, 2008), http://globaltextproject.blogspot.com/2008/04/building-network.html (accessed Apr. 8, 2008).

58. Josh Fischman, "Wiring Research to Developing Countries," *Chronicle of Higher Education* (July 12, 2007), http://chronicle.com/wiredcampus/index.php?id=2216?=atwc (accessed July 12, 2007).

59. Svetlana Shkolnikova, "Online 'Textbooks' See College Doors Opening," *USA Today* (July 9, 2008), www.usatoday.com/news/education/2008-07-09-open-textbooks_N.htm (accessed July 13, 2008).

60. Terry Anderson and Fathi Elloumi, eds., *Theory and Practice of Online Learning* (Canada: Athabasca University, 2004), http://cde.athabascau.ca/online_book/ (accessed Apr. 6, 2008).

61. Don Tapscott and Anthony Williams, *Wikinomics: How Mass Collaboration Changes Everything* (New York: Penguin, 2006), 35.

62. Corey Doctorow, "Giving It Away," *Forbes* (Dec. 1, 2006), www.forbes.com/2006/11/30/cory-doctorow-copyright-tech-media_cz_cd_books06_1201doctorow.html (accessed Apr. 8, 2008).

63. "Ender's Game," *Wikipedia*, 2008, http://en.wikipedia.org/wiki/Ender's_Game (accessed July 4, 2008).

64. Tapscott and Williams, *Wikinomics*, 35.

65. Corey Doctorow, "Think Like a Dandelion," *Lotus Magazine* (May 6, 2008), www.locusmag.com/Features/2008/05/cory-doctorow-think-like-dandelion.html (accessed June 10, 2008).

3. E-Demand Around the Globe

1. Jay Cross, *Informal Learning Rediscovering Natural Pathways That Inspire Innovation and Performance* (San Francisco: Pfeiffer, 2007).

2. Jeffrey G. MacDonald, "'Distance Learning' Gets Its Close-Up," USA Today (Nov. 27, 2007), www.usatoday.com/news/education/2007-11-27-distance-learning_N.htm (accessed Apr. 15, 2008).

3. Bizhan Nasseh, *A Brief History of Distance Education* (Muncie, IN: Ball State University, 1997): para. 4, www.seniornet.org/edu/art/history.html (accessed June 28, 2008).

4. Richard Schwier, "New Media in New Devices: The Democratization of Learning," *Rick's Café Canadian: Rick Schwier's Weblog* (June 23, 2004), http://omegageek.net/rickscafe/?p=166 (accessed May 1, 2008).

5. Ivan Illich, *Deschooling Society* (New York: Marion Boyars, 1970).

6. Ibid., para. 1.

7. Ibid., para. 3.

8. Stephen Heppell, "NotSchool.net," *Literacy Today*, 25 (Dec. 2000), www.literacytrust.org.uk/Pubs/heppell.html (accessed May 1, 2008).

9. See ACT Department of Education and Training, "Emerging Technologies—A Framework for Thinking," *Education.au* (2005), www.det.act.gov.au/__data/assets/pdf_file/0019/17830/emergingtechnologies.pdf (accessed June 3, 2008); and The Horizon Report, "The Horizon Report: 2006 Edition," report (A collaboration between The New Media Consortium and the EDUCAUSE Learning Initiative (ELI), an EDUCAUSE program, 2006).

10. Project Tomorrow, "Learning in the 21st Century: A National Report of Online Learning," report (Blackboard, 2008), www.blackboard.com/resources/k12/K-12_Learning_in_the_21st_Century.pdf (accessed Apr. 15, 2008).

11. John Watson and Jennifer Ryan, "Keeping Pace with K–12 Online Learning: A Review of State-Level Policy and Practice," *National Council for Online Learning* (Nov. 2007), www.nacol.org/docs/KeepingPace07-color.pdf (accessed Apr. 15, 2008).

12. Laura Devaney, "Reports Reveal Online Learning's Successes, Needs," *eSchool News* (Nov. 21, 2007), www.eschoolnews.com/news/top-news/?i=50614; _hbguid=6c7e3d93-fda9–41e4–941c-c83e6b4c7793 (accessed Apr. 15, 2008).

13. Kate Moser, "Online Courses Aren't Just for Home-Schoolers Anymore," *Christian Science Monitor* (Mar. 30, 2006), www.csmonitor.com/2006/0330/p14s02-legn.html (accessed Aug. 12, 2006).

14. Michigan Department of Education, "Michigan Merit Curriculum Guidelines: Online Experience," report (Michigan Department of Education, 2008), www.michigan.gov/documents/mde/Online10.06_final_175750_7.pdf (accessed July 2, 2008).

15. Watson and Ryan, "Keeping Pace with K–12 Online Learning."

16. Josh Jarmon, "Institute to Teach Mandarin Chinese: University, China Form Partnership," *The State News* (Apr. 24, 2006), www.statenews.com/article.phtml?pk=36024 (accessed Aug. 13, 2006).

17. Carol Huang, "Why China Wants You to Learn Chinese," *The Christian Science Monitor* (Jan. 4, 2007), www.csmonitor.com/2007/0104/p17s01-legn.html (accessed July 2, 2008).

18. Christine MacDonald, "State Teens Learn Chinese Online," *Detroit News* (May 11, 2006), http://sdkrashen.com/pipermail/krashen_sdkrashen.com/2006-May/000508.html (accessed June 3, 2008).

19. Sarah Harbison, "From Class to Computer: Students Learn Chinese Online," *The State News* (Jan. 18, 2007), www.statenews.com/index.php/article/2007/01/from_class_to_computer (accessed July 2, 2008).

20. Harbison, "From Class to Computer," para. 7.

21. Bill Perry, "At Michigan LearnPort, Teachers Tap Social Networking," *Chief Learning Officer* 7, no. 7 (July 2008): 52–53, www.clomedia.com/case-study/2008/July/2267/index.php?pt=a&aid=2267&start=3597&page=2 (accessed July 13, 2008).

22. "Cement City, Michigan," *Wikipedia*, 2008, http://en.wikipedia.org/wiki/Cement_City,_Michigan (accessed July 13, 2008).

23. Matthew Wells, "Urban Farming Takes Root in Detroit," *BBC News* (July 10, 2008), http://news.bbc.co.uk/1/hi/world/americas/7495717.stm (accessed July 13, 2008).

24. Lee H. Ehman, Curtis J. Bonk, and Lisa Yamagata-Lynch, "A Model of Teacher Professional Development to Support Technology Integration," *AACE Journal* (AACEJ) 13, no. 3 (2005): 251–270.

25. Tiffany Danitz, "Florida's Virtual High School Breaks the Mold," *Stateline.org* (Oct. 8, 1999), www.stateline.org/live/ViewPage.action?siteNodeId=136&languageId=1&contentId=13814 (accessed Apr. 27, 2008).

26. See Robert L. Jacobson, "State-Run Virtual Schools Gather Steam," *eSchoolNews* (Dec. 28, 2007), www.eschoolnews.com/news/showStoryRSS.cfm?ArticleID=7328 (accessed Dec. 28, 2007); and Florida Virtual School, "FLVS Fast Facts," Florida Virtual School (2008), www.flvs.net/educators/fact_sheet.php (accessed Apr. 13, 2008).

27. "Florida Leads Growth in Virtual Schooling," *eSchool News* (Aug. 17, 2007), www.eschoolnews.com/news/showStoryRSS.cfm?ArticleID=7315 (accessed Aug. 20, 2007).

28. Laura Green, "Districts Prepare Full-Time Online K–12 Schools Under New State Law." *Palm Beach Post* (Sep. 28, 2008), www.palmbeachpost.com/state/content/local_news/epaper/2008/09/28/a1a_virtual_school_0929.html (accessed Jan. 8, 2009).

29. Staci Hupp, "Virtual Charter Schools Celebrated and Targeted," *Indianapolis Star* (Mar. 7, 2007), www.k12.com/news/indianapolis_star_in__virtual_charter_schools_celebrated_and_targeted/ (accessed Apr. 13, 2008).

30. See Robert Zemsky and William F. Massy, "Why the E-Learning Boom Went Bust," *Chronicle of Higher Education* (July 9, 2004): B6, http://chronicle.com/weekly/v50/i44/44b00601.htm (accessed June 3, 2008); and Abtar Kaur and Ahmed Ansary, "Developing a Learning Mix for the Open University of Malaysia," in *Handbook of Blended Learning: Global Perspectives, Local Designs*, eds. C. J. Bonk and C. R. Graham (San Francisco: Pfeiffer, 2006), 311–324.

31. See Elaine I. Allen and Jeff Seaman, "Online Nation: Five Years of Growth in Online Learning," report (The Sloan Consortium (Sloan-C), Oct. 2007),

www.sloan-c.org/publications/survey/pdf/online_nation.pdf (accessed Apr. 15, 2008); and Curtis J. Bonk, *The Perfect E-Storm: Emerging Technologies, Enormous Learner Demand, Enhanced Pedagogy, and Erased Budgets* (London: UK: The Observatory on Borderless Higher Education, June 2004); and Curtis J. Bonk and Charles R. Graham, eds., *Handbook of Blended Learning: Global Perspectives, Local Designs* (San Francisco: Pfeiffer, 2006).

32. Bonk and Graham, *Handbook of Blended Learning*.

33. See Mica Schneider, "Distance Learning Closes the Gap," *BusinessWeek Online* (Aug. 19, 2004), www.businessweek.com/bschools/content/aug2004/bs20040819_8201_bs001.htm (accessed June 28, 2008); and Elaine I. Allen and Jeff Seaman, *Entering the Mainstream: The Quality and Extent of Online Education in the United States, 2003 and 2004* (Needham, MA: Sloan-C, 2004), www.sloan-c.org/resources/entering_mainstream.pdf (accessed Dec. 4, 2005).

34. Robert Jablon, "O'Neal Adds MBA to His NBA Title," *SFGate.com* (June 2005), http://sfgate.com/cgi-bin/article.cgi?f=/n/a/2005/06/25/state/n162712D89.dtl (accessed Aug. 13, 2006).

35. "Apollo Group, Inc.," Answers.com, 2008, www.answers.com/topic/apollo-group-inc?cat=biz-fin (accessed June 28, 2008).

36. Goldie Blumenstyk, "President of Apollo Group, Inc. Resigns to Join Competing For-Profit Institution," *Chronicle of Higher Education* (June 26, 2008), http://chronicle.com/daily/2008/06/3567n.htm?rss (accessed June 28, 2008).

37. Chronicle of Higher Education, "U. of Phoenix Draws Big Names to Advisory Panel on New Center on Teaching Adults," *Chronicle of Higher Education* (May 5, 2008), http://chronicle.com/news/article/4436/u-of-phoenix-draws-big-names-to-advisory-panel-on-new-center-on-teaching-adults (accessed June 28, 2008).

38. Goldie Blumenstyk, "For Online Students U. of Phoenix Opens Tutoring and Social Centers," *Chronicle of Higher Education* (June 24, 2008), http://chronicle.com/blogs/architecture/2200/for-online-students-u-of-phoenix-opens-tutoring-and-social-centers (accessed June 28, 2008).

39. See Blumenstyk, "President of Apollo Group, Inc. Resigns to Join Competing For-Profit Institution"; and Bill Breen. "The Hard Life and Restless Mind of America's Education Billionaire," *Fast Company* (Dec.19, 2007), www.fastcompany.com/magazine/68/sperling.html (accessed July 3, 2008).

40. "University of Phoenix," *Wikipedia*, 2008, http://en.wikipedia.org/wiki/University_of_Phoenix#cite_note-16 (accessed June 28, 2008).

41. Ibid.

42. Brian Lindquist, (2006), "Blended Learning at the University of Phoenix," in *Handbook of Blended Learning: Global Perspectives, Local Designs,* eds. C. J. Bonk and C. R. Graham (San Francisco: Pfeiffer, 2006), 223–234.

43. Bonk and Graham, *Handbook of Blended Learning.*

44. Susan Feyder, "The Halo Has a New Name: Capella Tower," *Star Tribune* (Mar. 20, 2008), www.startribune.com/business/16853701.html (accessed May 10, 2008).

45. "List of Tallest Buildings in Minnesota," *Wikipedia,* 2008, http://en.wikipedia.org/wiki/List_of_tallest_buildings_in_Minneapolis (accessed May 10, 2008).

46. Lynn Bronikowski, "Glenn R. Jones: Cable Pioneer Envisions Worldwide University," *AllBusiness.com* (Jan. 1, 2003), www.allbusiness.com/technology/internet-technology/440027–1.html (accessed May 10, 2008).

47. Steve Gorski, "Credits by Cable: The Mind Extension University," *EDUCOM Review* 29, no. 6 (Nov./Dec. 1994), www.educause.edu/pub/er/review/reviewArticles/29626.html (accessed May 10, 2008).

48. Linda Moss, "Discovery Buys Knowledge TV for Health," *Bnet* (June 1999), http://findarticles.com/p/articles/mi_hb4895/is_199906/ai_n17991879 (accessed May 10, 2008).

49. See Glenn R. Jones, *Make All America a School,* 2nd ed. (Englewood, CO: Jones 21st Century, 1991); Glenn R. Jones, *Cyberschools: An Education Renaissance* (Englewood, CO: Jones Digital Century, 1997); and Glenn R. Jones, *Free Market Fusion: How Entrepreneurs and Nonprofits Create 21st Century Success* (Englewood, CO: Jones Digital Century, 1999).

50. Jones, *Cyberschools.*

51. Ibid., xxvii–xxviii.

52. Marlowe Froke, "Glenn Jones Interview," *The Cable Center* (Sep. 1999), www.cablecenter.org/education/library/oralHistoryDetails.cfm?id=125 (accessed May 10, 2008).

53. Froke, "Glenn Jones Interview."

54. Michael R. Young, "Gas Prices Drive Students to Online Courses," *Chronicle of Higher Education* (July 8, 2008): para 5, http://chronicle.com/free/2008/07/3704n.htm (accessed July 13, 2008).

55. Associated Press, "High Gas Prices Fuel Boom in Online Classes," *Technology Review* (July 9, 2008), www.technologyreview.com/Wire/21063/ (accessed July 13, 2008).

56. Larry Abramson, "Online Courses Catch On in U.S. Colleges," *NPR* (Nov. 19, 2007), www.npr.org/templates/story/story.php?storyId=16638700 (accessed Feb. 21, 2008).

57. Jeffrey R. Young, "Minnesota State Colleges Plan to Offer One-Fourth of Credits Online by 2015," *Chronicle of Higher Education* (Nov. 20, 2008), http://chronicle.com/wiredcampus/article/3476/minnesota-state-colleges-plan-to-offer-one-fourth-of-credits-online-by-2015 (accessed Jan. 5, 2009).

58. "Indira Gandhi National Open University," *Wikipedia,* 2008, http://en.wikipedia.org/wiki/Indira_Gandhi_National_Open_University (accessed June 6, 2008).

59. CNNIC, "The 21st Statistical Survey Report on the Internet Development in China," report (China Internet Network Information Center, Jan. 17, 2008), www.cnnic.cn/uploadfiles/pdf/2008/2/29/104126.pdf (accessed Mar. 5, 2008).

60. CNNIC, "The 21st Statistical Survey Report on the Internet Development in China," (China Internet Network Information Center, Jan. 20, 2008), www.cnnic.cn/html/Dir/2008/02/29/4999.htm (accessed Mar. 5, 2008).

61. Ibid.

62. Daokai Ge, "The Practice and Future of Chinese Distance Education (in Chinese)," keynote speech at the International Distance Education Advanced Forum, Beijing, China, Oct. 2007, www.ideaforum.com.cn/english/default.aspx (accessed June 4, 2008).

63. Ibid.

64. Feiyu Kang and Gilsun Song, "E-learning in Higher Education in China: An Overview," in *E-learning in China: Sino-UK Insights into Policy, Pedagogy and Innovation* (in English), ed. H. Spencer-Oatey (Hong Kong: Hong Kong University Press, 2007), 11–32.

65. Ke Zhang, "China's Online Education: Rhetoric and Realities," in *Global Perspectives on E-learning: Rhetoric and Realities,* ed. A. A. Carr-Chellman (Thousand Oaks, CA: Sage, 2005), 21–32.

66. Lan Xue, "Reform and Expansion: Challenges and Opportunities for China's Higher Education System," presentation at Indiana University, Bloomington, IN, Feb. 28, 2008.

67. See China Department of Education, *China Education Yearbook 2007* (in Chinese) (Beijing: Peoples' Education Press. Dec. 2007); and China Department of Education, *The Public Bulletin of Statistics on the Development of Educational Enterprise in China in 2006* (May 2007), www.gov.cn/gzdt/2007–06/08/content_640905.htm (accessed Apr. 28, 2008).

68. "Web Game Provides Rice for Hungry," *BBC News Online* (Nov. 10, 2007), http://news.bbc.co.uk/2/hi/europe/7088447.stm (accessed Feb. 7, 2008).

69. Los Angeles Times, "FreeRice: Giving by Clicking." *Los Angeles Times* (Jan. 19, 2008), www.latimes.com/news/printedition/asection/la-ed-freerice19jan 19,1,2668923.story?ctrack=1&cset=true (accessed Feb. 26, 2009).

70. "FreeRice," *Wikipedia*, 2008, http://en.wikipedia.org/wiki/FreeRice (accessed Feb. 7, 2008).

71. Mike Leonard, "A Grain of Rice: Bloomington Man's Computer Vocab Game Feeding the World," *Herald Times* (Feb. 6, 2008), www.heraldtimesonline.com/ stories/2008/02/06/news.qp-7496993.sto (accessed Feb. 7, 2008).

72. Curtis J. Bonk and Vanessa Paz Dennen, "Teaching on the Web: With a Little Help from My Pedagogical Friends," *Journal of Computing in Higher Education* 11, no. 1 (1999): 3–28.

73. Mary Grush, "Changing the Gold Standard for Instruction: An Education Scholar's View of Teaching, Learning, and Technology Change on Campus," *Campus Technology* 19, no. 10 (June, 2006): 15, www.campus-technology.com/ article.asp?id=18568 (accessed Aug. 13, 2006).

4. It's a Free Software World After All

1. The Economist, "Open Source Business," *The Economist* (Mar. 16, 2006), www .economist.com/business/displaystory.cfm?story_id=5624944 (Accessed Feb. 24, 2009).

2. Chris Anderson, "Free! Why $0.00 Is the Future of Business," *Wired* (Feb. 25, 2008), www.wired.com/print/techbiz/it/magazine/16–03/ff_free (accessed May 27, 2008).

3. Mitch Kapor, "How Is Open Source Special?" *EDUCAUSE Review* 40, no. 2 (2005): 72–73.

4. Richard Stallman, "Why 'Open Source' Misses the Point of Free Software," *GNU Operating System* (2007), www.gnu.org/philosophy/open-source-misses-the-point .html (accessed July 2, 2008).

5. Eric S. Raymond, *The Art of UNIX Programming* (Boston: Addison-Wesley, 1992).

6. Steven Levy, *Hackers: Heroes of the Computer Revolution* (Garden City, NY: Anchor Press/Doubleday, 1984).

7. Steven Weber, *The Success of Open Source* (Cambridge, MA: Harvard University Press, 2004).

8. Richard Stallman, "Serious Bio," *Richard Stallman's Homepage* (2008), www .stallman.org/#serious (accessed June 29, 2008).

9. Richard Stallman, "The GNU Project," *GNU Operating System* (1985), www.gnu .org/gnu/thegnuproject.html (accessed Mar. 3, 2006).

10. Levy, *Hackers*.

11. Richard Stallman, "Initial Announcement," *GNU Operating System* (Sep. 27, 1983), www.gnu.org/gnu/initial-announcement.html (accessed June 29, 2008).

12. GNU Project, "What Is Free Software Foundation?" *GNU Bulletin* 1, no. 3 (June 1987), www.gnu.org/bulletins/bull3.html#SEC1 (accessed July 6, 2008).

13. Free Software Foundation, "The Free Software Definition," *Free Software Foundation* (Nov. 1, 2007): para. 3, www.fsf.org/licensing/essays/free-sw.html (accessed July 6, 2008).

14. Federico Biancuzzi, "RMS: The GNU GPL Is Here to Stay," *ONLamp.com* (Sep. 22, 2005), www.onlamp.com/lpt/a/6222 (accessed June 25, 2007).

15. Lawrence Lessig, "Free, as in Beer," *Wired Magazine* (Sep. 2006), www.wired.com/ wired/archive/14.09/posts.html?pg=6 (accessed June 23, 2007).

16. "The Free Software Definition," *Free Software Foundation* (Nov. 1, 2007), www.fsf .org/licensing/essays/free-sw.html (accessed July 6, 2008).

17. Richard Stallman, "Why Schools Should Exclusively Use Free Software," *GNU Operating System* (2003), www.gnu.org/philosophy/schools.html (accessed July 4, 2008).

18. Stallman, "Why 'Open Source' Misses the Point of Free Software," para. 3.

19. Ibid.

20. FM, "FM Interviews with Linus Torvalds: What Motivates Free Software Developers?" *First Monday* (1998), www.firstmonday.dk/issues/issue3_3/torvalds/ (accessed Mar. 9, 2006).

21. Linus Torvalds, "Linus vs. Tanenbaum," (1992), www.dina.kvl.dk/~abraham/ Linus_vs_Tanenbaum.html (accessed June 29, 2008).

22. Andy Tanenbaum, "Some Notes on the 'Who Wrote Linux' Kerfuffle, Release 1.5," (2004), www.cs.vu.nl/~ast/brown/ (accessed Feb. 25, 2006).

23. FM, "FM Interviews with Linus Torvalds."

24. Ibid., para. 4.

25. Ibid., para. 6.

26. See Guohua Pan and Curtis J. Bonk, "The Emergence of Open-Source Software in China," *International Review of Research in Open and Distance Learning* 8, no. 1 (Mar. 2007), www.irrodl.org/index.php/irrodl/article/view/331/762 (HTML), www.irrodl. org/index.php/irrodl/article/view/331/771 (audio file) (accessed July 16, 2008).

27. See Guohua Pan and Curtis J. Bonk, "A Socio-Cultural Perspective on Free and Open Source Software," *International Journal of Instructional Technology and Distance Learning* 4, no. 4 (Apr. 2007): 3–22, www.itdl.org/Journal/Apr_07/article01.htm (accessed July 16, 2008); Pan and Bonk, "The Emergence of Open-source Software in China"; and Guohua Pan and Curtis J. Bonk, "The Emergence of Open-Source Software in North America," *International Review of Research in Open and Distance Learning* 8, no. 3 (Nov. 2007), www.irrodl.org/index.php/irrodl/article/view/496/938 (HTML), www.irrodl.org/index.php/irrodl/article/view/496/971 (audio file) (accessed July 16, 2008).

28. Weber, *The Success of Open Source*, 47.

29. Gisle Hannemyr, "Technology and Pleasure: Hacking Considered Constructive," *First Monday* 4, no. 2 (1999), www.firstmonday.org/issues/issue4_2/gisle/index.html (accessed Feb. 27, 2006).

30. Hannemyr, "Technology and Pleasure."

31. Pan and Bonk, "A Socio-Cultural Perspective on Free and Open Source Software."

32. "Netscape," *Wikipedia*, 2008, http://en.wikipedia.org/wiki/Netscape_Communications_Corporation (accessed June 29, 2008).

33. Brad Wheeler. "Open Source 2007: How Did This Happen?" *EDUCAUSE Review* 39, no. 4 (2004): 12–27.

34. Kapor, "How Is Open Source Special?" para. 3.

35. Yochai Benkler, *The Wealth of Networks: How Social Production Transforms Markets and Freedom* (New Haven, CT: Yale University Press, 2006), 60.

36. Campus Computing Project, "The 2004 National Survey of Information Technology in U.S. Higher Education: Tech Budgets Get Some Relief, Cautious Support for Open Source Applications," *Campus Computing Project* (Oct. 2004), www.campuscomputing.net/sites/www.campuscomputing.net/files/2004-CCP.pdf (accessed June 28, 2008).

37. Eric Brown, "Is Ning the Next Facebook or MySpace?" *CMS Wire* (Apr. 14, 2008), www.cmswire.com/cms/enterprise-20/is-ning-the-next-facebook-or-myspace-002535.php (accessed June 16, 2008).

38. "Ning," *Wikipedia*, 2008, http://en.wikipedia.org/wiki/Ning (accessed June 16, 2008).

39. Michael Arrington, "Ning, Worth Half a Billion Dollars," *TechCrunch* (Apr. 18, 2008), www.techcrunch.com/2008/04/18/ning-worth-half-a-billion-dollars/ (accessed June 16, 2008).

40. Adam L. Penenberg, "Ning's Infinite Ambition," *Fast Company* (2008), www
.fastcompany.com/magazine/125/nings-infinite-ambition.html (accessed June 16,
2008).

5. MIT in Every Home

1. "MIT to Make Nearly All Course Materials Available Free on the World Wide
Web," *MIT News* (Apr. 4, 2001), http://web.mit.edu/newsoffice/2001/ocw.html
(accessed July 4, 2008).

2. Susan Kinzie, "Colleges Bring Class to Web," *The Journal Gazette* (Jan. 13, 2008),
www.journalgazette.net/apps/pbcs.dll/article?AID=/20080113/FEAT/801130382/
0/FEAT (accessed Apr. 16, 2008).

3. Jeanne C. Meister, "Three Learning Trends to Watch in 2008," *Chief Learning
Officer* 7, no. 1 (Jan. 2008): 54, www.clomedia.com/in-conclusion/jeanne-c-
meister/2008/January/2041/index.php (accessed Feb. 21, 2008).

4. Olaf Resch, "Can You Benefit from Open Course Ware?" *eLearn Magazine* (2007),
www.elearnmag.org/subpage.cfm?section=opinion&article=86–1 (accessed Feb.
21, 2008).

5. "MIT to Make Nearly All Course Materials Available Free on the World Wide
Web," para. 17.

6. "Learn for Free Online," *BBC News* (Sep. 22, 2002): para. 5–6, http://news.bbc
.co.uk/1/hi/technology/2270648.stm (accessed June 25, 2007).

7. Stephen Carson, "2005 Program Evaluation Findings Report—MIT
OpenCourseWare," MIT (June 5, 2006), http://ocw.mit.edu/ans7870/global/
05_Prog_Eval_Report_Final.pdf (accessed Apr. 16, 2008).

8. Carson, "2005 Program Evaluation Findings Report—MIT OpenCourseWare."

9. Ibid.

10. Kinzie, "Colleges Bring Class to Web."

11. Carson, "2005 Program Evaluation Findings Report—MIT OpenCourseWare,"
37.

12. Carson, "2005 Program Evaluation Findings Report—MIT OpenCourseWare."

13. BBC News, "Learn for Free Online," para. 10.

14. Meng-fen Lin and Mimi Miyoung Lee, "E-learning Localized: The Case of the
OOPS Project," in *Globalization in Education: Improving Education Quality Through
Cross-Cultural Dialogue*, ed. A. Edmundson (Hershey, PA: Idea Group, 2006),
168–186.

15. Sally M. Johnstone, "Open Educational Resources Serve the World," *Educause Quarterly* 28, no. 3 (2005): 15–18, www.educause.edu/apps/eq/eqm05/eqm0533 .asp (accessed Nov. 18, 2006).

16. See Meng-fen Lin, "Sharing Knowledge and Building Communities: A Narrative of the Formation, Development and Sustainability of OOPS," (PhD diss., University of Houston, 2006); and Lin and Lee, "E-learning Localized," 168–186.

17. Gavin Phipps, "Turning Fantasy into a Reality That Helps Others: Lucifer Chu's Obscure Interest in Fantasy Novels Ended Up Making Him an Unlikely Millionaire," *Taipei Times* (Mar. 6, 2006): 18, www.taipeitimes.com/News/feat/ archives/2005/03/06/2003225764 (accessed July 16, 2007).

18. See Noam Cohen, "M.I.T. Education in Taiwan, Minus the Degree," *New York Times* (Apr. 2, 2007), www.nytimes.com/2007/04/02/technology/02link.html?_r=1 &oref=slogin (accessed June 8, 2008); and Jeremy Wagstaff, "Free Online College Classes Are Proliferating: Asia Has Embraced the Global Movement to Spread Knowledge," *Wall Street Journal* (Mar. 27, 2008), http://online.wsj.com/article/ SB120664000282069051.html?mod=googlenews_wsj (accessed June 8, 2008).

19. "Opensource Opencourseware Prototype System," *OOPS Web site* (2005), http:// oops.editme.com/ (accessed Dec. 27, 2006).

20. "China Wins Quake Lake Victory," *BBC News* (June 10, 2008), http://news.bbc. co.uk/2/hi/asia-pacific/7445384.stm (accessed June 11, 2008).

21. Kathrin Hille. "Taiwan Shares Quake Lessons with Sichuan," *Financial Times* (June 9, 2008), http://us.ft.com/ftgateway/superpage.ft?news_id=fto 060920081256373940&page=2 (accessed June 11, 2008).

22. Tom Caswell, Shelley Hensen, Marion Jensen, and David Wiley, "Open Educational Resources: Enabling Universal Education," *International Review of Research on Open and Distance Learning* 9, no. 1 (2008), www.irrodl.org/index.php/ irrodl/article/view/469/1001 (accessed Apr. 1, 2008).

23. Kinzie, "Colleges Bring Class to Web."

24. Wagstaff, "Free Online College Classes Are Proliferating."

25. Josh Fischman, "Yale U. Puts Complete Courses Online," *Wired Campus: Chronicle of Higher Education* (Dec. 11, 2007), http://chronicle.com/ wiredcampus/article/2604/yale-u-puts-complete-courses-online (accessed Apr. 19, 2008).

26. Dan Coleman, "India's Answer to M.I.T. Presents Free Courses on YouTube (in English)," *OpenCulture* (2008), www.oculture.com/2008/05/indias_answer_to_ mit_presents_free_courses_on_youtube_in_english.html (accessed May 29, 2008).

27. United Nations General Assembly, "Universal Declaration of Human Rights," *Wikisource* (1948), http://en.wikisource.org/wiki/Universal_Declaration_of_Human_Rights#Article_26 (accessed Apr. 2, 2008).

28. The Open Knowledge Foundation, "The Open Knowledge Foundation: Protecting and Promoting Open Knowledge in a Digital Age," *Open Knowledge Foundation Website* (n.d.): para. 2, www.okfn.org/ (accessed July 31, 2008).

29. Online Education Database, "Skip the Tuition: 100 Free Podcasts from the Best Colleges in the World," *Online Education Database* (Jan. 28, 2008), http://oedb.org/library/beginning-online-learning/skip-the-tuition:-100-free-podcasts-from-the-best-colleges-in-the-world (accessed Apr. 6, 2008).

30. Online Education Database, "Skip the Tuition."

31. Andrea L. Foster, "Will Open-Access Publishing Free Enslaved Academics?" *Wired Campus: Chronicle of Higher Education* (Feb. 22, 2008), http://chronicle.com/wiredcampus/article/2765/will-open-access-publishing-free-enslaved-academics (accessed Feb. 26, 2008).

32. John Willinsky, *The Access Principle: The Case for Open Access to Research and Scholarship* (Cambridge, MA: MIT Press, 2005).

6. Portals for the People

1. Xavier La Canna, "Scientists Post Live Webcam of Giant Squid Thaw," *News.com* (Apr. 29, 2008), http://news.ninemsn.com.au/article.aspx?id=228877 (accessed May 2, 2008).

2. AAP, "Massive Squid to Be Shipped to Museum," *The West Australian* (Mar. 13, 2007), www.thewest.com.au/aapstory.aspx?StoryName=363776 (accessed June 26, 2008).

3. National Geographic, "Video: Colossal Squid Eyes Are the Biggest," *National Geographic News* (Apr. 30, 2008), http://news.nationalgeographic.com/news/2008/04/080430-eye-video-ap.html (accessed July 7, 2008).

4. Ray Lilley, "Colossal Squid Thaw to Be Webcast Live," *Discovery News* (Apr. 29, 2008), http://dsc.discovery.com/news/2008/04/29/colossal-squid.html (accessed May 2, 2008).

5. Dave Hansford, "Colossal Squid Has a Glowing 'Cloaking Device,' Huge Eyes," *National Geographic News* (May 1, 2008), http://news.nationalgeographic.com/news/pf/21812845.html (accessed June 26, 2008).

6. "Colossal Squid," *Wikipedia*, 2008, http://en.wikipedia.org/wiki/Colossal_squid (accessed May 2, 2008).

7. Josh Fischman, "Virtual Museum of African-American History Opens," *Wired Campus: Chronicle of Higher Education* (Oct. 4, 2007), http://chronicle.com/wiredcampus/article/2429/virtual-museum-of-african-american-history-opens (accessed Apr. 19, 2008).

8. Douglas Cruickshank, "Turning Pages into Classroom Gold: Ancient Texts Shine on the Web," *Edutopia* (Apr. 27, 2008), www.edutopia.org/british-library-ancient-texts-online (accessed May 24, 2008).

9. Josh Fischman, "19th-Century Science Online," *Wired Campus: Chronicle of Higher Education* (Dec. 11, 2007), http://chronicle.com/wiredcampus/article/2602/19th-century-science-online (accessed Apr. 19, 2008).

10. Carol Guensburg, "Daring Dozen 2007: Twelve Who Are Reshaping the Future of Education," *Edutopia* (June 2007), www.edutopia.org/daringdozen2007 (accessed Feb. 24, 2008).

11. Linnie Rawlinson, "Throw Away Your School Books: Here Comes Textbook 2.0," *CNN.com* (Nov. 8, 2007), http://edition.cnn.com/2007/TECH/11/08/connexions.learning/ (accessed Nov. 8, 2007).

12. Rawlinson, "Throw Away Your School Books."

13. Grace Rubenstein, "Toss the Traditional Textbook: Revamping the Curriculum," *Edutopia* (Oct. 2006), www.edutopia.org/toss-traditional-textbook (June 26, 2008).

14. Charlene O'Hanlon, "Content, Anyone?" *T.H.E. Journal* 35, no. 5 (May 2008): para. 24 and 26, from www.thejournal.com/articles/22568 (accessed May 26, 2008).

15. Corey Murray, "Curriki Offers New World of Course Content," *eSchool News* (Jan. 5, 2007), www.eschoolnews.com/news/top-news/index.cfm?i=45616&CFID=4093627&CFTOKEN=27950383 (accessed May 26, 2008).

16. Victoria Shannon, "A Group Approach to Teaching Teachers," *International Herald Tribune* (Nov. 25, 2007), www.iht.com/articles/2007/11/25/technology/curriki26.php (accessed May 31, 2008).

7. Making a Contribution

1. Stephen Downes, "E-Learning 2.0," *eLearn Magazine* (2006): para. 1–2, www.elearnmag.org/subpage.cfm?section=articles&article=29–1 (accessed Jan. 23, 2006).

2. John Dewey, "My Pedagogic Creed," *School Journal* 54 (Jan. 1897): 77–80, http://dewey.pragmatism.org/creed.htm (accessed May 30, 2008).

3. Michael Jensen, "The New Metrics of Scholarly Authority," *Chronicle of Higher Education* (June 15, 2007), http://chronicle.com/free/v53/i41/41b00601.htm (accessed June 6, 2007).

4. Downes, "E-Learning 2.0."

5. Yi-Wyn Yen, "YouTube Looks for the Money Clip," *Fortune* (2008), http://techland.blogs.fortune.cnn.com/2008/03/25/youtube-looks-for-the-money-clip/ (accessed June 2, 2008).

6. Yen, "YouTube Looks for the Money Clip."

7. Stephen Downes, "Places to Go: YouTube," *Innovate: Journal of Online Education* (2008), http://innovateonline.info/index.php?view=article&id=633&action= synopsis (June 2, 2008).

8. N'Gai Croal, "The Internet Is the New Sweatshop," *Newsweek* (July 7–14, 2008), www.newsweek.com/id/143740 (accessed July 4, 2008).

9. Yen, "YouTube Looks for the Money Clip."

10. Michael Kleeman, "Point of Disconnect: Internet Traffic and the U.S. Communications Infrastructure," *University of California, San Diego and USC Annenberg Center for Communications* (2007), http://cpe.ucsd.edu/assets/013/6535 .pdf (accessed Sep. 4, 2007).

11. Kleeman, "Point of Disconnect."

12. Bill Sheridan, "Corporate Talent Shortage: Are Colleges to Blame?" *CPA Success* (Mar. 25, 2008), www.cpasuccess.com/2008/03/corporate-talen.html (accessed Apr. 15, 2008).

13. Jeanne C. Meister, "Learning for the Google Generation," *Chief Learning Officer* 7, no. 4 (Apr. 2008), www.clomedia.com/in-conclusion/jeanne-c-meister/2008/ April/2142/index.php (accessed Apr. 14, 2008).

14. Josee Rose, "Recruiters Take Hip Path to Fill Accounting Jobs," *Online Wall Street Journal* (Sep. 16, 2007), http://online.wsj.com/article/SB119006634913930317 .html (accessed Apr. 14, 2008).

15. Malcom Gladwell, *The Tipping Point: How Little Things Make a Big Difference* (New York: Little, Brown, 2000).

16. Ella Powers, "A Lesson in Viral Video," *Inside Higher Ed* (Feb. 7, 2008), http:// insidehighered.com/news/2007/02/07/web (accessed Sep. 6, 2007).

17. David L. Margulius, "Tech Tops the Pop Charts: Music-Video Paean to Web 2.0 Burns Up YouTube, Puts Machines at the Center of Personal Expression," *Info World* (Mar. 15, 2007), www.infoworld.com/article/07/03/15/12OPentinsight_1 .html (accessed Sep. 5, 2007).

18. Jay Cross. *Informal Learning Rediscovering Natural Pathways That Inspire Innovation and Performance* (San Francisco: Pfeiffer, 2007).

19. Don Tapscott, *Grown Up Digital: How the Net Generation Is Changing Your World* (New York: McGraw-Hill, 2009).

20. Battelle, "A Brief Interview with Michael Wesch."

21. Downes, "Places to Go: YouTube."

22. Daily Star Staff, "AUB Launches Dedicated Channel on YouTube," *Daily Star (Lebanon)* (Apr. 18, 2008), www.dailystar.com.lb/article.asp?edition_id=1&categ_id=1&article_id=91149 (accessed Apr. 21, 2008).

23. Laura Devaney, "'Coursecasting' Now a Higher-Education Staple: Universities Increasingly Turning Lectures into Podcasts," *eSchool News* (Dec. 19, 2007), www.eschoolnews.com/news/top-news/?i=51181;_hbguid=0b8af8f9–649b-4696–98c2-f4366bd7aa00 (accessed Apr. 20, 2008).

24. Jeffrey R. Young, "Thanks to YouTube, Professors Are Finding New Audiences," *Chronicle of Higher Education* (Jan. 9, 2008), http://chronicle.com/free/2008/01/1159n.htm (accessed Apr. 9, 2008).

25. Jeffrey R. Young, "'Big Think' Video Site Not Attracting Much Feedback?" *Wired Campus: Chronicle of Higher Education* (Feb. 8, 2008), http://chronicle.com/wiredcampus/article/2730/big-think-video-site-not-attracting-much-feedback (accessed Apr. 10, 2008).

26. Lila Guterman, "Specially Made for Science: Researchers Develop Online Tools for Collaborations," *Chronicle of Higher Education* 54, no. 2 (Feb. 22, 2008): A9, http://chronicle.com/weekly/v54/i24/24a00901.htm (accessed Apr. 10, 2008).

27. Brock Read, "Scientists Get a YouTube of Their Own," *Chronicle.com* (2007), http://chronicle.com/wiredcampus/article/2323/scientists-get-a-youtube-of-their-own (accessed Aug. 31, 2007).

28. "Learning with Sound," *Chronicle of Higher Education* (July 11, 2007), http://chronicle.com/wiredcampus/index.php?id=2215?=atwc (accessed July 11, 2007).

29. Jack Kerouac, *On the Road* (New York: Penguin Books, 1959).

30. Jeff Howe, *Crowdsourcing: Why the Power of the Crowd Is Driving the Future of Business* (New York: Crown Business, 2008).

31. Kwaku Anom, "Offshore Outsourcing Blossoming in Ghana," *Ghana Cyber Group* (Feb. 7, 2007), www.ghanacybergroup.com/articles/getart.asp?MC=ART&cat=2&id=367 (accessed July 20, 2008).

32. "Videoconferencing," *Wikipedia*, 2008, http://en.wikipedia.org/wiki/Videoconferencing (accessed July 12, 2008).

33. Elizabeth Crane, "Global Nomads: At-Risk Students Connect with Peers Worldwide," *Edutopia, The George Lucas Education Foundation* (2006), www.edutopia.org/global-nomads-group-worldwide-videoconferencing (accessed Aug. 31, 2007).

34. Crane, "Global Nomads."

35. Ibid., para. 9.

36. Mimi Miyoung Lee and Deborah S. Hutton, "Using Interactive Videoconferencing Technology for Global Awareness: The Case of ISIS," *International Journal of Instructional Technology and Distance Learning* 4, no. 8 (2007): 3–14, itdl.org/Journal/Aug_07/article01.htm (accessed Apr. 10, 2008).

37. See Mimi Miyoung Lee, "'Going Global': Conceptualization of the 'Other' and Interpretation of Cross-Cultural Experience in an All-White, Rural Learning Environment," *Ethnography and Education* 1, no. 2 (June 2006): 197–213; and Mimi Miyoung Lee, "'Making It Relevant': A Rural Teacher's Integration of an International Studies Program," *Intercultural Education* 18, no. 2 (May 2007): 147–159.

38. Downes, "E-learning 2.0," para. 42.

39. Ibid., para. 43.

40. "Ward Cunningham," *Wikipedia*, 2007, http://en.wikipedia.org/wiki/Ward_Cunningham (accessed June 27, 2007).

41. Chris Anderson, "Jimmy Wales: The (Proud) Amateur Who Created Wikipedia," *Time* (May 8, 2006), www.time.com/time/magazine/article/0,9171,1187286,00.html (accessed June 28, 2007).

42. "Jimmy Wales," *Wikipedia*, 2007, http://en.wikipedia.org/wiki/Jimbo_Wales (accessed June 27, 2007).

43. Wikimedia Foundation, "Wikipedia Hits Milestone of 10 Million Articles Across 250 Languages," *Press Release of the Wikimedia Foundation* (Mar. 28, 2008), http://wikimediafoundation.org/wiki/Press_releases/10M_articles (accessed June 25, 2008).

44. "Wikipedia: About," *Wikipedia*, 2007, http://en.wikipedia.org/wiki/Wikipedia:About (accessed June 27, 2007).

45. Jonathan Dee, "All the News That's Fit to Print Out," *New York Times* (July 1, 2007), www.nytimes.com/2007/07/01/magazine/01WIKIPEDIA-t.html?_r=1&pagewanted=print&oref=slogin (accessed July 7, 2007).

46. "Wikipedia: About," *Wikipedia*, 2007.

47. Dee, "All the News That's Fit to Print Out."

48. Ibid.

49. Andrea Foster, "U. of California Researcher Holds Wikipedia Authors Accountable?" *The Wired Campus: Chronicle of Higher Education* (June 30, 2008), http://chronicle.com/wiredcampus/index.php?id=3127&utm_source=wc &utm_medium=en (accessed July 4, 2008).

50. Jim Giles, "Internet Encyclopaedias Go Head to Head," *Nature*, no. 438 (2005): 900–901, www.nature.com/nature/journal/v438/n7070/full/438900a.html (accessed Dec. 15, 2005).

51. Brock Read, "Middlebury College History Department Limits Students' Use of Wikipedia," *Chronicle of Higher Education* (2007), http://chronicle.com/weekly/ v53/i24/24a03901.htm (accessed July 5, 2007).

52. "Wikipedia: Stable Versions," *Wikipedia*, 2007, http://en.wikipedia.org/wiki/ Wikipedia:Stable_versions (accessed July 5, 2007).

53. Jeffrey R. Young, "Book 2.0: Scholars Turn Monographs into Digital Conversations," *Chronicle of Higher Education* (2006), http://chronicle.com/ weekly/v52/i47/47a02001.htm (accessed Sep. 27, 2006).

54. Toru Iiyoshi and M. S. Vijay Kumar, eds., *Opening Up Education: The Collective Advancement of Education Through Open Technology, Open Content, and Open Knowledge* (Cambridge, MA: MIT Press, 2008).

55. Yochai Benkler, *The Wealth of Networks: How Social Production Transforms Markets and Freedom* (New Haven, CT: Yale University Press, 2006).

56. Matt Marshall, "Scribd, the 'YouTube for Documents,' Copyright Violations," *Venture Beat* (Mar. 28, 2007), http://venturebeat.com/2007/03/28/scribd-the-youtube-for-documents-copyright-violations-and-all/ (accessed Feb. 26, 2008).

57. Dewey, "My Pedagogic Creed."

58. TMC News, "Scribd Secures $9 Million in Series B Financing, Bebo COO George Consagra Joins as President," *TMC News* (Dec. 19, 2008), www.tmcnet.com/ usubmit/2008/12/19/3868617.htm (accessed Jan. 4, 2009).

59. Benkler, *The Wealth of Networks*, 272.

8. Collaborate or Die

1. Don Tapscott and Anthony Williams, *Wikinomics: How Mass Collaboration Changes Everything* (New York: Penguin, 2006).

2. Diana Rhoten, "The Dawn of Networked Science," *Chronicle of Higher Education* 54, no. 2 (Sep. 7, 2007): B12, http://chronicle.com/weekly/v54/i02/02b01201.htm (accessed May 1, 2008).

3. Tapscott and Williams, *Wikinomics*, 31.

4. Ibid.

5. Reuters, "Skype Unveils 'SkypeCasting' Conference Calls," *PCMag.com* (May 3, 2006), www.pcmag.com/article2/0,1895,1956926,00.asp (accessed May 14, 2006).

6. Anick Jesdanun, "Disney Acquires Club Penguin for $350M," *Washington Post.com* (Aug. 2, 2007), www.washingtonpost.com/wp-dyn/content/article/2007/08/01/AR2007080101718.html?nav=rss_technology (accessed Sep. 8, 2007).

7. Stephanie Olsen, "What Kids Learn in Virtual Worlds," *CnetNews.com* (Nov. 15, 2007), www.news.com/What-kids-learn-in-virtual-worlds/2009-1043_3-6218763.html (accessed Apr. 26, 2008).

8. Andrew Yu, *Blog Post* (Apr. 2004), http://1kgweb.blogbus.com/logs/2005/04/1109333.html (accessed Feb. 22, 2008).

9. Andrew Yu, *Blog Post* (May 2005), http://1kgweb.blogbus.com/logs/2005/09/1468870.html (accessed Feb. 22, 2008).

10. Douglas Cruickshank, "Edwin Gragert: Bridging Borders, Both Real and Imagined," *Edutopia* (2008), www.edutopia.org/edwin-gragert (accessed May 31, 2008).

11. Steve Lohr, "A Capitalist Jolt for Charity," *New York Times* (Feb. 24, 2008), www.nytimes.com/2008/02/24/business/24social.html?_r=1&oref=slogin (accessed June 14, 2008).

12. eSchool News, "See Science in Action at the South Pole Through These Live (and Archived) Webcasts," *eSchool News* (Jan. 2, 2008), www.eschoolnews.com/news/site-of-the-week/site/index.cfm?i=51354;_hbguid=a9d5d040-8d6d-4eb6-89c7-75e426c9da15 (accessed May 28, 2008).

13. Anders Bylund, "Google's Writely Reopened for Public Access," *Ars Technica* (Aug. 18, 2006), http://arstechnica.com/news.ars/post/20060818-7542.html (accessed Apr. 4, 2008).

14. Josh Fishman, "Microsoft Opens Free Workplace for Student Collaboration," *Chronicle of Higher Education* (Mar. 5, 2008), http://chronicle.com/wired campus/index.php?id=2795&utm_source=wc&utm_medium=en (accessed Apr. 4, 2008).

15. Dian Schaffhauser, "Click Here to Chat Live," *Campus Technology* 21, no. 7 (Mar. 2008): 24, 26–27, http://campustechnology.com/articles/58853/ (accessed Apr. 10, 2008).

9. Who Are You?

1. Michel Marriott, "We Have to Operate, but Let's Play First," *New York Times* (Feb. 24, 2005), www.nytimes.com/2005/02/24/technology/circuits/24docs.html (accessed Apr. 28, 2008).

2. Jonathan Fanton, "New Generations, New Media Challenges," *St. Louis Post-Dispatch* (June 19, 2007), www.macfound.org/site/apps/nlnet/content2.aspx?c= lkLXJ8MQKrH&b=1137397&ct=3970699 (accessed June 3, 2008).

3. Tom Krazit, "Dell Sets Up 'Second Life' Shop, Offers PCs to Residents," *ZDNews .com* (Nov. 14, 2006), http://news.zdnet.com/2100–9595_22–6135497.html (accessed Apr. 26, 2008).

4. Stephen Shankland, "IBM to Give Birth to 'Second Life' Business Group," *CNET News.com* (Dec. 12, 2006), http://earthlink.com.com/IBM+to+give+birth+to +Second+Life+business+group/2100–1014_3–6143175.html (accessed Apr. 26, 2008).

5. Martin LaMonica, "IBM's Chief Steps into 'Second Life' for Incubator Launch," *CNET News.com* (Nov. 13, 2006), http://earthlink.com.com/IBMs-chief-steps-into-Second-Life-for-incubator-launch/2100–1014_3–6135109.html (accessed Apr. 26, 2008).

6. Stephen Hutcheon, "Workers Shape Up for Big Blue with IBM," *The Sydney Morning Herald* (Sep. 19, 2007), www.smh.com.au/news/web/ibm-workers-to-walk-out-in-second-life/2007/09/19/1189881553044.html (accessed Apr. 26, 2008).

7. Steve O'Hear, "IBM Workers Strike in Second Life; Twitter Keyword Alert Goes Live; Google Buys Mobile Zingku; Facebook Bubble?" *The Social Web* (Sep. 28, 2007), http://blogs.zdnet.com/social/?p=316 (accessed Apr. 26, 2008).

8. Mitch Wagner, "Virtual Worlds Getting Friendlier for Businesses," *InformationWeek* (Apr. 3, 2008), www.informationweek.com/news/personal_tech/ virtualworlds/showArticle.jhtml;jsessionid=VBRNNRUPK5FQ4QSNDLPCKH SCJUNN2JVN?articleID=207001420&_requestid=8991 (accessed July 4, 2008).

9. Wagner, "Virtual Worlds Getting Friendlier for Businesses," para. 12.

10. Christopher Dawson, "Harvard Prof Holds Law Class in the Virtual World of Second Life," *ZDNet Education* (Sep. 28, 2006), http://education.zdnet.com/? p=548 (accessed Apr. 26, 2008).

11. Rebecca Nesson and Charles Nesson, "In the Virtual Classroom: An Ethnographic Argument for Education in Virtual Worlds," *Space and Culture* (in press), www.eecs.harvard.edu/~nesson/ed-vw-1.3.pdf (accessed Apr. 27, 2008).

12. eSchool News, "Instructors Get Help Teaching in Second Life: Georgia State to Create Island in Second Life That Offers Guidance on Virtual Instruction," *eSchool News* (Dec. 6, 2007), www.eschoolnews.com/news/top-news/?i=50934 (accessed Apr. 26, 2008).

13. Catherine Price, "Sex Ed in Second Life: Could a Virtual Island Teach Students About Real-World Sex?" *Salon.com* (July 31, 2007), www.salon.com/mwt/broadsheet/2007/07/31/sex_in_second_life/print.html (accessed Apr. 26, 2008).

14. D. C. Spensley, "Full Immersion Hyperformalism by DC Spensley 8/07 to 4/08," *Blog: Dan Coyote* (Sep. 13, 2007), www.dancoyote.com/?p=29 (accessed Apr. 26, 2008).

15. Mike Musgrove, "The New Political Games Make a Point," *Washington Post.com* (June 10, 2007), www.washingtonpost.com/wp-dyn/content/article/2007/06/09/AR2007060900049.html (accessed Apr. 26, 2008).

16. William Sims Bainbridge, "The Scientific Research Potential of Virtual Worlds," *Science* 317, no. 5837 (July 2007): 472–476, www.sciencemag.org/cgi/content/abstract/317/5837/472 (accessed June 26, 2008).

17. Cisco, "Coventry University Creates a Unique Mobile Learning Environment in Its Serious Games Institute: Students to Synchronize Their Real-life Locations in a Virtual Campus with Cisco and Giunti Labs' Technology," *Cisco Systems, Inc.* (Nov. 28, 2007), http://newsroom.cisco.com/dlls/2007/prod_112807b.html (accessed Apr. 27, 2008).

18. eSchool News, "MacArthur to Invest $50 M in Digital Learning: Five-year Research Project to Explore the Impact of Digital Learning on Youth," *eSchool News* (Oct. 20, 2006), www.eschoolnews.com/news/top-news/index.cfm?i=41374&CFID= 818938&CFTOKEN=57205032 (accessed Apr. 20, 2008).

19. Colleen Long, "NY School Opens for Serious Games," *Boston.com* (Dec. 13, 2007), www.boston.com/business/technology/articles/2007/12/13/ny_school_opens_lab_for_serious_games/ (accessed Apr. 26, 2008).

20. Aili McConnon, "The MacArthur Foundation's Digital Drive," *BusinessWeek* (Nov. 7, 2006), www.businessweek.com/innovate/content/nov2006/id20061107_359889.htm (accessed June 30, 2007).

21. Byron Reeves, Thomas M. Malone, and Tony O'Driscoll, "Leadership Games Online," *Harvard Business Review* (May 2008), http://custom.hbsp.com/b02/en/implicit/viewFileNavBeanImplicit.jhtml?_requestid=9765 (accessed July 8, 2008).

22. Robin Wilson, "A Greenspan for Gamers," *Chronicle of Higher Education* (July 3, 2007), http://chronicle.com/wiredcampus/index.php?id=2199?=atwc (accessed July 6, 2007).

23. Curtis Bonk and Vanessa Paz Dennen, "Massive Multiplayer Online Gaming: A Research Framework for Military Education and Training," technical report #2005–1, (Washington, DC: U.S. Department of Defense (DUSD/R), Advanced Distributed Learning (ADL) Initiative), http://mypage.iu.edu/~cjbonk/GameReport_Bonk_final.pdf or from the ADL lab: http://adlcommunity.net/file.php/23/GrooveFiles/GameReport_Bonk_final.pdf (accessed July 18, 2008).

24. Reeves, Malone, and O'Driscoll, "Leadership Games Online."

25. John Kirriemuir, "Video Gaming, Education and Digital Learning Technologies," *D-Lib* 8, no. 2 (Feb. 2002), www.dlib.org/dlib/february02/kirriemuir/02kirriemuir.html (accessed Apr. 10, 2004).

26. Mike Snider, "Where Movies End, Games Begin," *USA Today* (May 23, 2002), www.usatoday.com/tech/techreviews/2002/5/23/e3.htm (accessed May 14, 2002).

27. See J. C. Herz and Michael R. Macedonia, "Computer Games and the Military: Two Views," *Defense Horizons* 11 (Apr. 2002), www.ndu.edu/inss/DefHor/DH11/DH11.htm (accessed May 3, 2004); and Kevin Delaney, "Are Videogames Ready to Be Taken Seriously by Media Reviewers?" *GameGirlAdvance Weblog and Online Journal: Wall Street Journal* (Nov. 3, 2003): B1, www.gamegirladvance.com/archives/2003/11/03/the_wsj_gets_it.html (accessed May 20, 2004).

28. Seeking Alpha, "The Video Game Industry: An $18 Billion Entertainment Juggernaut," *Seeking Alpha* (Aug. 5, 2008), from http://seekingalpha.com/article/89124-the-video-game-industry-an-18-billion-entertainment-juggernaut (accessed Jan. 10, 2009).

29. Kirriemuir, "Video Gaming, Education and Digital Learning Technologies."

30. Amanda Lenhart, Lee Rainie, and Oliver Lewis, "Teenage Life Online," report (Pew Internet and American Life Project, 2001), www.pewinternet.org/reports/toc.asp?Report=36 (accessed Apr. 10, 2004).

31. "Industry Facts," *Entertainment Software Association* (2008), www.theesa.com/facts/index.asp (accessed July 4, 2008).

32. See Steve Jones, "Let the Games Begin: Gaming Technology and Edutainment Among College Students," report (Pew Internet and American Life Project, 2003), www.pewinternet.org/reports/toc.asp?Report=93 (accessed Apr. 10, 2004); and Amanda Lenhart, Joseph Kahne, Ellen Middaugh, Alexandra Rankin Macgill, Chris Evans, and Jessica Vitak, "Teens, Video Games, and Civics," report (Pew Internet and American Life Project, Sep. 16, 2008), www.pewinternet.org/pdfs/PIP_Teens_Games_and_Civics_Report_FINAL.pdf (accessed Sep. 21, 2008).

33. Nicolas Ducheneaut and Robert J. Moore, "The Social Side of Gaming: A Study of Interaction Patterns in a Massively Multiplayer Online Game," proceedings of the 2004 ACM conference on Computer Supportive Cooperative Work, 2004, 360–369.

34. Andrea L. Foster, "Thought-Controlled Avatars Emerge in Second Life," *Wired Campus: Online Chronicle of Higher Education* (Oct. 15, 2007), http://chronicle.com/wiredcampus/article/2454/thought-controlled-avatars-emerge-in-second-life (accessed Apr. 26, 2008).

35. Erica Naone, "Moving Freely Between Virtual Worlds," *Technology Review* (Oct. 29, 2007), www.technologyreview.com/Infotech/19629/ (accessed Apr. 26, 2008).

36. Cade Metz, "Second Life Will Dwarf the Web in Ten Years," *The Register* (Aug. 1, 2007): para. 1, www.theregister.co.uk/2007/08/01/second_life_to_dwarf_web_in_ten_years/ (accessed Apr. 26, 2008).

37. Brad Stone, "Google Introduces a Cartoonlike Method for Talking in Chat Rooms," *New York Times* (July 9, 2008), www.nytimes.com/2008/07/09/technology/09google.html?ex=1216267200&en=68ad9e88cd355b9b&ei=5070 (accessed July 13, 2008).

10. U-Learning?

1. Cathie Norris and Elliot Soloway, "Get Cell Phones into Schools," *BusinessWeek* (Jan. 14, 2009), www.businessweek.com/technology/content/jan2009/tc20090114_741903.htm (accessed Jan. 15, 2009).

2. Michael Winter, "Soldier Saved by an iPod," *USA Today* (Apr. 4, 2007), http://blogs.usatoday.com/ondeadline/2007/04/soldier_saved_b.html and www.flickr.com/photos/tiki/445618364/in/pool-20083316@N00/ (accessed Apr. 20, 2008).

3. Sharon Weinberger, "Taser Goes Leopard Print, Plays Music," *Wired* (Jan. 7, 2008), http://blog.wired.com/defense/2008/01/taser-goes-leap.html (accessed May 3, 2008).

4. Susan Stellin, "On the Job, Everywhere," *New York Times* (Nov. 20, 2007), www.nytimes.com/2007/11/20/business/20laptop.html (accessed Apr. 16, 2008).

5. Zaib Kaleem, "Airplane WiFi Wireless Internet," *WLAN Book* (Dec. 17, 2008), www.wlanbook.com/airplane-wifi-wireless-internet/ (accessed Jan. 10, 2009).

6. Roger Yu, "Fliers with iPods May Soon Be Able to Plug In," *USA Today* (Nov. 15, 2006), www.usatoday.com/tech/products/services/2006-11-14-ipod-planes_x.htm (accessed Apr. 20, 2008).

7. Roger Yu, "Business Travelers Lighten Up on Tech," *USA Today* (June 19, 2008): 5B, www.usatoday.com/travel/news/2008-06-18-mobile-computing-travel-baggage-ultralight_N.htm?csp=34 (accessed June 19, 2008).

8. David Pogue, "Camcorder Brings Zen to the Shoot," *New York Times* (Mar. 20, 2008), www.nytimes.com/2008/03/20/technology/personaltech/20pogue.html?_r= 1&oref=slogin (accessed June 19, 2008).

9. Elliott Masie, "507—Chumby—Viewable Information and Support Device," *Learning TRENDS* (Mar. 5, 2008), http://trends.masie.com/archives/2008/3/6/507-chumby-viewable-info-and-support-device.html (accessed Apr. 6, 2008).

10. Keith Shaw, "Prepare for the SAT on an iPod," *Networkworld* (June 21, 2007), www.networkworld.com/community/?q=node/16575 (accessed July 2, 2007).

11. Bruce Meyerson, "Schools Crack Down on Cellphones," *MSNBC* (Sep. 19, 2006), www.msnbc.msn.com/id/14912068/ (accessed Apr. 19, 2008).

12. Thomas L. Friedman, *The World Is Flat: A Brief History of the Twenty-First Century* (New York: Farrar, Straus & Giroux, 2005), 184.

13. Jim McKay, "For the 'Zippies,' Life Is Good: High-Tech Workers Forge Lifestyles Very Different from Their Parents," *Pittsburgh Post-Gazette* (Mar. 21, 2004), www .post-gazette.com/pg/04081/288432.stm (accessed July 3, 2007).

14. Don Tapscott, *Grown Up Digital: How the Net Generation Is Changing Your World* (New York: McGraw-Hill, 2009).

15. "Reaching More Customers with Simple Text Message," *New York Times* (July 16, 2007), www.nytimes.com/2007/07/16/business/media/16ecom.html?ex= 1342238400&en=6d5ee743c2b85589&ei=5088&partner=rssnyt&emc=rss (accessed July 17, 2008).

16. See Reuters, "Global Cellphone Penetration Reaches 50 Pct," *Reuters UK* (Nov. 29, 2007), http://investing.reuters.co.uk/news/articleinvesting.aspx? type=media&storyID=nL29172095 (accessed Feb. 21, 2008); and Leslie Cauley, "Are Google, Yahoo the Next Dinosaurs?" *USA Today* (June 10, 2008): 1B, http:// news.yahoo.com/s/usatoday/20080610/tc_usatoday/aregoogleyahoothenextdino saurs (accessed June 2008).

17. Jim Dalrymple, "Analysis: iPhone Arrives Friday to Huge Expectations," *Macworld* (June 29, 2007), www.macworld.com/news/2007/06/29/iphonearrival/index.php? lsrc=mwrss (accessed July 3, 2007).

18. Elliott Masie, "Special 5 Minute Video Report: iPhones and Learning," *Learning TRENDS* (July 2, 2007), www.learning2007.com/iphone1 (accessed July 2, 2007).

19. Edward C. Baig, "Third-Generation iPhone Picks Up Speed," *USA Today* (June 10, 2008): 3B, www.usatoday.com/tech/columnist/edwardbaig/2008–06–09-iphone_N.htm (accessed June 10, 2008).

20. Steven Levy, "Dialing into the Future," *Newsweek* (June 9, 2008), www.newsweek .com/id/140786 (accessed June 10, 2008).

21. Jefferson Graham, "Let the iPhone Hype Begin Again," *USA Today* (June 10, 2008): 1B, http://usatoday.com/tech/wireless/phones/2008–06–09-iphone-3g_N .htm?imw=Y (accessed June 10, 2008).

22. Thomas P. Walron, "iPhone Reaps 6.9 million," *Bright Hub* (Dec. 9, 2008), www .brighthub.com/mobile/iphone/articles/18589.aspx (accessed Jan. 10, 2009).

23. Edward C. Baig, "iPhone 3G: Still Not Perfect, but Really Close," *USA Today* (July 9, 2008): 3B, www.usatoday.com/tech/columnist/edwardbaig/2008–07–08-iphone-3g-review_N.htm (accessed July 9, 2008).

24. Cauley, "Are Google, Yahoo the Next Dinosaurs?"

25. Clive Thompson, "Clive Thompson on How Twitter Creates a Social Sixth Sense," *Wired Magazine* 15, no. 7 (June 26, 2007), www.wired.com/techbiz/media/ magazine/15–07/st_thompson# (accessed July 12, 2007).

26. "Teaching with Twitter," *Chronicle of Higher Education* (2008), http://chronicle .com/media/video/v54/i25/twitter/ (accessed July 4, 2008).

27. Jeffrey R. Young, "Forget E-mail: New Messaging Service Has Students and Professors Atwitter," *Chronicle of Higher Education* 54, no. 25 (Feb. 29, 2008): A15, http://chronicle.com/free/v54/i25/25a01501.htm (accessed Feb. 26, 2008).

28. Young, "Forget E-mail."

29. Edward C. Baig, "Livescribe Pulse Digital Pen Brings Your Notes to Life," *USA Today* (May 7, 2008), www.usatoday.com/tech/columnist/edwardbaig/2008–05–07-smartpen-livescribe-pulse_N.htm (accessed May 28, 2008).

30. Miguel Helft, "Take Note: Computing Takes Up Pen, Again," *New York Times* (May 30, 2007): para. 20, www.nytimes.com/2007/05/30/technology/30pen .html?_r=1&scp=1&sq=livescribe&st=nyt&oref=slogin (accessed Feb. 8, 2008).

31. Rama Ramaswami, "Fill'er Up!" *T.H.E. Journal*, 35, no. 5 (May 2008): 33–34, 36, www.thejournal.com/articles/22571 (accessed May 26, 2008).

32. Gail Salaway and Judith Borrenson Caruso with Mark R. Nelson, "The ECAR Study of Undergraduate Students and Information Technology, 2007," (EDUCAUSE Center for Applied Research, Boulder, Colorado, 2007), www .educause.edu/ir/library/pdf/ers0706/rs/ERS0706w.pdf (accessed Apr. 19, 2007).

33. Chronicle of Higher Education, "Freshmen Arrive Bearing Gadgets and Great Expectations," *Chronicle of Higher Education* 55, no. 5 (Sep. 22, 2006): A30, http:// chronicle.com/weekly/v53/i05/05a03001.htm (accessed Nov. 20, 2006).

34. Edward C. Baig, "Analysis: Apple's Skinny MacBook Air Is Fat with Features," *USA Today* (Jan. 15, 2008), www.usatoday.com/tech/products/2008–01–15-macworld_N.htm (accessed Apr. 11, 2008).

35. Alexis Madrigal, "Terabyte Thumb Drives Made Possible by Nanotech Memory," *Wired* (Oct. 26, 2007), www.wired.com/gadgets/miscellaneous/news/2007/10/ion_memory (accessed Apr. 11, 2008).

36. Kevin Bullis, "Terabyte Storage for Cell Phones," *Technology Review* (Oct. 31, 2007), www.technologyreview.com/Nanotech/19643/ (accessed Apr. 12, 2008).

37. Dan Carnevale, "Email Is for Old People: As Students Ignore Their Campus Accounts, Colleges Try New Ways of Communicating," *Chronicle of Higher Education* 53, no. 7 (Oct. 5, 2006): A27, http://chronicle.com/free/v53/i07/07a02701.htm (accessed Nov. 20, 2006).

38. Tapscott, *Grown Up Digital*.

39. Candace Lombardi, "Penn State Offers Mobile News Service," *USA Today* (Aug. 16, 2006), www.usatoday.com/tech/products/cnet/2006–08–16-penn-st-text_x.htm (accessed Nov. 20, 2006).

40. Ashley Fantz and Jeanne Meserve, "Witness Survives by Pretending to Be Dead," *CNN.com* (Apr. 17, 2007), www.cnn.com/2007/US/04/16/vtech.shooting/index.html (accessed July 3, 2007).

41. Mark Owczarski, "University Agreement to Significantly Expand Campus Emergency Notification Systems," *Virginia Tech News* (June 21, 2007), www.vtnews.vt.edu/story.php?relyear=2007&itemno=363 (accessed July 10, 2007).

42. Campus Technology, "News Update: Stanford Debuts Wiki of All Things Stanford," *Campus Technology* (Oct. 10, 2006), http://campustechnology.com/news_article.asp?id=19384&typeid=150 (accessed Feb. 2, 2007).

43. ACU, "A Vision of Convergence in Higher Ed," *Abilene Christian University* (2008), www.acu.edu/technology/mobilelearning/index.htm (accessed Feb. 28, 2008); and Jeffrey R. Young. "Abilene U. to Give iPhones or iPods to All Freshman," *Chronicle of Higher Education* (Feb. 28, 2008), http://chronicle.com/wiredcampus/article/2782/university-to-give-iphones-or-ipods-to-all-incoming-freshmen?utm_source=at&utm_medium=en (accessed Feb. 28, 2008).

44. Jeffrey R. Young, "Another University to Give Away iPhones or iPods," *Chronicle of Higher Education* (Mar. 5, 2008), http://chronicle.com/wiredcampus/article/2796/another-university-to-give-away-iphones-or-ipods (accessed Apr. 5, 2008).

45. CBC News, "Text-Message Course Helping Newcomers Learn English," *CBC News* (Feb. 8, 2007), www.cbc.ca/canada/edmonton/story/2007/02/09/text-classes.html?ref=rss (accessed Apr. 19, 2008).

46. Howard Rheingold, *Smart Mobs: The Next Social Revolution* (Cambridge, MA: Basic Books, 2003).

47. Dan Balaban, "Japan's JR East Opens Up Mobile Ticketing Service After Disappointing Year," *Card Technology* (2007), www.cardtechnology.com/article .html?id=20070306FXK3K1E2 (accessed Apr. 30, 2008).

48. Associated Press, "Next Hot Trends for Cell Phones: Reading?" *MSNBC* (Mar. 18, 2005), www.msnbc.msn.com/id/7232995/wid/11915829 (accessed Apr. 19, 2008).

49. Sheila Franklin, "Sony Unveils Bendable Screens," *Gear Live* (May 28, 2007), www.gearlive.com/news/article/q107-sony-bendable-screens/ (accessed Apr. 30, 2008).

50. Yuri Kageyama, "Cell Phone College Class Opens in Japan," *USA Today* (Nov. 28, 2007), www.usatoday.com/tech/wireless/phones/2007–11–28-cellphone-college-japan_N.htm (accessed June 26, 2008).

51. Pete Cashmore, "Mixi, Japan's Biggest Social Network," *Mashable* (July 8, 2006), http://mashable.com/2006/07/08/mixi-japans-biggest-social-network/ (accessed Apr. 29, 2008).

52. "Mixi," *Wikipedia*, 2008, http://en.wikipedia.org/wiki/Mixi (accessed Apr. 29, 2008).

53. Yayoi Anzai, "Empowering English Learning by Utilizing Podcasts," *Proceedings of E-Learn 2007 World Conference on E-learning in Corporations, Government, Healthcare & Higher Education*, (Quebec City, 2007), 10–15.

54. Yayoi Anzai, "Web 2.0 and English Education—University Students' Created Podcasts," paper presented at the annual meeting of Kanto Chapter of Japan Association for Language Education and Technology (LET, 2008).

55. Emily Ng, "Mobile Wallet," *Mobile World* (Jan. 9, 2007), www.mobileworld.com .my/v1/content/view/219/62/ (accessed May 28, 2008).

56. Martin Fackler, "In Korea, a Boot Camp Cure for Web Obsession," *New York Times* (Nov. 16, 2007), www.nytimes.com/2007/11/18/technology/18rehab .html?_r=1&oref=slogin (accessed Apr. 3, 2008).

57. Jaz Hee-jeong Choi, Marcus Forth, and Greg Hearn, "Site Specific Mobility and Connection in Korea: Bangs in Between Public and Private," *Technology in Society* (in press), http://eprints.qut.edu.au/archive/00013004/01/13004.pdf (accessed Apr. 4, 2008).

58. International Telecommunications Union, "World Information Society Report. Chapter Three: The Digital Opportunity Index (DOI)," *Geneva: International Telecommunication Union* (2006), www.itu.int/ITU-D/ict/doi/material/WISR07-chapter3.pdf (accessed Apr. 4, 2008).

59. "The World Internet Users," *Internet Statistics Information System* (2007), http://isis.nida.or.kr/eng/ (accessed Apr. 15, 2008).

60. Korea.net, "Digital Textbook to Debut in 2008," *Korea.net* (Mar. 8, 2007), www.korea.net/news/news/newsview.asp?serial_no=20070308026 (accessed Apr. 4, 2008).

61. Associated Press, "S. Korea Wants People in 'Smart' Clothes," *USA Today* (Aug. 16, 2006), www.usatoday.com/tech/products/gear/2006–08–16-smart-clothes_x .htm (accessed Apr. 4, 2008).

62. Jin-seo Cho, "U-learning in Palm of Hand." *The Korea Times* (July 17, 2006), http://times.hankooki.com/lpage/biz/200607/kt2006071718464311910.htm (accessed Nov. 20, 2006).

63. Choi, "Approaching the Mobile Culture of East Asia."

64. Hyun-oh Yoo, "Cyworld Storm Heads for Asian Countries," *The Korea Times* (Feb. 23, 2005), http://times.hankooki.com/lpage/special/200502/ kt2005022320383545250.htm (accessed July 24, 2005).

65. Yoo, "Cyworld Storm Heads for Asian Countries."

66. See Jin-seo Cho, "Cyworld Members Reach 20 Mil," *The Korea Times* (Feb. 5, 2007), http://search.hankooki.com/times/times_view.php?term=cyworld+ +&path=hankooki3/times/lpage/tech/200702/kt2007020519364411810. htm&media=kt (accessed Apr. 15, 2008); and "The World Factbook: Korea, South," *Central Intelligence Agency* (2007), https://www.cia.gov/library/ publications/the-world-factbook/geos/ks.html (accessed Apr. 4, 2008).

67. Jaz Hee-jeong Choi, "Living in *Cyworld*: Contextualising Cy-ties in South Korea," in *Uses of Blogs*, eds. Axel Bruns and Joanne Jacobs (New York: Peter Lang, 2006): 173–186, www.nicemustard.com/files/jaz_c_cyworld_ch.pdf (accessed Apr. 3, 2008).

68. Agnes Kukulska-Hulme and John Traxler, *Mobile Learning: A Handbook for Educators and Trainers* (London and New York: Routledge, 2005).

69. Thea Payome, "Making Good Use of Mobile Phone Capabilities. Interview with John Traxler," E-learning Africa Conference, 2007, www.elearning-africa.com/ newsportal/english/news70_print.php (accessed Apr. 20, 2008).

70. John Traxler, "Mobile Learning in 'Developing' Countries—Not Too Different," *Vodaphone Receiver* (2008), www.receiver.vodafone.com/mobile-learning-in-developing-countries (accessed July 9, 2008).

71. UNDP, *Human Development Report 2004: Cultural Liberty in Today's World* (New York: United Nations Development Programme, 2004), http://hdr.undp.org/en/ media/hdr04_complete.pdf (accessed June 14, 2008).

72. Paul Kim, Miranda Talia, and Claudia Olaciregui, "Pocket School: Exploring Mobile Technology as a Sustainable Literacy Education Option for Underserved Indigenous Children in Latin America," *International Journal of Educational Development* 28 (2008): 435–445.

73. Carly Shuler, "Pockets of Potential: Using Mobile Technologies to Promote Children's Learning," *The Joan Ganz Cooney Center at Sesame Workshop* (Jan. 2009), www.joanganzcooneycenter.org/pdf/pockets_of_potential.pdf (accessed Jan. 16, 2009).

74. John Traxler, "Defining, Discussing and Evaluating Mobile Learning: The Moving Finger Writes and Having Writ . . . ," *International Review of Research in Open and Distance Learning* 8, no. 1 (June 2007), www.irrodl.org/index.php/irrodl/article/view/346/875 (accessed July 2, 2007).

75. "Video iPods Revolutionize Hotel Chain's Learning Program," *Chief Learning Officer* (Aug. 13, 2007), www.clomedia.com/in-the-news/2007/August/1930/index.php (accessed Apr. 20, 2008).

76. Ted Hoff, "Learning in the 21st Century: A Brave New World," *Chief Learning Officer* 7, no. 4 (Apr. 2008): 46, www.clomedia.com/features/2008/April/2146/index.php (accessed Apr. 14, 2008).

77. Grace Rubenstein, "Computers for Peace: The $100 Laptop," *Edutopia* (Feb. 2, 2007), www.edutopia.org/computers-peace (accessed June 26, 2008).

78. "The XO-1 (Laptop)," *Wikipedia*, 2007, http://en.wikipedia.org/wiki/$100_laptop (accessed July 2, 2007).

79. Jonathan Fildes, "Politics 'Stifling $100 Laptop.'" *BBC News* (Nov. 27, 2007), http://news.bbc.co.uk/2/hi/technology/7094695.stm (accessed Apr. 17, 2008).

80. Associated Press, "Developing-World Laptop to Be Available for Sale: Looking for Spark, Project to Let Donors Buy Two, Keep One," *Sydney Morning Herald* (Sep. 24, 2007), www.smh.com.au/news/Technology/Looking-for-a-spark-developingworld-laptop-project-to-let-donorsbuy-2-keep-1/2007/09/24/1190486170366.html (accessed Apr. 17, 2008).

81. Associated Press, "Little Laptop a Hit in Rural Peru," *CNN.com* (Dec. 24, 2007), www.cnn.com/2007/WORLD/americas/12/24/laptop.village.ap/index.html (accessed Apr. 17, 2008).

82. Wade Roush, "Colombian State Orders 65,000 XO Laptops," *Xconomy Boston* (May 29, 2008), www.xconomy.com/boston/2008/05/29/colombian-state-orders-65000-xo-laptops/ (accessed Jan. 10, 2009).

83. Darren Murph. "Uruguay Youngsters Receive Batch of OLPC XOs," *Engaget* (May 14, 2007), www.engadget.com/2007/05/14/uruguay-youngsters-receive-batch-of-olpc-xos/ (accessed July 3, 2007).

84. Rubenstein, "Computers for Peace," para. 1.

85. Ibid., para. 11.

86. John Ribeiro, "India Says It Is Developing a $10 Laptop," *Computerworld* (July 29, 2008), www.computerworld.com/action/article.do?command=viewArticleBasic& articleId=9110966 (accessed Aug. 3, 2008).

87. Mail Online, "Sony Unveils 'James Bond-style' Watch That Controls Phone and Music Player," *Daily Mail* (Sep. 28, 2006), www.dailymail.co.uk/pages/live/articles/news/news.html?in_article_id=407525&in_page_id=1770 (accessed Apr. 19, 2008).

11. Learning at Your Service

1. Yochai Benkler, *The Wealth of Networks: How Social Production Transforms Markets and Freedom* (New Haven, CT: Yale University Press. 2006).

2. Benkler, *The Wealth of Networks*, 376.

3. John Seely Brown and Richard P. Adler, "Minds on Fire: Open Education, the Long Tail, and Learning 2.0," *EDUCAUSE Review* 43, no. 1 (Jan./Feb. 2008): 16–32, http://connect.educause.edu/Library/EDUCAUSE+Review/MindsonFireOpenEducationt/45823 (accessed Feb. 23, 2008).

4. "List of Social Networking Sites," *Wikipedia*, 2008, http://en.wikipedia.org/wiki/List_of_social_networking_websites (accessed May 1, 2008).

5. John Schwartz, "73 and Loaded with Friends on Facebook," *New York Times* (Oct. 14, 2007), www.nytimes.com/2007/10/14/fashion/14facebook.html?_r=1&oref=slogin (accessed May 1, 2008).

6. Michael Morisy, "Facebook's New Take on Communications Should Be Embraced by Business," *Search Unified Communications.com* (Apr. 17, 2008), http://searchunifiedcommunications.techtarget.com/news/article/0,289142,sid186_gci1310144,00.html (accessed May 1, 2008).

7. Schwartz, "73 and Loaded with Friends on Facebook."

8. Eric Eldon, "Facebook Education App Gets Funding," *Venture Beat* (Dec. 3, 2007), http://venturebeat.com/2007/12/03/facebook-education-app-gets-funding/ (accessed May 1, 2008).

9. "Hi-Tech Tools Divide Social Sites," *BBC News* (Dec. 14, 2007), http://news.bbc.co.uk/2/hi/technology/7144143.stm (accessed May 1, 2008).

10. Paul McCloskey, "Stanford Hosts Course on Designing Apps in Facebook," *Campus Technology* (Sep. 18, 2007), http://campustechnology.com/articles/50319/ (accessed May 1, 2008).

11. Jason Lee Miller, "Facebook Widgets Cause Dramatic Traffic Increase," *WebPro News* (July 24, 2007), www.webpronews.com/topnews/2007/07/24/facebook-widgets-cause-dramatic-traffic-increase (accessed July 25, 2007).

12. Mark Franek, "Web Pulls World into Classroom," *Christian Science Monitor* (2007), www.csmonitor.com/2007/0910/p09s03-coop.htm (accessed May 1, 2008).

13. "Samuel Pepys," *Wikipedia*, 2008, http://en.wikipedia.org/wiki/Samuel_Pepys (accessed Apr. 21, 2008).

14. Riverbend, *Baghdad Burning: Girl Blogs from Iraq* (New York: Feminist Press, 2005).

15. BBC News, "'Why I Turned Pepys' Diary into a Weblog,'" *BBC News* (Jan. 2, 2003), http://news.bbc.co.uk/2/hi/uk_news/2621581.stm (accessed Apr. 23, 2008).

16. "John Evelyn," *Wikipedia*, 2008, http://en.wikipedia.org/wiki/John_Evelyn (accessed Apr. 23, 2008).

17. "History of Worldbridges," *Worldbridges*, 2007, http://worldbridges.net/node/76 (accessed July 10, 2007).

18. Erica Naone, "Learning Language in Context: Startup Live Mocha Leverages Social Networking to Teach Foreign Languages," *Technology Review* (Oct. 5, 2007), www.technologyreview.com/Biztech/19484/?a=f (accessed Feb. 8, 2008).

19. Anne Eisenberg, "Learning from a Native Speaker, Without Leaving Home," *New York Times* (Feb. 17, 2008), www.nytimes.com/2008/02/17/business/17novel.html?_r=1&ex=1360904400&en=1d0f905569d45e41&ei=5088&partner= rssnyt &emc =rss&oref=slogin (accessed Feb. 17, 2008).

20. Shirish Nadkarni, "Livemocha Secures $6 Million in Funding by Maveron," *Mochatalk* (Jan. 15, 2008): para. 2, http://blog.livemocha.com/2008/01/15/ livemocha-secures-6-million-in-funding-led-by-maveron/ (accessed Feb. 21, 2008).

21. Robert Goodwin-Jones, "Skype and Podcasting: Emerging Technologies for Language Learning," *Language Learning & Technology* 9, no. 3 (Sep. 2005): 9–12, http://llt.msu.edu/vol9num3/emerging/default.html (accessed Feb. 8, 2008).

22. Mike Butcher, "Babbel Acquires FriendsAbroad in Cash Deal," *Tech Crunch* (Nov. 6, 2008), http://uk.techcrunch.com/2008/11/06/babbel-acquires-friendsabroad-in-cash-deal/ (accessed Jan. 15, 2009).

23. Jamie Thompson, "A New Chapter for Those Learning Chinese, Thanks to Technology," *China Daily* (Sep. 28, 2006), www.chinadaily.com.cn/cndy/2006–09/ 28/content_698333.htm (accessed Feb. 20, 2008).

24. Elizabeth Weise, "As China Booms, So Does Mandarin in U.S. Schools," *USA Today* (Nov. 19, 2007), www.usatoday.com/news/education/2007–11–19-mandarin-cover_N.htm (accessed Feb. 21, 2008).

25. Weise, "As China Booms, So Does Mandarin in U.S. Schools."

26. Ken Carroll, "Here Comes ItalianPod," Ken Carroll's Weblog: Here Comes Everybody (June 10, 2008), http://ken-carroll.com/2008/06/10/is-italianpod-the-future/ (accessed July 10, 2008).

27. Ali Winston, "Homework Help NJ Has Tutors on Online: Library Program Helps Kids in Grades 4–12," *New Jersey Star Ledger* (Dec. 12, 2007), www.techlearning.com/story/showArticle.php?articleID=196604913#article2 (accessed Apr. 11, 2008).

28. See Hiawatha Bray, "Online Tutoring Pays Off at Home, Abroad," *The Boston Globe* (2006), www.boston.com/business/technology/articles/2006/03/28/online_tutoring_pays_off_at_home_abroad/ (accessed June 15, 2008); and Anupreeta Das and Amanda Paulson, "Need a Tutor? Call India," *Christian Science Monitor* (2005), www.csmonitor.com/2005/0523/p01s01-legn.html (accessed June 15, 2008).

29. Jeffrey R. Young, "Who Needs a Professor When There's a Tutor Available?" *Wired Campus: The Chronicle of Higher Education* (June 17, 2008), http://chronicle.com/wiredcampus/article/3095/who-needs-a-professor-when-theres-a-tutor-available?utm_source=at&utm_medium=en (accessed June 17, 2008).

30. Steve Lohr, "Hello India? I Need Help with My Math," *New York Times* (Oct. 31, 2007), www.nytimes.com/2007/10/31/business/worldbusiness/31butler.html (accessed June 15, 2008).

12. The Treasures and Traps of This Open Learning World

1. George Siemens, "A World Without Courses," (Mar. 6, 2008), www.elearnspace.org/media/worldwithoutcourses/player.html (accessed July 4, 2008).

2. George Siemens, "Connectivism: Learning Theory of Pastime for the Self-Amused?" (Nov. 12, 2006), www.elearnspace.org/Articles/connectivism_self-amused.htm (accessed July 4, 2008).

3. Gavriel Salomon, "Cognitive Effects With and of Computer Technology," *Communications Research* 17, no. 1 (1990): 26–44.

4. Elisabeth Wasserman, "Cyberspace-Age: Interplanetary Internet Is Final Frontier," *CNN.com* (July 23, 1998), www.cnn.com/TECH/computing/9807/23/interplanet.idg/index.html (accessed Apr. 29, 2008).

5. See Barry Levine, "Coming Soon—Mind-Reading Computers," *Sci-Tech Today* (June 26, 2006), www.sci-tech-today.com/story.xhtml?story_id=44079 (accessed

Apr. 29, 2008); and Erica Naone, "Software That Learns from Users," *Technology Review* (Nov. 20, 2007), www.technologyreview.com/Infotech/19782/ (accessed Apr. 29, 2008).

6. Andrew Peters, "Bill Gates Speaks on Farewell Tour," *The Tartan* (Feb. 25, 2008), www.thetartan.org/2008/2/25/news/gates (accessed Apr. 29, 2008).

7. Michael Laff, "The Future of Learning and Work: Big Thinkers Forecast the Next Big Moves," *T&D* 61, no. 12 (Dec. 2007): 40–45, www.cedma-europe.org/newsletter%20articles/ASTD/The%20Future%20of%20Learning%20and%20Work%20(Dec%2007).pdf (accessed Apr. 29, 2008).

8. Don Tapscott and Anthony Williams, *Wikinomics: How Mass Collaboration Changes Everything* (New York: Penguin, 2006).

9. Siemens, "Connectivism: Learning Theory of Pastime for the Self-Amused?"

10. M. Johnson, O. Liber, S. Wilson, P. Sharples, C. Milligan, and P. Beauvoir, "Mapping the Future: The Personal Learning Environment Reference Model and Emerging Technology," in *Research Proceedings of the ALT-C 2006: The Next Generation Conference*, eds. D. Whitelock and S. Wheeler (Edinburgh, U.K.: Heriot-Watt University, Sep. 2006): 182–191.

11. Stephen Downes, "E-Learning 2.0," *E-Learn Magazine* (Oct. 2005), http://elearnmag.org/subpage.cfm?section=articles&article=29-1 (accessed Oct. 26, 2006).

12. See "What Percentage of the World Speaks English?" *Answers.com,* 2007, www.answerbag.com/q_view/53199 (accessed July 16, 2007); and "List of Languages by Number of Native Speakers," *Wikipedia,* 2008, http://en.wikipedia.org/wiki/List_of_languages_by_number_of_native_speakers (accessed June 17, 2008).

13. Henry Jenkins, Katie Clinton, Ravi Purushotma, Alice J. Robison, and Margaret Weigel, *Confronting the Challenges of Participatory Culture: Media Education for the 21st Century* (Chicago: The John D. and Catherine T. MacArthur Foundation, 2008), http://digitallearning.macfound.org/atf/cf/%7B7E45C7E0-A3E0-4B89-AC9C-E807E1B0AE4E%7D/JENKINS_WHITE_PAPER.PDF (accessed Apr. 18, 2008).

14. Sir John Daniel, "Technology and the Media Have Transformed All Aspects of Human Life—Except Education," *Economist.com* (Oct. 24, 2007), www.economist.com/debate/index.cfm?action=article&debate_id=1&story_id=9968827 (accessed Apr. 18, 2008).

15. Jeffrey Zaslow, "A Beloved Professor Delivers the Lecture of a Lifetime," *Wall Street Journal* (Sep. 20, 2007), http://online.wsj.com/public/article/SB119024238402033039.html (accessed May 26, 2008).

16. Randy Pausch with Jeffrey Zaslow, *The Last Lecture* (New York: Hyperion, 2008).

17. Curtis J. Bonk and Ke Zhang, *Empowering Online Learning: 100+ Activities for Reading, Reflecting, Displaying, and Doing* (San Francisco: Jossey-Bass, 2008).

18. Thomas L. Friedman, *The World Is Flat: A Brief History of the Twenty-First Century* (New York: Farrar, Straus & Giroux, 2005).

19. Don Tapscott, *Grown Up Digital: How the Net Generation Is Changing Your World* (New York: McGraw-Hill, 2009).

20. Bonk and Zhang, *Empowering Online Learning*.

21. Gavriel Salomon, "Novel Constructivist Learning Environments and Novel Technologies: Some Issues to Be Considered," *Research Dialog in Learning and Instruction* 1, no. 1 (1998): 3–12.

22. "Time Magazine Person of the Year," *Time Magazine* 168, no. 26 (Dec. 25, 2006/ Jan. 1, 2007).

Index